THE BIOSPHERE
AND THE BIOREGION

D1602438

Bioregionalism asks us to reimagine ourselves and the places where we live in ecological terms and to harmonize human activities with the natural systems that sustain life. As one of the originators of the concept of bioregionalism, Peter Berg (1937–2011) is a founding figure of contemporary environmental thought.

The Biosphere and the Bioregion: Essential writings of Peter Berg introduces readers to the biospheric vision and postenvironmental genius of Berg. From books and essays to published interviews, this selection of writings represents Berg's bioregional vision and its global, local, urban, and rural applications.

The Biosphere and the Bioregion provides a highly accessible introduction to bioregional philosophy, making Berg's paradigm available as a guiding vision and practical "greenprint" for the twenty-first century.

This valuable compilation lays the groundwork for future research by offering the first-ever comprehensive bibliography of Berg's publications and should be of interest to students and scholars in the interdisciplinary fields of environmental humanities and environment and sustainability studies, as well as political ecology, environmental sociology, and anthropology.

Cheryll Glotfelty is professor of literature and environment at the University of Nevada, Reno. She is cofounder and past president of the Association for the Study of Literature and Environment (ASLE).

Eve Quesnel is a lecturer at Sierra College in California and writes for an independent newspaper in the Lake Tahoe region of California.

Helmuth Trischler, Deutsches Museum, Munich and Co-Director, Rachel Carson Centre, LMU Munich University, Germany

Mary Evelyn Tucker, Yale University, USA

Kirsten Wehner, Head Curator, People and the Environment, National Museum of Australia

The *Routledge Environmental Humanities* series is an original and inspiring venture recognising that today's world agricultural and water crises, ocean pollution and resource depletion, global warming from greenhouse gases, urban sprawl, overpopulation, food insecurity and environmental justice are all *crises of culture*.

The reality of understanding and finding adaptive solutions to our present and future environmental challenges has shifted the epicenter of environmental studies away from an exclusively scientific and technological framework to one that depends on the human-focused disciplines and ideas of the humanities and allied social sciences.

We thus welcome book proposals from all humanities and social sciences disciplines for an inclusive and interdisciplinary series. We favour manuscripts aimed at an international readership and written in a lively and accessible style. The readership comprises scholars and students from the humanities and social sciences and thoughtful readers concerned about the human dimensions of environmental change.

Rethinking Invasion Ecologies from the Environmental Humanities
Jodi Frawley and Iain McCalman

The Broken Promise of Agricultural Progress
An environmental history
Cameron Muir

The Biosphere and the Bioregion
Essential writings of Peter Berg
Cheryll Glotfelty and Eve Quesnel

THE BIOSPHERE AND THE BIOREGION

Essential writings of Peter Berg

Edited by
Cheryll Glotfelty and
Eve Quesnel

Karen,

November 1, 2014 –

To my fellow bioregionalist
and hiker – hope you
enjoy Peter's words as
much as Cheryll and I did.

Lots of love,

Eve

Routledge
Taylor & Francis Group

LONDON AND NEW YORK

First published 2015
by Routledge
2 Park Square, Milton Park, Abingdon, Oxon OX14 4RN

and by Routledge
711 Third Avenue, New York, NY 10017

Routledge is an imprint of the Taylor & Francis Group, an informa business

British Library Cataloguing-in-Publication Data

A catalogue record for this book is available from the British Library

Library of Congress Cataloging-in-Publication Data

Berg, Peter, 1937–2011.
  [Works. Selections]
  The biosphere and the bioregion : essential writings of Peter Berg / edited by
Cheryll Glotfelty and Eve Quesnel.
     pages cm. — (Routledge environmental humanities)
  Includes bibliographical references and index.
  1. Bioregionalism.   2. Biosphere.   3. Berg, Peter, 1937–2011—Interviews.
I. Glotfelty, Cheryll, editor of compilation.   II. Quesnel, Eve, editor of
compilation.   III. Title.
  GE43.B58   2014
  304.2—dc23
  2014004841

ISBN: 978-0-415-70440-3 (hbk)
ISBN: 978-0-415-70441-0 (pbk)
ISBN: 978-1-315-89007-4 (ebk)

Typeset in Times
by Apex CoVantage, LLC

Printed and bound in the United States of America by
Edwards Brothers Malloy on sustainably sourced paper

To Peter Berg and other activists of his generation

FIGURE 1 Peter Berg, San Francisco, 2001
Source: © Jean-Marc Lubrano

"Peter Berg set in motion an entirely new realm of environmental thinking and social action by establishing the bioregion as the best location and scale for sustaining human and non-human life. His pioneering work needs to be broadcast widely, and this book accomplishes that task."

Robert Thayer, University of California, Davis, USA

"With global initiatives providing only tepid solutions to the problems of environmental destruction and economic insecurity, Berg's empowering vision of how people can live fulfilling lives in the context of local, sustainable communities is more relevant than ever."

Richard Evanoff, Aoyama Gakuin University, Japan

"Berg's Pacific-rim vision of reinhabitation is articulated with poetry, verve, and wit. An explorer and advocate of complexity, he speaks alike to 'densely-creatured food chains' and to the cultural ecologies of expanding cities. In this guide to one of the best ideas of the past forty years, one also finds a manual for the decades ahead."

Jonathan Skinner, Warwick University, UK

"*The Biosphere and the Bioregion* is a captivating, stimulating collection of essays drawn from the work of Peter Berg, internationally known bioregional thinker and activist and founder of Planet Drum Foundation. This brilliant selection, interlaced with original tributes from prominent writers and thinkers, brings to the student or general reader many of the most urgent and pressing issues of our time."

Ann Fisher-Wirth, University of Mississippi, USA

"Peter Berg was a true visionary—a foundational thinker in the fields of bioregionalism and sustainability. Cheryll Glotfelty and Eve Quesnel have produced a careful and engaging introduction to Berg's important work. This book shows how Berg offers a vivid counterpoint to sanguine representations of the global tilt of contemporary society."

Scott Slovic, University of Idaho, USA

"Peter Berg reads the land through the soles of his feet, reads watersheds with his heart—yet guides us to re-inhabiting with sensitive practicality. We are now fortunate to have his work gathered in this impressive guidebook."

Laurie Ricou, The University of British Columbia, Canada

"Peter Berg took a stand as an activist, and these essays reflect his unique position in life as one of the first bioregional poets and practitioners for a new millennium. To take a stand for resilience requires that we know when to draw the line in terms of our unsustainable behaviour, join with others to adapt and sustain the cultural values inherent to home place, and forge a new economy that can restore the self-generating capacity of a living community and bioregion."

Michael Vincent McGinnis, Monterey Institute of International Studies, USA

"Want to make the world a better place? These lively short essays will get you thinking, talking, imagining, and acting to that end."

SueEllen Campbell, Colorado State University, USA

CONTENTS

CELESTIAL SOULSTICE 2010

Peter Berg

Circles, ellipses, curves
bring us to this turn point

lunging unquenchable bulged desire
(eating to live)

hosting millions of organisms
without knowing them
until all left alive
still feed without knowing us

each our own planet
out of cold space and witless unknowing

this parabola of another year
completes again what remains
to flame our sensing souls.

PREFACE: MEETING PETER BERG

Eve Quesnel

"You can't really change what you do until you change your idea of who you are. And your idea of who you are should stem from the place where you are" (Berg, Personal Interview, 10 Dec. 2010).

How does one define a principal leader of a movement or life philosophy? By his or her intellect? Demeanor? Ideologies? Communication skills? These questions and others came to mind when I began to consider writing about Peter Berg, a leading advocate of bioregionalism and founder of Planet Drum Foundation. During a dinner conversation with friends one night I was reminded of the memorable impression Peter made on people, which got me thinking: What was it that made Peter stand out? "I'll never forget it, the night he gave that talk at Tahoe, the things he said and the way he said them," one friend recalled. "Just like this summer when we were on the reservation in Arizona and people were learning old native practices on how to grow and cook food. Peter Berg would have loved that." Another friend, whose husband, John, had joined Cheryll Glotfelty and me on one of our trips to San Francisco to meet with Peter and his lifelong partner, Judy Goldhaft, chimed in: "John was really taken aback. He will never forget that day with Peter. He thought Peter was brilliant. He made a lasting impression on him." These conversations and others, and reading through the contributions of Peter's peers included in this book, reveal a unique quality that only certain people possess, that of an innate insight into the workings of the world coupled with the ability to connect with people.

The many complexities Peter embodied were both admired and scrutinized, his above-average intelligence apparent to all who knew him, many of his acquaintances referring to him as "Genius." Gary Snyder said of Peter, "he is a hard and scrappy, super-smart guy, a probing alpha" ("Peter Berg, Counterculture, and the Bioregional Impulse"). Other contemporaries described the overtly ambitious bioregionalist as "a force of nature" and "a provoker." Of himself, Berg proclaimed: "It's a pain in the ass being thirty years ahead" (Personal Interview, 24 May 2011). Added to Peter's intelligence was a sort of sassiness. David Simpson, a contributor to this project, says it best when describing Berg's bristly behavior: "If from time to time friends and nemeses of Peter found annoyance in his outpouring of rhetoric, it was usually in terms of form more than of meaning. The barrages he regularly unleashed on audiences, witting or otherwise, were sometimes thunderous and intimidating." Beyond these passionate diatribes, Simpson maintains, is "a man of visionary ideas" ("The Mechanics of Reinhabitation").

Cheryll Glotfelty, professor of literature and environment at the University of Nevada, Reno, and I, one of Cheryll's students in her graduate seminar "Regionalism and Bioregionalism," met Peter and Judy Goldhaft at the Planet Drum Foundation office in San Francisco, on a field trip that ended the course. This was in 2006. We were greeted by Peter, approximately five feet seven, with straight silver hair pulled back in a small Samurai bun and almond-shaped hazel eyes hidden behind black framed glasses, in the basement of his Victorian home. In the office, a cluttered eagerness prevailed, much like Peter and his stream of untidy, unconventional ideas. A big, burly copy machine boasted the largest presence in the room, sitting high above random chairs, some wood with tattered pillow cushions, others black leather on wheels, facing all directions as if no chair could decide which way to direct itself. Electrical wires from computers and lamps and a printer wound around the edge of the room like a group of snakes, intertwined, slithering behind each piece of furniture to the closest outlet, where they became even more entangled. Books, the main gravity of the room, stuffed into narrow wooden or flimsy metal shelves and stacked haphazardly, vertically and horizontally, threatened to spill over the edges at any moment, their subjects—natural science, ecology, poetry, literature, and green cities—revealing Peter' passions. At one point in our office tour, Peter pointed to a calligraphy print on a wall, with a 1964 poem by Lew Welch: "Step out onto the planet. / Draw a circle a hundred feet round." Within the circle, Welch stated, three hundred things are waiting to be seen for the very first time. With a careful eye and a curious mind, the poem implies, we can learn about our bioregions directly underfoot. "Poetry changes consciousness," Peter said, "It can be politically radical."

As Peter began to tell us about bioregionalism, it became clear he had done this a million times, and in fact we learned later that he had spoken all over the world to other classes and political and cultural organizations. He was a skilled orator, an actor after all, or, as Peter said of himself, "I'm an actor . . . inside" (Personal Interview, 24 May 2011). He also described himself as "an agent provocateur who is pursuing my own survival in a trance-driven society. . . . I simply try to create a mental condition that will have the effect of an explosion in the brain" (Evanoff 4).

Peter explained to our small group the precepts of bioregionalism, a philosophy he and ecologist Raymond Dasmann illuminated in an essay titled "Reinhabiting California" in the environmental journal *The Ecologist* in 1977. How does one define a bioregion? Peter asked the class. How do we, as a culture, learn and interact with the places we live in, in a cogent and respectful manner? Well, get to know your place. Ask, who were the indigenous people in your area? How did they live? Then ask yourself what you can learn from them. Other questions to pursue: What defines your watershed? What native plants and animals surround you? What direction do storms come from? Once you've determined your bioregion, often formed by a watershed, restore and maintain its natural systems, and find ways to satisfy basic human needs such as water, food, energy, and materials. And within bioregionalism, another precept. Engage artistically. Write. Dance. Sing. Act. Are you with me? Can you dig it?

As one example of bioregionalism, Peter took us outside for a tour of their sidewalk garden, a group of native plants set in a narrow strip of steep sidewalk next to his Victorian home. In one of the strips of dirt with wild bushes, trees, and flowers, a sign was posted next to the street: "Backyard Wildlife Habitat. National Wildlife Federation. This property provides the four basic habitat elements needed for wildlife to thrive: food, water, cover, and places to raise young." Peter beamed with pride at the notion of planting native plants in an area previously covered with concrete. "It was a small but honest gesture," he recounted. "I was reprimanded by the city government for allowing weeds to grow up through cracks in the sidewalk outside the Planet Drum office. The plants that grew there seemed to me a hopeful sign of nature returning to the asphalt and concrete drabness of city streets." Peter was given permission from the city to break up half of the sidewalk to plant a natural garden, a wild patch in the middle of a metropolis: coyote bush, yarrow, sword fern, douglas iris, soaproot, sticky monkey flower, dune tansy, California fuchsia, and oak trees. Peter scanned the garden and added, "With the wild comes an influx of insects and birds." Greening a city, one part of Peter's legacy, was made real by this one demure gesture.

Not far from Peter and Judy's house, at Glen Canyon Park, a city park with a large eucalyptus forest, our small group was led to our next place of bioregional education. Peter told us that eucalyptus, so common as to seem native to San Francisco, was transported from Australia in the late 1800s. Other species, such as the dry tall grass we walked on, a European grass, came to the bay on explorers' ships as filling for their mattresses. While some visitors and San Francisco natives might believe the green areas of the city to be natural, there's a history to be learned on what is native and what is not.

Leaving the eucalyptus forest, we turned toward a dirt road that led to a narrow path in a wooded area that was so thick with brush that the tangled blackberry bushes and overhanging moss forced us to bend forward in order to clear the brushy ceiling. In this dark bristly tunnel, we proceeded through a dense, mythical landscape and experienced on the most visceral level what was once San Francisco. Everything around us was messy and everything was wild, undergrowth, overgrowth; the lines were seamless. An algae-ridden creek trickled below the trail, and above us rose layered, twisted sedimentary rock. The air was dominated by birds' lively chatter as we watched sporadic flights into and out of the tangled creek bed. To think: *This* was what San Francisco looked like before the pervasion of concrete and steel; this was native San Francisco!

After we left the troll-like woods and returned to the organized, clean eucalyptus forest, emerging from the wild to the civilized, Peter asked, "Do you smell the difference?" The scent changed from earthy-must to mint-oregano. We had just learned another lesson; the eucalyptus grove remained a monocrop, whereas the native brush was rich in biodiversity.

Our last activity on the field trip involved a map-making exercise that Berg regularly employed in his workshops all over the world, a lesson easily taught to those who were unable to read and write (he realized this benefit when he introduced the exercise to rural farmers in Tepoztlán, Mexico). We were handed large pieces of paper, and then Berg gave a list of instructions. First, mark an x in the middle of your paper to represent your home. Write N for North, and draw arrows that show the direction of storms. Draw the high ground, hills or mountains that cause rain to flow downward. High ground sheds water, so the term "watershed" is used to describe an area of land that drains into a body of water, such as a river, lake, or ocean. Next, draw nearby bodies of water—streams, rivers, ponds, lakes, ocean, and so on—and then add geological characteristics such as granite cliffs or caves. Sketch plants and animals that are native to your place, and then draw two aspects of the human relationship to the features you have drawn, the worst things people are doing (e.g., pollution, soil erosion) and the best things people are doing (e.g., river restoration, recycling). This is your bioregion, and this is what's going on within it.

While the activity may seem simple, it was a humbling experience. At each step, we were shocked at what we *didn't* know about our places. But Peter knew. He knew exactly where he lived: "When people ask where I'm from I say that I am from the confluence of the Sacramento River and San Joaquin River and San Francisco Bay, of the Shasta bioregion, of the North Pacific Rim of the Pacific Basin of the Planet Earth" ("Bioregion and Human Location" 96).

In a bioregional state of mind

Four years later, in July 2010, Cheryll and I returned to San Francisco to visit Peter and Judy, to check in and to continue a friendship whose seeds were planted in 2006. We had kept in touch by reading the Planet Drum Foundation website, keeping up to date on bioregionalism coursework and a continuing revegetation project in Ecuador, bioregional gatherings around the country, and workshops in the Bay Area.

During that visit, we discussed our lives, personal projects, and future goals, slipping into bioregionalism concepts, Peter philosophizing. After a few hours spent in their home, we took a short drive to a restaurant called Serpentine, well known for its local food offerings, located in a semi-industrial area near the bay called Dogpatch. Once seated at the hip eatery, Peter asked, "Do you know why it's called Serpentine? Serpentine outcrops were common in San Francisco until they were covered with streets and buildings." "Serpentine," he continued, "is a metamorphic rock that has a light green tint to it. A lot of the California coastal ranges are made up of long bands of it." While driving around Dogpatch and other adjacent areas near the bay, Peter played our personal bioregional tour guide, describing the geography of the past: "Underneath us were streams, and over there, portions of the bay were filled in for development." This was Peter looking at the world. He ruminated on what once was, what nature and culture had become, and how best to address nature and culture in healthy, sustainable ways. He was also always asking questions: What kind of vegetation used to grow here? What grows here now? Where do streams come from and where do they go? What practices did native people use?

Peter saw indigenous people, listening to, learning from, and engaging with the natural systems surrounding them; he saw a pervading monoculture, homogenizing the ways we think and live; he saw a promising world where one raindrop fallen from the mountains, flowing down a stream, into a valley, into a river, and finally ending its journey at a bay, determined a watershed and a lifeline to a variety of ecosystems. He saw us as part of, not separate from, natural systems. And he strongly believed, whether we lived in a sleepy rural community or in a bustling city, whether we lived in America or Japan or Ecuador, we lived in particular bioregions in one place, the biosphere, whereby we could live sustainably, by *bio* means.

At one point during the day after we returned to their home and engaged in further discussions, a sudden awkwardness filled the air, and Peter stopped talking. He became quiet and stern and then he looked directly at Cheryll and me, leaned forward and said, "So, Cheryll and Eve, why are you *really* here?" His question took us by complete surprise. Why were we there? To see Peter and Judy, of course, and to learn about Planet Drum's current activities. But, after further questions and conversation, we all came to the same conclusion. Cheryll and I were there to put together a book, a book that would help get Peter's words out into the world.

Three years later, *The Biosphere and the Bioregion: Essential Writings of Peter Berg* has found a home, and now Peter can speak for himself, our visits to San Francisco and the University of Nevada, Reno, library, trips of the past, our e-mail correspondences, quieted. We started the book with Peter in that initial return visit, but when we finished we finished without him. Peter passed away in July 2011 in his beloved San Francisco, with Judy and their daughter, Ocean, by his side. Two months later, on October 1, 2011, Peter's birthday, a celebration of his life was held at the Josephine Randall Museum, on a high hill overlooking the city, the place where he had raised his family and tried to turn the world on its axis, spin it into some kind of sense.

It is our hope that through Peter's words and stories and through the essays from those who "ran with him," the ideas of bioregionalism spread like seeds, much as this "agent provocateur's" wily coyote self was disseminated into different parts of the world, with passion, good intention, oftentimes an abrasion that rubbed the wrong way, but always with inspiration that made you look at the world in a whole different light and then changed your life forever.

"We didn't play it for the Big Time. We didn't play it for the Small Time. We played it for the Real Time."

(Quote from Peter, written in the initial announcement of Peter's death, posted on the Planet Drum Foundation website.)

Works cited

Berg, Peter. "Bioregion and Human Location." 1983. Rpt. in *Envisioning Sustainability*. San Francisco: Subculture Books, 2009. 91–97. Print.

———. Personal Interview. 10 Dec. 2010.

———. Personal Interview. 24 May 2011.

Evanoff, Richard. "Bioregionalism Comes to Japan: An Interview with Peter Berg." *Japan Environmental Monitor* 97.4 (June 1998). Web.

Simpson, David. "The Mechanics of Reinhabitation: Remembering Peter Berg Along the Bioregional Trail." In this volume.

Snyder, Gary. "Peter Berg, Counterculture, and the Bioregional Impulse." In this volume.

ACKNOWLEDGMENTS

It takes a large circle of support to see a book through from inception to completion. We would like to thank the following people and programs for contributing to Peter Berg's legacy and far-reaching principles and activism.

At the University of Nevada, Reno (UNR) we gratefully acknowledge the College of Liberal Arts Scholarly and Creative Activities Grant Program, the Mountain and Desert Research Committee, and the English Department's Summer Research Assistant program for generous support. Donnie Curtis, Betty Glass, and Jacque Sundstrand in Special Collections at the Mathewson–IGT Knowledge Center ordered and catalogued Planet Drum Foundation publications, which were a great help.

This book would not have been possible without the support and dedication of Judy Goldhaft, who spent countless hours combing through Peter's writings and files of photographs. Judy's precision of language and meticulous attention to detail have been both exacting and essential. Our thanks to Ocean Berg for permission to print many of the essays collected here. With much appreciation we thank the photographers and tribute writers for being part of this project and for the time and effort spent on their pieces. It has been a privilege to work with such a talented and accomplished cast. Artist Mona Caron generously allowed us to use a photograph of her Noe Valley East mural at the Noe Valley Farmers' Market in San Francisco for the book cover; Peter admired this mural, which resonates with his vision of a green city.

Louisa Earls and Helen Bell at Routledge are a dream come true. Enthusiastic about the project from the beginning, they have been prompt, clear, and courteous in their communication, professional at every turn, and utterly delightful. We feel fortunate indeed that our project found a niche in Routledge's new Environmental Humanities series. This book benefited from the advocacy and constructive suggestions of several anonymous outside reviewers, whom we thank for their careful reading.

UNR graduate research assistants Andy Ross and Tyler Nickl ably performed a variety of book-related tasks, and alumna Lauren Yero translated the Ecuador plaque. Thank you to Amy Anderson for transcribing audio tapes and to John Echols for filming an interview with Peter. Sandra Marshall, our indexer, has been a pleasure to work with.

For providing lodging for our trips to the Bay Area, we would like to thank Dorrie Wick and Jim Peikon for allowing to us to stay in their Marin home, Ann Mullen for her gracious hospitality in the city, and Gary Snyder for his warm accommodations and invigorating discussions on San Juan Ridge. Mayumi Elegado, editor of the Tahoe independent newspaper *Moonshine Ink*, believed Peter's words had a place in journalism and sponsored a talk by Peter on the shores of Lake Tahoe.

Peter said to us during one of our last visits to his home, after a few hours discussing not only his past but also, and more important, his ideas for the future, "We're becoming friends, aren't we?" Our goal had always been to get Peter's name and ideas out into the world, but little did we know that we would become friends along the way.

I [Eve] would like to thank the following friends and family members for their support. Good friends and mentors Mike Branch, Ann Ronald, Suzanne Roberts, and Ray March for their leadership, inspiration, and encouragement, and Candy Blesse, who listened patiently to *every* stage of the book while on our daily dog walks. Also, much gratitude to other friends who lent an earnest ear. My mother and brother, Paul, for supporting my life choices and the Stroys, Quesnels, and Barretts, who also reinforce my passions. My husband, Quiz, who works hard every day to make our lives in the mountains a beautiful one and who was always patient for the time this project took away from our time together. Our daughter, Kim, who shares with me in the most sincere way the successes and setbacks of life. Last, a most wholehearted thank you to Cheryll Glotfelty for organizing the Planet Drum Foundation field trip, the impetus for this book, and for being consistently professional at all phases. Her camaraderie and friendship along the way made this journey a special one, and I will fondly remember these years we worked together. DS and MS unite!

I [Cheryll] learned about bioregionalism by teaching it. I am grateful to the UNR English department for the opportunity to develop classes that reflect my emerging interests, and I want to thank my students for exploring new terrain together, challenging my thinking and making the journey so enjoyable. I'd like to thank my enormously supportive department chair, Eric Rasmussen; the genial geographer, Paul Starrs; and my close colleagues and friends, Mike Branch and Scott Slovic, who have shared ideas, texts, and troubles. I deeply appreciate my family and my friends Eileen and Laura, who for fifty years have seen me through the ups and downs of life, and Matthew, who shares my love of Nevada. My husband, Steve, and daughter, Rosa, give me a sense of *home* that cannot be found in books or even in nature. With them life is good. Finally, I'd like to thank Eve Quesnel, my collaborator and friend, who turned what could have been a lonely road into a shared adventure.

EDITORIAL POLICIES

In preparing Peter Berg's published essays for reprinting in this volume the editors have adopted the following policies:

- We retain Berg's punctuation because he was very deliberate.
- If we deleted a passage from the original, the omission is indicated by an ellipsis in square brackets, e.g. [. . .] or [. . . .]. If an ellipsis is not in square brackets, it occurred in the original.
- Most of the essays use American spelling, but we retain British spelling if the original essay was published in a British publication.
- Typos and misspellings have been silently corrected.
- For a few of the pieces that had generic titles such as "Interview," we retitled the piece to reflect its contents. Original titles appear in the Permissions page in the Appendix.
- We use MLA style for documentation in the editor's essays and bibliography. However, we retain the citation style of the original for reprinted essays.
- Peter Berg's partner is known as "Judy Berg" to some and "Judy Goldhaft" to others. We use "Judy Goldhaft" in our writing, but we retain the original in reprinted material and tributes.

CONTRIBUTORS

Saul Yale Barodofsky, born in 1939, is a former street theater activist and social revolutionary. He presently divides his time between his professional life as a Tribal textile collector, dealer, and lecturer and his spiritual work in "noncommercial" healing, both individual and planetary.

Peter Coyote is an actor who has appeared in more than 120 films. A writer whose first book, *Sleeping Where I Fall,* is still in print after fourteen years and whose second, *The Rainman's Third Cure*, is recently finished. Coyote is a founding member of the Diggers, past chairman of the California State Arts Council, father of two, and a grandfather.

Jim Dodge, a founder of the bioregional movement, is emeritus director of the Writing Practices Program at Humboldt State University in Arcata, California. His published novels include *Not Fade Away* and *Stone Junction*. *Rain on the River* is a collection of poetry and prose by Dodge. His modern fable, *Fup*, has delighted readers for thirty years.

Susan Griffin is an award-winning poet, essayist, playwright, and screenwriter. Her writings, which include the ecofeminist classic *Woman and Nature*, critique the interlinked domination of women, minorities, and nature; probe the root causes of war; and measure the gap between democratic ideals and actual practice. Griffin has been named by *Utne Reader* as one of a hundred important visionaries for the new millennium.

David Haenke moved to the Ozarks bioregion in 1971 and has been immersed in whole-systems ecological design in the context of bioregions ever since. Haenke is the cofounder/organizer of the Ozark Area Community Congress (OACC; 1977–present) and helped to found and coordinate the continental bioregional congress movement. Haenke currently directs the Ecological Society Project of the Ozarks Resource Center and an eco-forestry education and management organization.

Robert Hass served as poet laureate of the United States and chancellor of the Academy of American Poets. Hass has written seven books of poetry and translated eight. His collection *Time and Materials* won both the Pulitzer Prize and the National Book Award. He lives in California with his wife, poet Brenda Hillman, and is a professor of poetry and poetics at the University of California, Berkeley. His poetry explores our connectedness with the natural world and its reverberations in the emotions of our lives.

Joanne Kyger is a native California poet and teacher with ties to the Beat Generation and the San Francisco Renaissance. The author of more than thirty books of poetry, her collected *ABOUT NOW* was a winner of the 2008 Pen Oakland–Josephine Miles Award in Poetry. She also received a Small Press Traffic Lifetime Achievement Award in 2007, and a Contemporary Arts Award in 2005.

Martin A. Lee is the author of several books, including *Acid Dreams*, *The Beast Reawakens*, and, most recently, *Smoke Signals: A Social History of Marijuana— Medical, Recreational and Scientific*. He is cofounder of the media watch group FAIR and director of Project CBD, an information service that focuses on cannabis science and therapeutics.

Malcolm Margolin is founder and executive director of Heyday, a nonprofit publisher specializing in California's cultures, natural history, social justice, and the arts. He is the author of several books, including *The Ohlone Way: Indian Life in the San Francisco-Monterey Bay Area*, and is the recipient of many awards, including a Cultural Freedom Award from Lannan Foundation, a Community Service Award from the San Francisco Foundation, and a Chairman's Commendation from the National Endowment for the Arts.

Duncan McNaughton is a poet living in San Francisco and Bolinas, California. He taught for many years at the New College of California in San Francisco's Mission District, heading its poetics program. McNaughton edited the small-press journal *Fathar*. His books include *The Pilot, Kicking the Feather*, *Valparaíso*, *Capricci, Bounce*, and *Altoon's Frog*.

Stephanie Mills first met Peter Berg and Freeman House in 1972 when they were Diggers and she was Editor-in-Chief of *EarthTimes*. In 1978 as Editor of *Not Man Apart*, Mills reprinted Peter Berg and Raymond Dasmann's "Reinhabiting California," introducing bioregional ideas to a mainstream environmentalist audience.

Mills has seven books to her credit, including *Whatever Happened to Ecology?* and *Epicurean Simplicity*.

Giuseppe Moretti lives in the middle/lower portion of the Po river watershed in northern Italy, where he is an organic farmer, having converted his parents' farm into an organic farm. Since 1992 he has worked to spread the bioregional concept in Italy through the pages of his biannual review, *Lato Selvatico*. In 1996 he was among the founders of the Rete Bioregionale Italiana and in 2010 of Sentiero Bioregionale.

Clayton Plager-Unger is the Ecuador program director for Planet Drum Foundation's projects in Bahía de Caráquez. Clay supervises the Revegetation Project, an ongoing effort to put bioregional theory into practice by planting native trees for erosion control and habitat restoration in and around the coast city. Clay works with a team of national and international volunteers, interns, and employees on expanding the scope of the Revegetation Project through increased tree production at the nursery and education campaigns. He also collaborates with the local government on promoting issues related to the Bahía eco-city.

Kirkpatrick Sale is the author of a dozen books, including *Dwellers in the Land: The Bioregional Vision* (1985), which is still in print. He was a contributor to several of the books in the New Society publisher's bioregional series. In his writings Sale critiques technology, considers appropriate scale, and advocates decentralization. He is founder and director of the Middlebury Institute, which studies separatism, secession, and self-determination.

David Simpson has served as president of the Institute for Sustainable Forestry and the Mattole Salmon Group, perhaps the most successful citizen-run effort in the American West to restore the resources of an entire watershed. He is also a writer, performer, and producer for Human Nature, a touring theater company that has brought comedy about crucial environmental and social issues all over the planet.

Gary Snyder—Pulitzer Prize poet, essayist, teacher, and bioregional thinker—makes his home among the manzanita, oaks, and pines in the foothill country of northern California. Snyder's work blends watershed consciousness, Zen Buddhism, and indigenous, old-new ways of thinking. Notable books include *Turtle Island*, *Axe Handles*, *Practice of the Wild*, *A Place in Space,* and *Mountains and Rivers Without End*. Snyder recently gave the annual Hopwood Lecture on Writing at the University of Michigan.

Starhawk is a veteran of progressive movements, from antiwar to antinukes to Occupy. A highly influential voice in the revival of Goddess religion, she is the author of twelve books on earth-based spirituality and activism, including *The

Spiral Dance and *The Fifth Sacred Thing.* Her latest book, *The Empowerment Manual: A Guide for Collaborative Groups,* examines power, process, and conflict for groups that organize without top-down leadership.

Kimiharu To, a Planet Drum Foundation board member since 2001, is an environmentalist and translator, who lives in Aomori, Japan. Kimiharu launched Guard Fox Watch with Peter Berg during the 1998 Winter Games in Nagano, Japan. Currently, he teaches courses on environmental studies at Aomori University and serves as a regent of the Aomori Yamada Educational Foundation.

Robert Young is an assistant professor of community and regional planning at the University of Texas at Austin. He has served as director of planning of the Philadelphia Recycling Office, executive director of the New Jersey Office of Sustainability, board member of the New Jersey State Planning Commission, and adviser to several state governors on issues of sustainable economic development.

Seth Zuckerman coauthored *A Green City Program for San Francisco Bay Area Cities & Towns* with Peter Berg and Beryl Magilavy. He has chaired the Mattole Restoration Council and directed its Wild and Working Lands Program. Zuckerman's writing has appeared in numerous publications, including *Orion, Sierra, Whole Earth,* and *The Nation.* He is coauthor and coeditor of *Salmon Nation: People, Fish and Our Common Home.*

INTRODUCTION

Cheryll Glotfelty

Peter Berg tells a story: Two guys are sitting in a bar. A TV news story shows a chunk of Antarctica floating away that is the size of Delaware. One guy turns to another guy and says, "How the hell did we get ourselves in this place?" His friend says, "Well, everything we do seems to point to doing more of this. So have another beer."

This book introduces readers to Peter Berg, a precocious post-environmentalist who bridged the gap between knowing how bad things are and doing something about it. As early as the 1970s, Berg observed that the environmental movement was becoming institutionalized in big-ten environmental organizations and government agencies as a primarily defensive force that might regulate but would never replace industrial civilization. He began articulating a more positive, pro-active alternative, founded on the concept of bioregions. In brief, bioregionalism asks us to become conscious of ourselves and the places where we live in ecological terms and to harmonize human activities with ecological realities. *The Biosphere and the Bioregion: Essential Writings of Peter Berg* makes Berg's bioregional paradigm available as a guiding vision and practical "greenprint" for the twenty-first century.

The bioregional movement is a decentered, grassroots movement of people and communities in diverse locations that are making an effort to craft a way of life and a means of support appropriate to the natural characteristics of the particular places where they live. The ideas that emerge from these scattered groups differ in terms of emphasis, with groups focused on permaculture, ecological restoration, wilderness, spirituality, autonomy, social ecology, and watershed politics. Bioregionalism is, as a chronicler of the movement, Doug Aberley, writes, "a story from many voices, [...] a body of thought and related practice that has evolved in response to the challenge of reconnecting socially-just human cultures in a sustainable manner to the region-scale ecosystems in which they are irrevocably embedded" (13). The core concepts of bioregionalism were collaboratively developed in conversations and publications, and not all practitioners agree on every point.[1] This book focuses on the perspective of Peter Berg, a seminal thinker and organizer, acknowledged by his peers as a founder or even *the* founder of the bioregional movement (Mills, "Standing in the Places" 41). Berg's vision is planetary, relevant to cities, practical, cultural, and empowering. He expresses this vision with the utmost cogency and poetic precision.

Peter Berg's bioregional paradigm arrived as an illumination, a flash of understanding in which he saw things in a new light. A cross-country circuit drive he made from 1970 to 1972 revealed environmental disasters in every corner of North America, penetrating into even the most remote locations. Attending the 1972 United Nations conference on the human environment in Stockholm convinced Berg that solutions to environmental destruction were not going to come from the top. What could be done? Berg envisioned a movement for change starting from the ground up, led by people such as those he had met along his travels and in Stockholm, whom he dubbed "the planetariat." Indigenous peoples had inhabited particular places for thousands of years, evolving a way of life exquisitely adapted to local conditions. To "inhabit" implies fitting into and being a part of a *habitat*, a living place composed of plants, animals, organisms, soil, water, landforms, and climate. Perhaps people could learn to *reinhabit* Earth by learning about the natural conditions of the particular place where they live and evolving ways to fit into the ecology of that place. For example, people living in a windy area might produce energy from wind turbines, while those in a sunny climate might develop solar power.

In this model people must reimagine places from geopolitical to primarily ecological terms. Just as a plant or animal does not pay attention to county, state, or national borders but rather attends to ecotones, so too human "reinhabitants" would identify with the place where they live in terms of its natural properties and "soft borders," watersheds being a salient feature. Emerging from conversations with Allen Van Newkirk, Raymond Dasmann, and others, Berg proposed the term *bioregion* to designate these reimagined territories where reinhabitation could take place. As Berg argues, "If you want to get down to the hard bolts of breaking down this oil economy, you want to have political, agricultural, economic, social, and energy decentralization. What is going to be the locus, the site for alternate energy? [. . .] Bioregions make appropriate locations for decentralization" ("Bioregion and Human Location" 94).

If reinhabitation is a process, *bioregion* is a concept that posits places as alive, each place a complex ecological web. As Berg explains, bioregions are

> "unique life-places with their own soils and climates, native plants and animals, and many other distinct natural characteristics. Each characteristic affects the others and is affected by them as in any other living system or body. And bioregions are all different from each other: not just 'mountains' but Appalachian Mountains or Rockies; not just 'river valley' but Hudson or Sacramento" ("Watershed-scaled" 5).

"Everyone lives in a bioregion," Berg explains. "Every place has its own unique set of natural characteristics. [. . .] People can fit into their bioregion by learning to adapt to these features" (Kisseloff 150).

Berg traced the root of the environmental crisis to industrialism, which has transformed civilization, culture, and consciousness in both capitalist and communist countries. Berg cites Lewis Mumford in dating the Industrial Age as beginning in the seventeenth century with the first iron bridge in England. As Berg explains,

> Since that time, Western consciousness has been dominated by the idea of taking natural systems apart for their ingredients and then reassembling the ingredients to make other things. This is a chemical trick that has been enormously powerful—I'm not going to say "successful" because the end product is *garbage*. The end product of the cars and refrigerators, all the rest of it, is a landfill or a *dump*. But the trick of it was that you were no longer bound by the restrictions of the natural resources of the place where you live. Once this Industrial Age consciousness became the main consciousness, inhabitation was no longer thought to be necessary or useful or practical. It became limited to the people with "insufficient intelligence" to be able to participate in the industrial trickery, the transformation of nature's ingredients into products. Consumer identity came from this.
>
> Well, this has been the ruination of the biosphere. And it won't do any good to *protest* industrial consciousness. What's necessary is to regain a consciousness that fits people into the biosphere. How else can you exist in a place for ten thousand years? So it's necessary to get traction with inhabiting the biosphere again. And that's what reinhabitation is about. In fact, there wouldn't be any reason for the term "bioregion" if the idea of the biosphere and the necessity of reinhabitation didn't exist. You put those two together, the middle part is the bioregion. (Personal Interview, 24 May 2011)

With the ultimate objective being sustainability, Berg envisioned bioregionalism as pursuing three goals, realized locally. First, reinhabitation requires restoring and maintaining natural systems. Ecological restoration projects might include replanting clearcuts, stabilizing stream banks to stop erosion, improving water quality by halting pollution, and re-creating marshlands. Second, the people of each bioregion should find ways to meet basic human needs sustainably, relying as much as possible on local materials and resources. Needs include food, shelter, energy, transportation, and health care. Third, and linked to the other two, there must be support for individuals engaged in the work of sustainability. People need ways to make a living, and those working toward reinhabitory goals need support for their efforts. Berg's vision rested on the insights that "your head can be any place, but your feet have to be *some* place" and that "we all live in some life-place, and [. . .] maybe if we save those parts we can save the whole" (*Envisioning* 97; "Post-Environmentalist").

Berg's bioregional paradigm provides the basis for redefining human identity. For Berg, the fundamental questions of identity are "Who am I? Where am I? And what am I going to do about it?" The bioregional alternative suggests the following answers:

- You are a member of *Homo sapiens*, a mammal species sharing the biosphere interdependently with other species and natural systems that support them.
- You are in a bioregion, an ecological home place that has distinct continuities that affect the way you live and are affected by you.
- You can reinhabit the place where you live by restoring and maintaining natural systems, finding sustainable ways to satisfy basic human needs such as water, food, energy, materials, and culture, and [. . .] support[ing] other people involved with the process of reinhabitation. ("SFMT Talk" 7)

To develop and disseminate bioregional ideas and practice, Peter Berg and his partner, Judy Goldhaft, founded Planet Drum in 1973, incorporating as a 501c3 federal nonprofit in 1978 as Planet/Drum Foundation, a "grassroots organization that emphasizes sustainability, community self-determination, and regional self-reliance" (Berg and Goldhaft 16). Berg directed Planet Drum Foundation for nearly forty years, from its founding to his death, in 2011. His overarching goal was to "develop a place-located ecological philosophy and movement to restore bioregions that could eventually replace the disinhabitory view of industrialism" (*Envisioning* 51).

Bioregionalism could reasonably be viewed as a strand of the environmental movement. Philip Shabecoff, for example, in *A Fierce Green Fire: The American Environmental Movement*, regards bioregionalism as one manifestation of social ecology, a "minor tributary" of the US environmental movement (116). Berg, however, thought of bioregionalism as postenvironmental. By the first Earth Day, in 1970, there was broad popular support for protecting the environment. Sweeping environmental protection laws were passed in the United States at this time in history, including the National Environmental Policy Act (1969), a Clean Air Act (1970), the Clean Water Act (1972), and the Endangered Species Act (1973), among others. Berg did not oppose these acts, but he felt that their thrust was misguided. Rather than overturning industrial civilization, such laws merely made it "nicer" (Berg, "Ecology Emerges"). Berg likened environmentalism to "a hospital that only has an emergency room. It doesn't have a maternity ward. Doesn't have long-term care. Doesn't have child care—it just has a trauma section. That's environmentalism. [W]e need a nonindustrial perspective of human beings and the biosphere. Nonindustrial. Postindustrial" (Wilson 2). In his view, while the environmental movement aimed to conserve, protect, and preserve natural resources, what was needed was a movement to *harmonize* human activities with natural systems.

The problem with environmentalism is encoded in the word "environment" itself. By definition, "environment" separates humans from the "environment" that surrounds and is outside them. "Environment" rests on the premise of a duality between humans and nature, and environmentalists want to protect nature from humans. According to Berg, this view is fundamentally flawed. He prefers the word "ecology" to "environment." Ecology is a whole-systems vision that sees humans as a species in the biosphere, a part of nature. Speaking of environmentalists, Berg said, "it seemed to me that they were spectators of nature rather than involved in it. They weren't willing to give up the benefit of the anthropocentric viewpoint of dominating the earth. [. . .] They wanted to keep that but also be nice to nature" ("Ecology Emerges"). Berg wanted to replace industrial civilization with an ecological civilization, and from his perspective environmentalism amounted to little more than cleaning up environmental messes rather than transforming civilization into one that does not damage natural life-support systems in the first place. In his critique of the environmentalist paradigm, Berg shared the outlook of deep ecologists such as Arne Naess, and he wanted to create a social movement that would transform society and *enact* a biocentric philosophy. To do that required grounding. Berg's idea of the bioregion described a territory where a culture based on principles of deep ecology could *take place*.

Berg wanted to replace the protest approach of environmentalist politics with a proactive approach of ecological politics ("Ecology Emerges"). While protest had its place, Berg preferred an orientation that took positive steps to restore damaged ecosystems and push for sustainability. And he wanted to do it "in a communal way—interactive, mutualistic, participatory" ("Ecology Emerges"). As he saw it culture change comes from the bottom up, not from the top down. For Berg, the environmental movement became less interesting and engaging as it became institutionalized with Earth Day and the founding of the US Environmental Protection Agency (EPA) in 1970. At that point environmentalism became the domain of lawyers and professionals, reflecting middle-class values. He recalled receiving a mailer from the Sierra Club, inviting Planet Drum Foundation to place an ad with *Sierra* magazine. In an effort to attract Planet Drum's business, the mailer characterized the demographic of Sierra Club membership. The average Sierra Club member, Berg learned, had an income *way* above the normal income and had $15,000 of disposable money per year for excursions to places like Tierra del Fuego. The common cars were Volvos and Mercedes-Benzes, and the liquor of choice was scotch. Berg balked: "To me it seemed like these were the very people I was rebelling against" ("Ecology Emerges"). Throughout its history Planet Drum Foundation has aimed to facilitate communication among grassroots groups and to find ways for a wide spectrum of people of all colors and incomes to become directly involved in projects where they live.

From its inception to the present, Planet Drum Foundation has sponsored projects and activities related to "restoration ecology, green cities, sustainable agriculture, renewable energy, watershed consciousness, and ecology education" ("Planet Drum's Vision"). Planet Drum has pursued an active publishing program, producing more than fifty publications, including early "Bundles"; books; the Planet Drum review, *Raise the Stakes*; *PULSE* newsletter; *The Green City Calendar*; booklets; workbooks; pamphlets; broadsides; posters; videos; a website; and online articles and "Dispatches."

Under Berg's leadership, Planet Drum has offered hundreds of workshops, cosponsored bioregional gatherings both regional and continental, and organized numerous community events. Berg has given talks at Harvard University, Vassar, Pratt Institute, the University of North Carolina, Stanford, and the University of California (at Berkeley, Santa Cruz, Santa Barbara, and Davis), as well as at the Library of Congress in Washington, DC, where he was an invited speaker at the *Watershed: Writers, Nature and Community* event organized by poet laureate Robert Hass.

Planet Drum's activities extend beyond North America and include educational and organizing tours in South America, Europe, Japan, China, and Australia. Berg has lectured at the Chinese Academy of Sciences in Beijing, King Abdul Aziz University in Saudi Arabia, numerous universities in Japan, the University of Barcelona in Spain, the University of Rome in Italy, the Open University in Norwich, England, and the Universidad Espiritu Santo in Ecuador. He has spoken to an unusually wide range of groups, including the American Association of Anthropologists, the Association of Landscape Architects, the Brisbane and Melbourne city councils in Australia, the Center for Democracy in Germany, city council members of Tepoztlán, Mexico, the City Ecology Conference in Moscow, the Eco-City Conference in Brazil, the International Forum on Globalization (in Washington, DC, New York, and California), the Pollution Probe Foundation in Canada, the Smithsonian Institution, and hundreds of other locally based groups. In 2000 Planet Drum opened a field office in Bahía de Caráquez, Ecuador, to assist in transforming that city into an ecological city based on bioregional principles.[2]

Berg has been recognized with honors and awards that include a Gerbode Professional Development Program Fellowship for Outstanding Non-Profit Organization Executives in 1998 and inclusion in Greenwood's *Environmental Activists* in 2001. In recognition of Berg's vision, dedication, and leadership, the City and County of San Francisco proclaimed October 1, 2011, Peter Berg Day ("Proclamation"). A memorial ceremony for Berg was held in 2012 by the city of Bahía de Caráquez, Ecuador, and a plaque honoring him hangs in the entrance of Bahía's city hall.

But Peter Berg deserves more recognition than he has yet received. Richard Evanoff, author of *Bioregionalism and Global Ethics*, compares Berg to Aldo Leopold, "whose *Sand County Almanac* presented embryonic ideas that would form the basis for much current environmental philosophy and would later be more fully developed by others" (e-mail correspondence). Berg chose to work outside of and often against the mainstream, on the ground and in the streets, with ordinary people, and under the radar of the establishment. His influence on people in many parts of the world has been profound, and the ripple effect from his thinking, writing, and organizing has crossed the oceans to embrace the whole planet.[3]

Indeed, Berg's ideas have caught on, even as the specific term "bioregionalism" has been eclipsed by the related term "sustainability," a word that Berg began using in the '70s, a generation ahead of his time. The farmers markets, organic farming, local foods, and community-supported agriculture movements emerge from a bioregional paradigm. Green City initiatives ("green city" is another term we owe to Berg) are being implemented all over the world, leading to the daylighting of streams, energy conservation in public buildings, fuel-efficient public transportation, community gardens, plantings in median strips, remanufacturing industries, biological treatment systems for sewage, and recycling programs. Ecological restoration efforts are under way via revegetation projects, wildlife corridors, bioremediation of polluted waterways, dam removal, river-course re-engineering, invasive-species control, and native plant landscaping. People enjoy a range of local seasonal celebrations, such as spring and fall bird migration festivals, wildflower walks, whale watches, salmon runs, wolf howls, and solstice and equinox observations. In addition, hyperlocal websites and apps, local blogs, and regional magazines are proliferating, part of a vibrant DIY movement and an emerging focus on resilience.

But do people know *why* they are doing these things? Are these trends just passing fads, or are they more deeply rooted in an emerging ecological identity? *The Biosphere and the Bioregion* pursues interlocking goals in four areas:

Philosophy: The essays collected here provide a highly accessible introduction to bioregional philosophy, a paradigm that integrates, undergirds, and gives direction to emergent new localisms, envisioning these activities and human identity in an ecological context.

History: This book contributes to the history of the environmental movement by documenting the work and reprinting selected writings of Peter Berg. Berg moved to San Francisco in the 1960s, wrote and acted in productions of the San Francisco Mime Troupe, cofounded the Diggers, and became an internationally known bioregional thinker and activist. Despite Berg's importance, his significance has yet to be registered by scholars.

Policy: Berg's essays offer hands-on, practical guides for urban sustainability, habitat restoration, and life-place education by establishing a conceptual framework, setting forth specific mandates, and providing helpful examples.

Scale: This book enters a current debate about whether the global scale of environmental problems requires that we develop a "sense of planet" rather than a "sense of place."[4] Berg's dispatches—from North America, Japan, China, and Ecuador—reveal how each place (bioregion) is a functional part of the life of the planet (biosphere), requiring place-specific ways of harmonizing culture with nature. Berg was ahead of his time in realizing that globalization and localization are occurring simultaneously and in striving collaboratively to envision a way for the two trends to make an ecological turn.

Regarded as a genius by his peers, Berg possessed a lightning mind, a trickster's wit, and a poet's sensitivity to language. His essays are the precise and poetic pronouncements of a radical intellect, and discerning readers will relish Berg's double entendres, epigrams, and insights/incites. Peter Berg was a charismatic performer whose delivery was tailored to the stage of the hour, from street theater to outdoor bioregional gatherings to college classrooms to press clubs to a United Nations conference. Some of Berg's most engaging publications originated as talks or taped interviews. Many of the essays and transcripts featured in this book retain a fresh, performative quality, a readerly taste of "Berg live." While this book includes some foundational essays from the late 1970s and 1980s, most of the pieces date from the late 1990s and 2000s. Berg did not waver from the bioregional paradigm that he proposed in the early '70s, but he did deepen it conceptually and extend it to new contexts. Cheryll Glotfelty's essay "Peter Berg: Living a Making" establishes these contexts by tracing the evolution of Berg's thinking and documenting his accomplishments.

The lead essay of this collection, "Reinhabiting California," by Peter Berg and Raymond F. Dasmann, one of the world's preeminent conservation biologists, was published in *The Ecologist* in 1977 and has been reprinted many times as a foundational essay in bioregional thought. Few people realize that this classic coauthored essay is a revised version of an earlier piece authored solely by Peter Berg, which appeared in *Seriatim: Journal of Ecotopia* earlier the same year. For the historical record and to facilitate comparison between the two versions, Berg's original essay is reprinted in the appendix of this book.

Berg's more recent writings document bioregional initiatives, such as an ecological report card of the winter Olympics in Nagano, Japan, and a revegetation project in Bahía de Caráquez, Ecuador. From Berg's books, essays, and published interviews, which together number well over two hundred, this volume collects pieces that represent his bioregional vision and its urban and international applications.[5] These brisk essays and dispatches, from a single page to a dozen pages in length, are grouped chronologically within each of four sections; a fifth section includes tributes written about Berg:

Part 1 – Peter Berg's Bioregional Vision

These essays introduce Peter Berg's bioregional philosophy, establish core concepts, distinguish bioregionalism from environmentalism and "planetarianism" from globalism, and show bioregional ideas in action through a fresh mix of examples.

Part 2 – Transforming Cities from Gray to Green

These readings bring bioregionalism to the city, with the aim of reintegrating urban areas into the natural systems in which they are embedded. At once pragmatic and visionary, Berg provides a feasible plan for urban sustainability and imagines an ecological identity for urban dwellers.

Part 3 – Bioregional Travels around the Pacific Rim

Peter Berg has traveled to most of the continents on the planet. The dispatches from Asia and Hawai'i featured in this section show Berg exchanging ideas with citizens from a variety of places, from depopulated mountain villages in Japan to overpopulated megacities in China.

Part 4 – Ecological Restoration in Ecuador

A bioregional approach can be applied anywhere, and it is instructive to witness its versatility and effectiveness. In 2000 Planet Drum Foundation began doing ecological restoration work in Bahía de Caráquez. The readings in this section tell the story of how Bahía transformed itself from a storm- and earthquake-ravaged disaster area to an eco-city, and Berg expresses admiration for forward-thinking Ecuador, whose newest constitution grants rights to Nature.

Part 5 – Tributes

Peter Berg's friends and associates are a varied and accomplished group, including a Pulitzer Prize-winning poet, a poet laureate of the United States, a movie star, publishers, activists and organizers in different parts of the world, and many published authors. Twenty of Berg's gifted comrades and contemporaries agreed to write original tributes for this book. Their eloquent reflections illuminate Berg's character, affirm his significance, contextualize his work, and place him in good company.

A gallery of photographs located in the center of the book captures gestures from Berg the life-actor and agent provocateur.

Just two months before his death, after Berg had undergone chemotherapy and was sometimes tethered to an oxygen machine, he was asked, "What is your message to the world?" Pausing, he then replied thoughtfully:

> There is a tremendous need to not only transform our consciousness about the relationship of people to nature but to actually begin living a different kind of life that is geared toward blending with nature. There needs to be a new idea or a more fleshed out idea of what a human being is in reference to sharing the biosphere with other life. The current notion of that, even in its most benevolent form, isn't adequate to the problem. The problem has always been at the fringe of social, political, and economic considerations, and I'm not going to attribute this to any ideological deliberation. It just is the way it is, and it's got to move, not only more towards the center, it's got to *become* the center. Ecological identity of a human being has to become the *central* identity of a human being in order to get through the crisis that we're presently involved with. Most people aren't aware of the depth of the crisis. I don't want to trot out all the reasons why this century has this particular burden, which is to change the identity of who people are, but it is the case and it's an enormous job. The task of it is almost overwhelming to consider. Like how are we going to get from the present idea of a person who is consuming resources and creating a garbage planet to a person who is interdependent with other species and the natural processes of the biosphere? The word "sustainability" will have no meaning unless *that* can be achieved. (Personal Interview, 24 May 2011)

In *The Conservation Alternative* Peter Berg's friend and mentor Raymond Dasmann observes that "the first law of the environment for today [is], 'no matter
how bad you think things are—the total reality is much worse'" (99). Peter Berg
was aware of the severity of environmental problems, and he dedicated his life to
envisioning and enacting a way out of the crisis, a way that entails a fundamental
change in the way humans think of themselves and relate to the biosphere, specifically the part of the biosphere where they live. Bioregionalism equips society to
make the leap from the industrial era into the ecological era, one place at a time.

Notes

1. Several important introductory books on bioregionalism were published during the
   height of the bioregional movement, from the late 1970s through 1990. Key works from
   this period include *Reinhabiting a Separate Country*, edited by Peter Berg (Planet Drum
   Foundation, 1978); Kirkpatrick Sale's *Dwellers in the Land* (Sierra Club Books, 1985);
   Home! A Bioregional Reader, ed. Van Andruss, et. al. (New Society, 1990); and *The
   Practice of the Wild* by Gary Snyder (North Point Press, 1990). Noteworthy books since
   1999 include Michael Vincent McGinnis's edited collection *Bioregionalism* (Routledge,
   1999); Mitchell Thomashow's *Bringing the Biosphere Home* (MIT Press, 2002); Robert
   Thayer Jr.'s *LifePlace: Bioregional Thought and Practice* (U of California Press, 2003);
   Richard Evanoff's *Bioregionalism and Global Ethics* (Routledge, 2011); *The Bioregional Imagination: Literature, Ecology, and Place*, co-edited by Tom Lynch, Cheryll
   Glotfelty, and Karla Armbruster (U of Georgia P, 2012); and Molly Scott Cato's *The
   Bioregional Economy: Land, Liberty and the Pursuit of Happiness* (Routledge, 2012).
2. For additional information on Peter Berg's travels and accomplishments contact Planet
   Drum Foundation.
3. Information on the achievements of Peter Berg and Planet Drum was drawn from "Biographical Note," "Planet Drum's Vision," "Proclamation," and Clay Plager-Unger's
   "Field Report #6."
4. Ursula K. Heise's *Sense of Place and Sense of Planet* (Oxford UP, 2008) opened this
   important debate in the context of risk theory and literary studies.
5. Berg's 2009 collection, *Envisioning Sustainability*, features essays, poems, broadsides,
   posters, and screeds from the 1960s to 2004. We hope that our book will spark wider
   interest in Peter Berg and will lead readers to *Envisioning Sustainability*.

Works cited

Aberley, Doug. "Interpreting Bioregionalism: A Story from Many Voices." *Bioregionalism*.
   Ed. Michael Vincent McGinnis. London: Routledge, 1999. 13–42. Print.
Berg, Peter. "Bioregion and Human Location." 1983. Rpt. in Berg, *Envisioning Sustain-
   ability*. Print.
———. "Ecology Emerges" oral history interview collection. Interview by Chris Carlsson
   and David Martinez. *Shaping San Francisco: Excavating the City's Lost History*. Aug.
   2009. Web. 28 May 2013.
———. *Envisioning Sustainability*. San Francisco: Subculture Books, 2009. Print.
———. Personal Interview. 24 May 2011.
———. "The Post-Environmentalist Directions of Bioregionalism." *Poetics of Wilderness
   Proceedings*. Wilderness Issues Lecture Series 2001. Ed. Roger Dunsmore. Missoula:
   University of Montana, 2001. 166–173. Web.

————. "SFMT Talk." Unpublished manuscript. No date.

————. "Watershed-Scaled Governments and Green Cities." *Land Use Policy* 4.1 (Jan. 1987): 5–10. Print.

Berg, Peter, and Judy Goldhaft. "Peter Berg and Judy Goldhaft." *Environmental Activists*. Ed. John Mongillo and Bibi Booth. Westport, CT: Greenwood Press, 2001. 16–20. Print.

"Biographical Note." 11 March 2012. *Planet Drum Foundation Blogs*. Planet Drum Foundation, 2012. Web. 15 June 2013.

Dasmann, Raymond F. *The Conservation Alternative*. New York: Wiley, 1975. Print.

Evanoff, Richard. E-mail correspondence. 1 Feb. 2013.

Kisseloff, Jeff. "Peter Berg: The Digger." *Generation on Fire: Voice of Protest in the 1960s, An Oral History*. Lexington: UP of Kentucky, 2007. 137–51. Print.

————. "Standing in the Places We Live: Some Sketches of Bioregionalists." *E Magazine* (September/October 1991): 40–43, 56. Print.

Plager-Unger, Clay. "Field Report #6." Reports from Planet Drum Staff Eco-Ecuador Project 2012–2013. *Planet Drum Foundation*. Planet Drum Foundation, 2013. Web.

"Planet Drum's Vision." 2011. *Planet Drum Foundation*. Planet Drum Foundation, 2013. Web. 15 June 2013.

"Proclamation. October 1, 2011 as Peter Berg Day in San Francisco." City and County of San Francisco. Ross Mirkarimi, Supervisor, Board of Supervisors. 20 Sept. 2011. Print.

Shabecoff, Philip. *A Fierce Green Fire: The American Environmental Movement*. Revised edition. Washington, DC: Island Press, 2003. Print.

Wilson, Josh. "Another Green World. 1970s-Spawned Planet Drum Foundation Presages Today's Green Renaissance." *San Francisco Chronicle* 5 Feb. 2004: 2. Web. 11 Jan. 2014.

PETER BERG: LIVING A MAKING

Cheryll Glotfelty

Peter Berg's genius lies not only in his ideas—available in this collection—but in how he implemented them. He was, by his own self-description, a *life-actor*. Rather than aiming to make a living, he strove to "live a making." He is the consummate "Be the Change" agent. And he was extraordinarily effective. The following essay chronicles Peter Berg as thinker and activist, tracing the evolution of Berg's ideas and documenting how he *enacted* those ideas to bring about change. In an interview late in his life Berg compared a person's growth to tree rings, and he identified the layers of his own life as being civil rights, Mime Troupe and Diggers, early bioregional work, Green City, and Ecuador (Berg, "Ecology"). The following account begins by surveying Berg's early activities through the Digger period, then focuses in greater detail on Berg's bioregional work, including his Green City and Ecuador activities.

I. Early years

Peter Berg was born in 1937 in the town of Jamaica, Long Island, New York, the youngest of four children. His mother moved with her two youngest children to Florida when Berg was in grade school. In 1954 Berg entered the University of Florida on a work-study scholarship. Among the subjects that interested him were psychology, philosophy, drama, and English. At the University of Florida in the segregated South in the mid-1950s, Berg was one of a dozen or so students who agitated for civil rights. Black students were not permitted to attend the University of Florida at that time, and Berg and some fellow students were hauled into the dean's office and reprimanded for putting up signs around campus that read "Integrate in '58" (Wolf and Wolf 255).

In college, Berg became friends with Marvin Longton, a Korean War veteran who read British novels, was a jazz fanatic, and became a mentor to the younger

Peter (Kisseloff 141). Through Longton, Berg discovered Allen Ginsberg's *Howl* and felt an immediate kinship with beat poetry, electrified by its hip language and rebellious spirit. After college Berg chose to enlist in the army rather than be drafted. The United States was between the Korean War and the Vietnam War, so he did not see combat. He was assigned to conduct a psychological study of soldiers' morale (Personal Interview, 24 May 2011). Berg took advantage of his desk job in the army to read all the books he could find on Indian, Chinese, and Japanese poetry, prose, and plays as well as contemporary Asian-influenced writing, including poetry by Gary Snyder. He memorized parts of the *Tao Te Ching*, some poems of Li Po, haiku by Bashō, and some lines from Snyder's "T-2 Tanker Blues" (Berg, "Beating" 376–77).

After his discharge from the army, in 1961, Berg moved to New York City, where he reconnected with his college friend Marvin Longton. In New York Berg took a job as a statistician for the American Bankers Association and became involved with radical black activists in the civil rights movement. One day he was riding the subway and glanced up at some lettering inside the subway car. The green-lit words read, "If you don't know who you want to be, somebody will tell you who to be" (Personal Interview, 24 May 2011). The words were a wake-up call. So Berg left New York, and he hitchhiked, rode buses, and hopped a freight train, eventually landing in the San Francisco Bay Area.

II. Mime Troupe and Diggers

In 1964 Berg arrived in San Francisco and began working with the San Francisco Mime Troupe, a theater company that performed outdoor shows in the Commedia dell'Arte style to satirize contemporary politics and society. Berg worked as an actor, director, playwright, and producer for the Troupe. He adapted Giordano Bruno's sixteenth-century play *Il Candelaio* so that it could be performed in the park. The Mime Troupe's celebrated arrest for performing without a permit occurred during a public performance of this play. While Berg was working with the Mime Troupe he also wrote several original plays—*Centerman*, *Output You*, *Search and Seizure*—and cowrote the Obie-winning *Olive Pits*.

In 1966 Berg, his partner, Judy Goldhaft, and others split off from the Mime Troupe to form the Diggers, a more radical anarchist street-theater group. Two aspects of Peter Berg's Digger activities are worth noting here, his theory of theater and his awareness of ecology. As a spin-off of the Mime Troupe, which presented theater in public parks and usually for free, the Diggers pushed the idea of what Berg had dubbed "guerrilla theater" even further, beyond a designated stage and into the streets, where lines blurred between acting and life and between actors and audience. The Diggers stated, "Everything is free and do your own thing." Positing that "No play can change your life unless you are in it," Berg advocated that people become "life-actors" and perform "life acts": "*Acts that can create the conditions of life they describe!*" ("Free City Bloodlight" 22). Berg wrote numerous anonymous broadsides and "street sheets" with the Diggers, some of which were printed in *The Digger Papers*, including his manifesto "Trip without a Ticket":

> *Theater is territory.* A space for existing outside padded walls. Setting down a stage declares a universal pardon for imagination. But what happens next must mean more than sanctuary or preserve. How would real wardens react to life-actors on liberated ground? How can the intrinsic freedom of theater illuminate walls and show the weak-spots where a breakout could occur?
>
> *Guerrilla theater intends to bring audiences to liberated territory to create life-actors.* It remains light and exploitative of forms for the same reason that it intends to remain free. It seeks audiences that are created by issues. It creates a cast of freed beings. It will become an issue itself.
>
> This is theater of an underground that wants out. Its aim is to liberate ground held by consumer wardens and establish territory without walls. Its plays are glass cutters for empire windows. [...]
>
> Not street-theater, the street *is* theater. ("Trip" 3–4)

Berg named damage to the environment as one of the high costs of the US standard of living, with "death, slavery, and psychosis" as collateral damage. In "Trip without a Ticket" Berg asks, "Who paid for your trip?," answering that "Industrialization was a battle with 19th century ecology to win breakfast at the cost of smog and insanity. Wars against ecology are suicidal" ("Trip" 4). Printed in 1966, "Trip without a Ticket" used the word "ecology" before Paul Krassner, the publisher of *The Digger Papers*, had heard the term and before the word appeared in some dictionaries. In 1968 the city of San Francisco cracked down on the counterculture, and by 1969 many members of the Digger free family and counterculture left San Francisco and spread out across North America in the back-to-the-land movement.

Berg and Goldhaft next spent several years living with and visiting rural communes. They began their odyssey in northern California in Siskiyou County, spending some of winter 1970–71 at Black Bear Ranch, a Free Digger-esque commune, where they lived off the grid. According to Berg, the orientation of the Diggers at this time was changing from "Everything is free. Do your own thing" to "Everything is interdependent. Act responsibly with nature" (Kisseloff 149). During that same winter Berg was invited to visit the set of the Hollywood movie *McCabe and Mrs. Miller* as the final episodes were being filmed in Canada. The art director of the movie, Al Locatelli, gifted Peter a Sony Portapak, the first portable reel-to-reel video camera and player. Berg wanted to document back-to-the-land communes around the country, places where people who had moved out of the cities were exploring homesteading and new social forms (Personal Interview, 24 May 2011). By the summer of 1971 Berg and Goldhaft and some cohorts decided to make a caravan of rolling house-trucks "in an attempt to discover whatever common threads might be running through other land-based communities" ("Beating" 383). At each commune of "new settlers" Berg planned to make a "video postcard," which he would show to the next group as a way to introduce these land-based communities to each other. He called this project "Homeskin Video Postcards."

An early stop on the caravan journey was the San Juan Ridge above the Yuba River in the Sierra Nevada foothills of northern California, where a Zen-practicing community had formed on "the Ridge" with Gary Snyder as a nucleus. Berg, an "inveterate outsider," found spiritual practices of any sort, "whether public rituals or solitary meditation, [to be] anathema" ("Beating" 382). Peter Berg, whom others referred to as "The Hun," could be an intimidating guest. Peter Coyote in his memoir *Sleeping Where I Fall* recalls Berg as "a penetrating thinker, hypnotically articulate and animated by a moral outrage expressed in rapid-fire, highly associative dialogue and mad humor of the low-German, slapstick variety. Mercurial, charming, coercive, subliminally menacing, and intellectually uncompromising, he frightened people who did not know him well" (18). Berg recalls asking a challenging question during one of Snyder's Zen teaching circles; Snyder parried elegantly, answering Berg's question and then making a point of his own ("Beating" 382–83). Indeed, Berg and Snyder, two of the most prominent individuals of the bioregional movement, form a fascinating contrast—Berg urban, Snyder rural; Berg East Coast, Snyder West Coast; Berg confrontational, Snyder composed; both extremely intelligent. As Berg recalls of the caravan stopover in the summer of '71:

> Snyder and I talked over the apparent conflict in what each of us was doing. Although he was making a local stand and concentrating on community and regional issues and I was setting out to view as many places as possible, there was an intimate connection between our approaches. I would learn if there was real potential for a widespread land-based ecology movement. He would discover whether the Ridge community could strengthen and mobilize its own ecological concerns. We would share experiences when we met again. ("Beating" 384)

Snyder and Berg would meet again many times, and their work would intertwine over the next forty years. Like oil and vinegar, they gave flavor to the bioregional movement.

In southern Colorado most of the truck caravan returned to California, but Berg and Goldhaft and their children continued on to Maine that year and then to what ultimately became a "coast-to-coast circuit ride around North America" (Berg, "Beating" 383). Everywhere they encountered ecological disasters, with even the most remote places suffering damage (Personal Interview, 11 March 2011). For example, at the end of a dirt road in the Ozarks, just the place you would go to get away from civilization, a group of new settlers was distressed that the government was providing Agent Orange to their nearest neighbors across the road to defoliate the hardwoods. The group was very concerned that Agent Orange would pollute their drinking water (Personal Interview, 24 May 2011).

III. Thinking about bioregions

The year 1972 was a milestone in the history of bioregionalism. During the winter of 1972 in Maine, Berg and Goldhaft traveled to Nova Scotia so Berg could rekindle a relationship with a poet named Allen Van Newkirk, an expatriate American living in Canada ("Ecology Emerges"). Van Newkirk and Berg shared a concern that environmental degradation was more widespread than most people realized. Both agreed:

> [T]he environmental movement as it had proceeded until then was completely inadequate to deal with the underlying problems that industrial society created for the biosphere. Cleaning up after larger and larger disasters wasn't going to keep them from happening in the first place. The only way to succeed at preventing them was to restructure the way people satisfied basic materials needs and related to the natural systems upon which their own survival ultimately depended. (Berg, "Beating" 385)

On his trip Berg had already observed many instances of ecological disasters that straddled political jurisdictions such as state and county lines, thus stymieing efforts to create long-range solutions ("Beating" 384). Van Newkirk was interested in researching, cataloguing, and preserving the plants, animals, and ecology of naturally defined as opposed to politically defined regions. He liked the term "bioregions" to designate regions whose borders could be determined by natural properties such as native plant and animal communities, climate, landforms, and soil type. The term apparently originated in nineteenth-century German natural science investigations (Berg, "Ecology Emerges"). Van Newkirk planned to start an Institute for Bioregional Research to begin mapping bioregions as a basis for conservation. Van Newkirk told Berg about Dr. Raymond Dasmann, a UC Berkeley–trained ecologist who was working in Switzerland for a unit of the World Wildlife Fund called the International Union for the Conservation of Nature and Natural Resources (Berg, "Beating" 384). Dasmann and Miklos Udvardy had produced maps of "biotic provinces" based on communities of native plants and animals. All three men, Berg, Van Newkirk, and Dasmann, were attempting to see beyond existing political boundaries—often straight lines imposed on the land irrespective of natural properties—in order to identify territories or conservation management areas in tune with habitat types and natural systems.

Despite their shared concerns, Berg and Van Newkirk disagreed on the role of people in bioregions. As Berg recalls, "[Van Newkirk] had grown very disaffected about being involved with people in politics. [. . .] He did not want human beings in bioregions" ("Ecology Emerges"). Van Newkirk envisioned bioregions as a way of classifying and conserving natural areas in scientific terms, preferring to "develop concepts and information that could be used on an academic and agency level" (Berg "Beating" 385). Berg, however, "wanted a new cultural and political formulation that would put ecological concerns at the center of society" (385). He thought that "bioregion" would be a good *cultural* term, maybe even popular culture. His vision was to "include people and their culture in a geography in [. . .] an ecologically restorative way" ("Ecology Emerges").

While Van Newkirk thought of bioregions in strictly scientific terms and strongly disagreed with Berg's idea to inject the idea of bioregions into popular culture, Dasmann thought the idea had merit. As Berg tells the story,

> Ray had expert information about ecologically defined geographic areas and knew firsthand how far destruction of the planet had progressed. He had worked with enough state, national, and international agencies to know their limits and distrust their capability to come to grips with ultimate ecological realities. When I proposed that new land-based and other groups could identify with and restore their local areas in ways that were more thorough-going and socially transformative than were possible through established governments he was enthusiastic about the prospect and wanted to help. ("Beating" 386)

When Dasmann was on leave in the United States in 1973 and interested in moving to the country, at Berg's suggestion he bought some land and eventually built a house on the San Juan Ridge near where Gary Snyder lived (Jarrell 82). Dasmann and Berg spent time together exploring there and other places around northern California. Dasmann provided an ecologist's view, filled with wonder and questions, noticing details such as coyote scat on a tree stump. Berg, Dasmann, and Snyder carried on a "trialogue" that extended to other activists about how to reverse the way society was headed. They combined Dasmann's idea of defining regions based on their natural characteristics, Snyder's interest in locally specific subsistence practices, and Berg's intuition that the solution had to involve putting people back into nature.

Berg thought that the best way to reverse environmental damage was to change culture and consciousness, moving society from an industrial model of human relation to the biosphere to an ecological model. Dasmann agreed, but as a scientist he lacked experience in changing culture. For his part, Berg was a seasoned activist, but he needed Dasmann's scientific expertise and reputation to give these ideas legitimacy and clout. Their co-authored "Reinhabiting California" appeared in *The Ecologist* in 1977, introducing the bioregional perspective as a science-culture model for maintaining the health of the biosphere. As Berg explains, Dasmann took the bioregional idea "out of the hippie, back-to-the-land, Indian-loving, fringe area and put it into science. Major. Something you could base a policy on. And as soon as he did that the State of California based policies on it" (Personal Interview, 24 May 2011). Together Berg and Dasmann made a formidable team. "We were really hell on wheels," Berg recalls, "You couldn't get past us if [we] were in a room of people trying to convince them of something. We had them. We had them from both directions" (Personal Interview, 24 May 2011).

While the visit with Van Newkirk kindled the idea of bioregions in Berg's imagination, his 1972 trip in June to attend the first United Nations Conference on the Human Environment, in Stockholm, Sweden, convinced him that environmental solutions would never come from the top. In Stockholm, there was a class divide between the official representatives of nations along with UN-recognized environmental organizations, both of whom convened inside the conference building, and the thousands of ordinary citizens gathered outside in the streets, denied entry to the conference building. These people had made their way to Stockholm from all over the world to express concerns about environmental problems affecting their lives, but they were given no voice in or access to the official proceedings. Nevertheless, to Berg's way of thinking, "the planetariat" represented the future. As he recalls,

> The presence of thousands of activists and demonstrators who somehow managed to transport themselves to Stockholm proved that ecology wasn't just a North American cause. Included in the wide range of uninvited attendees who I dubbed "the planetariat" were Japanese Minamata disease (mercury poisoning) victims, Vietnamese Buddhist monks, Eritrean rebels, Sames (Laplanders) from the Arctic Circle, Native Americans, and Swedish anarchists with black and green flags. For most of them no real answers to the issues they represented came out of the official gathering. Instead, the conference crystallized the frustration people were feeling about the inability of any established institutions to deal with planetary problems. Snyder blasted it as an exercise where "robot nations [. . .] argue how to parcel out our Mother Earth." And if the U.N. couldn't provide an effective forum, what body could? I came back determined to find a method for constructing a human-species-on-the-planet-together politics from the ground up. ("Beating" 385)

After Berg returned from the UN, the widespread ecological damage he and Goldhaft witnessed across the country and their lack of faith that the government would address these problems solidified their determination not to "contribute to this crap," Berg recalls. As their circuit drive continued Berg remembers looking at Goldhaft and saying, "We're not going back [to San Francisco] unless we can reverse this process. I'm not going to live in this country. I don't want to do anything unless we can change this" (Personal Interview, 11 March 2011). He returned with determination and a new sense of direction.

IV. Planet Drum

Berg and Goldhaft decided to form something like a "green guerrilla network," which would link the many back-to-the-land communities they had met on their drive and learned about while traveling. The idea was that if one community needed immediate assistance to protect its area from an environmental threat, others in the network would come to its aid (Personal Interview, 24 May 2011). The plan ultimately did not materialize because each community had so many challenges in its own region that people couldn't rush to aid another location. Nevertheless, this network bore fruit and played a key role in starting the bioregional movement.

Working in the years before personal computers and the Internet, Berg and his associates needed a medium that could help to form a network out of a large and diverse number of new settler groups in North America and similar groups elsewhere on the planet whose commitment to their place went well beyond "conventional governmental consciousness" (Berg, "Beating" 386). Berg wanted to avoid a top-down editorial approach and the hierarchical structure of conventional magazines. His solution was to create "Bundles," envelopes containing separately printed pieces that reflected a common theme but each of which could also stand on its own. The contents of each Bundle varied but might include articles, maps, posters, photographs, a calendar, and even a piece of cloth. The publishing of Bundles was originally expected to move from group to group, but it became clear that their production and distribution needed to be coordinated.

Both the Bundles and the fledgling bioregional networking organization that published and distributed them free of charge were called Planet Drum. Berg explains the origin of the name:

> In Sweden I had learned about the reindeer-herding Sames who seemed to be European Indians and represented a link between indigenous people on both sides of the Atlantic. When I saw a drawing of one of their shamans playing a hoop drum painted with natural symbols and singing about the connections between them as a moving reindeer bone pointed them out, I decided to make it the publication's logo. The drum's symbols were like the pieces in the envelope. The order they were read in and the interpretation each person gave to them were similar to the shaman's song. It made perfect sense to call it *Planet Drum*. ("Beating" 386)

The first Planet Drum Bundle was published in 1973 and included six items:

1. A booklet entitled "Redwood's journal (Northern Colombia Notes)," documenting the lifestyles of the Indian people in La Guajira and the Cabo, noting "the relationships between characteristics, customs and natural surroundings."
2. "A page in the notebook of planeteye explorations" by David Empfield.
3. Drawing of the head of a Lapp shaman's drum, with description and explanation.
4. Black and white photographs of the Hausa tribe of Kano, West Africa, illustrating their cloth-dying technique, by Edmund Shea.
5. A poster with sections entitled "States" and "Two Rivers" by David Simpson, sharing local analysis from "reinhabitants of North America."
6. "Rain's cloth," a poem by Barbara LaMorticella silk-screened onto a nineteen-inch by fifteen-inch muslin cloth designed by Luna Moth Robbins, which might be used as part of a shirt or a piece of a quilt. ("Bundles, Spare Parts, and Illuminations" 1)

As the international contents of the first and subsequent Bundles—and indeed the very name of the organization, Planet Drum—suggest, Peter Berg's bioregional vision was from its inception planetary and not provincial. He sought to promote awareness of diverse cultures fitting in with the unique characteristics and natural systems where they live. As the Planet Drum facilitator, Berg solicited an eclectic range of genres, including art, poetry, manifestoes, essays, scientific reports, economic analysis, maps, photographs, interviews, jail notes, memoirs, watershed planning models, cyclical calendars, public policy recommendations, and geopsychic studies. He also maintained a high aesthetic value, and each Bundle is beautifully designed and produced. From 1973 to 1985 Planet Drum published nine Bundles (often as collaborations with bioregionally oriented locals), whose materials include pieces about specific places in North America, South America, the Arctic Circle, West Africa, Morocco, the Pacific Rim, Japan, and China. Issues explored include land-based identity, trade routes, phytogeography, totemic species, illness, recycling of wastes, low-impact technology, population, regional self-sufficiency, economics, colonialism, food, nuclear power, sustainability, watershed planning, renewable energy, and region-specific issues. The writings in these Bundles by authors such as Peter Berg, Peter Coyote, Raymond Dasmann, Jeremiah Gorsline, Freeman House, David Simpson, Gary Snyder, and George Tukel helped to develop and express bioregional principles. These Bundles, now thirty to forty years old, will strike even today's readers as radical and visionary.

In addition to their far-reaching publishing and networking activities, Berg and Goldhaft contacted local activists, natural scientists, writers, and artists to pool their knowledge of the San Francisco Bay watershed. The group, which met monthly beginning in 1975, called itself the Frisco Bay Mussel Group and explored hydrology, local culture, weather systems, political history, native plants and animals, and geological features. When the Mussel Group learned that the state of California planned to divert water from the Sacramento River to southern California by building a "Peripheral Canal" around the northern California inland delta, the group converted from a study group to a political action gadfly to protest the proposed water grab. The Sierra Club had gone on record as approving the project, and Friends of the Earth had expressed neutrality. From a bioregional perspective, water is the essential ingredient for the life of a place, and the "Vampire Ditch" plan would deprive the Sacramento Delta and San Francisco Bay of more than a million acre feet of water per year. The Mussel Group placed a full-page ad in the *San Francisco Chronicle* in 1977 against the canal—"*ACT NOW TO STOP THE PERIPHERAL CANAL.* Your entire water supply and 3.5 billion of your tax dollars are about to go down the Southern California drain" (rpt. in Berg, *Envisioning Sustainability* 72). The ad included coupons that could be clipped and sent to legislators. As a result of the public pressure aroused by the Mussel Group, the Sierra Club dropped its endorsement and Friends of the Earth began to openly oppose the diversion scheme, which was ultimately defeated by California voters.

The Mussel Group produced and Planet Drum published a booklet entitled *Living Here* and a *Watershed Guide* map-poster to evoke the natural amenities of the

San Francisco Bay Area watershed. Berg's introduction to *Living Here* is entitled "Borne-Native in the San Francisco Bay Region," a clever reversal of the concept that someone must be "native-born" to have the authority to speak for a particular place (1977, rpt. in *Envisioning* 71). Berg's memorable opening paragraphs poetically evoke the natural rhythms that unite the species of the watershed:

> We who live around the San Francisco Bay-Sacramento River Estuary, all species ranging this watershed on the North Pacific Rim, feel a common resonance behind the quick beats of our separate lives; long-pulse rhythms of the region pronouncing itself through Winter-wet & Summer-dry, Something-flowering-anytime, Cool Fog, Tremor and Slide.
>
> The region proclaims itself clearly. It declares the space for holding our own distinct celebrations: Whale Migration & Salmon Run, Acorn Fall, Blackberry & Manzanita Fruit, Fawn Drop, Red Tide; processions and feasts which invite many other species, upon which many other species depend. The bay-river watershed carries these outpourings easily. They are borne, native, by the place. Their occurrence and the full life of the region are inseparable. (rpt. in *Envisioning* 73)

In the mid 1970s Judy Goldhaft oversaw the creation of The Reinhabitory Theater Show *Northern California Stories*, which toured northern California performing renditions of stories from the region's Pomo, Maidu, Karok, and Pit River oral tribal traditions. The multispecies performances with actors performing animals (recognizable only by their physical movements and activities) were both informational and extremely funny. Berg was memorable as Lizard.

Berg notes in "Reinhabitory Theater," his philosophical guide to producing these shows, that the humor evokes deeper ecological realities. Berg ranks Native American "coyote stories" with Zen koans and Hasidic parables for "stimulating illuminations into the nature of being" and asserts that in order to do justice to the stories actors must assert "a multi-species vision that gives implicit credence and equality to all living things" (186, 187). "Coyote stories" work on several levels—visceral, interpersonal, multispecies, and cosmological—and the live performances aimed to evoke these levels simultaneously (187).

In this essay as in his other work, Berg attempts to forge a path from industrial to indigenous consciousness. "Each role should become a door which the actor opens to permit us to tumble back thousands of years in the history of that species," Berg explains. "Repeated gestures, repeated postures and repeated sounds that move through thousand-year cycles. Repetitions which are supported by the story line and by the fact that the principal phenomena of life occur over and over again" (191). Berg further observes that:

> "Coyote stories" are apparently about animals with the attributes of humans, but in essence they are about the consciousness of all living things in time. The sense of time that is revealed in tree rings, strata of rock, migrations of

> salmon, annual blossoming and fruiting of plants. Reinhabitory performers
> must create the sense of that which lives from generation to generation and
> is immutable. (191)

Reinhabitory Theater was an early experiment in ecological theater, intended to
help us "focus local community attention on bioregional concerns" and "invoke
a spirit of perpetual creation to show the interdependent relationship between
human beings and other species" ("Beating" 387; "Reinhabitory" 190). *Northern
California Stories* was staged in theaters, grange halls, and open-air pastures and
included a history of European settlement in California. Performances were often
accompanied by local community empowerment workshops, which later evolved
into Berg's acclaimed bioregional mapping workshops. Berg's central involvement in Reinhabitory Theater speaks to his belief in the importance of art in promoting change in culture, society, and ecological understanding.

Planet/Drum Foundation incorporated in 1978 as a federal 501c3 nonprofit
educational organization to "pursue research, organize workshops, create forums
and publish information about the relationship between human culture and the
natural processes of bioregions and the planetary biosphere" (Berg, "Creating"
159). From a small cluttered space, Planet Drum Foundation has served as an
incubator and nerve center for the bioregional movement.

In the second half of the 1970s Planet Drum gathered stories, poems, oral
histories, photographs, maps, art, and natural history information for a planned
Bundle about the Shasta Bioregion (northern California). The material outgrew
the constraints of a Bundle. Gary Snyder, who at the time chaired the California
Arts Council, encouraged Berg to apply for a publications grant. Berg was leery of
being affiliated with state-level government, but Snyder persisted, and the newly
minted Planet Drum Foundation received funding to produce *Reinhabiting a Separate Country: A Bioregional Anthology of Northern California* (1978), edited
by Peter Berg ("Beating" 388). As Berg's introduction explains, the "separate
country" of the title refers to distinct bioregions, whose "soft borders" are founded
on "specific soils and land forms, exposed to particular climate and weather, and
populated by native plants and animals which have endured since the last Ice Age"
(*Reinhabiting* 1). Each of these "natural countries" is "a separate part of the unified planetary biosphere; tissues and organs in the current manifestation of Earth's
anatomy" (1). Berg observes that on average Americans change residences every
three years. Rather than lamenting American transience, Berg encourages newcomers to learn and adapt to the "live geography" of their new home: "Wherever
they arrive, people are in a specific place and they are part of the natural country
holding them. Unless there is a culture and governing spirit that is informed by the
long-term life-continuities of that place to show them ways to reciprocate with it,
people usually become a negative part of the place" (1).

When the bioregional movement began to take off in the late 1970s, Planet
Drum started its review *Raise the Stakes*, published from 1979 to 2000, to explore
bioregional realities and reinforce the necessity for action. *Raise the Stakes* sought

to expand environmentalism to include radically proactive ideas and a long-term perspective. Throughout the 1980s Planet Drum served as a "mother-networking" organization for a movement that by the early 1990s comprised more than 250 bioregionally oriented groups in North America, including Canada and Mexico, with emerging movements in Australia, Latin America, Italy, and Spain (Weinberg 54).

Even as Berg penned a steady stream of writings that shaped the conceptual landscape of the bioregional movement, including articles for *Raise the Stakes* and its eventual successor, *PULSE*, he was equally active as an editor and organizer with a gift for involving people. In 1979, for example, Planet Drum convened a four-day public symposium in San Francisco, titled *Listening to the Earth: The Bioregional Basis of Community Consciousness*. Approximately one thousand people listened to discussions on such topics as "Grounding: New Approaches to the Problem of Energy"; "Technological Influences on American Culture"; "Our Place in the Water Cycle"; and "A New Context for Growth and Development." Speakers included leading environmental thinkers and authors, including Morris Berman, Murray Bookchin, Ernest Callenbach, Raymond F. Dasmann, Jerry Mander, Stephanie Mills, Roderick Nash, and Gary Snyder; scholars in the humanities; innovators in alternative energy and agriculture; and representatives of government agencies ("Beating" 389–90; *Listening to the Earth*). The text of the symposium's poster posed a conundrum that remains fundamental to bioregional thought (and that Berg had earlier expressed in his essay "Grounds and Surrounds"):

> Our society is heading in two conflicting directions. One is to preserve regional culture, community identity, natural resources and political autonomy. The second involves an expanding economy, increased urbanization, and the spread of a global way of life.
>
> The conflict between these is expressing itself in crises in energy, natural resources, growth and development, and cultural priorities.
>
> What could a bioregional perspective hope to achieve? Could it extend the concept of local identity to include a recognition of planetary interdependence? (*Listening to the Earth*)

In 1981 Berg and Stephanie Mills coedited a special issue of *CoEvolution Quarterly* on bioregions. This publication includes the often reprinted "Where You At?" bioregional quiz, compiled by Leonard Charles, Jim Dodge, Lynn Milliman, and Victoria Stockley, as well as important essays by Jim Dodge ("Living by Life"), Murray Bookchin ("The Concept of Social Ecology"), Peter Berg ("Devolving beyond Global Monoculture"), Jerry Mander ("Kit Carson in a Three-Piece Suit"), Winona La Duke ("Succeeding into Native North America"), Wes Jackson ("The Moral Dilemma of Keeping the Plains Alive"), Paul Hawken ("Intelligence, Not Heaven, Will Protect the Working Stiff"), and Gary Snyder ("Ink and Charcoal"). The Bioregions special issue, which advocates decentralization and supports home-rule movements, also includes maps ("Devolving Europe" and "Indian Land Claims & Treaty Areas of North America"), art, poems, interviews, fiction, book reviews, and bibliographies representing many regions of the Earth. Mills writes in the introduction to this issue, "The resistance of people to colonization and cultural destruction is a constant of human history. A loyalty to the planet, a detailed sense of place, and an informed love of homeland will save us" ("Planetary Passions" 5).

V. Green City

The 1980s also saw Planet Drum launch a Green City initiative for San Francisco that helped to introduce the concept of urban sustainability and sparked similar programs in other metropolitan areas. The Green City idea alone—notwithstanding Berg's other bioregional work—has had an enormous impact worldwide. One must pause to recall how forward-thinking the Green City idea was. In the 1980s most bioregionally inclined people were living rurally, many in back-to-the-land communities founded in the '60s and '70s. By the same token, environmentalists—most of whom lived in cities—tended to view cities as environmental scourges, polluted, noisy, dirty, densely populated, paved over, car choked. Environmental efforts were to a large extent directed toward wilderness preservation, saving pristine places to which city dwellers with sufficient means could retreat to find weekend solace. When Planet Drum launched its Green City program, there wasn't "a single realistic plan in operation to ecologically redirect and thereby advance the quality of life for any sizable urban area in North America" (Berg, Magilavy, and Zuckerman, *Bay Area and Beyond* xii). What Peter Berg did—what Planet Drum did—was to rethink cities. After all, having spent time in back-to-the-land settlements across the country, Berg *chose* to live in a large city. Rather than resisting or bewailing demographic trends toward urbanization, Berg accepted that fact and sought to make cities "into places that are life-enhancing and regenerative" (xii).

Proceeding collaboratively and inclusively, Planet Drum organized a series of topically defined "Green City" symposia in spring and summer of 1986, held at San Francisco's Fort Mason Center. Fund-raising for these meetings kicked off with an event, called *Celebrate the Longest Night*, that Planet Drum Foundation organized for the winter solstice of 1985 at the California Academy of Sciences. "Join us for the start of a campaign to green Bay Area cities and towns," read the event poster, which showed a green swash superimposed over a blue-and-white photograph of San Francisco and the Bay (*Celebrate*). Emceed by Peter Coyote and Scoop Nisker, the event featured speakers and poets (Peter Berg, Ernest Callenbach, Bob Carroll, Susan Griffin, Sibella Kraus, Jerry Martien, and Michael McClure), jugglers, belly dancers, acts, music, and tables displaying "Things that Work," native plants gifts, wines of the bioregion, and "Best of the Bay" desserts. In keeping with the invitation to "observe a planetary holiday," people gazed through telescopes to look for Halley's Comet (*Celebrate*). The event was a rousing success and was the first time that a wide assortment of Bay Area environmental action groups had convened under one roof. Berg reported afterwards that "Nearly a thousand people celebrated the longest night as cultural activists, waving the flag of ecological populism [. . . .] They were declaring planethood, and they came to revel in it" ("Celebrate" 2).

For the Green City meetings Planet Drum invited groups and individuals from actional fields of interest and asked them to contribute suggestions and visions on the specific topic of that particular meeting. More than 150 representatives attended these symposia on urban sustainability, and an equal number added recommendations to the written reports that emerged from the discussions. Session topics included "Urban Planting"; "Smart Transportation"; "Sustainable Planning"; "Renewable Energy"; "Neighborhood Character and Empowerment"; "Recycling and Re-use"; "Celebrating Life-Place Vitality"; "Urban Wild Habitat"; and "Socially Responsible Small Businesses and Cooperatives." Planet Drum brought together representatives from an unusually broad spectrum, stimulating an exchange among sectors that normally had little interaction with one another. For example, at the " Recycling and Re-use" meeting there were representatives from the city and county recycling agencies, private and re-use businesses, citizen groups opposed to waste, youth employment agencies, and professional scavenger companies (Berg et al., *Bay Area and Beyond* xiv).

Each meeting began with the moderator asking attendees to describe the current situation vis-à-vis the day's topic from that representative's point of view. The picture of the current situation was both quite dismal and also helpfully specific. Next, participants were asked what alternatives were possible. The conversation then began to brighten as practical, implementable suggestions emerged that would make a positive difference and would not only halt the decline of the region but actually improve it. Short-term and long-term practical suggestions bubbled up from these citizen brainstorming meetings and were captured in notes taken during the proceedings. From these notes, Peter Berg, Beryl Magilavy, and Seth Zuckerman produced a user-friendly seventy-page book entitled *A Green City Program for San Francisco Bay Area Cities and Towns*, published by Planet Drum Books in 1989. Chapters correspond to meeting topics, and each chapter follows a format similar to those of the meetings. Each chapter opens by characterizing "The way things are now" (i.e., how bad), briefly defines and clarifies the topic, describes the benefits that stand to be gained if improvements are made, offers a bulleted list of things that cities can do, suggests longer-term visions for municipal action, links the topic to related fields, and then adds a fable suggesting ways to get from "the way things are" to the optimum Green City vision of what is possible.

Despite its San Francisco focus, *A Green City Program for San Francisco Bay Area Cities and Towns* became the most widely distributed publication that Planet Drum produced, and the initial print run nearly sold out within a year. Citizen and service groups in Chicago, New York, Washington, DC, Mexico City, and Vancouver, Canada, requested copies. City governments and planning departments in the United States and other countries ordered copies. University libraries across the country ordered copies. People recognized that a Green City program could be applied anywhere. A revised edition, *A Green City Program for the San Francisco Bay Area and Beyond*, followed in 1990, adding a chapter on Green City Realities that shared a sampling of successful efforts for each topic of the book, with examples from around North America and other parts of the world. Under "Recycling and Re-Use," for example, one entry reads, "A cooperative apartment building for the elderly in Copenhagen, Denmark was replumbed so that gray water from showers, laundry and dishwashing is re-used to flush toilets" (63).

These books became the basis for the formation of the San Francisco Department of the Environment. *A Green City Program* continued to enjoy high demand, and it is still sometimes used in university courses. But after the second reprinting Planet Drum reissued the book only in a photocopied version, because most of the forward-thinking suggestions set forth it in had become realities by the late 1990s.

Targeting cities allowed Berg to work within the existing power structure of municipal governments without abandoning the bioregional vision. Berg on behalf of Planet Drum was invited to take part in the United Nations Conference on Mayors for Urban Sustainability, held in San Francisco in 2005. Berg saw the UN Mayors conference as "an end run around nation-states that are reluctant to take the large steps necessary for the betterment of planetary ecology. If the nation-states don't do it then the Urban Environmental Accords contains the promise that cities—large and small—will" ("United Nations" 4). Twenty-one accords in areas such as energy, waste reduction, urban design, urban nature, environmental health, and water were signed by the mayors of major cities, including Delhi, India; Vancouver, British Columbia; Shanghai, China; Rio de Janeiro, Brazil; and Sydney, Australia, as well as San Francisco.

In 1989 Planet Drum began the Green City Project in San Francisco to carry out the plans set forth in *A Green City Program*. The project developed four main areas.

1. A volunteer network promoted public involvement by connecting interested individuals with active groups related to urban sustainability.
2. A Green City calendar, published bimonthly and eventually on the Planet Drum website, detailed day-to-day activities and projects in the San Francisco Bay region.
3. The Education + Action project in local K-12 schools brought bioregional awareness to kids and created hands-on ecology-oriented activities at school.
4. Workshop/Workdays helped to connect residents with their life-place; the day began with discussion/education and moved to work on an onsite project, such as restoring a creek or planting a rooftop garden on a hotel for formerly homeless people.

Overall, Planet Drum's Green City Project put ideas into action, moving toward the Green City future forecast in the book (Berg, "Planet Drum Foundation").

Building on connections in rural California and combining them with urban activists was the next step for Planet Drum and Peter Berg. In 1991 Planet Drum convened the first Shasta Bioregional Gathering/Big Time in Napa County and cosponsored subsequent gatherings in Shasta, Mendocino, Sonoma, and Humboldt counties through 1995. Somewhat similar in purpose to the Ozark Area Community Congresses founded by David Haenke in 1977, these annual bioregional gatherings became a forum for urban and rural activists from throughout northern California to discuss successes and problems, with special emphasis on the host location (Berg, "Planet Drum Foundation"). Thinking in terms of the continent, Planet Drum in 1994 began planning for a Bioregional Association of the North Americas (BANA), a membership organization intended to be a forum for addressing issues and policies, putting a public face on the bioregional movement, providing aid to bioregional groups, and being a clearinghouse for bioregional information and volunteer opportunities. Additionally, Berg conceived that BANA could enable bioregions to voice opposition to globalizing trends such as NAFTA and GATT while simultaneously looking toward a planetary federation composed of member organizations such as BANA that were based on other continents (Carr 274). In short, the BANA idea was in line with Berg's efforts to create a new society within the shell of the old and to forge a democratic, participatory society anchored in bioregions and confederating at appropriate levels from bioregion to continent to planet. Founding meetings for BANA were held in San Francisco in 1996, but other bioregionalists were not yet ready for this idea, fearing that a continental organization would become a form of centralized power that undermined the bioregional value of decentralization, so the idea was discontinued.

Nevertheless, in the 1990s, with trips to Australia, Mexico, Europe, and Japan, and in the 2000s, with trips to Asia and Ecuador, Berg worked to bring the bioregional perspective to other continents and helped to catalyze bioregional groups throughout the world. In Australia, the bioregional idea became a basis for the country's Interim Biogeographic Regionalisation for Australia (IBRA), a biogeographical provinces map and report that informs Australia's National Reserve System and conservation efforts. In Japan, made aware by local residents of the strain put upon the local bioregion by the 1998 Winter Olympics being planned for Nagano, Berg cofounded Guard Fox Watch, a watchdog group that monitors and exposes the negative local environmental impacts of the winter Olympics and proposes ways for the winter Olympics to create sustainability where they are held.

VI. Ecuador

In the late 1990s Berg received an invitation that would shift Planet Drum's focus to South America in the new millennium. After attending a presentation by Peter Berg in Japan, Motohiko Kogo invited him to help build community support for the First International Mangrove Day being held at the end of February 1999 in Bahía de Caráquez, an equatorial city of forty thousand on the coast of Ecuador. Without community support for the replanting of mangroves Kogo feared that the local people would cut down the newly replanted mangrove trees and replace them with shrimp farms as had been done previously. He felt Berg and his bioregional outlook would be able to involve the community in understanding and protecting the mangroves, so he financed a trip for Berg to Bahía a month before the celebration was to be held.

In Bahía Berg met local eco-activists who were organizing an Eco-Gathering in conjunction with the International Mangrove Day. In the previous year Bahía had suffered from severe flooding and mudslides as a result of heavy El Niño rains from December 1997 to May 1998. A 7.2 earthquake in August 1998 left Bahía in ruins. Local eco-activists wanted to rebuild the town as a sustainable eco-city, and Berg became involved in that effort, reporting on events in a series of dispatches posted on the Eco-Ecuador pages of the Planet Drum website. (See Works Cited for the titles of individual "Dispatches from Ecuador" listed by date.) As Berg observed in an early dispatch, "Bahía must now reassemble itself after nearly complete ruin. And it is choosing to do so in a history-making way as an eco-municipality within the context of its bioregion" (11 Feb. 1999). At one point in the initial planning meetings, the mayor of Bahía asked Berg, "What do we have to *stop* doing if we become an eco-city?" Berg assured him that "the thrust of bioregional Green City planning was proactive, saying 'yes' to new ideas and efforts that can replace harmful ones" (12 Feb. 1999).

During the eco-city planning meetings many action items were suggested, such as separating trash, picking up litter on the beaches, composting kitchen scraps, and making signs that read "Bienvenidos a Bahía, La Ciudad Verde." Berg supported these ideas while urging planners to keep in mind the bioregional foundation that must undergird the rebuilding effort:

> Water, energy, sewage, garbage, and transportation systems have to be reconstrued in ways that match the bioregional realities here. So does education and media, arts and architecture, and other aspects of public life. Most importantly, Eco-Bahía must undertake these short and long term changes in ways that provide economic advantages for the destitute victims of natural calamities and otherwise impoverished people, and encourage their participation in creating what can ultimately become a better way of life in all respects. (16 Feb. 1999)

As he became more involved in this exciting early phase of Bahía's strategic planning process, Berg was asked, "Have you ever worked to achieve your eco-municipality goals in a Third World country before?" The question prompted him to think about what we mean by "First World" and "Third World." He noted that there are so-called Third World conditions in the blighted areas of any major city in the First World. But then his musings turned cosmological, suggested by the title of the dispatch, "3rd World or 3rd Planet?":

> At this point in human history, what is any place on the third planet in the solar system anyway? It is inevitably part of the planet's skin, the biospheric web of life. New York City, Ecuador and the Kalahari Desert are all the

same in this. Any of them are redolent and ambient, paradisical and misera-
ble, known and mysterious, rainy and dry, inhabitable and visitable, tedious
and exciting, revelatory and monotonous. Anyplace is any place. (Isn't it
astounding that so many different ones exist and that they co-occur at the
same time?) (18 Feb. 1999)

Helping the eco-activists build community support, Berg spoke at a public meeting that attracted people from many sectors, including "barrio representatives,
students, some mothers with small children, the city's priest, the vice-mayor, tour
company operators, hotel and restaurant owners, [and] a uniformed officer of the
Ecuadoran navy" (21 Feb. 1999). He explained the bioregional concept and how
being an eco-city would benefit Bahía. Berg writes that at these meetings:

> My role was to put Eco-Bahía into a worldwide (or in this case, biospheric)
> context starting with the probable contributing effect of global warming on
> the severity of last year's El Niño rains. The mammoth mudflows they cre-
> ated are an immediately tangible example of the necessity to live more eco-
> logically everywhere. Bahía's ruin can now be viewed as an opportunity to
> rebuild as a recognizable model for other places.
>
> Eco-Bahía is a community process rather than an outside or top-down
> operation, and it requires everyone in the community in order to succeed. It
> can bring better living conditions, create employment, attract visitors, and
> become a continuous source of participation and pride. (21 Feb. 1999)

Just before the International Mangrove Day celebration and just before Berg was
to leave Bahía, the city council members and mayor signed a by-law declaring
Bahía de Caráquez a "Ciudad Ecologica" (Ecological City) and setting forth specific policies toward that goal (23 Feb. 1999).

Berg's initial visit in February 1999 led to Bahía's mayor requesting him to act
as an eco-city planning consultant, and Berg committed to continue working on
eco-city planning and implementation for five years, setting up a field office in
Bahía in 2000. Those five years would extend to ten and beyond as Berg remained
active in Ecuador until his death in 2011, and Planet Drum continues to maintain
a field office and carry out ecological restoration and sustainability projects in
Bahía to the present day. Berg explains in an early dispatch how Planet Drum's
bioregional work in Ecuador has biospheric significance:

> And if [Bahía] is located in the "undeveloped world" and thereby offers a
> working model for the entire planet (including the "developed" world), it
> presents a glowing vision of sustainability to tempt any fervent reinhabitant,
> an irresistible opportunity to help create the first truly bioregional Green
> City. [. . .] Although the Ecuador projects involve different places and con-
> ditions, this isn't a total change for Planet Drum. We have always advocated
> recreating urban environments so that they can become sustainable within

the restored natural systems of bioregions. Now we intend to help design and build a practical model that will embody this vision. (Aug. 1999)

Peter Berg helped to prepare an Ecological City Plan for Bahía, a final version of which was approved at a public meeting in February 2001. The plan outlines short- and long-term bioregional goals for sustainability in infrastructural areas of consideration that include water, food, energy, transportation, recycling, sewage, wild habitat, human resources, education, culture, and business development (9 Sept. 2000).

One of Planet Drum's earliest projects in Bahía was to revegetate an area of hillside in the Maria Auxiliadora barrio that had been denuded by the mudslides that destroyed a dozen houses and killed sixteen people (23 Jan. 2001). Planet Drum used only native dry neotropical forest species in the revegetation project, grown from seeds nurtured in seed beds, gathered as cuttings from local stands, or purchased as seedlings from local sources. Plant species were chosen to represent each stage of natural succession in the forest system (27 Sept. 2000). Community volunteers and local workers became involved in the project, which stabilized soil and provided a local source of native plants that are used by local residents in a variety of ways. The revegetated area became an officially designated public park named "El Bosque en Medio de La Ruinas" (The Forest in the Ruins). Planet Drum Foundation helped to create placards that identify native species and pedestrian paths and stairways that connect the hillside to the coast (23 Jan. 2001). This first revegetation project of a few hectares became a testing ground for a later, larger revegetation effort along roughly eight kilometers of eroded hillsides leading into Bahía. Seedlings are grown in a greenhouse that Planet Drum built on the property of a local university, and since 2003 there have been ongoing work-learning classes in which students help to care for and transplant the seedlings. Planet Drum's bioregional goal is to create wildlife corridors of native dry tropical forest vegetation to prevent erosion and restore ecosystems in the Rio Chone watershed.

Since its initial commitment in 1999, Planet Drum has provided technical assistance, planning ideas, and community outreach for a number of other projects that have helped Bahía transform itself into an eco-city. In 2001 Planet Drum initiated a composting project, in partnership with the city, in the Fanca barrio. Fanca Produce was a first step in what ultimately became a citywide recycling and composting program. In 2004 Planet Drum collaborated with a local NGO to develop a Bioregional Education Program curriculum for local teachers and students. Participants complete a course of study that covers reading and writing projects, nature study, sciences, handicrafts, field trips, and hands-on projects including recycling, composting, plant propagation, and revegetation work. As Berg explains, Planet Drum's Eco-Ecuador work is "directly based on restoring and maintaining natural systems while delivering human benefits. This is not just urban ecology, environmentalism or natural resources improvement as they are typically considered and followed. Certainly benefits occur during our process which are similar to those pursuits, but they aren't the main accomplishments. The real goal is to establish a deeply bioregional pattern of practical public activities for achieving true long-term sustainability" (17 Jan. 2003).

In 2010 Planet Drum launched a major new initiative in Ecuador, the Bioregional Sustainability Institute (BSI), announced in Berg's November 2010 dispatch, "A School to Retrieve the Future." By 2010 Bahía was becoming internationally recognized as an ecological city, listed in the top ten by *Grist* magazine. It seemed the right time and the right place to establish an institute "to teach effective ways for achieving balance between human activities and our ultimate basis of support in Nature's web of life" (18 Nov. 2010). The BSI curriculum includes "Ancient Culture Practices into the Present"; "Revegetation"; "Permaculture Farming and Gardening"; "Sustainable Land Development Practices"; "Bioregional Education"; and "Community Outreach." Built into the vision for BSI are the foundational principles of bioregionalism as envisioned by Berg: location in and study of a specific bioregion; integration of theory with hands-on practice; restoration and maintenance of damaged natural systems; creation of sustainable means to secure basic human needs, including water, food, energy, shelter, production and manufacturing, and culture; support for the activities of allied groups; and an urban and rural focus. The bioregional idea is "templatable," and BSI views its graduates as peers who can help to establish bioregional practices and teach the bioregional perspective wherever they may return to after their training at BSI.

In the last days of his life Berg was still busy getting the Bioregional Sustainability Institute up and running, acquiring land for the campus, discussing plans for buildings, creating the curriculum, meeting with teachers, pursuing accreditation, seeking grants, and recruiting students. As the project gained momentum, Berg was delighted to see it becoming a collective endeavor:

> When a vision of this potential scale becomes a reality it takes on a life of its own. There may have been an author at first, but as soon as others begin to share the dream and become involved, proprietorship fades. The idea becomes an identifiable entity that represents more than individual interests. It takes on the equivalent of personhood. (10 Nov. 2010)

These words are a fitting farewell to Peter Berg himself, whose bioregional vision, first articulated in the early 1970s, has been absorbed into the collective consciousness of persons sharing the planet together.

Works cited

Berg, Peter. "Beating the Drum with Gary." *Gary Snyder: Dimensions of a Life*. Ed. Jon Halper. San Francisco: Sierra Club Books, 1991. 376–91. Print.
———. "Celebrate the Longest Night." *Raise the Stakes! The Planet Drum Review* 11 (Summer 1986): 1–2. Print.
———. "Dispatches from Ecuador." *Planet Drum Foundation*. Planet Drum Foundation, 2013. Web. 21 June 2013. The following dispatches, cited in the text, are listed chronologically:
"Latitude 0 Degrees, 36 Minutes South" (11 Feb. 1999).
"'Will It Rain Forever?' (Flor-Maria Tamariz)" (12 Feb. 1999).
"Two and a Half Doses of Realidad" (16 Feb. 1999).
"3rd World or 3rd Planet?" (18 Feb. 1999).
"'Put some air into our lungs!' (Bahía audience member)" (21 Feb. 1999).

"Ecuador Green City Revisited, August 1999" (Aug. 1999).

"The Restoration of Bahía Is Underway" (9 Sept. 2000).

"Why 'Revegetation' Rather Than 'Reforestation' . . . and Where?" (27 Sept. 2000).

"Moving Several Levels Higher" (23 Jan. 2001).

"Ecuador and Planet Drum Undergo Major Transitions" (17 Jan. 2003).

"A School to Retrieve the Future" (18 Nov. 2010).

———. "Ecology Emerges." Oral history interview collection. Interview by Chris Carlsson and David Martinez. *Shaping San Francisco: Excavating the City's Lost History.* August 2009. Web. 28 May 2013.

———. *Envisioning Sustainability.* San Francisco: Subculture Books, 2009. Print.

———. "Grounds & Surrounds." *Planet Drum* Bundle #2. San Francisco: Planet Drum, 1974. n.p. Print.

———. Personal Interview. 11 March 2011.

———. Personal Interview. 24 May 2011.

———. "Planet Drum Foundation." 1995. *Shaping San Francisco's Digital Archive @ Foundsf.* Shaping San Francisco, 2012. Web. 15 June 2013.

———, ed. *Reinhabiting a Separate Country: A Bioregional Anthology of Northern California.* San Francisco: Planet Drum Foundation, 1978. Print.

———. "Reinhabitory Theater." *Reinhabiting a Separate Country.* Ed. Peter Berg. 186–91. Print.

[Berg, Peter.] "Free City Bloodlight." *The Digger Papers. The Realist* 81 (August 1968): 22. Web.

[———.] "Trip without a Ticket." *The Digger Papers. The Realist* 81 (Aug. 1968): 3–4. Web.

Berg, Peter, Beryl Magilavy, and Seth Zuckerman. *A Green City Program for San Francisco Bay Area Cities and Towns.* San Francisco: Planet Drum Foundation, 1989. Print.

———. *A Green City Program for the San Francisco Bay Area and Beyond.* San Francisco: Planet Drum Foundation, Wingbow Press, 1990. Print.

Berg, Peter, and Stephanie Mills, guest eds. Special issue on "Bioregions." *CoEvolution Quarterly* 32 (Winter 1981).

"Bundles, Spare Parts, and Illuminations." Order form for Bundles #1 through #9 (1973–1985). *Planet Drum.* San Francisco. 6 pp. n.d. Print.

Carr, Mike. *Bioregionalism and Civil Society: Democratic Challenges to Corporate Globalism.* Vancouver: U of British Columbia P, 2004. Print.

Celebrate the Longest Night. Poster. Art by Thomas Morris. Superior Press, 1985. Web. *Oakland Museum of California.* Oakland Museum of California, 2013. 10 Jan. 2014.

Coyote, Peter. *Sleeping Where I Fall: A Chronicle.* Washington, DC: Counterpoint, 1998. Print.

Jarrell, Randall, ed. and interviewer. *Raymond F. Dasmann: A Life in Conservation Biology.* Oral history. Santa Cruz: University of California, 2000. Print.

Kisseloff, Jeff. "Peter Berg: The Digger." *Generation on Fire: Voice of Protest in the 1960s, An Oral History.* Lexington: UP of Kentucky, 2007. 137–51. Print.

Listening to the Earth. Symposium Poster. Art Michael Myers. Berkeley, CA: Designed by Sharpshooter Studios. 1979. Web. *Oakland Museum of California.* Oakland Museum of California, 2013. 17 June 2013.

Mills, Stephanie. "Planetary Passions: A Reverent Anarchy." *CoEvolution Quarterly* 32 (Winter 1981): 4–5.

"United Nations' Mayors Conference and Planet Drum." *PULSE* Fall 2005: 4–9. Print.

Weinberg, Bill. "Peter Berg: High Times Interview." *High Times* April 1993: 50–55. Print.

Wolf, Leonard, and Deborah Wolf. "Peter Berg." Interview. *Voices from the Love Generation.* Boston: Little, Brown, 1968. 246–63. Print.

PART 1
Peter Berg's bioregional vision

REINHABITING CALIFORNIA

Peter Berg and Raymond Dasmann

"Reinhabiting California," published in The Ecologist *in 1977 and reprinted many times since, represents a collaboration between Peter Berg and Raymond Dasmann, chief ecologist at the Union for the Conservation of Nature and Natural Resources in Switzerland. Dasmann and other scientists, such as Miklos Udvardy, had created maps of biotic provinces for purposes of conservation and wildlife management. Peter Berg, having encountered the term* bioregion *through Allen Van Newkirk in Nova Scotia, adopted that term and reimagined it to include humans. This flagship essay memorably defines* bioregion *as "geographical terrain and a terrain of consciousness," introduces the concepts of* living-in-place *and* reinhabitation *and applies this biocultural model to northern California. This powerfully imagined manifesto grounded Berg's actions and articulations for the rest of his life and remains a fountainhead of environmental thought.*

Living-in-place

Living-in-place means following the necessities and pleasures of life as they are uniquely presented by a particular site, and evolving ways to ensure long-term occupancy of that site. A society which practises living-in-place keeps a balance with its region of support through links between human lives, other living things, and the processes of the planet—seasons, weather, water cycles—as revealed by the place itself. It is the opposite of a society which "makes a living" through short-term destructive exploitation of land and life. Living-in-place is an age-old way of existence, disrupted in some parts of the world a few millennia ago by the rise of exploitative civilization, and more generally during the past two centuries by the spread of industrial civilization. It is not, however, to be thought of as antagonistic to civilization, in the more humane sense of that word, but may be the only way in which a truly civilized existence can be maintained.

In nearly every region of North America, including most of California, natural life support systems have been severely weakened. The original wealth of biotic diversity has been largely spent and altered toward a narrow range of mostly non-native crops and stock. Chronic misuse has ruined huge areas of once-rich farms, forest, and range land. Wastes from absurdly dense industrial concentrations have left some places almost unlivable. But, regardless of the "endless frontier" delusion and invader mentality that came to dominate in North America, removing one species or native people after another to make-a-living for the invaders, we now know that human life depends ultimately on the continuation of other life. Living-in-place provides for such continuation. It has become a necessity if people intend to stay in any region without further changing it in ever more dangerous directions.

Once all California was inhabited by people who used the land lightly and seldom did lasting harm to its life-sustaining capacity. Most of them have gone. But if the life destructive path of technological society is to be diverted into life sustaining directions, the land must be reinhabited. *Reinhabitation* means learning to live-in-place in an area that has been disrupted and injured through past exploitation. It involves becoming native to a place through becoming aware of the particular ecological relationships that operate within and around it. It means undertaking activities and evolving social behaviour that will enrich the life of that place, restore its life-supporting systems, and establish an ecologically and socially sustainable pattern of existence within it. Simply stated it involves becoming fully alive in and with a place. It involves applying for membership in a biotic community and ceasing to be its exploiter.

Useful information for reinhabitants can come from a wide range of sources. Studies of local native inhabitants, in particular the experiences of those who have lived there before, both those who tried to make a living, and those who lived-in-place can contribute. Reinhabitants can apply this information toward shaping their own life patterns and establishing relationships with the land and life around them. This will help determine the nature of the bioregion within which they are learning to live-in-place.

Reinhabitation involves developing a bioregional identity, something most North Americans have lost, or have never possessed. We define bioregion in a sense different from the biotic province of Dasmann (1973) or the biogeographical province of Udvardy (1975). The term refers both to geographical terrain and a terrain of consciousness—to a place and the ideas that have developed about how to live in that place. Within a bioregion the conditions that influence life are similar and these in turn have influenced human occupancy.

A bioregion can be determined initially by use of climatology, physiography, animal and plant geography, natural history and other descriptive natural sciences. The final boundaries of a bioregion are best described by the people who have lived within it, through human recognition of the realities of living-in-place. All life on the planet is interconnected in a few obvious ways, and in many more that remain barely explored. But there is a distinct resonance among living things and factors which influence them that occurs specifically within each separate place on the planet. Discovering and describing that resonance is a way to describe a bioregion.

The realities of a bioregion are obvious in a gross sense. Nobody would confuse the Mojave Desert with the fertile valley of Central California, nor the Great Basin semi-arid land with the California coast. Between the major bioregions the differences are sufficiently marked that people do not usually attempt to practise the Sonoran desert way of life in the Oregonian coastal area. But there are many intergradations. The chaparral covered foothills of Southern California are not markedly distinct from those of the coast ranges of Northern California. But the attitudes of people and the centers to which they relate (San Francisco vs. Los Angeles) are different and these can lead to different approaches to living on the land.

The northern California bioregion is ringed by mountains on the north, east and south and extends some distance into the Pacific Ocean on the west. Since the boundaries depend in part on human attitudes they cannot be clearly mapped. These attitudes, however, have been persistent since prehistoric times. The region is separated from Southern California by the barrier of the Tehachapi Mountains and their extension through the Transverse Ranges to Point Conception on the seaward side. Flora and fauna change to some extent on either side of this boundary, but human attitudes are more important in the separation. Eastward, the region is enclosed by the Sierra Nevada which stops the rain and defines the dry Nevadan bioregion. Northward the volcanic Cascade Range and the geologically ancient Klamath Mountains separate the Oregonian bioregion. Along the coast the boundaries are fuzzy, but one could draw a line at the northern limit of the coastal redwood forests, at Oregon's Chetco River.

Within the bioregion is one major watershed, that of the Sacramento-San Joaquin river system which drains from all of the Sierra-Nevada, Cascade, and interior Coast Ranges and flows through the broad plain of the Central Valley. Coastally, smaller watersheds are significant, those of the Salinas, Russian, Eel, Mad, Klamath and Smith rivers. The Klamath River is anomalous in that it drains from an area that belongs to a different bioregion. So too does the Pit River which joins the Sacramento. Otherwise the drainage systems help to define and tie together the life of the bioregion, and the characteristics of watersheds point out the necessities which those who would live-in-place must recognize.

Biologically the California biotic province, which forms the heart of the bioregion, is not only unique but somewhat incredible—a west coast refuge for obscure species, full of endemic forms of plants and animals. It is a Mediterranean climatic region unlike any other in North America. It is a place of survival for once widespread species as well as a place where other distinct forms evolved. Anthropologically, it is also unique, a refuge for a great variety of non-agricultural peoples on a continent where agriculture had become dominant.

During the century and a half that invader society has occupied northern California, a primary sense of location has been provided by surveyors dividing up the land. We know more about property lines than we do about the life that moves under, over, and through them. People are bombarded with information about the prices of things, but seldom learn their real biospheric costs. They are encouraged to measure the dimensions of things without ever learning their places in the continuity of bioregional life.

Our real "period of discovery" has just begun. The bioregion is only barely recognized in terms of how life systems relate to each other within it. It is still an anxious mystery whether we will be able to continue living here. How many people can the bioregion carry without destroying it further? What kinds of activities should be encouraged? Which ones are too ruinous to continue? How can people find out about bioregional criteria in a way that they will feel these exist for their mutual benefit rather than as an imposed set of regulations?

Natural watersheds could receive prominent recognition as the frameworks within which communities are organized. The network of springs, creeks and rivers flowing together in a specific area exerts a dominant influence on all non-human life there; it is the basic designer of local life. Floods and droughts in northern California remind us that watersheds affect human lives as well, but their full importance is more subtle and pervasive. Native communities were developed expressly around local water supplies and tribal boundaries were often set by the limits of watersheds. Pioneer settlements followed the same pattern, often displacing native groups with the intention of securing their water.

Defining the local watershed, restricting growth and development to fit the limits of water supplies, planning to maintain these and restore the free flowing condition of tributaries that are blocked or the purity of any which have been polluted, and exploring relationships with the larger water systems connecting to it could become primary directions for reinhabitory communities. They could view themselves as centered on and responsible for the watershed.

The Central Valley has become one of the planet's food centers. The current scale of agriculture there is huge; thousands of square miles under constant cultivation to produce multiple annual crops. Fossil-fuel dependent heavy equipment appears at every stage of farming operations, and there is a steadily rising rate of artificial fertilizer use. Most of the land is owned or leased by absentee agribusiness corporations. It's a naturally productive place. Northern California has a temperate climate, a steady supply of water, and the topsoil is some of the richest in North America. But the current scale of agriculture is untenable in the long-term. Fossil fuel and chemical fertilizer can only become more expensive, and the soil is simultaneously being ruined and blown away.

There needs to be massive redistribution of land to create smaller farms. They would concentrate on growing a wider range of food species (including native food plants), increasing the nutritional value of crops, maintaining the soil, employing alternatives to fossil fuels, and developing small-scale marketing systems. More people would be involved, thereby creating jobs and lightening the population load on the cities.

Forests have to be allowed to rebuild themselves. Clearcutting ruins their capability to provide a long-term renewable resource. Watershed-based reforestation and stream restoration projects are necessary everywhere that logging has been done. Cut trees are currently being processed wastefully; tops, stumps and branches are left behind, and whole logs are shipped away to be processed elsewhere and sold back in the region. Crafts that use every part of the tree should be employed to make maximum use of the materials while employing a greater number of regional people. Fisheries have to be carefully protected. They provide a long-term life-support of rich protein, if used correctly, or a quickly emptied biological niche, if mishandled. Catching fish and maintaining the fisheries have to be seen as parts of the same concern.

Reinhabitory consciousness can multiply the opportunities for employment within the bioregion. New reinhabitory livelihoods based on exchanging information, cooperative planning, administering exchanges of labor and tools, intra and inter-regional networking, and watershed media emphasizing bioregional rather than city consumer information could replace a few centralized positions with many decentralized ones. The goals of restoring and maintaining watersheds, topsoil, and native species invite the creation of many jobs to simply undo the bioregional damage that invader society has already done.

Politics

Beginning with the Spanish Occupation, the distinctiveness of northern California's ongoing bioregional life has been obscured by a succession of alien super-identities. The place to fit into simply wasn't recognized.

First, it was part of "New Spain" a designation that tells nothing of this specific place and lumps it with a dozen barely related bioregions radiating out from the Caribbean. "California" was a fictional island created by a 16th century Spanish novelist and it became the next rough label pasted over the bioregion when it was adopted for the Pacific side of New Spain. "Alta California" actually approximated the bioregion by accident; its real use was simply to acknowledge further Spanish explorations above the "baja." Mexico held it (along with half the western U.S.) in the early 19th century, but since the middle of last century almost the whole bioregion has been included in the annexed portion of Mexican territory that was sliced out as the state of California along with totally foreign pieces of the Great Basin desert and similarly dry stretches below the Tehachapi Mountains.

The bioregion that exists largely in what is now called northern California has now become visible as a separate whole, and, for purposes of reinhabiting the place, it should have a political identity of its own. It is predictable that as long as it belongs to a larger state it will be subject to southern California's demands on its watersheds. Its rivers already run through pipes to Los Angeles. Its control over use of the Central Valley is pre-empted by policies tailored for southern monocultures. From a reinhabitory point of view, both are bioregional death threats. Elections over the last decade have shown a distinct difference in voting sentiments between northern and southern California. It is likely that this difference will continue and increase on vital bioregional issues on which the population weight of southern California will prevail.

The bioregion cannot be treated with regard for its own life continuities while it is part of and administered by a larger state government. It should be a separate state. As a separate state, the bioregion could redistrict its counties to create watershed governments appropriate to maintaining local life-places. City-country divisions could be resolved on bioregional grounds. Perhaps the greatest advantage of separate statehood would be the opportunity to declare a space for addressing each other as members of a species sharing the planet together and with all the other species.

References

Berg, Peter, editor. (1977) *Reinhabiting a separate country.* California Arts Council. Planet/Drum, San Francisco (in press).

Dasmann, R. F.; 1973 *A system for defining and classifying natural regions for purposes of conservation* IUCN Occ. Paper 7, 47 pp., IUCN, Morges, Switzerland.

Forbes, Jack D., 1971. The native American experience in California History. *California Historical Quarterly* September, pp. 234–242.

Udvardy, Miklos D.F., 1975 *A classification of the biogeographical provinces of the world.* IUCN Occ Paper 18, 48 pp., IUCN, Morges, Switzerland.

GLOBALISTS VERSUS PLANETARIANS

An interview of Peter Berg by Michael Helm

Peter Berg is at his brashest in this lively 1978 interview with Michael Helm, pub-lished in Berkeley's City Miner. *In a no-holds-barred rant, Berg critiques globalism, argues that "ecologics" must replace economics, supports separatist movements in Europe, insists on political autonomy for northern California, condemns undersea mining and nuclear tests, rails against colonialism, and sees "future primitive" as a way to move forward to planetary consciousness. While Berg became more states-manlike in later years, this early exchange reveals a core of radicalism that never waned, and his words will continue to challenge readers today.*

Peter Berg is a fellow who generates controversy. In the 1960's the focus of his creativity centered around the renowned San Francisco Mime Troupe and the largely anonymous, but not ineffective, Diggers. Beginning in the early 1970's, he and his partner, Judy Berg—also an ex-Mime Trouper—synthesized their the-atrical, political orientation with a growing interest in ecology. The result was the innovative, San Francisco based, Planet/Drum Foundation.

A non-profit organization, Planet/Drum was set up in 1972 [*sic*] as an open network for people interested in exploring the emergent idea of regional reinhabi-tation from a planetary perspective. Since then, through its subscriber supported *bundles* of thoughtful, attractively designed articles, posters and poems, Planet/ Drum has developed a quiet but significant international readership. Among its contributors are included people like Raymond Dasmann, Gary Snyder, Robert Curry, and Linn House. In addition to the *bundles*, the foundation also circulates an ongoing planetary newsletter and will publish its first book, *Reinhabiting a Separate Country: A Bioregional Anthology from Northern California*, early this summer.

Besides Planet/Drum, Peter is also involved with the independent, but philo-sophically related, *Frisco Bay Mussel Group*—which studies the watershed of the San Francisco Bay-Sacramento River Estuary—and with the *Reinhabitory Theatre*—directed by Judy Berg—which dramatizes regional watershed con-sciousness through the use of indigenous tales, myths, and existing "wildlife." Regarding all these activities Peter has said:

"We are in the midst of a crucial struggle between globalist and planetarian interests regarding our ongoing mutual inhabitation of this planet.

"Globalism perceives our species as possessing the primary intelligence and consciousness in the biosphere. Wants and needs of human beings are important to the degree that they should actually control the entire biosphere. The planet is a warehouse of resources in which agricultural and industrial production proceed to deliver commodities. Although the diversity of regions and biospheric influences over the planet provide the essential elements of those commodities, differences in creating distinct cultural groups form obstacles to smooth global operations. Centralization and monoculture are necessary to keep the warehouse-factory at peak efficiency. Globalists are rushing to complete an edifice-habitat.

"Planetarians, people who view themselves from within the biosphere rather than from the top of it, extend importance beyond the human species to include other life and the processes by which all life continues. The planet is organismic and expresses itself through diversity. People adapt to differences in the biosphere by developing *in situo* cultures that express regional characteristics naturally. Variations on the means for fulfilling fundamental human wants and needs are seen as providing richness to our existence. Planetarians are anxious about main-taining distinct regions, cultures, and species, and look forward to experiencing full ranges of planetary diversity without destroying them."

In the interview which follows, Peter talks about such things as Northern Cali-fornia Secession, the concept of *future primitive*, and the natural ties, extending to China and Japan, of Pacific Rim peoples. . . .

CITY MINER: Why did you start Planet Drum?

PETER BERG: To encourage discussion of a regional/planetary identity as opposed to a national/global one. I wanted to say something about the planet within a context that was appropriate to it. I also wanted to provide a forum for natural scientists, poets, writers, and political thinkers who were becoming impatient with the limits of a globalist view. The thing that excited me was that the planetary perspective was and is an emergent cul-tural phenomenon which somehow overcomes all the prob-lems traditionally associated with cultural chauvinism.

CM: How did Planet Drum emerge from your interest in theatre? What is the relationship between your current activities and your work with the San Francisco Mime Troupe?

PB: I wasn't doing the Mime Troupe exclusively as theatre. I would never have done theatre except as a way to express a radical political consciousness.

CM: So you see Planet Drum as being an extension of your political consciousness?

PB: Of course. Planetary identity is an emergent dimension of human identity. I want the full range of human identity to be expressed without oppression. That is why I was a political radical, why I came to see the U.S. as the most oppressive agency on the planet.

CM: Both to its own people and worldwide?

PB: Exactly. The Vietnam War was a symptom of that. But, I also came to see that a Marxist definition started from much the same place as Capitalism as far as "world" identity was concerned. It wasn't inclusive of other species, it wasn't based in natural processes. I came to see *ecologics* as replacing economics. Engels says that the final note is always economics. I came to see ecologics as the final one. In the late 60's when so many confrontations were occurring, globalist maneuvers and ideology were getting unbridled license. Population control, the publication of *Limits to Growth*—which was presumably an introduction to the planet actually introduced a liberal/globalist world view. I saw that view as being the next camp for oppression. I saw the globalists, in conjunction with the trans-national corporations, taking away the potential for planetary/regional consciousness.

CM: There seems to be something about the globalist perspective that enervates thinking about regional consciousness.

PB: Oh man! Talk about regional consciousness to a globalist and he'll call you a feudalist; he'll say, "We have the whole world to talk about, to think about. You know starvation is a worldwide problem." Everything is on a world scale. Well, it's on a world scale if you're controlling the products and inputs of labor. But it's on a very regional scale if you are in *place*. That's the way the planet arranges itself; in places.

CM: It's unusual for someone who has come out of radical Marxist perspective to be interested in the scientific community and developments from that perspective. What sparked your interest?

PB: I started noticing that if I asked a natural scientist who has roots, who wasn't in a position where his career came first and his enquiry came second, asked him about social and political realities; his kinds of answers were quite different from the kinds of answers I always heard before. If I asked a geologist who refused to work for the petroleum industry and who loved geology what the geological underpinnings of the political and social system were, he would talk about the availability of soil, about the activity of the place in terms of soil, and the activity of the soil in terms of food, and amounts of food that could be produced to support a certain number of people. It had nothing to do with whether or not there should be a dictatorship of the proletariat on the one hand or whether the place should be developed from a capitalist point of view on the other. It had to do with a planetary phenomenon like the availability of soil.

CM: In that sense Marxism is really locked into industrialism and rather inimical to the development of indigenous culture. Or do you think that's going too far?

PB: I don't think it's useful or appropriate to cast Marxism as being anti-human. I don't think it has been. I think that it's been just the opposite. I am talking about the limits of it, and I am talking about where we're going. If there's going to be a post-Marxist phase of human identity, it will be globalist or planetary. If there is some element of Marxism that can be used to sprout globalism, then that element or perspective isn't worthwhile. I want the planetary element. Marxism was a valuable step in the evolution of human identity.

CM: But still politically tied to nationalism?

PB: Tied to nationalism, yet many nation-states now have movements to cause regional separatism. I personally think that's the most interesting development in contemporary European politics. These fifty-odd separatist movements.

And of course one of the most successful separatist movements on the planet right now is in North America, in Quebec. That's going to have an incredible impact on North America, and I think it's the wave of the future.

Most of the nation-states that exist today are amalgams of regional cultures and tend, because they are all centralist, to overplay one regional culture in regard to the others. They recognize this in Communist China as Han chauvinism, which is at least given lip-service as a major problem; the domination of the Han culture over all the other Chinese cultures. There are Muslim camel-riding Chinese, Canton Boat People—dozens of other cultures.

CM: Let's talk about the Bay Area as a region. What are the implications in terms of politics, in terms of economics, in terms of the direction of change that would flow from a planet/regional perspective for this area?

PB: The first dimension would be seeing ourselves here in the Bay Area as part of the S.F. Bay-Sacramento River estuary watershed.

CM: So watershed is the key concept in terms of regional identity.

PB: Just as the planet tends to describe itself in regions, so regions organize themselves in terms of watersheds. Our large watershed is the S.F. Bay-Sacramento River watershed; so we would want the unity, wholeness and continuity of that watershed to be a primary interest.

CM: Could that unity and wholeness sustain the existing population in the Bay Area or do you think population would have to be reduced?

PB: Why is there always pessimism when people talk about that? No one has tried, because of the dominant super technological world-view and lack of a planet-view, to assess what the regional limits of a human population actually are. That has never been assessed for any region. We just don't know and don't have any way of knowing unless we study it. Then we would have a basis for *adaptive* technology. We would know how many people can appropriately fit within the regional limits of technology and other species. We do know that one of the densest native populations in North America lived in the Sacramento River-San Francisco Bay region. Adaptive technology, which also considered the continuity of native species, *could* possibly sustain the population we have now.

CM: Would the implications of a planet/regional perspective require that each region be self-sufficient as an economic unit?

PB: Self-sufficient is an ambiguous phrase. Planetary interdependence is actually what we're looking for—we are not looking to be independent of the planetary biosphere; we are looking to continue contributing to the planetary biosphere. For example, I'd rather have the definition of climax that's used in ecology as our definition; the greatest amount of diversity along with the widest range and greatest number of population per species. Why don't we use *that* as our definition instead of self-sufficiency which already throws you into an independent versus inter-dependence slot. Why don't we think of ourselves in organismic terms. What's the greatest number of people and greatest number of other species, native species, that we can have here with the greatest amount of diversity. What is that number?

CM: That relates to what is the optimum *quality* of life that we can create for ourselves.

PB: Exactly. Why not have that as the definition of an ideal social system? A social system that delivers—that will deserve our adherence. And let's continue thinking about our regional contribution to the planetary biosphere.

CM: What about the concept of *future primitive*? How does that relate in terms of the lifestyle that would evolve in a planet/regional consciousness?

PB: I was talking before about psychic deprivation, about how much deprivation results from our perpetual tourism. The phrase *future primitive* refers to human beings as Mutualist members of a species who in the future would ensure for themselves the full dimensions of consciousness that a regional identity would provide, a regional/planetary identity. It doesn't mean wearing loincloths. It doesn't mean trying to become Indians. It means reinhabitation; inhabiting places rather than occupying them as if we were the agents of some kind of fucking Western Army, Western World Army, with an obligation to hold down North America for the Queen of England or General Motors.

CM: What's the relationship between technology and this concept of regional inhabitation and future primitivism?

PB: In a world-global-view new technology has tremendous priority, because new technology—or technology which does not yet exist—has the potential to take advantage of some "surplus" situation, some niche; and to drain that niche for temporary "benefits." There are no studies of the real interactions among bioregions. So there are no studies as to how technology can fit bioregional or biospheric perspectives. There are all kinds of *old* technologies. All kinds. Eskimo technology, for example, is incredibly rich.

Adapting existing technology to bioregional continuities would be reinhabitory.

JUDY BERG: There are people in the South Pacific who can navigate by counting the waves, counting the frequency of waves hitting the bow; and if there's an off wave, every ninth wave then you know how far you are from the island, because the waves are going around the island and setting up a sphere of tear-drop design, and they count the beats.

CM: That's an incredible feat of observation.

PB: Technology isn't new. There are huge inventories of human technology to draw on.

CM: There is that bias that technology is necessarily physical and mechanical rather than perceptual.

PB: People tend to think of so called primitive technology as being what pre-industrial people were forced to do—what they had to put up with. They never notice how exquisite it is. How exquisitely designed it is for the place. As though it had endured in a wind tunnel shaken down for a test of forty thousand years.

CM: You're defining technology as a subdivision of knowledge essentially.

PB: I think it always is. One of the things that has happened to us in the West, one of the reasons we have this tourist sense and feel so hopeless about ever having a *place identity* is that we've taken technologies from all over the planet and deposited them in one place.

As far as alternative technology is concerned, if you didn't have a bioregional reason for doing it you would be mad. For instance, if you set up only solar collectors on the Olympic Peninsula where there are two hundred inches of rainfall a year, you would be crazy. Water turbines would be more appropriate there. Two of the tallest windmills in the world were built to pump water for Golden Gate Park. That was very bright! Now nobody uses wind here anymore. Instead we use natural gas from Alberta, which is very dumb.

To elaborate on future primitive, I don't see it as something to go back to, I see it as a place to go forward, and what we are going forward to is a planetary consciousness. We are going to identify ourselves as part of a species in a bioregion on the planet. That's actually a new place. We've never been in that consciousness terrain before.

And the social corollary of planetary identity is *reinhabitation*, learning to be in the bioregion as part of the bioregion contributing to the biosphere. There's nothing arcane or Indianola about future primitive.

CM: Do you use the term future primitive mainly to show deference to the consciousness that previous cultures have had of a bioregion, rather than to exactly duplicate their form of dealing with it?

PB: So-called primitive cultures are a good model for reinhabitation. There's no reason everyone should be eating corn flakes for breakfast: corn doesn't grow everywhere, it doesn't grow everywhere the same way. There are things to eat for breakfast which are native to a place. Why not have them as part of your regional identity? Otherwise, we become agents of global monoculture.

CM: Like eating cornflakes in the Hong Kong Hilton?

PB: Exactly. Beautiful.

CM: I want to ask you a question about monoculture and the whole corporate world that exists. Obviously they have a vested interest in reducing diversity; how do we deal with that? They've got political power and they're highly organized.

PB: Well, for example, we could put limits on what could be done within our own watershed; for example, the watershed of the greater S.F. Bay-Sacramento River Estuary. There are immediate corporate invaders to pinpoint. Multi-national corporations which have huge farming tracts in our Central Valley—that's *OUR* Central Valley, part of *OUR* watershed. The water comes from the Sierra Nevada, comes through there, goes through the Delta and comes into S.F. Bay. That's our watershed and if corporate farming is not the best way to use that land we could decide that on a watershed basis. Thinking of the watershed can be a very powerful political agency, because if you're thinking about things that are continuous with the watershed, multi-national exploitation of the region is impossible. You have controls on whether something which happens within the watershed is continuous with it or not.

CM: Well, you have examples like, say, the California Water Project or the Colorado River . . .

PB: California's present political definition includes two major bioregions. One of the first moves we would make would be to insist on political autonomy for the Northern California bioregion. We should separate from the rest of California.

CM: But, politically how do you realize that goal? There's a tremendous vested interest . . .

PB: How did residents of Martha's Vineyard recently decide to separate from the state that held it? Martha's Vineyard just had a referendum about whether or not they wanted to continue being a part of the state or join another.

CM: So you would say that the sheer act of organizing a referendum on the question of the secession of Northern California, whether or not it was allowed, would create a consciousness that would be positive?

PB: Exactly. To gain an eventual change from the way it's set up now, we'd have to convince a lot of Southern Californians to let us go.

CM: Do you think they'd buy that? They're pretty dependent in some ways on Northern California water. Given the fact that it's a desert area, unless they went to desalinization or some such, it would require a major population relocation don't you think?

PB: Well, a major population relocation occurred over the last 50 years to create L.A. That's a very short time. 50 years ago there wasn't one one-hundredth of the present population in L.A. Those people haven't been there very long. I don't know where they want to be. I don't know if they know where they are now. Maybe if they knew it was a desert they wouldn't want to be there anymore. Maybe if they couldn't grow ivy and Bermuda grass on their lawns they would want to move. They could. To Bermuda or England or Yucatán. There are some wonderful abandoned cities in Yucatán that could be reinhabited.

CM: The Mexicans might object to that.

PB: Well, if you really want to push this, I think it would be a good idea if L.A. became part of Mexico. They're already connected by the Sonoran biotic province.

CM: Let's move back to the Bay Area. Tell me a little about the *Frisco Bay Mussel Group*. How does that fit into the perspective of planet/region and reinhabitation.

PB: The goal of the Frisco Bay Mussel Group is to develop a background of information. It's a study group to explore the natural and cultural history of the region.

CM: Who are some of the people involved with it?

PB: When it became apparent that the S.F. Bay-Sacramento River Estuary was of interest as a greater area in which environmental problems, for example, could be understood; people who were already members of other environment groups: S.F. Ecology Center, people from Bolinas, Oakland, Berkeley who were active, the Berkeley Community Gardens people—when I contacted them they were willing to sit down once or twice a month and listen to information about the Bay Area and decide what to do. We decided to put this information in a map which we call *Water-shed Guide*, and a little booklet called *Living Here*, a book that is a collection of original essays by Mussel Group members.

CM: When will that be available?

PB: Within a month. Hopefully while the drought still has people's consciousness on water, so that they can see the relationship of water to the entire watershed and all the life systems in it. I wouldn't like to see a lot of native watershed life wiped out by dams built from hysteria about the drought. People can learn to appreciate the watershed as their life-place and think of how they can live within the limits that are imposed by it. [. . . .]

CM: What's the next step up from the watershed?

PB: The San Francisco Bay/Sacramento River Estuary is one *watershed*. Northern California is one *bioregion*. San Francisco should see itself as a Pacific Rim city; its allegiance is with the Pacific Rim. Rather than thinking of San Francisco/New York, we should be thinking of San Francisco/Tokyo. We should be sure that multinational corporations do not go forward with plans that jeopardize the Pacific Rim.

CM: For instance?

PB: Undersea mining. We should ban nuclear tests in the Pacific Ocean. The Pacific Ocean has been used as a primitive dump for a lot of things. Agent Orange is stored on an island in the Pacific. It leaks.

CM: What is Agent Orange?

PB: It's the herbicide which caused mutations of fetuses in Vietnam and was eventually banned from its use to defoliate Vietnam. It's stored in drums and the drums are kept on an island in the Pacific Ocean. Hundreds of thousands of gallons and the leakage is about 10%. Drums of radioactive waste also dumped in the Pacific Ocean off the Farallones. They leak. They're leaking!

CM: Is the Atlantic being similarly used?

PB: Yes, but the Pacific is being used worse. There's an illusion of wildness, a frontier mentality about the Pacific that is unmatched. For example, blatant colonialism exists in the Pacific. The way we hold Micronesia. The colonialism of American trade, American shipping.

CM: Do you consider Japan, especially Honshu, to be a kind of neo-colonial outpost of the trans-national corporations?

PB: Definitely. But just as there is the S.F. Bay Mussel Group as the rein-habitory agency of the San Francisco Bay/Sacramento River estuary, there is a group in Japan anxious to have Japan be restored as a biologically responsible place. They refer to the Japanese islands as Yapanesia, and they're moving for the reinhabitation of the Japanese Islands. Planet Drum helps present their information.

CM: Do you think the situation in Japan is worse than it is here?

PB: Tokyo is the most polluted city on the planet.

CM: Can that trend be reversed?

PB: The Japanese are attempting to do that. There's alarm about the mercury poisoning and research into it: original research by Japanese. There is a move in Japan to counteract industrial giantism.

    We should identify more with political movement and places around the Pacific Rim. Vancouver is a natural sister city. We should be thinking of Mexico City, the Chilean coast, the Australian coast: that's our planet place. The future of our identity here will be with the "East." It's an example of globalism that we refer to Asia as the East. Asia isn't East of us, it's east of Europe. It's west of us. When we stop referring to Asia as the East, we'll be Pacific Rim people.

CM: What about the apocalyptic perspective that seems to be associated with a global/national view of the world? How do you relate to apocalypse; is it real?

PB: Well, I think world crisis is real; but "world" is a "national cultural" point-of-view. It means that people's national points of view are undergoing crisis. There are world crises from a national perspective.

CM: That tends to be interpreted as synonymous with extinction of the human race. Is that valid do you think?

PB: I think that an apocalyptic perspective stampedes us into things like . . . insisting on population control when we don't even know what the population limits of a region are. I think that is what we should be finding out.

CM: Judy, tell me something about the *Reinhabitory Theatre*.

JB: It consists of a couple of different kinds of things. One of them is a paper movie that's really a story about the watershed. It's a discussion of where we are and the changes that have happened where we are in the last two hundred years. We tell stories that are enacted; and the stories are stories of the people of the watershed. Some of them are the old stories of the indigenous peoples and some are new stories of those who are here now. They all deal more or less with reinhabitation. Some of them deal with understanding where we are; some of them deal with perceiving all life forms as part of an inter-connected situation. So that rather than human beings being at the top of the system, they are just another piece of the puzzle.

CM: One species among many, rather than a mono-species dominating everything.

JB: Right. Most of the enacted stories deal with other species; coyotes, foxes, moles, chickens, bobcats, all fitting in together.

CM: You used the phrase paper movie, can you give a more graphic sense of what that means?

JB: It's like a big scroll, inside a box, with pictures drawn on it. We also call it "Cranky" because it moves by cranking the handle. Our Cranky moves from the bottom up. Various pictures pass on the screen and Peter is the one who does the talking with Cranky.

CM: What, for example, might be shown as an image?

JB: Rain. Raindrops. Raindrops fall on some mountains and make a stream in the mountains and you see the stream go through a valley and down into the bay and down to the ocean. Mostly our Cranky's story is about the different feet that have stood on this earth, and so there's a lot of feet in ours; there's bare feet and feet in rubber and feet in mining boots. All different feet. Dog feet.

CM: Typically how long are the performances?

JB: About 1½ to 2 hours, and when we do performances we also do workshops. We feel that the workshops are integral to the performances. The workshops involve theatre games and movement explorations and verbal explorations that pertain to "living in place."

CM: Is there anything unusual in the audience's relationship to the performers?

JB: We don't really consider that it's an audience like an audience at a theatrical production. We hope that the audience will participate, because, for one thing, we ask for stories from the audience.

In situations where it's possible we like to have our performance as part of a pot luck—sharing food, sharing stories. A community event. We don't even have costuming so we're not very different from the audience. In an outdoor situation you couldn't tell the actors from the watchers.

PB: It's a cultural prototype. We're thinking there'll be a larger regional fabric eventually.

JB: It's really my hope that we'll turn people on to investigate where they live and the stories that have gone down in the place where they live. Maybe in a year or two we could come back through and they could tell us lots of stories.

PB: Then you would have a sub-regional theatre for that place.

JB: There's lots of exciting theatre going on in small towns now anyways.

PB: Give him an example of what we're going to be doing at San Juan Ridge.

JB: Well, at San Juan Ridge there's a community of people and they've done some investigations of theatrical forms, I guess more as ceremony than as theatrical forms. When they heard about the theatre we've been doing they invited us to come up. They've set up what is almost the perfect situation for our theatre to happen in. They've set up an in-town performance in Nevada City where we can charge people at the door. Then they've set up outdoors, at their community which is about ten miles from Nevada City, where people can make some kind of contribution but won't *have* to pay. Then the next day they've arranged for a workshop that will give people an opportunity to see what kind of theatre it is that we're dealing with. It gives us a chance to discuss, with the people who are interested, how we arrived at the kind of theatre we're doing and how they might arrive at a theatre for where they are.

CM: So the theatre is a kind of vehicle for helping to both create and recreate a cultural identity from a regional perspective?

JB: Yes.

PB: We see the theatre as helping to create a network among the communities.

FIGURES OF REGULATION: GUIDES FOR RE-BALANCING SOCIETY WITH THE BIOSPHERE

On a finite planet, it serves our mutual interests to live within limits and not plunder the very source of life. But how limits are determined and implemented presents a conundrum for anyone who values freedom. Berg looks beyond law, religion, and ideology, suggesting that social customs be developed to guide human behavior. Just as an embryo regulates cell activity to repair internal damage, and just as a dance is a figure in the mind, which dancers make visible, so too human activities in the post-Industrial era might be directed by new customs—figures of regulation—that maintain and restore bioregions while making visible values of interdependence. This treatise on cultural forms appears with essays by John Todd and George Tukel in Eco-Decentralist Design *(Planet Drum Foundation, 1982), whose major themes are energy and sustainability. Berg's contribution links sustainability to social values and customs in the context of the human species' need to reproduce and survive.*

The South African Army is now inducting Bushmen into its ranks, teaching them to forsake traditional bows and arrows for R-1 rifles. And their phenomenal tracking skills, gleaned from centuries of stalking animals over the vast roadless stretches of southern Africa, are being used to track down black nationalist guerrillas contesting South Africa's control of this disputed territory [Caprivi Strip, Namibia] . . .

In return for fighting SWAPO, the Bushmen are paid about $400 per month by the South Africans—a considerable sum in these parts, and a staggering amount for people unaccustomed to cash. In addition, the SADF [South African Defense Forces] provides housing for some 900 women and 1,500 children of the Bushmen troops . . .

Lieutenant Wolff concedes that a cash economy once baffled the Bush-men. "When they first arrived here, their sense of money was very poor," he explains.

But now, he says, they are being taught to invest their earnings. Indeed, Bushman wives are even being offered insurance plans as a hedge against the death of their husbands in combat . . .

Lieutenant Wolff admits that the Bushmen have "no political sense" and know little about the causes in the war which they are helping to fight.

Indeed, when this reporter asked a Bushman trooper why he was involved in the conflict, he replied simply, "For the money."

Gary Thatcher, "Bushmen: The Hunters Now Fight Guerrillas,"
The Christian Science Monitor, March 1981

Prior to the Industrial Revolution, most decisions about activities that affected natural systems were guided by custom. The traditional hunting practices, agriculture, house designs and uses of tools that evolved in distinct regions over long periods of time were maintained to be consistent with the "right way" to do things. It's not surprising that under analysis with contemporary criteria of efficiency and appropriateness these customs often yield the best way, if regional availability of materials and local conditions are retained as limiting factors. After all, customs incorporate the intelligence and experience of many people over generations of dealing with those limits. Taken as a whole, a traditional culture's customs also represent sensitive understandings of the relationship between human needs and the requirements of the overall life-community. The practical evidence of this is that these cultures continue to exist and maintain themselves in their home regions.

In order to restore and maintain bioregions, we need to develop frameworks of understanding that are equivalent to customs but even more attentive to balance points between human needs and the requirements of the natural community that ultimately supports us. We need a basis for limits to our undertakings that like social customs are not of a specifically religious, legal or ideological mold. Our species' interdependence with all life provides the ultimate justification for these limits: it absolutely forbids us from wantonly destroying life that sustains us if we expect to continue to live. These limits should be seen as serving our mutual interests rather than as restricting individual freedom. Stanley Diamond points out about tribes who are dedicated to maintaining traditional customs, "Freedom as a concept does not exist among primitive people because society is not perceived as oppressive." These limits can obtain a benefit that none of us could secure alone.

The frameworks of understanding, or areas of social rapport, that would be appropriate for reinhabitory activities could be thought of as regulating them, but not as a machine is regulated by an operator. In biology the term "regulation" describes the process of redistribution of material within an embryo to restore a damaged or lost part without the necessity of new tissue growth. The embryo is thus able to continue developing in the face of abnormal conditions by filling in the features of a disturbed stage further along in the growth process. This sense of regulation should apply to limits on activities that threaten natural systems.

These regulatory understandings needn't be restricted to a list of "dos and don'ts." Their representation can be as varied as the activities themselves. The term "figure" is especially relevant to this kind of representation because it connotes a diverse range of meanings besides mathematical numbers: an object seen mainly in outline; a painting, carving or drawing of an object; an analogous person, place or thing; an imagined form; a conspicuous or impressive aspect; or a series of movements that make part of a dance.

Figures of regulation is a workable phrase for the new equivalents to customs that we need to learn. Late Industrial society with its misplaced faith in technological solutions is out of control. Our social organism is like an embryo that is suffering damage but there are no internal checks on our activities to re-establish a balance with the capacities of natural systems. The point of figures of regulation is that they would incorporate the concept that individual requirements and those of society are tied to the life processes of a bioregion. A bioregional model can identify balance points in our interactions with natural systems, and figures of regulation can operate to direct or limit activities to achieve balance.

The idea of a figure as a series of movements in a dance is useful for understanding the multi-layered nature of figures of regulation. The performance of a dance follows a distinct sense of rightness that would otherwise exist only as an idea, and it suggests connectedness with many other activities and ideas. It is a process that makes the invisible visible. As a dance unfolds it implies further action that is self-referenced by what has gone before. Figures of regulation are assemblages of values and ideas that can similarly become ingrained in patterns of activity.

Some examples of shared practices in Late Industrial society can illustrate how social activities based on mutual understandings of value operate.

Shoveling snow from house paths and sidewalks is an activity left over from an earlier period that shows how an unorganized set of individual activities results in fulfilling a social objective. Each householder shovels only a single path to the house and the length of sidewalk in front of it, but these increments eventually clear the entire sidewalk for everyone's benefit. Snow shoveling requires obtaining special tools, storing and learning how to use them. It is a regional practice that is specific to a particular season, and is still followed faithfully in small towns.

Heavy morning water use in urban areas is a practice by individuals that society accommodates in ways that have surprisingly great effects on natural systems. Toilets, showers and sinks being used nearly continually by everyone in a large city for an hour in the morning establishes a peak level for which water systems are designed. Peak levels dictate the maximum capacities of water supply and distribution systems, and consequently the extent to which water is diverted from natural courses and the uses of native ecosystems. Water management involves eco-cultural decisions on a scale that ranges up to damming major rivers and the creation of deserts. Figures of regulation should interrelate individual, social and bioregional requirements in new cultural practices for priority areas in the transition from high energy and resources consumption to reinhabitory society. The results of these practices would be:

1) Construction of new renewable energy housing or redesign of current houses with recycled materials
2) Participation in community transportation systems that eliminate most uses of private automobiles
3) Using intermediate power generating facilities scaled to local watersheds
4) Developing small-scale agriculture while restricting food imports and large-scale agribusiness methods
5) Restructuring water supply, use and disposal around considerations of regional native ecosystems through recycling, conservation and waste water utilization

In constructing new renewable energy housing, for example, figures of regulation like those shared by the "barn raising" participants in new greenhouse construction groups can come into play. These groups are assembled for a weekend to learn how to build a greenhouse addition to a house that can provide both food and passive solar heat by actually building one. The owner is a working participant and the crew members will eventually lead groups to build their own and other greenhouse additions. Recycled materials are used whenever possible. The crews cook meals and eat together while becoming a community of renewable energy practitioners and activists. Figures of regulation guide their ethics: They want to raise some of their own food and unplug from fossil fuel powered utilities. And the practice of participating in "barn-raising" groups becomes a new custom for starting toward that goal.

A greenhouse addition, like any of the other possibilities for alternative energy, could be constructed entirely through Late Industrial practices. A contractor could be hired to handle the whole job, for example. And the ethical motives could be completely consistent with Late Industrial ethics: do anything to make or save money. Figures of regulation, however, relate the implementation of renewable energy technology to broad aspects of energy flows that include human labor and community interaction.

Figures of regulation can be elaborated further in building new renewable energy housing or retrofitting houses by arranging labor or materials exchanges between workers, development of small-scale cooperative "cottage industries" for supplying recycled materials, and many other aspects of the housing transition process. Community design itself could eventually be determined by figures of regulation. The specific practices would be those of the particular community as it responds to its own circumstances.

Figures of regulation can help organize disparate ideas about energy, food, water, agriculture and transportation that will be connected together in a sustainable society. They can do this by providing the ethical underpinning for recognizing the overall life-community in seasonal celebrations that stress multi-species relationships. Memorial Day is recognized in Late Industrial society as a time to commemorate the victims of war. Observation of equinox or solstice days can become reinhabitory events to celebrate our interdependence with natural life processes.

Our function as individuals in society, as well as society's overall function, has been seen in progressively more mechanistic terms. Individuals are adjusted to society, society is rated for success by statistics of unemployment and GNP. It is a configuration of smaller machines within a big machine. Figures of regulation can't be relevant as long as society is viewed as a machine. It is essential to re-establish the roots of society in natural processes in order to develop reciprocal relationships between society and the biosphere.

The main biological root of society grows from the need to reproduce and maintain our species. The interaction of individuals relating to each other at each state of growth and development (ontogeny) provides the essential foundation of social relationships:

- Conception to birth, a continuous relationship with a mother.
- Early nurturing, assistance from many individuals during a state of helplessness.
- Learning to communicate with symbols learned from others.
- Puberty and ultimate sexual differentiation.
- Mating, mingling personal identity with another.
- Birthing and nurturing offspring.
- Full adulthood, attainment of social trust to represent and affirm values to offspring.
- Death, absorption of identity into social memory and species history.

Regardless of the degree to which these stages are obscured from their direct biological significance by contemporary mechanisms (birth certificates, school degrees, marriage licenses, death certificates) they nevertheless root our identity as mammals in the biosphere.

A second source of necessary social relationships is the immediate locale. Without ways to understand the unique conditions presented by natural places in regard to obtaining food and water, dealing with topography and climate, building shelters and securing needed resources, we wouldn't be able to survive. Relationships and symbolic communication are necessary to convey methods for obtaining sustenance, report variations in natural characteristics, and maintain regular practices. An abundance of natural life in an unscarred environment will provide evidence that figures of regulation are working. Social success or progress would also be measured by increased quality of life such as providing diverse work opportunities for individuals to interact with natural systems. Rather than feeling alienated from society and the life-community as many do currently, people would be able to view themselves as belonging to both.

Smaller, more naturally defined political entities would present many more opportunities for participation in the political process than currently exist, and decisions resulting from direct democracy would be more prevalent. The spirit of these governments could be mutualistic and nonhierarchical as a reflection of the operation of the biosphere itself.

Although an understanding and grasp of every aspect of natural processes isn't available to everyone all the time, figures of regulation nevertheless allow people to have confidence that they are approaching things in the best way. Their increased certainty and sense of belonging to a place in the biosphere implies a social vision quite different from that of Late Industrial preoccupation with space travel and technological breakthroughs. Emphasis would be placed instead on discovering more about biospheric processes and how they apply to unique bioregions (an area of investigation which has been neglected during Late Industrial fascination with physics). Research and experimentation would be directed toward aligning technology with those processes.

Finally, faith in natural cycles and the life-affirming purpose of the biosphere implies revitalized spiritual ties with our planet, and development of many cultural forms and events to express celebration of our reciprocity with the places, living things and delicate connecting life-web of Earth.

A RIVER RUNS THROUGH IT

"Do you know where your water comes from? Or what the rainfall in your area is? Can you point to the direction storms normally come from in your area?" So begins this compelling piece on the supreme importance of water, the Earth's most distinctive and essential element. In this essay, which appeared in Environmental Action *in 1983, Berg introduces readers to a diverse range of groups throughout the United States that are applying a watershed perspective to local problems, goading people to take a more-conscious-than-ever look at their own watersheds.*

"I have thought many times about where this rain is born. . . . Where in the ocean does the water rise up to fill the pores of the air? Where do the winds first breathe the air back to the land?

"The Bull Run watershed is a catchment area in the Mt. Hood National Forest where the clouds deposit their gifts and the gifts begin the journey through the stream and filter and pipe in house and body. It is good water . . . But . . . very few people know where their water came from."

Michael Soulé in *Clearing, a Journal of the Northwest*

Do you know where your water comes from? Or what the rainfall in your area is? Can you point to the direction storms normally come from in your area?

Perhaps you're an expert on water issues, but if you can't answer questions like these you have a woefully inadequate sense of place. Of course, water doesn't originate "from the faucet" any more than it disappears "down the drain." It is the lifeblood of a watershed system, and we are *part of*, not merely *in* that system.

Some activists around the country have begun to apply a watershed perspective to local problems. They're looking at their area as a "bioregion" or life-region, a geographically continuous area with similar plant and animal life. The wet Gulf of Maine bioregion, for example, is distinctly different from the arid Sonoran Desert in Arizona, and each has unique climatic and geological characteristics.

The National Water Center in Eureka Springs, Arkansas is a prime example of this new perspective. Eureka Springs residents founded the center when natural springs that flow through the town became polluted by sewage. Members of the center have researched alternatives to "disposing" of effluents by letting them flow directly into the Ozark Mountains' fractured limestone subsoil. It now advocates waterless compost toilets and sponsors National Water Week to involve other communities in "healing the waters." The group is also active in the Ozarks Area Community Congress, an organization that has described itself as, "the bioregional shadow government for the Ozarks."

In Northern California, forest restoration and salmon enhancement groups take a whole watershed view of their activities, involving local residents in their work and aiming toward long-term recovery from deforestation, erosion, depletion of native wildlife and misuse of the land. Even in New York City, the Hudson Estuary group has begun collecting materials to use in making residents of that metropolis aware of a natural home base in the shadow of the World Trade Center.

The strength of grassroots support for watershed-bioregion planning shouldn't be underestimated. In 1982, Northern California voters helped defeat a ballot proposition to divert vast amounts of Sacramento River water to the southern Central Valley and Los Angeles by voting an unprecedented 90 percent (and greater in some local areas) against it. Ranchers in Utah, usually staunchly pro-national defense, were disturbed enough by the potential water consumption of an MX missile basing proposal to help disqualify Utah as a possible site. Where issues are sharply focused on regional availability of water, local people are most likely to become strongly protective of their resources.

Water is the most urgent life-resource issue of the 1980s—and the next century. Its full impact will affect more people in greater ways than any previous ecological concern. Water quality problems, particularly in the old industrial Northeast and new industrial South, will force decisions about manufacturing practices and use of materials. Limited availability of water, particularly in the growth-staggered Southwest and West, and agriculturally over drawn Mid-west, will radically alter and restrict modes of life and work in those areas. The scale of water problems that is looming lifts the issue above what could be otherwise labeled "just another environmental consideration."

Throughout human history water has been the *sine qua non* of stable civilizations. It is now a fundamental issue for determining the future course of our Late Industrial society. Late Industrial solutions for re-securing water supplies, such as the oversized schemes proposed to drain the Great Lakes or divert the Columbia and Colorado Rivers, are not only capable of creating more problems than they resolve—as Egypt's Aswan Dam did—but will collide directly with increasingly protective local sentiments.

Legislative approaches that have been used to resolve environmental problems in the recent past aren't enough to deal with all the profound implications of the water issue. New regulations to control point source discharges or reduce emissions from smokestacks and prevent acid rain, for instance, are only single notes in reharmonizing with the delicately interwoven strings of the water web. We need to transform the way we look at water supply and use if we are to make the transition to stable interdependence with Earth's most distinctive and essential element.

Start with a fresh look at the watershed where you live. It's probably been viewed as the province of a musty-officed water or sewage department while you've lived there, but in reality that watershed is the principal designer of life patterns around you, including many of your own.

A watershed's foundation is the literal ground of any life-place. Are there steep mountains sharply thrust up from ancient periods of mountain-building such as in the Rockies or Sierra Nevada? Are there even older peaks that have been rounded off like the Appalachians? Barely rolling hills of windblown mountain dust in the Great Plains? Those rises and valleys are the underpinning for the action of a watershed.

Water is the community actor. Water frozen in glaciers may have smoothed the land surface millennia ago as in the Dakotas and New England, and each winter's ice will continue to break down remaining boulders. A dried-up lakebed may stretch for flat miles in the Great Basin. This year's rain will find an imperceptible low place to float cars down small town streets in Nevada. The minutely gradual sinking of North America's eastern shore will lower a coastside pasture just enough so that a rain-swollen creek will spread to become a new marsh, mixing fresh water with the Atlantic.

People respond to watersheds in both conscious and unconscious ways. If a house is close to a river floodplain or built over a dried-up creek, the occupants probably know that the basement will flood in heavy rains. But most people aren't aware when driving that highway engineers try to follow water courses whenever possible because watershed patterning has made the ground flatter there.

Most Northern Californians, for example, didn't recognize the region's dependence on winter rain and snow for the entire year's water supply until a severe drought four years ago forced residents to count gallons. Old-timers in Arizona know they live in a desert and don't expect (or want) English-style grass lawns, while transplants to the Sunbelt who think a lawn is essential are severely overtaxing the available water base for everyone who lives there.

Only by taking a fresh and more-conscious-than-ever look at our own watersheds can we address the water shortages and pollution problems we must face. The ways that we interact with water during its entire course through the watersheds where we live—from its arrival as rain or up from wells to its departure as sewage or downstream to the next watershed—are the ultimate measures of how well we can adapt to the broad challenges of the water issue.

BIOREGIONS

Contending that the fate of the Earth is the central issue that civilization must address, Berg succinctly explains the two core concepts of the bioregional paradigm: bioregions *and* reinhabitation. *This brief essay, which originally appeared in a 1983 issue of the British periodical* Resurgence, *presents bioregionalism in a nutshell for readers new to the concept, serving as a helpful starting point and a handy reference.*

Where do any of us actually live? Since the advent of Industrial Age consciousness only about two centuries ago (and for only the last few decades in most of the world) the answer to this literally basic question has been framed in progressively more urban, statist and technological terms, rather than in those of the processes of life itself. Ask the next person you meet and expect at least part of this reply, "In a numbered house on such a street, in some section of a city, in a particular state or province or department, of . . . nation-state, in a First, Second or Third World power bloc. That is, when I'm not at . . . another place where I commute to work by car, bus, train, or airplane."

We all live within the web-of-life, of course. Our bodies and senses are those of mammals in the biosphere. All of our food, water and materials come from processes of the biosphere. But during the Industrial Age, reaching a climax in the Late Industrial period dating from World War II, the fact of our interdependence with all life became a vague abstraction. We have suffered from the delusion of believing that our lives were safely in the care of machines. The separation between conscious human identity and locatedness, and the planetary life-web of which our species is part, is now critical enough to threaten the survival of both. We are in the absurd and tragic position of someone who sets fire to the house to keep warm in a freezing blizzard, destroying ever-widening ranges of life without consciousness of our ultimate bond with them.

How do we rediscover where we actually live?

Bioregions are geographic areas having common characteristics of soil, watersheds, climate, and native plants and animals that exist within the whole planetary biosphere as unique and intrinsic contributive parts. Consider them as possessing the diverse and necessary distinction of leaves from roots, or arms from legs. The Amazon jungle, for instance, provides so much oxygen that it can be counted as a lung of the biosphere. The Nile delta is a kidney for the Mediterranean Sea. Underneath and around the industrial grids of row-houses and factories, streets and sewers, highways and railways, oil and gas pipelines, legal jurisdictions and political boundaries, this natural geography of life continues to endure.

Everyone lives in some bioregion or other. Prior to industrialism the reality of inhabitation in a unique life-place was reflected in adaptive cultures that reciprocated with cycles and conditions of that place. Some strong examples still remain such as the Hopi's deeply sacred involvement with and cultivation of corn, rain, mesas, and respectful grace in the American Southwest. Some vestiges continue to haunt the designs of nation-states such as the heroic persistence (after eight centuries' domination) of Welsh language and culture on the western side of England's principal topographical divide. Thoroughly adaptive cultures are native human mammal interactions, as natural as any other aspect of the life of a bioregion.

For most people, however, inhabitation of a unique bioregion has lost pre-eminence as a fact of survival. While this condition prevails no bioregion is secure from the threat of being crippled in its ability to nurture life. "Cut down the Amazon jungle for newspaper pulp, we need to read about fluctuations in oil prices." "Level the Hopi's Black Mesa, we need coal to produce electricity so Los Angeles's lights can burn all night." There is no way to ensure the survival of the biosphere without saving each bioregion, and it is especially important for anyone living within industrial society to begin cultivating bioregional consciousness.

Reinhabitation is a term for undertaking the practice of living-in-place, becoming part of a bioregion again. A first step is to become familiar with the specific natural characteristics of the place where one lives. Wet and green northern California, for example, isn't continuous with the dry desert portion of the state. Northern California is a separate natural country, "Shasta." The Ozark Mountains are a distinct raised limestone formation with a unique natural identity of watersheds and vegetation straddling the border of Arkansas and Missouri, the bioregion of "Ozarkia." Ocean-influenced areas of northern Maine in the United States and New Brunswick in Canada share the same bioregion, "The Gulf of Maine."

Any place is within a bioregion. Every metropolis exists in a natural locale: Manhattan in the lower Hudson River valley; London in that of the Thames. Suburbs, towns, villages, rural farming areas, forests and national parks are all within specific bioregions.

Once the extent and character of a life-place is determined, reinhabitory approaches can be taken to an impressively large number of activities and problem areas. Education and awareness have a special priority at present, and bioregional study groups have already emerged in over fifty areas of the United States and

Canada. They produce newsletters and information "bundles" on their bioregions, and often choose particularly immediate political issues for emphasis. In Shasta, for example, the Frisco Bay Mussel Group evolved into an adamant voice for opposing inter-basin transfers of northern California water to the south and Los Angeles, and in the 1982 election was active in defeating what up until now was a common practice (over 90% of Shasta voters opposed the latest diversion scheme; the largest single-side vote in California history).

For decentralists in general the concept of a bioregion answers the question, "Decentralize to where?" Antinuclear activists are becoming pro-bioregionalist. Local food co-operatives and local natural resources defense groups are finding that organizing along watershed and bioregional lines makes them more effective.

Bioregionalism is a significant step beyond either conservationist or environmentalist thinking. It is directly addressed to the fate of the earth, not as merely an "ecological" issue, but as the central issue that human civilization must address.

THE POST-ENVIRONMENTALIST DIRECTIONS OF BIOREGIONALISM

The biosphere, a thin skin of life that surrounds the planet, becomes a verb in Berg's opening gambit, "How do we biosphere?" One way to biosphere is to become fully engaged in the bioregions, or specific "life-places," where we live. While environmentalism had protest as its reigning activity, bioregionalism promotes the positive activities of urban sustainability and restoring habitats and ecosystems. Berg offers inspiring examples of these two directions for bioregional practice, instilling the hope that by saving the parts we can save the whole. This important lecture was delivered at the University of Montana in 2001 in the Poetics of Wilderness series. Note: Ellipses in the text indicate where Berg showed and discussed slides, not included here but available on the Planet Drum website.

The central subject I'm going to be talking about is the biosphere, the thin skin of life that surrounds our planet. A very thin covering, like our own skin. And the question is: how do we biosphere? It sounds like a verb, doesn't it? This is an interesting idea for two reasons. One is that we're all coming out of the Industrial Era beginning from roughly the 17th century to the present. We're at the beginning of late industrial or even post-industrial society. The second thing is that biosphere in the sense of "the blue planet" seen from space is a relatively new idea. It's not exactly the same idea as the older sense of Mother Earth. For example, a Hopi or Navajo representation of the universe would be from the Southwest Desert. Navajo sand paintings are done on sand; they're not done on Everglades muck. That's a local-cosmological vision of Mother Earth. But a planet-wide biosphere is a somewhat different concept.

There is a potential for some major considerations that can come into play when you begin thinking about the fact that we all share the earth together. One is that we are a species. Homo sapiens is a mammalian species. We are animals. The other forms of life that we share the planet with are similar to us in many ways. We evolved in the biosphere, we weren't spirited down from a spacecraft to colonize Earth. We are interdependent with all the other life forms and forces on the Earth. Which even includes interdependence with fleas and scorpions.

How does one grasp this? Well, it's not easily graspable. It's not the same kind of thing as knowing what's happening on channel four. Take as an example the nitrogen cycle. We know that the nitrogen cycle is active in the biosphere, we know that in fact that we participate in the nitrogen cycle. The nitrogen cycle is one of the most important gaseous phenomena in the biosphere, but we don't know exactly how it operates with us in this room right now. It's necessary to have a little faith about this. We're not going to know what happened with everything we eat or where everything we eat goes. Or what happens with all of the elements that move in and out of us. The exact nature of our total interdependence with natural systems in the biosphere will remain a large-scale mystery.

Another aspect of being in the biosphere is that you have to be some place. This has sometimes gone right by people who are involved with environmental causes. Environmentalism has largely been an activity that was parallel to industrial society, which is essentially dislocated. All of us at every moment are some place in the biosphere, a bioregion. You may have noticed, in just the last ten years, that most major ecologically oriented organizations have begun to fit the notion of a biogeographic region into their programs. The Sierra Club, possibly one of the most conservative environmental organizations, has been persuaded by its membership to start an ecoregion program. It is becoming a more widely acknowledged idea that we all live in some life-place, and that maybe if we save those parts we can save the whole.

I want to tell a couple of stories from an urban context that point to ways we can fit into bioregions as a way to biosphere. Zeke the Sheik lived in Altadena, California. I learned about Zeke from a newspaper article that related how a man had been arrested in Altadena and charged with three civic crimes which were arson, violating the zoning laws, and operating a business without a license. This is what Zeke the Sheik did. He had built a compost pile that was over 25 feet tall in his backyard, and it worked so well that it broke into flames. The top of it caught on fire and necessitated the fire department to come and put it out. That was the arson charge. The business without a license was that he was distributing compost to his neighbors at an extremely small cost to cover his transportation expenses. He was giving out barrels of almost-free compost. He violated the zoning laws by having chickens on his place. He had simply decided to eat his own eggs. Altadena is a semi-suburban town so he was brought up on charges and treated as a criminal. Are you having the same thought I am, that he should have been appointed the minister of sustainability for Altadena? Instead of being arrested for doing these things?

In San Francisco currently there are explosions of feathers taking place outside of office building windows. Secretaries and CEO's turn and look out the window at a burst of feathers. They might believe that they are in the midst of some supernatural phenomena. It's actually the result of peregrine falcons diving down from the tops of office buildings and hunting pigeons. One of them has the poetically true name, Mutual Benefit Life Building. The birds are taking pigeons up to the rooftops and at the end of the day they fly back to where they roost under the bridge between San Francisco and Berkeley. The falcons have not only adapted to an urban environment, but they're commuting to work!

I could really go on at length about these native hunting birds because they are so inspiring. They are doing us a service by symbolizing what we can be. We are animals too. And we are wild at heart. Our dreams are wild. Our bloodstream is wild. We shouldn't solely cultivate postures and behaviors that are appropriate for operating machines, getting backaches and neck aches from driving cars or operating computers. We are human animals. The falcons are showing us that we can be wild in an urban environment with a high degree of elegance as well. Not wild like crazy, but the kind of wildness our predecessors possessed who made beautiful cave paintings in southern France thousands of years ago.

There are two directions that I think post-environmentalism should and will follow. The first is urban sustainability. To many people large cities are simply bad. New York and Los Angeles are not environments that they really enjoy. I also don't generally like cities that are over about 100,000 in population, and there have been some cities that had populations of less than 50,000 and still produced great music and art. The bad news is that our present large cities can be awful environments, and the necessary news is that they are becoming the dominant habitat for our species. Our population is increasing at an extremely rapid rate and within a few years more than 50% of all homo sapiens on the planet will live in cities of 25,000 or more. The World Watch Institute estimates that this will probably occur at around 2010, but it may happen faster. There are some ridiculously overblown populations in cities today. Almost half the population of the entire nation of Mexico lives in Mexico City. China is planning to build 100 new cities of one million population or more in the next few decades. They're moving the majority population of rural people off of the land in China to become urban dwellers.

Cities are not sustainable at present. They haven't been sustainable historically and they're not sustainable now. There are outstanding examples of great ruined cities. The Tigris-Euphrates Valley which is allegedly the cradle of human civilization is at this point incapable of supporting much more than goats. It's been completely deforested, the rivers have been diverted, and the soil was ruined. Some ruined cities are still incredibly beautiful. One wonders why people would abandon Machu Pichu or Angkor [sic] Wat? They are like whole pieces of exquisite sculpture. The reason is that their inhabitants destroyed their local regional bases of support to fill basic human needs.

The only thing that keeps our present large metropolitan areas going is that they can still exploit their region or other regions for their continued support. For example, Los Angeles gets water from the Colorado River and northern California. Its liquid natural gas is from Indonesia. A large percentage of its labor comes from Mexico. Its electrical energy is derived from coal that comes from the Four Corners area of the Southwest. It is completely dependent, like a hospital patient. LA is alive because it is getting continuous transfusions from other places.

If we don't attempt to transform these cities, we are performing a form of suicide for our species. I want you to answer the following questions as though you live in New York. Where does your water come from? A Manhattanite might say, "It comes from the faucet, stupid!" Where does energy come from? "The wall switch!" And food? "Everybody knows food comes from the store." And garbage? "I've been thinking about garbage. Garbage goes out. There's a parallel universe called out." And the stuff in the toilet? "This is a real miracle of civilization. It disappears. Totally!" That is a suicidal view of the basic underlying resources that are essential for our lives.

The transformation of cities is perhaps the greatest challenge that I can imagine a person undertaking. The bigger a city gets the bigger this challenge is. How would NYC get its energy, food and water sustainably? How would it deal with its garbage and sewage sustainably? These are really formidable problems. Urban sustainability is an enormous transformative proposition and I encourage all of you to begin thinking of how this can be done. You may question the particulars of what is meant by "urban," or question the term "sustainability," but making cities harmonious with the regions where they exist and with the planetary biosphere is undeniably a major problem for our time and our species.

The other direction for post-environmentalism is the restoration of habitats and ecosystems. I just attended a memorial for David Brower. The older generation of conservationists was there to make tributes. Some of the ways they described being in nature were touching and beautiful, and also essentially different from what motivates people today. They were primarily Sierra Club hikers, backpackers and yodelers. These aren't bad activities, of course, but they are different from what we think of now as the spirit of wilderness or wildness. We're moving toward a different consideration of the natural world. Frankly, there isn't a lot of it left. Have all of you seen the book from the Foundation for Deep Ecology titled *Clear Cut*? Please take a look at it. It's the most brutally honest view of forests destroyed by logging that you could possibly imagine. It's also a view that any one of you can have fairly easily just by taking a plane ride from San Francisco to Seattle, which I did this morning. You'll fly over many of the clear cuts photographed for this book. In winter they're particularly visible as checker board-like squares full of white snow that stand out from the uncut green trees around them. There is extremely little of the original primary forest left in North America.

We are even running out of water now. Naturally pure water is disappearing fast. In the American west, the biggest ecological question is becoming: where will sufficient water come from? We're polluting water, diverting water, and consuming water to a degree that will soon outpace available supplies. A lack of potable water may be the biggest limiting factor on the quality and numbers of human lives everywhere on the planet in the future.

Environmentalism wasn't really addressing the issue of "we are the human species sharing the biosphere together interdependently with other species and should have the long-range goal of doing so harmoniously." The previous directions of environmentalism were mainly to stop polluting air and water, to protect human health, and to slow down the destruction of nature. This was essentially from the mental perspective of industrial society surrounding nature. Actually, nature surrounds industrial society. We're in the biosphere, not in the Boeing aircraft factory parking lot. We're not in a human created environment, we are animals in the wild biosphere.

Cities need to become more self-reliant. Suburban-type communities like Altadena, California need to develop a public presence or governmental presence about sustainability and restoring the ecosystems in that area. How do we sustain them? How do we restore the natural systems that have been destroyed in them?

First of all, we need to start seeing these sites for human inhabitation as existing in bioregions. What is a bioregion? This idea doesn't come from pure natural science. Bioregionalism is a cultural idea. It's an attempt to answer, "Who am I, what am I, and what am I going to do about it?" It's a way for people to look at the place where they live in terms of fitting into natural characteristics.

[. . . .]

These are the major characteristics of a bioregion; watershed, landform, native plants and animals, soils, climate, and an adaptive human relationship about living in that place. [. . . .] [T]he idea of a bioregion is based on natural characteristics and natural science, but it is a cultural view that's not only held by people in parts of North America, but also Europe. There are active bioregional groups in South America, Australia and Japan. Bioregionalism is becoming a popular movement that roughly follows the idea that people who live in a place have a certain inhabitory obligation to live in harmony with the natural systems that are there. We call this reinhabitation, becoming inhabitants again.

What are some of the things these groups do? They are really quite diverse. It might be a group of Catholic sisters living on a communal farm in New Jersey. Or tree sitters who are resisting logging in northern California. It might be a group of farmers in the Great Plains who want to find a way to stop destroying the soil and water resources of that area, by finding human food and materials resources from native plants, rather than the present monoculture of grain crops such as wheat, corn, soybeans. There are actually several groups doing this including the Land Institute which has a basically bioregional perspective. Also an organization named the Kansas Area Watershed Council, or KAW, the sound a crow makes. There is a group in the Ozarks called the Ozarks Area Community Congress, or OACC after oak, the dominant tree form there. There are several bioregional groups in Mexico. The most inspiring one for me is near the town of Tepoztlan in Morelos where local people resisted a multinational globalist invasion by land developers to build a golf course resort using their water resources. They called their resistance "The Golf War," and they were successful after five years and half a dozen people killed. They prosecuted the governor of the state on charges of bribery, and the new president of Mexico has given them back the rights to the water in a legal form so that they hopefully won't have this problem again.

From a bioregional perspective, water is one of the first things to consider. How can we live with available water sources without diverting or destroying them?

Agriculture. What kind of agriculture is important to this life-place? The most appropriate form of agriculture for a bioregional context is "permaculture." For example, you aren't able to grow the same kinds of things with natural means in the Sonoran Desert Bioregion in Arizona as you could in Cascadia Bioregion around Seattle. Agriculture needs to be bioregionally reconfigured.

Energy. We can't keep thinking that our future is going to be dependent on fossil fuels and nuclear power. We have to develop renewable energy sources. You can see right away that those are going to be bioregionally determined. For example, in Cascadia using mini-hydropower makes sense because there is abundant flowing and falling water there. But you wouldn't think of using small-scale, local hydropower in the Sonoran Desert where there is little water. That's a good place to be using direct solar energy instead.

We can't think of sustainability in a jingoistic, economic determinist way. We have to think of it in terms of regional realities, and the grounding for that has to be in harmony with local natural systems as they occur where you live.

About borders of bioregions, these aren't strict boundaries. They aren't straight lines. [. . .] They are usually soft, and can be 50 miles wide. They could in some cases be as sharp as the crest of the Cascade Mountains where you can actually step over from one bioregion to another, from the wet side of the mountains to the dry side. But in most places, the phasing between bioregions is more gradual.

The practice of living in a bioregion is proactive, and I think this is an important point for making an aside. Environmentalism had protest as its reigning activity. Most people have the view that environmentalism is somebody telling them, "no." Urban sustainability, and restoring habitats and ecosystems, are positive activities. People can actually make their livings doing these things. Unfortunately it's not a lot of people yet, but at some point in the future when hopefully there will be more subsidization and more local community support for it, there will be a great many ways that people can support themselves in this way. At present, for most people, it's mainly pursuit of a life-way. Most of the bioregionalists I know are following a path that leads towards bioregional connectedness and identity.

The implications for bioregionalism are numerous. Politically, governmental borders should follow natural watershed lines. In terms of education, school children would learn the bioregional realities of where they live. Isn't it amazing that we don't teach that in school? That we've gotten to this point in environmental awareness and ecological destruction, and we're not teaching children the bioregional characteristics of where they live, or their connectedness with them, or the activities that are appropriate for living in a specific life-place? In terms of philosophy and literature there are obvious implications. Paintings can easily relate to the natural phenomena of the place where the artist lives, or poetry. Gary Snyder is a writer who will be known in the future for leading a transition for North American literature: from Europe to the Pacific Rim, and to life-places like his own Shasta Bioregion in northern California. Culture can go straight to wilderness for inspiration rather than just relying on industrial civilization.

[. . . .]

LEARNING TO PARTNER WITH A LIFE-PLACE

The planet-wide ecological crisis demands a redirection of society, which will require knowledge, which in turn means that we need life-place education. In this practical piece, which opens on a fog-wet spring morning in San Francisco in a partially undeveloped park, Berg designs a hands-on, first-year curriculum, whose subjects include restoring a habitat or watershed, producing food and energy through renewable means, utilizing native and recycled materials in making products, and creating life-place culture. Life-place education, Berg contends, is a constructive way to begin learning to identify with and actually become a part of a place in the biosphere.

On a fog-wet spring morning in San Francisco, our unusual urban group climbed to the top of a rock promontory midway along a canyon trail to get a clear view of the standout feature in a partially undeveloped park. The expedition of city explorers consisted of a wilderness enthusiast who arrived on a motorcycle with his realtor girlfriend riding behind, three environmental students from Minnesota, Connecticut and New Jersey, and myself as guide. This park presents a jarring contrast between native and exotic vegetation, plants that grew there naturally and those brought from another part of the world. Eucalyptus trees originating in Australia were planted over a hundred years ago and subsequently spread invasively over the hillsides along the trail. Then they stopped short as though a border had been drawn as part of a landscaper's design. It was actually a natural effect, attributable to a flat spot where water from a creek spread out to nourish a wide swath of yellow willows and dozens of other native plants. Willows thrive where their roots are constantly wet, and here they had become too large and dense to be crowded out by past or present intruders. The same group of indigenous species had probably occupied this identical place starting some time after the Ice Age, perhaps as long as ten thousand years. It didn't take specialized knowledge to see how the tall, straight, shaggy trunks of the sparsely leafed non-natives differed from low, impenetrably dense willows that had prospered so well they had grown to medium-size trees. An inescapable trace of the difference appeared when the sharp cough drop scent of eucalyptus nuts that we had all noticed along the trail suddenly yielded to an inviting humus perfume of dark brown decaying willow leaves. It was as complete a transition as when a chapter ends and a new one begins.

We sat on outcrops of what had once been the compacted floor of the Pacific Ocean. The edge of the sea bottom was twisted and thrust upward millions of years ago by the force of the North American and Pacific Tectonic Plates colliding during Continental Drift. As ancient as the foundations for natural life here might be, the stand of willows that we had just walked through looked narrow and vulnerable from above. Newly built houses looped ominously around the rim of the canyon like an encircling noose. What we were seeing was only a minuscule refuge. A sense of thoughtful sadness came over the group.

One of the college students had been quiet until our stop. Now her low voice broke the silence. "This isn't the way they taught me botany."

What an off-center remark! She had our complete surprised attention and quickly obliged with an explanation. She had taken the course because of an impulse toward Nature as a relief from conflicting social and personal directions. She even planned a trip to Ecuador soon to volunteer working with forest revegetation projects. The botany class had been a way to get a little background. "From the beginning we just learned about uses for plants and making them as productive as possible. The professor said it definitely wasn't an ecology class and that they liked poisons, herbicides, fertilizers, and so forth. I got put off and didn't get much out of it."

The rest of us looked at each other and nodded affirmation with the relieved understanding that comes from solving a puzzle together. "Well, at least he was honest for a change," blurted out the wilderness loving biker, speaking what the rest of us felt. "Things may actually be changing for the better if they feel it's necessary to make that distinction," someone else asserted wryly.

We had taken the walk to see some broad aspects of northern California as a unique natural place. Having been left in its original condition, this small section of the park retained some of the classic essentials. Just walking through brought the unique experience of a coastal canyon watershed. Chert stones in several shades of red crunching beneath our feet proclaimed the soil underpinnings. Native plants grew in their chosen natural habitats: watercress in the creek, piggyback plants in the shade, yellow blue-eyed grass in a sunny patch of marsh. A red-tailed hawk's nest darkened the crotch of some tree branches.

We even had a view of the built-up, paved over city stretching out beyond the park. The same native elements in this refuge persisted there in some form as well, traveling in the air or lying dormant beneath the sidewalks and streets. The creek might disappear down a storm drain and into an underground sewer at a point farther on but it still ran free here. How many of these things could be seen in other places of the city outside the park? How much could be restored? Our conversation until the walk ended was occupied with similar atypical urban observations, seemingly coaxed by the living generosity of the creek.

But the student's dissatisfaction implied a different kind of question.

Meaningful ecological learning, fast

The present planet-wide ecological crisis is foremost in the minds of an ever-widening circle that encompasses groups as different as scientists and business planners, academics and construction workers, and even some politicians. Our concern has moved beyond self-serving quibbling to identify this calamity as a primary problem in urgent need of solutions. Denial of crucial indications such as global warming is deluded and dangerous. It only contributes to public unease through increased frustration and suspicion.

More and more of the national and international issues of the 21st century can be directly traced to ecologically rooted causes. Struggles over energy availability and use, limitations on water and other essential resources, food shortages, and increasing population have already become the basis for wars that jeopardize reasonable approaches to ecological imbalances.

We can't delay in reversing our rampant destruction and learning to live integrally with the rest of life. Ecological sustainability can't continue to be viewed as a luxury that only the richest countries can afford. It is an essential goal for every human society regardless of economic level, geographic location, or culture. It can no longer be compartmentalized as just an environmental concern either. We have to learn to live within the limits of the biosphere, and this is such a serious problem that it requires a thorough going redirection of the central course of society.

We desperately need to gain knowledge that enables individuals and communities to make ecologically beneficial decisions about what to do and how to do it. This has to become a primary function of contemporary information media and education at all levels. At present in even the best institutions of learning, general access to useful information about sustainability is as remote as Antarctica. It needs to become as close as a radio, a television set, or a neighbor's conversation. It definitely needs to be taught at every level of schooling. If classes in specific natural sciences such as botany aren't required to teach these things, where can a student learn?

A personal, local start

Learning how to develop solutions at the level of the whole biosphere may be too far a reach for most people, but at least they can find out what needs to be done in the particular place where they live. Work to become compatible with local life systems in a home place. These are both comprehensible and realistic goals. Each person lives in a specific bioregion, a life-place that is an essential part of the planetary web of life. Even small outlays of effort locally can genuinely benefit some aspect of the mutuality of life. They result in tangible outcomes that are there to live with and watch while their impact on other natural features grows. There is no question that this kind of involvement will stimulate the expansion of personal ecological consciousness. Salutarily, it is a genuine and necessary remedy that will aid more wide-ranging cures such as decreasing carbon dioxide in the atmosphere or reducing global warming.

We need to gain knowledge about regional ecology with an emphasis on social and cultural implications. How do we identify the basic starting points for maintaining and restoring life where we live?

Active projects have a priority

Because rapid action is required to harmonize with local natural systems and to remedy damage already done, there have to be hands-on projects: learning by doing essential work to achieve natural health in our life-places.

Choosing these projects can follow simple guidelines. Because the educational core is lit by an ecological imperative, there are *three clear sources* for activities. These are primary colors that will make up all the shades and blends of a full spectrum of possible projects.

The first is restoration and maintenance of natural features to whatever extent is immediately possible. These rehabilitory efforts to restore life-place health must be undertaken with a sensibility for continuous improvement. They are the cornerstones for more projects aimed to eventually regain the highest possible level of original vitality. For example, planting native trees on an eroded hillside can be the first step toward restoring habitats for native plants and animals, and might eventually lead to creating a wild corridor.

Next is developing sustainable means to satisfy basic human needs. Food, water, energy, shelter, materials, and information are essential, and they can be elaborated in numerous variations. Some possibilities: growing indigenous plant species for food, reusing wastewater, using renewable energy to power households, building with recycled or regenerated native materials, creating new products from indigenous resources, and heightening bioregional awareness through public media. And those are only single entries from long "to do" lists in each area.

Finally there needs to be support for living in place in the widest possible range of ways from economics and culture to politics and philosophy. This involves both proactive undertakings that create positive alternatives as well as protests against ecological devastation and disruption.

What else is different about life-place education?

The main focus for life-place learning is on the ecologically bounded place itself. It isn't difficult to locate this spot. Identify the climate, weather, landforms, watershed, predominant geological and soil conditions, native plants and animals, and sustainable aspects of the traditional culture along with ecological practices of present day inhabitants. Your life-place is the geographic area where those things converge. Lessons, workshops, and exercises need to be directed toward identifying and harmonizing with the specific features of that place, and they should do this while assisting to carry out public projects that foster ecological sustainability.

If participants include children, young adults and seniors, all the better because that will mean the whole range of generations within the community is involved. Each age group brings essential ingredients for the ultimate success of the educational program.

Another new feature for life-place schooling is that it operates to some extent throughout the year. This is important because it is the only way everyone can witness the effect of each season on what is being learned and the work that's done. Students need to observe the movement that takes place within life processes over time, and responses to different seasonal conditions. Otherwise they won't perceive characteristics that are indispensable; cycles of change and how forces of life vary from month to month.

A first year's worth of learning/doing

The first year needs to be as basic as possible because of its foundational role for future studies and projects. A valuable starting place is the fact that every life-place has lost some of the original trees and plants that provided habitats and were essential members of ecosystems. Revegetation projects to replant native plants are undoubtedly needed. Due to the massive displacement of these species by timber cutting, farming and land development, it is likely that their identities and inter-workings will be relatively unknown. In fact, the overall ecological life patterns of the place will need to be rediscovered. To address these problems set two practical objectives: 1) propagate indigenous plants in local neighborhoods, and 2) create a map and guide that shows characteristics of local natural systems.

To cover four seasons the program can be divided into quarters of three months each.

First quarter

a) Native plant species. Locate and identify, obtain seeds through gathering and other sources, plant seeds.
b) Watershed. Begin to identify natural landforms and water bodies from available charts and direct outdoors observation.
c) Arts and handicrafts. Research existing examples of arts and products created from local materials. Create planters for seeds from recycled containers.
d) Mapping. Create individual maps showing landforms, watersheds, water bodies, soils, native plants and animals, and major human interactions with them (*Discovering Your Life-Place: A First Bioregional Workbook* contains this exercise).

Second quarter

a) <u>Native plants for habitat restoration</u>. Grow indigenous plant seedlings prefer-ably in local neighborhood greenhouses.
b) <u>Soil exploration</u>. Hike through different locations to observe landforms, geo-logical characteristics, and soils. Test for soil types, study erosion, and learn stages of compost cycle.
c) <u>Food consciousness</u>. Learn what native foods are presently available and how they are prepared. Grow vegetable seedlings.
d) <u>Begin a consolidated large-scale map of the bioregion</u>.
e) <u>Determine revegetation sites and begin planting native trees</u> (at that time or in a more appropriate season).
f) <u>Continue First Quarter</u> identification of native species and watershed, and arts and handicrafts research.

Third quarter

a) <u>Climate and weather characteristics</u>. Identify seasonal variations and effects. Emphasize annual periods of rain or snow for water availability, create means for collecting rain or snow melt water, relate water availability to growth and development of plants, learn water sources and human utilization.
b) <u>Energy sources and uses</u>. Identify and contrast renewable and non-renewable forms of energy, relate human energy needs to climate and weather, build model solar rooftop water-heating system.
c) <u>Continue First and Second Quarter activities</u>.

Fourth quarter

a) <u>Indigenous culture</u>. Research archeological sources for information and explore sites. Create awareness about indigenous people (speakers, visits, interviews, oral histories, etc.) Assist museums and indigenous peoples' ser-vice agencies or groups.
b) <u>Literature</u>. Read works by past and present local writers. Write stories, poems and journals using life-place themes. Explore at least one other language that is used besides the dominant tongue of the place.
c) <u>Continue First, Second and Third Quarter activities</u>.
d) <u>Plan next year's work</u> to continue present projects and initiate new ones.

To accommodate conventional school and job schedules of students, it may be necessary to hold classes (whatever number of sessions per week proves most workable) for only two hours in the late afternoon, and two hours in the early eve-ning. (Perhaps with a dinner break in between.) The first session should be spent working on outdoor projects to take advantage of daylight, while the second can be indoors for lessons, study, writing, and workshops.

The teacher is primarily a guide to the work/learning process. A background in ecology and the natural sciences is essential, but this can be from practical experience or personal study as well as formal instruction. The teacher-guide should also have a working experience with previous restoration and sustainability projects. Because potential candidates for teachers may come from many fields, and life-places themselves vary so widely, it would be inappropriate to advise a universal work plan. Let the subjects be chosen to follow a direction that is organic in the specific place, and determine their order, amount of study, and seasonal duration by the needs of projects at hand.

The one imperative for a teacher is to avoid the trap of determining student results through evaluations such as examinations or tests. Rebuilding a role for human beings in the natural flows of the place where they live will not be achieved by a grade at the end of the term. This goal can only be measured by the degree of a student's involvement in the accomplishment of direct, practical results. With class subjects ranging from restoring a habitat or a watershed, producing food and energy through renewable means, utilizing native and recycled materials in making products, and creating life-place culture, each member has started on a life-long exploration. What is learned can even transfer to benefit other places where a student may visit or live in the future.

This is a constructive way to begin learning to identify with and actually become part of a place in the biosphere. It is overdue. And needs to start immediately.

PART 2

Transforming cities from gray to green

A WHITE PAPER ON SAN FRANCISCO'S FUTURE AND THE NATURAL INTERDEPENDENCE OF PACIFIC PEOPLE

This op-ed article, published in 1975 in City of San Francisco *magazine, urges San Franciscans to think of their city not in globalist but in planetary terms. Rather than inviting multinational corporations to move to downtown San Francisco, the city should encourage industries that produce products from regional materials to serve Bay Area markets. San Francisco's future, Berg contends, is as a true Pacific Rim City, affiliated not with Europe but with other places around the Ring of Fire, from South America to the Aleutian Islands and from Siberia's Kamchatka Peninsula to New Zealand. By "switching from a globalist to a planetary viewpoint," Berg asserts, "San Franciscans can be transformed from residents to inhabitants." In this piece about San Francisco Berg provides a template for rethinking the location and identity of every major city on Earth.*

San Francisco has aspired to be a Western City, a great American City, and an International World City; it has been flattered to be included among important cultural centers in the Euro-American tradition—with a little moldering, perhaps a North American Vienna. This flattery has tilted San Francisco's head eastward. It has failed to accept its Pacific shore identity as its primary one. But San Francisco's future is as a true Pacific Rim City.

San Francisco has always faced two directions: it looks back at the rest of the U.S. from a far edge of the continent, and it gazes dreamily across the Pacific toward Asia. Until Hawaii and Alaska came into the Union, San Francisco was the last stop going west and the first coming in from the Far East. It still acts as a kind of Byzantium for the American Realm—a loose town and a passage from West to East.

A more realistic identity for San Francisco grows out of its actual planetary location. East and West might have been essential distinctions for globalist empire-builders, but they are no longer appropriate terms. Rather than a Western beach on a foreign ocean or a West-East transition point, the city should be seen as a significant place on the great living circle of the Pacific Basin.

Planetary San Francisco

Planetary San Francisco still lies beneath the pavement of Globalist San Francisco. A natural coast-bay peninsula has become San Francisco, California—USA—World. We can reconnect with Bay Estuary, Coast Range—Pacific Rim—Earth. The mental space stocked with World News, World Affairs, and World Events can fill with planet references instead.

Globalism tears life from its niches, destroys natural land forms, and wipes out locally in-tune cultures to keep itself going. A base is protected in one place and every place else is subjected to deadly forays. Eventually even the protected base is rendered unlivable by wastes.

Globalists have developed a uniform culture, a monoculture that replaces richer and more diverse elements evolved in the planet's unique places. Overlaying part of North America with the United States meant covering topsoil with artificial lakes to power hydroelectric plants, robbing topsoil to produce endless rows of tobacco that deliver the US nicotine tax base, and destroying topsoil as in the Great Plains with single-crop grain farming.

Monoculture has the same effect on the creativity of people as it has on the fecundity of the land.

San Francisco is currently searching for globalist corporations to move in downtown. Instead, it should be encouraging industries that draw their materials from northern California and the Bay region, finish products from them here, and find markets among the region's population.

Relocating the city from globalist to planetary terrain, from world-nation to planet-region, and joining the biosphere by participating in our local ecosystem would restore our human species identity and transform San Francisco into a Pacific Rim City.

Whoever fights the planet loses: our species loses the rich diversity of multiple indigenous cultures to thin out-of-place monoculture; the biosphere loses its vulnerable moment-to-moment capacity to maintain in the regions where we live.

Americans are children of the Flying Dutchman, rootless migrants on a voyage of lethal global tourism.

San Francisco has nothing to gain by being a force for Americanizing the Pacific. Its allegiance should go to maintaining the long-term continuities that are common to places and peoples around the Rim. The Pacific Coast of North America has always been east of Asia from a round planet perspective anyway, and San Francisco's people don't really come off as Eastern or Western. They should see themselves most clearly as citizens of the Pacific Rim. Switching from a globalist to a planetary viewpoint, San Franciscans can be transformed from residents to inhabitants.

We come into a mixed legacy as a Pacific Rim City. The Basin is potentially one of the most bountiful areas on the planet, but it has been badly ripped-off. Globalism separates the people and habitat of a place from the natural resources which can be extracted from it. The Pacific has lost much of its ocean life—fish, sea mammals—and the Rim has been stripped of forests, minerals, and most importantly, cultivatable soils. Globalism justifies its predations with two deadly attitudes: cultural superiority and the idea that there is always somewhere else to go.

No place to go

For a Pacific Rim City, there is no place else to go and a planetary attitude of sharing the locale with other cultures and species is ultimately justified by continued life.

Fortunately, San Francisco possesses a force for dispelling this cultural superiority. The make-up of its population already reflects the wide range of peoples around the Pacific Rim.

There were more Chinese-origin people here than in any other U.S. city when the 1970 census was taken. Nearly as many Filipinos lived in San Francisco as in Honolulu, their largest U.S. city, and the third largest Japanese community in the United States lived here.

Actual numbers were variously under-represented because there are more living situations among Pacific Islanders and Asian mainlanders than census sampling methods took into account. Both groups tend to have large extended families that stay close together; census-takers miscalculated their density. Whole distinct-origin groups were never counted. The Pacific-Asian Coalition estimates the total figure at around 175,000. Included are over 10,000 Samoans, an equal number of Koreans, and groups from Tonga and Fiji.

That's one quarter of San Francisco's people.

Another 25 percent are from Mexico or Central and South American countries facing on the Pacific. Nicaraguans alone number roughly 40,000.

The Soviet Union has a Pacific shore, but probably only some of the 30,000 Russians in San Francisco would claim an origin near the Rim. There's no question about the coastal credentials of several thousand Yuroks and other Pacific Northwest native Americans (including Eskimos) living in the city.

Over half the population comes from someplace else around the Pacific.

Full representation for pan-Pacific people has been slow coming while San Francisco tried on various identities. This year the city ballot was printed in three languages spoken around the Rim for the first time. To be sure most of the candidates can't personally campaign in anything but English, and there are still at least a half-dozen more languages unrepresented, but the ballot is definitely a step in planetary direction.

Greater space for Rim cultures would show their planetsense value to a Pacific Rim City. They cover an amazing range—China to Easter Island—and hold enough symbols, divination, lore, and techniques concerning habitation generally and Pacific living in particular to occupy any curiosity.

"First peoples" of the Pacific migrated onto the Rim and out to ocean islands with the other species of plants and animals, exploring a rich and growing habitat.

All mid-ocean people first glimpsed their new homelands from boats or rafts and most of them retain stories of their crossing and arrival. Water people who never really left the sea, they fused their early boat-life with the new land-life they found and continued to look out on the waves or down at the beach for food and sheer pleasure. Micronesian, Polynesian, and Hawaiian cultures stand waist-deep in the water, heavy with the moon and sharply aware of how volcanoes mother their islands.

Closer-to-shore island and mainland coastal peoples are much less recent and hardly as definite about their origins. Malaysia and the Japanese islands were once part of the mainland and contain some very early human sites. Java Man's skull is nearly a million years old. North and South American Pacific coast civilizations (there's no more reason to call them "tribes" than to apply that term to ancient Babylonians) were around at least 50,000 years ago and one theory holds that divers could find earlier evidence of their inhabitation sunken offshore beyond the San Andreas Fault.

Pacific peoples

Regardless of their time-in-place or even distance from the shore, Pacific Rim peoples kept alive links with the sea in forms that span the range of human culture. It was an ever-present theme in religion, stories, designs, and dances. New Guinea highlanders and Australian aborigines are still-living "first peoples" who have no direct face on the Pacific but temperate ocean-current weather, occasional stormy collisions of sea-cool and land-warm air and river life that migrates out to coastal lagoons. Fruits whose seeds originally drifted to them are recognized and hold important places in their cosmology.

There is a World War II image of shining metallic bombers taking off through the palm fronds on unknown islands like Tinian that haunts a globalist view of the Pacific—the most sophisticated and deadly equipment used in the most "primitive" places. The Pacific Basin has been a nuclear test site for the last thirty years; a storage dump for lethal Agent Orange after it was banned for offensive use in Viet Nam (the latest proposal for getting rid of Agent Orange is to burn it in ships' hulls stripped down as floating garbage cans in the Pacific); and a target point for everything from ICBM test firings to spacecraft re-entrys.

It is as though the West's very definition of "modern" depended on assaulting the Pacific.

The West is a state of mind that arose through displacement of people from their regional identities; Europeans transferred to America; indigenous people exterminated or removed from their land in America, Australia, and the Pacific Islands; Africans snatched from their continent and enslaved in America; home-based Europeans losing their regional cultures to global monoculture.

The West is no place on the Earth.

The planet is young in the Pacific Basin.

The Ring of Fire, a string of volcanic beads connecting the Pacific Rim from the bottom of South America to the Aleutian Islands and from Siberia's Kamchatka Peninsula to New Zealand, continually coats the coast with new cauterized layers of skin. Most of the Earth's five hundred or so active volcanoes pour onto the Rim, and even cool jewels like Fuji in Japan can suddenly liven in an eruption of steam and boiling mud. Washington's Mt. Baker is staging one this year.

A ring of burning and temporarily quiet cones, a trembling circular coast of youthful eruptions and quakes, growing slides and faults. Island chains are often mere protruding tips of huge undersea heaps of accumulated ash, cooled lava and cinders that rank among the planet's tallest mountains—Mauna Loa in Hawaii rises five miles from the sea bottom.

Evidence of how tightly the continents press on the Basin, how the whole bowl's lip puckers under the weight of Eurasia and the Americas drifting toward each other across the Pacific floor.

A young land

Enormous loads of new land shoot and ooze up from flaming soupy magma at the planet's core to make building platforms for successive pioneering forms of life; tiny corals whose single skeletal specks build up brilliant pink and purple reefs, floating seaweed pods that sprout forests beneath the surface of new lagoons. First steps soon followed by whole ranges of aquatic and terrestrial life.

Potently rich topsoil churns down rivers on the steep volcanic shore, fertilizing coastal valley bottoms and rushing succulent micro-organisms to densely-creatured food chains that multiply at sea.

The Basin catches a concentration of the juices of evolution that flow over the Rim. New niches of life open; old ones deepen.

Kuro Siwo, the Japanese Current, coils like a voluptuous warm body in the midst of the Pacific's waters to connect the sea as the Ring of Fire joins points along and around the Rim. A master stream for smaller currents swirling to cold reaches of the ocean and a leveling influence on benign temperatures that are characteristic of the Pacific.

Geopolitical opportunities are becoming even more globally extended in their attempts to retain an exploitative advantage over "the rest of it." Multinational corporations jump political boundaries in pursuit of raw materials and cheap labor. Nuclear power plant schemes move through bought government officials over protests from regional people who must live near lethal radiation hazards. Binational deals deliver ripped-off water and minerals in return for payoffs to central government treasuries which people in the regions of origin seldom see. National armies recruited from regional populations are called out to defend globalist interests abroad.

Reinhabitants of North America see the bright colors of inhabitory people, feel the strength and seek the long-time vision of people native to the land.

They see the salmon and sturgeon returning to swim under the Golden Gate Bridge up into streams of the Sierra Nevada; clams and oysters out of the Bay again served at city tables; a checkerboard of block-size connecting gardens over-laying the urban scenes so no corner lacks vegetables. They smell an odor of woodworking in the air.

It can happen. If we manage to make the transition without being forced into it by apocalyptic crisis, we'll be worthy of a voyage throughout the Pacific Basin to catch up on pure planetary gossip.

GREEN CITY

To Peter Berg, who originated the term, "green city" is an adjective, a verb, and a concept. People who live in cities, towns, and suburban areas, where the overwhelming majority of the population lives, have a more difficult time understanding the bioregional idea than do rural people, and even when urban dwellers begin to intellectually comprehend "living-in-place," they find putting the concepts into practice problematic. In this witty talk, originally presented to the Urban Panel of the North American Bioregional Congress (NABC) in 1986, Berg tells the story of establishing the Green City program in the San Francisco Bay Area—"You'll see how successful being naive can be." (Thanks to Peter Berg, San Francisco is now a leading green city in the United States.) Besides being an entertaining historical account, this piece offers savvy advice to others for starting Green City programs in their own areas.

The development of the concept "Green City" is a work in progress that I think would be valuable for other people to do where they live. You'll see how naively we began it, and how successful being naive can be. I'm going to discuss what's been done so far in this process in the San Francisco Bay Area. The bioregional idea makes so much sense to the people that live in rural areas today, that as soon as they hear it, they either say, "That's what I am," or the next day they say, "You know, I just had this idea . . ." Instant bioregionalism, or instant bioregional revelation.

The problem is that people in cities, towns and suburban areas, where the overwhelming majority of the population lives, have much more difficulty understanding the bioregional idea, and when they do understand it intellectually, they find it very difficult to apply. In fact, some of the people in the bioregional movement today are people in urban areas who write about bioregionalism and haven't yet found ways to apply it. Not that I'm saying that that's a negative situation, I'm just saying that it's a difficult thing to do. The next step is this:

There exists a certain attitude of why bother with cities anyway, for perfectly justifiable reasons. People have abandoned them for the country because they felt they were deathly, and they want to try a different notion of what human civilization and society is.

Secondly, the active bioregionalists who have done that, have been working so hard where they are that they really don't have time to go back to the city and proselytize. It's very difficult to restore a nearly extinct salmon population into a river. When people are working on ideas like self-sustainability, they have to actually take care of their gardens. So those people with experience in applying the bioregional idea often can't leave where they are to help others learn how to apply it.

The third reason is that cities are hard. Cities are the hardest obstacle for the bioregional idea to crack. Look at it: Los Angeles is a bioregion. The bioregion of the World Trade Center in Manhattan. The rivers have been turned backward, turned into running sewers; these places, you look at them and think, "There isn't a single reason to retain Newark." Arid cities are terribly designed. Almost any attempt to deal with them runs into so many built-in structural conditions that you think working with them would just be cosmetic—just putting pancake make-up on Detroit.

Cities are all in bioregions and their strain on life-places is probably the primary negative effect on all bioregions, especially the one where they're located. Los Angeles sends tentacles out to Four Corners for coal, Indonesia for liquid fuel, South America for vegetables, and northern California for water—some of these cites are really mechanical octopuses. They destroy forests, farmland, water and minerals in all the bioregions where they exist. They pollute all the bioregions with wastes, toxins, garbage, sewage. There has to be a way to make urban populations realize the necessity of large-scale reinhabitory activity or they will continue to threaten everything that is done positively outside their urban boundaries. We in the bioregional movement will miss the popular effectiveness of involving truly significant numbers of the population. We'll remain a rural, sparsely populated, land-based phenomenon and we could be destroyed by not being able to relate to urban populations.

So the trick is how do we do it? I had no sense of how to do it. I was asked to go to a rock concert in Golden Gate Park and address people about whatever was on my mind . . . I don't know how many of you have addressed people at a rock concert but you'd better not use too many words of more than one syllable. I heard poets throwing themselves against the airplane propellers of the crowd and I heard political activists try to speak to them about causes. They go "Arwaaugh, nye grue. Rwaaugh gruero. Hey man, rwaaugh gwae." So I got up to the microphone and I said, "I'm having a lot of trouble realizing a vision called green city. I'd like you to help me."

"Gwaaaayeh." "OK, when I say something, say 'green city.'"
"Green city (slurred)."
"OK, you ready? Salmon are going to swim through the streets of San Francisco."
"Green city."
"Half the city is going to look like Golden Gate Park."
"Green city!"
"We're all going to grow our own food."
(More coherently now), "Green city!"

I went through about 10 of these, "green city," and I thought, "These are my people." That's how green city began. The next part of this was that I got a ticket for having a sidewalk in ill repair. One of our favorite images has been that the grass will grow through the sidewalks again, and the city caught me at it. Our sidewalk had so much grass growing through it that people couldn't walk down the sidewalk anymore. A nice Chinese-American gentleman came out and very politely wrote me a ticket, "You will have to replace most of this sidewalk," and Judy [Goldhaft] and I were in despair. We had worked for years on not repairing that sidewalk, and the only possibility was to get a permit to plant half of the sidewalk. And not just half of the sidewalk, but more of the sidewalk area than San Francisco has ever allowed a permit for. The sidewalk is 10 feet wide. We wanted 5 feet of it to be garden, and we wanted the garden to be 20 feet long, two of them, if you don't mind.

So we asked for a permit to do this, and we were told that it has never been done, and "you are a minor sidewalk encroachment." I had always thought that the sidewalk was an encroachment on the hill that we live on. But it would be a minor sidewalk encroachment if I did this. I couldn't understand that. I wasn't going to build anything, I was going to *not* build things. It took three months to get them to suspend the $300 they wanted to charge me to do this. We finally did it. We put in new sidewalk where we had to, we left the rest in soil, and we put in native California plants. I have the most ragged-looking native California plant garden in all of San Francisco. But I think the neighbors like it, because they walk right up to it and they say, "That's manzanita, I know manzanita." Or they have arguments about the plants. They were arguing about a dune tansy, whether or not it's an invading fennel or a baby eucalyptus. We have actually heard them arguing out on the sidewalk about this. So that was the second thing—some act that will authenticate what we do. This story hit the newspapers because it was one of the largest gardens that had ever been permitted.

So the next thing was how to fund anything like green city? Here's where our friends the East Bay Greens came to stalwart assistance. We thought it would be a good idea to have a winter solstice celebration. People live in the city, but the solstice occurs everywhere, right? It's a natural event that people can relate to, and in San Francisco people will go to a party for anything. Do we tell them this is to fund a political campaign to overthrow the United States as it is presently constituted? No, we made a poster that said, "Celebrate the Longest Night." Well, nearly a thousand people went for that. Alex de Grassi, an acoustic guitarist, got up and said, "The name of this song used to be 'City Streets,' but now it's called 'Green City Streets.'" Peter Coyote, a film actor who used to be with the Diggers, got up and said, "I don't know what Green City is, I want you to tell me what it is. Let's just dream it into existence." Susan Griffin said, "I'm not sure I have any green city poems, but then, I think all my poems are green city poems." And they were chanting "Green city!"

So I said, "You live in San Francisco, what watershed do you live in?" And they would start saying, "Polk Gulch," "Yeah, I live in the Precita Park drainage." Some people really knew the creeks which are now covered with storm sewers. "Matriotic" I called it. They were matriotic about where they live. That raised about $7,500 to fund holding meetings.

Point 1 is that if you want to do green city, try to keep it simple and very participative, so that everybody thinks that they're thinking up this idea. Green city belongs to them. The second one is, find existing groups that fit with bioregional goals. In cities there are people already doing things who feel as though they're the only ones doing it. Find them and tell them that you think it's green city. I like green city as a kind of a verb: "Let's go green city;" or as an adjective, "What a green city thing to do," all lower case—green city.

So we found areas of urban sustainability:

Renewable Energy was the first one. We asked people, would you come to a meeting to formulate policies for cities and towns in the San Francisco Bay Area that would be green city. They were very convivial, everyone was respected for the valuable things they had to say, and toward the end of it we asked them to modestly suggest a few changes in local governments. Sim van der Ryn modestly proposed that all municipal buildings be demonstrations of renewable energy use. Hospitals, libraries, police stations, firehouses, government buildings, schools, we're talking about a massive program. And we said, modestly, yes, let's make that one of the renewable energy proposals for the green city program.

Urban Planting came next. Everybody from the Native Plant Society to the radical back-to-the-urban-landers, who in San Francisco are called SLUG—San Francisco League of Urban Gardeners—these are the Maoists with shovels. They have red bandanas, they have work-shirts, you know, Bette Davis black pants, and they are there to tear up the city streets and plant wholesome food. I love 'em. SLUG.

Urban Wild Habitat was next. That might have been our most popular meeting. Urban Wild Habitat people were Nancy Morita, who was at NABC I, the Wild in the City Project. There were also people from the zoo, people who were into bird watching, animal protection, all kinds of groups that have things to say about providing more habitat in cities for native plants and animals. And we came up with suggestions like tear up one-half of each existing street. That would limit traffic to one-way, and it would also be possible to expose native watercourses. San Francisco has a lot of hills, so when it rains, we have creeks. We would be able to plant native plants and have neighborhood community orchards. Why not take up half of the streets? Modest proposal, and very innocently arrived at.

Transportation. Cities should ban single-passenger privately owned automobiles and replace them with sophisticated shuttle services called point-to-point transportation. We should find ways to penalize single-passenger cars, encourage public transportation, and have more automobile-free zones.

Recycling. The maniacs from the Berkeley recycling yard called Urban Ore modestly proposed that there be goals of 85 percent recycling of everything. The garbage people, I'm talking about the Italian garbage men of San Francisco, sent a representative who said, "We are considering banning plastic. Eventually we want to go into recycling as a business and you can't recycle plastic. They're going to do it in Italy in two years anyway. So let's get rid of plastic." No plastic containers sold in Bay Area cities and towns when we have green city.

Cooperatives and Collectives. They were the least cooperative. There's a reason: when you send them a letter, they put it on the bulletin board. Nobody comes. They put it on the bulletin board because that's participatory non-hierarchical democracy. They don't come because they don't pay attention to the bulletin board. We got a couple of people and what they wanted was to stop gentrification zoning that was no longer allowing them to live and work in the same spaces. They wanted the cities and towns to establish small business bureaus explicitly for cooperatives and collectives like they do in Europe.

Sustainable Planning. We called it the Blue Sky meeting—what would be the most far out thing you could think of that cities might do. There were intentional community planners like the people that are putting out a new Sierra Club book called *Sustainable Communities*, by Peter Calthorpe and Sim van der Ryn. They came up with the idea that transportation patterns had determined the complex nature of cities today. Cities should be replanned without the transportation system of private automobiles so that there would be many nodal downtown areas, multiple purpose uses in several different sectors, in other words, villages. Most people agree that in the Bay Area, there is no little village as beautiful as North Beach, the Italian section, which is the most threatened neighborhood in the city. See how these things work? The Neighborhood Empowerment meeting had North Beach citizens at it, and you go to Sustainable Planning and people say really, we can't plan a better community than North Beach used to be.

Arts & Communication was our last meeting. There was the poet Michael McClure, who actually sees wood nymphs and gazelles jumping off of Twin Peaks all the time—he sees them in the clouds, he talks about them constantly. There were people who were environmental news writers. They talked about how can we get more people involved thinking in terms of human identity in a city as a natural thing.

Now from these meetings have come statements. Seth Zuckerman, who's at this congress, has been helping to put the thoughts of the meetings into a format that we hope will appeal to people in a published green city program.

[. . . .]

Winners and losers in green city

People who pay utility bills are big winners in the transition to renewable energy—their bills are cut in half. Everyone benefits from cleaner air and water, and everyone is spared the fear that is part of living with the threat of nuclear accidents and oil spills. Some dislocations may occur as the number of jobs in the fossil fuel industry declines but many of those people can be retrained and taught skills that are more appropriate to the way of energy in green city. Utilities and fossil fuel companies may find that their assets are worth less. But many farsighted utilities have already diverted resources into the development and use of renewable energy and have begun the switch into it—ARCO is a major manufacturer of solar cells, and both Southern California Edison and PG&E emphasize renewable energy in their strategic plans.

I hope all of you noticed that the word "bioregion" was never used in this. I didn't find it ever necessary at any of these meetings with these people who are working so hard to try to transform urban lifestyles and landscapes to bother them to feel that they had to join the First Fundamentalist Church of Bioregionalism. I appreciate what these people do, and they appreciated us providing them with an umbrella because there is no overview with the social-political content that they can relate to. They very often find themselves competing with each other for the small little dog-biscuit grants that are available for this kind of work. So they develop personality conflicts and animosities. But when they're invited to come have biscotti and tea and treated as though their ideas are valuable, they look at each other and say, we're really on the same side, there just hasn't been a common way for us to behave before. They appreciate green city.

What I've tried to say is, make green city participative. Deal with existing groups, invite them to meetings in similar areas of concern, so their expertise is appreciated and they actually meet each other. Try to steer it toward changes in policy. Try to deal with what's actually going on. Now we're this far, we know what's good, we know what's bad, now how could policies of city governments be changed to accommodate what you would like to see?

We can afford to wait to realize the dream of those natural bioregional areas becoming self-governing and autonomous. Immediately, what we can do is change the governance of cities, towns, and sometimes counties. (There are a couple of California counties that are on watershed boundaries.) A federation of green city constituencies in the Bay Area is the urban component of a bioregional council. That's my hidden agenda. I don't expect the people coming to these meetings to be bioregionalists, but if we keep the framework bioregional, eventually they could see the validity of a federation of the nine Bay Area counties. Local governments could come together, sending representatives as the green city plank, or program, to a bioregional council/congress/federation/whatever for northern/ Shasta/Alta California.

City people think about voting a lot more than people in sparsely populated, rural areas, because in fact you affect much more of your own life in sparsely populated, rural areas through your actions than you do through voting. But city people almost always have to go to the polls to get their problems solved, they almost always have to go to the hospital to get taken care of, and they have to almost always go to city government to get zoning abated, automobile traffic stopped, etc. They're used to thinking that way, and green city programs should be directed toward candidates that will run on these platforms, constituencies that will stand for these platforms and maintain the umbrella of them, because it's the context, not the individual actions, that are going to make them work.

Judy would like to see little decals that we put on things that we think are green city, establish green city awards, say to the 85-year-old woman who collected the most aluminum cans for resale and recycling in San Francisco last year, a green city award. There are a lot of cultural ways to spread these ideas—through things like solstice benefits, concerts, collections, shows, performances. So that green city becomes a way of thinking of yourself in the city. We have to rehabilitate these folks. We have to give them an authentic, positive identity. That's really the point of green city.

And finally, I'd like to do it here. Will you bear with me?

Salmon will swim in the streets of San Francisco!

[Audience, chaotically] "Green city!"

Thank you.

BIOREGIONAL AND WILD!

An interview of Peter Berg by The New Catalyst

In 1989 British Columbia's The New Catalyst *magazine interviewed Peter Berg, pressing him to anticipate the next phase of the bioregional movement. Berg replies that "a tsunami of ecology is running through human consciousness," transforming our priorities and reshaping politics, culture, society, and human relationships. He suggests that whereas the image of material progress was a beacon of the industrial era, the image of wildness might inspire the ecological era. Wild is a good image for the city, too, Berg maintains. Wildness is a vision that could revitalize both the urban landscape and the aspirations of urbanites.*

What do ecology, nation states, wilderness, and a new breed of urban settler have in common? Through the eyes of bioregional agent provocateur, Peter Berg, of San Francisco's Planet Drum Foundation, they are all elements of an emerging human consciousness, a transformation of society crucial for the continued survival of the planet.

THE NEW CATALYST: You've been one of the originators of the bioregional concept, over a decade ago, and the movement has come a long way since then. Where do you think it's heading in the next phase, the 1990s?

PETER BERG: Probably in a number of different cultural and social and political directions, but the ones that interest me most are those that have to do with human consciousness in general.

One of the things that inspired me to try to conceive of an alternative to nation states, for example, in bioregions, was that in the United States, environmentalism effectively came to an end as a broad volunteer movement with the creation of the Environmental Protection Agency in the early 1970s. After that, environmentalism has only lingered on as a branch of the legal profession, whose primary job now is to bring injunctions, suits, etcetera—to prevent things from happening. But the pro-active element of "what should we do instead?" was obviously not going to be provided by environmentalism, but by ecology . . .

TNC: Let's talk about this bioregional ecological consciousness. How does it differ fundamentally from the nation state consciousness?

PB: Take the term "ecology" for a moment. The biological sciences are rather late developing in full bloom. Darwin is about a century after Newton. Physics is really well-developed before biology even gets its basic concepts going. And ecology is a late twentieth century word. It was Rachel Carson who put the word on the bookshelf with *Silent Spring*. She put it in people's hands and she did it authoritatively, with the credentials of a scientist. This is 1962! Ecology is a very recent idea.

The natural sciences and biology developed for a while like physics, in the sense that they were going to be used for industrial purposes (to take natural processes apart, disassemble them). But then, after *Silent Spring*, ecology started rolling in human consciousness. These ideas from the natural sciences started to come over into popular consciousness not as tools to disassemble nature, but to see it, to see its sanctity. So we hear the word "watershed" (which is just water basin terminology to a hydrologist). All of a sudden when people say "watershed," they lower their voice a little bit. Or they say, "natural succession" realizing what a beautiful idea this is. And it's not human; it exists out there. "Old-growth forest"—ooh, magical ideas! And becoming sacred to people. In bioregional workshops, I've said learn these words like watershed and throw them at these scientists. Say, "Not in my watershed, you don't!" Say it like your body, or your home or your family. Identify with that watershed, identify with the bioregion, identify with those native plants and animals!

Why? You don't even have to know why intellectually. It's where your allegiance lies. What is your homeland? Well, it's these plants and animals and natural systems that are in this life-place, in this bioregion. That's what it is.

Ecology as an idea has become that way too. It's not just a natural science concept. A tsunami of ecology is running through human consciousness. We're beginning to be aware: what are our connections? What am I really? What are my ties? Is there a future? Well, there's no future unless it's an ecological future: we know this deeply! Ecology is beginning to bend and reshape and transform every thought that we've had previously about human priorities. For politics, culture, society, human relationships.

So we're beginning to ask, what is the role of the nation state? It seems that it's a very destructive one from a biospheric point of view. Not only is it replaceable, it probably must be replaced by another view. Should my considerations be humanity? Or should they be human species in the biosphere? Probably human species in the biosphere. Is it the workers of the world? No, the managers have to lose their chains, too. What is the purpose of growth in the economy? What is the purpose of progress? It seems that they're destructive purposes. So sometimes I and other people—Thomas Berry, for example—will tell you that he's the conservative. He's not cutting down the forests; radicals cut down forests. He's not doing open-pit mining; radicals do that. He's a real conservative, he wants to conserve the biosphere. And in a way, we have to start selecting out ways to be with each other as human beings where our shared values are being part of the same species together in the biosphere. My own feeling is that the greatest shared value for the necessary upcoming ecological era is wilderness. Because wilderness already embodies systems, designs, purposes that are workable, are demonstrably eco-energetic—efficient in terms of using energy and resources and so on. And they weren't designed by people . . .

The way that plants and animals use resources is extraordinarily conservative. Lean and mean, if you like, not excessive. A lot of those images can come over into human affairs. But the reason why I think wilderness has such value for the pattern of values of the ecological era is that it is shareable, it is non-hierarchal. Wilderness has been outside the management of human consciousness.

In the industrial era, the image was material progress, transforming things, mutating things, changing their being, their shape, their chemistry, their nuclear components, changing everything about them! Whereas I think self-reliance, sustainability, climax, stages of succession—those are good images for the ecological era. And a lot of people can relate to them. They have a lot of lessons to teach about human interaction. Because what we have done in the last 250–300 years as a species on the planet is beyond the effects of the last ice age. We've destroyed more species, we've re-arranged more features of the Earth's surface, we've changed the atmosphere more, so we had better preserve what wilderness there is, and we had better attempt to restore as much as we can.

TNC: How can human activities be redefined in the light of this new consciousness?

PB: Well one of the ways is in terms of political locatedness. I think the bioregion is going to continue to manifest itself in consciousness, even for those people for whom bioregion at this point is just an adjective. Pretty soon they're going to start saying the noun of it, and they're going to begin seeing that it is a life-place that they owe their allegiance to. So they're going to want political autonomy for bioregions.

There are some places on the planet where this already exists. In Europe the boundaries of ethnic peoples can often be considered roughly bioregional. On the western side of the Penine Rise of the British Isles, for example, you run into Cornwall which is a bioregion, Wales, which is a bioregion. The Bretons; it's obvious that they're very different from the rest of France.

As nation states become more desperate to control their situations, they impose more on the regions, bioregions, and ethnic peoples, and by so doing create in them a desire for a separate identity, and a feeling of deliberate repression of their values. In North America this rule of foreign language and cultural domination was thrown down so heavily on the land, I think the places themselves are crying out. The places have more authority than the governments do!

TNC: The industrial state used to be the image of civilization. If we're to have a wilderness consciousness, I guess we'd be moving in the direction of having wild culture. What would that look like?

PB: That's what I spend most of my time thinking about; wildness in people. Wild people—the people that we call primitive—actually have very ordered lives. The differences aren't in the quantity of what they do but in the quality of what they do. They have deeper relationships with the things that they're involved with. Their cultural horizons are horizontal compared to how vertical ours are, where we always think in terms of ascendancy (get a better job, make more money, go up the ladder, get to the pinnacle of success – we have all these expressions). Whereas what wild people do is learn more about the horizon, more about what's out here, what's possible: "Success" would be more like filling in things you didn't have before, as skills, or experiences. Those are key differences. If they were magnified just a bit, we'd have a whole different society.

For example, right now, the idea of having a wild median strip that nothing could be built in, that was for wild plants and animals, run through an urban center is frightening to at least 95% of city-dwellers! But if you have more horizontal perspectives, this is an addition, something to go for. Planet Drum's current Green City Program, thinking of how urban areas might be in bioregions, is a very horizontal idea. With median strips for wild habitat, and block-scale solar retro-fitting of houses with maybe one little solar retrofitting shop per block, with secondary materials industries in neighborhoods. And small-scale, so that you're not only collecting aluminum cans, you're making something out of them . . .

Wild is a good image for the city, too. As cars begin to diminish, I would see a really cheery cultural prospect of tearing up streets, or at least tearing up half the street. And recreationally restoring creeks and springs in urban areas. And in a horizontal, wild way, planting gardens, having a little grove of citrus trees, or peach trees.

TNC: What about the harder, more mundane question of how people would make a living?

PB: Well, live a making is what we're looking for here. It doesn't take much to live. I mean we don't work for food! But outside of food, if you're cutting down on your expenditures, I think maybe Ivan Illich said that 25% of an automobile owner's salary goes to preserving that automobile? Take out the automobile and there's one quarter of your workday that you don't need to toil!

I would also like to regain the notion of neighborhood culture. Before our urban areas got as run together as they are now, there used to be little villages. And eventually these villages just overlapped with each other. But they were little villages serving all the necessities that people require: you would be able to live simply within that one area and not have to travel. I can see regaining that as an image of urban dwelling. I think there's a new urban settler, a new urban person who belongs in the ecological era, who is much more conscious of resources, what they use, what they require, what they provide for themselves, what they do with their time …

TNC: The city has always been a vacuum for resources from the hinterland, and it's been viewed by progressive people somewhat negatively. What I hear you doing is reidentifying the city in positive terms?

PB: It has to happen. Because it has become the overwhelming habitat for human beings on the planet—fairly recently. Seventy five percent of North Americans now live in cities and towns of 25,000 or more. It's a growing trend and they're not going to go back in volume to the countryside. So they have to change. And from a bioregional perspective, they also have to change because they're such a tremendous drain on bioregions. Living in the city— I'm an urbanite—I had to address the problem: how do you get cities off the bioregional back? And the way you do that is to have people in cities become bioregional and mindful of their connections to natural systems. I think things are changing rather quickly in the direction of post-industrial era that I would call ecological.

TNC: Do you see the idea of wilderness as having the power to liberate people?

PB: When I think of the worst image of contemporary society it's not necessarily one of destruction, in ecological terms, that this society causes, but the control of the people it imposes. So that what makes me most indignant is the enslavement of potentially creative individuals to mass systems of information, or mass systems of political domination— satellite television, for example, or so-called "global" communication. Global doesn't mean that everybody talks to everybody; global means that somebody talks to everybody. Somebody controls "global," that's why that word is to be avoided in bioregional parlance.

For us to become liberated from such late-industrial forms of control, it seems to me that we need an image, a vision without which we cannot survive. That's what "freedom" was, beginning in the 18th century. Freedom suddenly became a flame. People would die for freedom. Think of the Paris Commune: people were so desperate to revise society in an egalitarian way that they seized part of Paris and said we will live or die to be this way. Well, I see us literally dying and not living if the depredations on the planet continue. And so a vision that is worth living for is what I'm hoping to get from wilderness.

When I saw eight species of raptors in one valley the other day—obviously making a spring migration north; I saw about 50 individuals, but there were hundreds—I was looking at the survival of wildness. And it was such a positive image that I called a friend and said, "It's the best sign I've seen in months that it's still working out there, still working without us!" So I see those as hopeful images and as culturally supportive images.

I think our working together to discover our own wildness, the wild homo sapiens being within us, is very liberating, very exciting. It is the future from my point of view, and it's pivotal in terms of human civilization. We're making a swing from where we've been—disassembling natural systems—to seeing them as possessing more for our not having been involved with them. The wilderness is more for our not having been part of it. And we can see it as a model for ourselves: wild society! Bioregional and Wild!

A METAMORPHOSIS FOR CITIES: FROM GRAY TO GREEN

First published in San Francisco's City Lights Review *in 1990, "Metamorphosis" presents a comprehensive agenda compressed into an outline form. Offering both a rationale and a bulleted list, this essay reviews basic principles that govern all ecosystems: interdependence, diversity, self-regulation, and long-term stability. It then provides a detailed set of achievable steps and municipal policies that would have powerfully transformative effects to make urban dwelling much richer and cities more livable.*

Once a rare and privileged way of life supported by a large agriculturally-productive rural population, city-dwelling is fast becoming the norm. In spite of the fact that they are grotesquely overgrown compared with the recent past, overextended, and subject to crippling disruptions, urban environments will soon be the primary inhabitation sites for our species. As late as 1950, less than 30 percent of the world's population lived in cities and towns of 25,000 or more. But by the year 2000, half of humanity will no longer live on the land. In some places the figure will be much higher: over 75 percent in Latin and North America, Europe, East Asia and Oceania. Fewer people are remaining in direct contact with nature at a time when more urbanites need to somehow produce part of the resources they consume. Cities not only restrict beneficial contact with nature, they inexorably surround and destroy it. Open spaces that previously separated urban areas fill in with new development to encircle natural areas like cages in a zoo. A nearly unbroken megalopolis that runs down North America's eastern seaboard from Boston to Atlanta is, in effect, a wall barricading wildlife from the ocean. Cities bordering on rivers sprawl further and further along banks to thinly stretch and finally break the all-important water links of ecosystem chains. A profound transformation is needed in the way cities are conceived. This can't be merely an administrative reform or change in the design of systems or structures because it needs to involve a completely new set of priorities and principles. The future purpose and function of cities and the activities of city-dwelling must become the focus of social and political consciousness on a primary level. The first step toward reconceptualizing urban areas is to recognize that they are all situated in local bioregions within which they can be made self-reliant and sustainable. The unique soils, watersheds, native plants and animals, climate, seasonal variations, and other natural characteristics that are present in the geographical life-place where a city is located constitute the basic context for securing essential resources of food, water, energy and materials. For this to happen in a sustainable way, cities must identify with and put themselves in balanced reciprocity with natural systems. Not only do they have to find nearby sources to satisfy basic human needs, but also to adapt those needs to local conditions. They must maintain the natural features that still remain, and restore as many of those that have been disrupted as possible. For example, restoring polluted bays, lakes, or rivers, so that they will once more be healthy habitats for aquatic life can also help make urban areas more self-reliant in producing food.

Different geographical areas have different conditions depending on their natural characteristics. Bioregionally-founded values that are appropriate to each place should be agreed upon and then used to direct municipal policies. Guides for doing this can be transferred over from some basic principles that govern all ecosystems:

- **Interdependence**—Heighten awareness of interchanges between production and consumption of resources so that supply, re-use, recycling, and restoration become more closely linked. Reduce inequitable exploitation;
- **Diversity**—Support a wide range of means to satisfy basic human needs and a multiplicity of cultural, social, and political expressions. Resist single-interest solutions and monoculture;
- **Self-Regulation**—Encourage decentralized activities carried out by groups in neighborhoods and districts. Replace top-down bureaucratic agencies with grassroots assemblies;
- **Long-term Stability**—Aim policies to work under various conditions and for several generations. Minimize short-term programs and patchwork remedies.

When interdependence, diversity, self-regulation and long-term stability are consulted, it is possible to make much more ecologically coherent and therefore more practical decisions than are generally seen today. Applied to the cycle of food production and consumption, for example, these values could lead to beneficial features:

- more small-scale farms and gardens near or in the city that employ greater numbers of people;
- preserve and restore green spaces;

- reduce transportation costs;
- provide fresher produce;
- wider use of permaculture (permanent agriculture) and native food plants to conserve and build topsoil;
- lower water use;
- maintain natural habitats;
- subscription buying by institutions and groups of individuals who spend a certain yearly amount to receive a specified quantity of produce thereby stabilizing farm incomes and levels of food production (community-supported agriculture);
- collection of tree and yard trimmings, food scraps, and other organic wastes to create compost fertilizer;
- re-use of urban grey water on farms and in gardens to reduce fresh water consumption;
- some type of food production on everyone's part ranging from backyard, rooftop, window box and community gardens to work-sharing on farms.

Each urban area needs to develop an ecologically-oriented Green City Program that delivers a high quality of life for all its residents in harmony with its bioregion. City greening includes urban planting but extends to much more than re-vegetation. It also means:

- conversion to renewable energy;
- development of suitable transportation;
- extensive recycling and re-use;
- greater empowerment of neighborhoods;
- support for socially responsible small businesses and cooperatives;
- restoration of wild habitat;
- wide participation in planning for sustainability;
- creation of new civic art and celebrations.

There are already many separate groups working in various sectors of urban sustainability that can supply pieces of an overall program. They should help in drafting sections of it to authenticate a grassroots approach, introduce disparate elements in the same field, and eventually join together differing concerns under an overarching "green umbrella" to accomplish the massive governmental changes that are necessary. In planning the transition from polluting fossil fuels and dangerous nuclear power to renewable sources such as solar, hydro and wind, for example, representatives can be drawn from:

- businesses that manufacture, distribute and install renewable energy equipment;
- labor groups who will benefit from jobs in those areas that regulate energy production and use;
- alternative energy advocacy and environmental groups.

Here are some examples of changes in municipal policies that might be recommended in different parts of a Green City Program whose implementation would have powerfully transformative effects:

Retrofit public buildings for renewable energy

- Equip city office buildings, schools, libraries, fire and police stations, and all other structures with some means to produce their own energy from renewable sources.

Develop suitable transportation through a wide front of new approaches including:

- company buses and vans to transport workers directly to job sites,
- point-to-point conveyances to replace use of automobiles for shopping and appointments,
- in-neighborhood transit such as ride switchboards for local businesses and institutions to operate close to where people live and thereby reduce the need to travel to work.

Initiate full-scale recycling and re-use

- Curbside pickup of household organic and manufactured recyclables.
- Stringent reprocessing of all wastes from industrial processes.
- Establishment of small-scale neighborhood secondary-materials industries.
- Require municipal government to purchase recycled materials whenever possible, preferably from local sources.
- Create grey water treatment facilities so hot water now wasted can be used to water lawns and trees, wash vehicles, clean buildings, flush toilets, and for other uses that don't require fresh water.
- Install household units to recycle used wash water for similar purposes.

Empower neighborhoods

- Devolve a large percentage of tax revenues to neighborhood councils and assemblies for direct local use.
- Provide space and materials to greatly enhance neighborhood communications ranging from meeting places to bulletin boards and even FM radio and cable TV facilities.

Assist socially responsible businesses and cooperatives

- Greater employment and higher levels of prosperity are possible through the creation of sustainability-oriented small business and co-ops by providing "incubators" where offices, equipment, and materials can be shared.
- City government should also establish priorities for procuring supplies from these new companies.

Restore wild habitat

*   Establish new corridors of native vegetation in the city, linking habitats so that wildlife can move unimpeded through urban areas.
*   To make these corridors, restore creeks where possible by bringing them up from storm sewers.

Open the process of planning for sustainability

*   Solicit neighborhoods' visions of their futures and use these as standards for determining changes.
*   Adopt "statutes of responsibility" that charge officials to maintain the health of cities and their inhabitants. Citizens could take legal action against officials if air, water, and soil aren't kept free of poisons.

Celebrate life-place vitality

*   Assist the creation of small-scale localized media (murals, billboards, markers) that feature natural characteristics.
*   Stage public celebrations of natural events such as seasons and animal migrations.
*   Provide guides to natural sites.

Some of these measures reduce costs and eliminate waste on a vast scale. Most are directly related to greatly improving the health of local bioregions. All of them involve new job opportunities and contribute to self-reliance. And they are only a few examples of the many changes that should be made.

Although cities as we know them are on the verge of collapse, people aren't aware of the great changes that are coming. Media coverage is restricted to isolated situations like the plummeting decline of Detroit, of abysmal lack of public services in East St. Louis, and politicians are reluctant to air the bad news even as they quietly move to the suburbs. In fact, the city is a point of major transition. We are beginning to see an historical shift comparable to the birth of the modern industrial city.

To reclaim a positive outcome from deteriorating situations, city-dwellers have to become "urban pioneers" in a concrete, steel, and glass wilderness, developing new urban forms and remaking their own lives as they simultaneously recreate the urban landscape. To do this they need to learn new skills, redirect their energy and inventiveness, and align their efforts with the more self-reliant and sustainable vision offered in Green City Programs. The profile of an urban pioneering life includes these elements:

*   working several part-time jobs rather than a single-employment, 40-hour week;
*   growing some food on a continuous basis;
*   recycling household waste and water;

- re-fitting dwellings for energy conservation and maintaining some means for producing energy from renewable sources;
- restoring wildlife habitats;
- reducing or eliminating the use of a personal automobile;
- developing new cultural expressions that reflect bioregional and planetary themes;
- participating in a neighborhood council to decide everything from planning and justice to social services and celebrations.

Urban pioneers will replace the often deadening and escape-seeking urban existence of the present with stimulating, highly varied and creative pursuits that are more related to artists and nature-seekers than to factory and office workers. Even in a densely populated metropolis, these new urbanites will be able to claim personal home-neighborhood-villages and be fully involved with them. Many people are already doing some of the things that lead to this transformed urban life. When most people are doing all of them, urban-dwelling will be much richer and more livable.

A SAN FRANCISCO NATIVE PLANT SIDEWALK GARDEN

To Peter Berg the image of plants pushing up through cracks in concrete is a metaphor for the greening of the city. But to the City of San Francisco, the weeds that grew tall in the sidewalk cracks next to Berg's house were deemed an unsightly nuisance, and he was issued a ticket and told to repair the sidewalk. This order presented Berg with a dilemma, which he solved with characteristic trickster ingenuity. This piece, published in Growing Native Newsletter *(1991), is a transcript of a tour that Berg led of his sidewalk garden. This article points out the ecological folly of ordinances that prohibit the use of native plants for landscaping, while revealing Berg's wily tenacity and sharing his love of wild nature— wherever it may take root. The biographical note reads, "Peter Berg is a founder of the bioregional concept who keeps trying to bring the country into the city."*

This is San Miguel Hill. This used to be Rancho San Miguel, part of the Islais Creek watershed.

When I began, in Summertime, all the way down the sidewalk, dry weeds were growing through the cracks as high as your shoulder. People had to walk through 25 foot long rows of them, along each break in the sidewalk pattern.

I liked it. I saw it as grass breaking through the concrete, the greening of the city.

The neighbors complained.

And as a homeowner, the city required me to keep up the sidewalk in front of my house. So they came and literally wrote me a ticket for having plants growing through the cracks of "my" sidewalk—which was my favorite metaphor for regreening the city.

So I thought, this is intolerable. I can't just clean up the sidewalk to satisfy the city and ruin my metaphor.

So I called them up and said,

"What if I give you half a sidewalk and I take half for native plant gardens?"

They said they would have to see how wide the sidewalk was, and they didn't want to do it. So I said,

"Come and see. We have more sidewalk than we need. You'll see." I think I measured it. It's ten or twelve feet wide. And you can see there's no traffic. Nobody's walked by since we've been out here. So why is this sidewalk needed?

They sent someone. He said,

"That's what the city decided. Besides, what you're proposing would be the biggest sidewalk garden in San Francisco."

I said, "I don't want to plant in the middle. That's where the sewer lines run. Just give me two beds on the outer edge, five to seven feet wide, and fifteen to twenty feet long." He said he'd go back and talk to his office.

The next thing, an urban arborist came out with a list of plants that were approved and disapproved. No natives were approved because they might turn brown in summer, or have unfriendly fruits, like Buckeyes, or because their roots may get into the sewer lines.

So everything they had on the list was like that one across the street, an Australian tree that died in the freeze. Were you pleased when all those Eucalyptus died? You know what the plague is in Australia? Monterey Pines. Only they call them by their Latin species name, *Radiata*.

The guy had a Grateful Dead decal on the cab of his truck, so I said,

"Wait a minute. You're not just an urban arborist for fun."

He said, "That's right. I'm a dedicated native plant enthusiast."

I said, "OK. Between you and me, we're going to figure out a way to write this so that I repair half the sidewalk—you give me the gardens, and whatever it was I planted was OK. Right?"

And he said, "Right." And that's the way he wrote it up.

We dug up the whole sidewalk, and put all new concrete in this part, then took the other half and dug it out. It was pure clay.

We found some people excavating a basement on a lower slope, where all the soil that was originally here had gone to gather. Native. Took that soil and put it in this upper bed and left (the lower) one to see what could fend for itself in pure clay.

A friend put in recycled redwood boards here, out of a construction job.

The city never came back to look again. So I don't have Russian Olive. I don't have Peppermint Willow. I don't have any Scotch Broom—none of the approved plants. I have unapproved, disenfranchised natives. They have a franchise now, to operate in this plot of land.

What amazed me was having Buckeye on the list of unapproveds. Buckeye is such a gorgeous tree.

There are two gardens. One is sort of a show garden, which has really taken off. These plants are doing fabulous. All except this one, which I transplanted;

I'm sure it will be better when it gets in there. And the other one is a sort of experiment garden. That's the one that costs money. I keep buying plants for it and seeing if they will survive.

People have taken cuttings of these plants. We've found birds in them. They see it from the air. Put in natives and right away the birds come.

The neighbors are back and forth about it. One time a woman walked by—she had read an article about this in a local newspaper—and said, "I don't think those look good. Those don't look good to me."

She wanted roses.

So I turned a metaphor of grass growing in cracks in the sidewalk into growing and maintaining a native plant garden that has all these benefits, like less water and really beautiful blooms. That manzanita, with its pink-white, tiny little flower, is gorgeous. Even the Coyote Brush looks nice when it's in bloom. The Grindelia puts out hundreds of little yellow flowers, like tiny daisies.

There are certain northern California plants that, unlike the scrubby, brushy look that people often refer to, have an elegant French look, like Dune Tansy. It looks like a French plant. Rousseau would have painted it. Buckeye is like that, too. It always looks French to me. You know, delicate, leggy, long-limbed, with patchy leaves, and those incredible white racemes, like filigree.

Have you ever been in Buckeye Canyon on San Bruno Mountain? That looks like a Japanese gardener and an Ohlone Indian planned it. I've never seen anything as perfectly arranged, and it's completely wild.

We started the garden four years ago. What has succeeded has been what can endure clay. The Dune Tansy has done extraordinarily well, which surprised us. That manzanita could possibly be twice the size it is if it were someplace else. It's a 'Captain Bob,' a selection from around Santa Rosa. I've generally tried to get things that are in this vegetation formation. That's an exception.

This Coyote Brush is about the size it should be. The Douglas Iris surprised me by being so successful because it's so dry here. Irises tolerate dryness amazingly well. These go about half dormant. They tolerate people stepping on them as they get out of their cars.

There are perils of sidewalk gardening. The hazards are significant. I've lost Ceanothus from people stepping on them. People not only step on them, but they rip them apart with their car doors, and dogs and cats pee on them. Sometimes I call them our native plant dog toilets.

That oak is an interesting story. The Friends of the Urban Forest have a list of trees that they'll put in. None of those is a native. None. They tend to be Australian: acacias and eucalypts—under euphemistic names like "Peppermint Willow"—and Russian Olives are what they'll put in.

I asked for a native, and they said, "We don't have one."

I like everything about Friends of the Urban Forest, by the way, except this. I like the way they do things. They won't give just one person on a street a tree. You all have to do it together. We all planted these trees. Like that one across the street: Judy and I helped plant that, and that one there. It's done as a neighborhood work party. So you get to know your neighbors, which is valuable in terms of maintaining the trees.

Judy and I planted that one down on the corner because the people who live there were gone that day. They just happened not to be there to be part of the work party. It grew better than any of the others, and they really love it. That made a sort of a bond between us. We were the surrogate parents of their tree.

Fortunately, the Peppermint Willow we chose—because the choices were so poor—died. So I called and told them, "The tree died. Don't you have some sort of guarantee? Isn't there some way I can get the hundred dollars or so it's cost—not the money. Can you help me out with another tree?"

They said they remembered me, and would. "Actually," I said, "I want a native tree."

And this guy, for some reason, said, "Look, you've helped us out, you've had your tree die, we're just going to cut red tape about this."

One weekend they put this in. I asked, "What did you find for me? What did you plant?"

They said, "That's a Coastal Live Oak. Good luck."

That's how I got that native tree. Otherwise it would have been impossible. It is an exception.

If you have an eye for what they are, and if you know what the obstacles are, you know what this means. I am secretly pleased to believe that seeds from these plants blow out and into other sidewalk cracks and are propagating more of these natives all over the place, instead of the European invaders.

CITY PEOPLE

An interview of Peter Berg by Derrick Jensen

Urban sustainability is the number one environmental issue for the twenty-first century, contends Berg in this interview with author and environmental activist Derrick Jensen, published in Listening to the Land *(1995). But how do we go about persuading city people to know the place where they live in natural terms? Berg discusses networking efforts, service projects, eco-friendly design principles, and the value of urban wild habitat—"Human brains need the interaction of other kinds of squiggly, furry, many-legged, able-to-fly, fierce, slinky species." We must inflame people with a desire to relate to and protect regional natural systems. Urban sustainability must become a new kind of consciousness.*

Peter Berg has written, "Wherever you live, the place where you live is alive, and you are part of the life of that place."

Founder (1973) and director of Planet Drum Foundation—an organization helping people to become "native to a place through becoming aware of the particular ecological relationships that operate in and around it"—Peter Berg is a noted ecologist, speaker, activist, and writer. He is acknowledged as an originator of the use of the word *bioregion* to describe land areas in terms of their interdependent plant, animal, and human life. He believes that the relationships between humans and the rest of nature point to the importance of supporting cultural diversity as a component of biodiversity.

> **PETER BERG:** The bioregional perspective, the one I've worked with for nearly twenty years, recognizes that people simply don't know where they live. Generally when you ask people what their location is, they give it in terms of a number on a house on a

street in a city in a county in a state in a nation-state in some
political division of the world. But if you were to answer in
bioregional or ecological terms you might say, "I'm at the
confluence of the Sacramento and San Joaquin Rivers and San
Francisco Bay in the North Pacific Rim of the Pacific Basin
of the planetary biosphere in the Universe." Very few people
know where they live, and fewer think it's important.

But unless we think it is important, we're going to destroy
the places we live. If you destroy the place you live, you have
to move someplace else. And there isn't someplace else left
anymore. Unless you understand the place where you live in
terms of its natural system, you're not going to understand
anything, anyplace.

Is this a big problem? Yes, because 75 percent of Americans live in cities, and the biggest human migration in history in the shortest time has been since 1950 from the old
industrial Northeast to the Sunbelt. Towns have to pass out
pamphlets telling people, "You're now a resident of Tucson,
Arizona, and what we have here are saguaro cactus and mes-
quite. We don't have English lawns here, and if you try to
have one, you're going to run us all out of water in the next
five years. So don't do that. Love your jojoba tree."

This process of finding out who you are in terms of place
is probably the principal consideration of contemporary civilization. Who am I, where am I, and what am I going to do
about it? I am a member of the human species. I am in the
Shasta Bioregion, roughly northern California. And what am
I going to do about it? I am going to attempt to reinhabit the
place where I live, attempt to become an inhabitant again.

There are a lot of ways to do this. Through natural sciences.
Through stories of native peoples. Through early settlers'
records. Through experience, which is probably the best way.
What happens on the summer solstice in Shasta Bioregion?
What happens when the rains come, in our Mediterranean
winter-wet/summer-dry climate form? What happens to various soils? What's the role of earthquakes here?

A lot of this is understandable to somebody who lives in the
country, because rural people tend to be more in contact with
elements and natural situations and systems. If somebody
says it's called Goose Valley, it's because geese go through
it, whereas if you ask somebody in Los Angeles, "Why is this
called Chavez Ravine?" they might not even know there's a
ravine there.

Not everything country people tend to do is divine. I've
seen a lot of rural situations that couldn't exist without a

hyperexploitation of energy sources. And in the past, people in the country were pretty much tied to resource exploitation, cutting down the trees, digging up the ground, taking out the minerals, killing the fish, and so on.

But that's not our problem anymore, from a bioregional perspective. Our problem now is city people. They are the majority population, and unless they agree with practices that are bioregionally coherent, bioregionally coherent practices just aren't ever going to be carried out, for voting and economic reasons.

So how do we go about persuading urban dwellers to know the place where they live in natural terms? That's difficult, because urban dwellers are so divorced from the sources of their fundamental requirements of life. For example, if you ask somebody from the city where the water comes from, they say . . .

DERRICK

JENSEN: The faucet.

PB: And where does the water go?

DJ: Down the drain.

PB: When you flush the toilet where does the stuff go?

DJ: Away.

PB: Where does the garbage go? Out. Food comes from—the store. So our task is to try to engage urban dwellers in activities that lead them to greater perception of how they are involved with interdependence in the planetary biosphere. What we at Planet Drum have been doing, besides publishing books and issues of our review, *Raise the Stakes*, is undertaking various activities here in the San Francisco Bay Area under the title Green City.

We've realized that city people want to do things to not feel guilty about their relationship with ecology. So we've established something called the Volunteer Network. Interested people can call us to find out about the activities of 240 Bay Area groups that work in areas ranging from urban wild habitat to recycling to transportation to neighborhood empowerment. The callers say what they want to do, whether it's rescue marine mammals, replant native vegetation, recycle, participate in transportation coalitions or bicycle demonstrations, whatever. Our service raises ecological consciousness.

But we also have to raise consciousness within the groups themselves, because they may not feel as though they're all connected the way we think they are. We see Green City as a big umbrella— urban sustainability as a new kind of consciousness. The people who collect the curbside recycling in San Francisco are hired by the garbage company, and they may not think they have anything to do with restoring wild habitat. We think they do, and we want to convince them of that fact.

Another thing we've done is to develop a Green City Calendar of activities going on in San Francisco and the Bay Area, activities you can join on your own. We've also developed a youth directory to connect high school and middle school students with activities.

That's all in the area of public information. The second realm of this is what we call workshop/workdays where in the morning we give a talk about bioregionalism and about a specific project we'll work on that day. Then we have lunch together. In the afternoon we all go out and work on the project. Things like taking garbage out of a creek, pulling up invasive plants, digging up asphalt to free the headwaters of an urban creek in Berkeley. We dug out scotch broom and put in native grasses on a piece of city-owned land. And we're going to build planter boxes for rooftop gardens in the Tenderloin District, which has about the highest unemployment and homeless rates in the city.

DJ: You've used the word *bioregional* several times. Can you say more about what bioregionalism is?

PB: The bioregional concept has three main goals. One is to restore and maintain local natural systems. The next is to find sustainable ways to satisfy basic human needs—food, shelter, energy, water, culture. The third is to support the work of reinhabitation, of people becoming native to the places where they live. These goals are very simple, and not overtly radical, but satisfying basic human needs in sustainable ways has a lot of social, political, and economic implications about sharing and cooperation and carrying capacities, and judgments as to what is too much.

In addition, supporting the work of reinhabitation doesn't only mean growing some of your own food. It also means, for example, preventing offshore oil drilling, stopping things that will destroy the possibility of reinhabitation.

DJ: And reinhabitation seems to be accomplished at least partly through making personal connections to a sense of life, even in the midst of a city.

PB: To be disassociated from the rest of life is totally alien to our species. To urbanites, though, nature is like a frightened bird that flies through the window into the living room, something you encounter by accident. Urbanites have to begin making the connections—this house is made of Sonoma County redwood, the electricity that comes into this house is from a hydroelectric plant on a tributary of the Sacramento River, and we use natural gas from Canada. The place where the non-recyclable garbage goes is a horrifying landfill in Altamont. Our food is increasingly standardized and regimented and poisoned.

In the history of human civilization, the sustainability of cities has seldom been an issue. Cities have destroyed themselves and the countryside around them. That's why there are magnificent ruins in jungles—the people who lived there stripped the capacity of the land to support them.

Sustainability of cities has to become a major gauge for whether or not we're succeeding at becoming harmonious in the planetary biosphere. In fact, I believe urban sustainability is the environmental issue of the nineties and the next century, because not only have cities generally been unsustainable, no American cities are presently sustainable. And major infrastructure collapses of cities are already happening.

City governments have to take the ecological sustainability of the city as their central topic of governance. And city dwellers have to look at being an urban person differently than they did previously. They have to think about providing some of their own food, some of their own energy, participating in local decentralized neighborhood government, undertaking different modes of transportation, carrying out different activities to make a living.

DJ: Can you get more specific on sustainable practices cities can undertake?

PB: In most Asian cities, human waste is collected daily and carried to nearby farms to be used as fertilizer on the fields. That's a sustainable agricultural practice.

Another is for every urban household to have a dual water system. One of fresh water for cooking and bathing, and the other of gray water—water left over from bathing—for other purposes such as flushing toilets, watering lawns and gardens, washing cars, et cetera. We could reduce water use in the average American household by probably 75 percent.

Gray water is already used this way in most third world countries. Most water, whether gray or not, is undrinkable in Mexico. But people have practices for dealing with that, such as boiling water before they use it or putting a drop of iodine in water used for soaking vegetables overnight. Rather than having a huge plant that pours hundreds of pounds of chlorine and fluoride into water so that the substance I flush down the toilet is nearly the equivalent of bottled water, we should be asking ourselves why we don't use our shower water to flush the toilets.

Similarly with electricity, or any of the energy that's consumed. If city governments would decide that public buildings should feature renewable energy, not only would taxpayers save money in the long run—not that much, between 5 and 10 percent of the energy used—but the agencies would be making a wonderful statement, much as when governments print on their agencies' letterhead, "We are an equal opportunity employer."

And food production in the city could be hugely amplified by a couple of simple techniques. One is greenhouses. Another is that every open space could feature some aspect of gardening, such as a community garden, cooperative gardens, privately owned gardens, and so on. This includes rooftops and planter boxes. In some third world cities it's not unusual to see fava beans coming over the sides of the roof or to see a goat eating grass on top of the building. These goats are going to be milked and eaten, and those fava beans are going to go into stews.

I feel you shouldn't give a permit for constructing a building unless 10 percent of the space bought for construction is designated as garden space—gardens, orchards, grape and other arbors of various kinds, whatever.

DJ: Two themes connect all these practices. One is the idea of reducing waste, and the other is the importance of self-sufficiency.

PB: Those seem to me to be design principles. And while, for example, it interests me that a Japanese sliding door saves space over Western hinged doors, probably five or ten apartments' worth in an apartment building, I'm much more interested in examining what our sense of limitless resources has done to us.

For example, we drive a car to have fun. Well, sure, I think everybody has driven in a car and had fun at some point. But driving a car for fun should be on the same level as taking a roller coaster ride for fun. It should be the kind of thing you pay for. And not just at the pump. If you're having fun driving the car, then it's an amusement park event. Go to an amusement park, pay some guy two bucks, and drive a car. But the idea that the price of fossil fuels should be kept at less than two dollars a gallon so that you can take a Sunday drive is inane. It's not even that much fun.

Hiking is fun. Hiking in the country would be a revelation to most urbanites. Most inner-city people don't know there is a naturally governed world outside the human domain. And if they did, they might find more reasons to live. I have taken inner-city kids out where they wouldn't get off the path because they were sure something huge and horrible would eat them.

Which takes us back to consciousness, and how to change consciousness. I have a story about that. Urban sustainability is especially important in Mexico, because Mexico City is the most polluted and overcrowded city on the planet. One day I asked one of the brave people trying to make Mexico City into Ciudad Verde (Green City), "How do you reach all these people driving these Volkswagen vans without exhaust pipes, and all of these homeless people burning railroad ties full of creosote to cook their dinner?"

She responded, "To reach them, you show them a man and a woman in a kitchen making dinner, and show that the water comes from a waterfall, the energy comes from a forest, the food comes from the soil, and the garbage goes back to being compost. Show them that the dinner they make is the earth's, that the earth gave them that dinner. You tell them, 'Your kitchen is the earth. Your grandmother knows this. She knows the kitchen is the place where you worship the earth.'" That's a wonderful perception.

DJ: That seems very similar to everything you've described you're doing here.

PB: We're trying to. The fact that we're all connected is a planetary reality. The fact that we don't know it is a huge condition of disability. We're in a hospital, and we're not getting better. The way to get better is to start finding out what these things are and relating to them again.

It was the popularity of physics in the industrial era that removed people from thinking that relatedness to natural systems was important. People have been enamored of physics because of what it could do to natural systems. What physicists told people was, "We no longer have to be bound by what nature gives us."

And this is a trick, an illusion, the fossil fuel illusion, the Industrial Era illusion. And we're coming to the end of it. When you have a hole in the ozone layer, that's like saying there's a hole in the milk pail. And it doesn't matter how much milk you put in the pail, it's going to run out. So wake up. We've got to do something about that hole. And the way to mend that hole is to mend our consciousness.

DJ: Does restoring wildlife habitat to cities help mend consciousness, by allowing people quick access to the natural world?

PB: Typical of all the other mistakes urban dwelling has caused is the presumption that wildlife does not belong in the city. Human beings have a kind of prescription for living in an urban environment, and that's to systematically destroy invasions by other species or systems. We should be doing just the opposite. If there are other systems in the place, plants and animals, the place is viable. Without them it isn't. Just to begin with, plants and animals are fantastic biological monitors. Keeping birds from dropping dead or moving out means keeping an environment you can live in.

But it's more than that. Human brains need the interaction of other kinds of squiggly, furry, many-legged, able-to-fly, fierce, slinky species. Our brains need this, not just for metaphors, but for stimulation. If we're surrounded by sheetrock walls all the time, we dry up. If we're surrounded by other kinds of creatures, they start to fill our consciousness.

Think about what I said a while ago about being in a hospital. Whenever patients are allowed to sit in the sun or on the grass, cure rates go up tremendously. Ask any honest doctor in a hospital and he'll say, "The best thing you could possibly do is get the hell out of here." Cities make people sick, the way hospitals make people sick.

So the value of urban wild habitat is that it's our legacy. It's not that we should allow it to be. It's that we deserve it. That is the highest level we can operate at. It's silly to say it's a question of anthropocentrism or biocentrism. It's mutually interactive. We need each other.

For better or worse, I have a bird feeder in the back yard. Now that it's spring, no birds come near it. They don't need it now. And besides, I wasn't saving the birds last winter. I was just trying to help them, because I like them. A friendly gesture on my part. I'm encouraged by the way they look, their beauty, the way they move, their migrations through here. Cedar waxwings were just through. Yellow-breasted finches are here. It's marvelous to watch these tides of animals.

It's a democracy of species. It's not a situation where we save them or they save us.

DJ: Say a person lives in New York City and doesn't have access to an organization like Planet Drum. How would this person go about reinhabiting place?

PB: Find a couple of other people like him- or herself. They can be found among fishermen, naturalists, teachers, artists. Start a study group to find out what the natural systems are and begin to understand how they relate together, as well as what the priorities are for restoring and maintaining that place.

And find out what issues are most pressing. For example, in northern California, the thing that really galvanized the bioregional movement was the state's proposal in the late 1970s to transfer a million acre-feet per year of the Sacramento River down to the southern Central Valley and Los Angeles. We encouraged people to oppose it, to look at what effect it would have on San Francisco Bay. We even encouraged them to quit the Sierra Club if the Sierra Club didn't oppose it.

Ninety percent of the people in the Bay Area voted against the proposal. It was the biggest one-sided vote on any issue for an area in the state's history. This means we really hit a chord of consciousness. A sociology professor at the University of California at Davis was asked afterwards, "Why did the people vote against it?" He said, "We just don't want to pay to support their lifestyle anymore." That's a hell of a comment. Very bioregional.

DJ: And very encouraging.

PB: Afterwards there was no stopping us, in terms of confidence that this is an appropriate point of view. People all over northern California—the Shasta Bioregion—say, "This is our watershed. We want to restore and maintain native animals and plants and native systems here." This is a new language for grassroots politics.

So, people interested in reinhabiting their place can find a galvanizing issue, and they can find out facts about where they live. They can decide not to move, regardless of the real estate values or the winters. They can decide to live there, decide that people *do* live there, and they can have a different consciousness, an inhabitory consciousness, and they can realize there are inhabitory rights that come with that, and they can strive to get those rights.

In northern California, for example, I would require that people do a weekend's worth of ecosystem restoration activity per month for six months before they are allowed to have a driver's license. The restoration work would qualify them to be inhabitants. I'm not suggesting that as a restriction. Instead it's a trade-off. You want to drive on the stuff, you've got to find out what it is. After everybody got through groaning and moaning about it, you would notice a tremendous shift in consciousness. People would start saying, "I don't want a freeway to go through there. It would disrupt too much of the native vegetation." They're going to know what it is and how rare it is.

And we need to begin teaching bioregional studies in schools K-12 as an accredited course along with literature and mathematics. Bioregional Studies 101. Make it required. If you're going to go to school here, you've got to find out about the place. Graduates would be inflamed with a desire to protect natural systems where they are, and to relate to them.

Even little things like that would shock people out of their disinhabitory coma. It would let people know they are a part of the place where they live. And that it's their true legacy.

SAN FRANCISCO BIOREGIONAL CHANT

FOR THE SERPENTINE ROCK FOOTING

      beneath the sewers and cables
      beneath the basements of these buildings

SHOVED UP FROM AROUND SAN LUIS OBISPO
AN INCH A YEAR

      for the last 60 million years

CHINKING COASTAL FAULTS

BROUGHT THROUGH THE HUGE GENEROUS
PRESSURE OF NORTH AMERICA

      sliding downhill over the Rocky Mountains

TO MAKE A WARM BAY WHICH SUCKS CLEAN WHITE FOG

      off the California Current fed by Asian Kuro Shio

SWEEPING EVENINGS AND MORNINGS HERE
IN SAN FRANCISCO

      with grey hooded intimacy

A CLOAK FOR EXPECTANT GEOPSYCHICS POISED
BESIDE A QUAKE

      of the North Pacific Rim

𝔓roclamation

City   and   County   of   San   Francisco

Whereas, San Francisco has consistently demonstrated its commitment to environmental sustainability, greening the city via its many parks, along its streets, and infrastructure, its promotion of green jobs and renewable energy sources; and

Whereas, Peter Berg, Founder and Director of Planet Drum Foundation since 1973, was one of the first ecologists to recognize the importance, on an increasingly urbanized planet, of developing sustainable cities and was the originator of the concepts in current usage of the terms "bioregion" and "reinhabitation;" and,

Whereas, In 1986 Peter Berg, via Planet Drum Foundation, brought together knowledgeable individuals to discuss sustainable urban public policy goals which led to the publication of *Green City Program for the San Francisco Bay Area* which in turn led to the creation of the San Francisco Department of the Environment and its Sustainability Plan; and,

Whereas, Peter Berg developed the Green City Project to educate, coordinate and network the involvement of the general public in environmental activities including the Green City Calendar, a central clearinghouse for environmental, sustainable activities and a vital source of information for all San Francisco Bay Area residents; and,

Whereas, From 1993-2011, Peter Berg through Planet Drum Foundation and the Green City Project carried out Education + Action Programs and Bioregional Education Workshops for teachers, students and residents that have included a broad array of activities: watershed restoration, planting school gardens, initiating recycling systems at schools, and materials reuse in art projects; and,

Whereas, Peter Berg's work has awakened personal ecological consciousness, fostered increasing environmental awareness, and aided residents in developing ecologically sustainable lifestyles; and

Whereas, Peter Berg unexpectedly transitioned to his next plane of existence on July 28, 2011 leaving behind a lasting legacy that will be sustained by both the Planet Drum Foundation and the Eliot and Peter Berg Endowment Fund; it has now, therefore, been

Resolved, That, in recognition of his vision, dedication, and leadership, the people of the City and County of San Francisco by and through their Board of Supervisors honors Peter Berg, for his powerful contribution to the residents, government, and civic life of San Francisco, and hereby proclaims:

October 1, 2011 as Peter Berg Day in San Francisco.

Enacted by the Board of Supervisors on September 20, 2011
Witness my hand and official Seal:

Supervisor Ross Mirkarimi

FIGURE 2 Proclamation by the City and County of San Francisco, declaring October 1, 2011 Peter Berg Day in San Francisco
Source: City and County of San Francisco

PROCLAMATION

City and County of San Francisco

Whereas, San Francisco has consistently demonstrated its commitment to environmental sustainability, greening the city via its many parks, along its streets, and infrastructure, its promotion of green jobs and renewable energy sources; and

Whereas, Peter Berg, Founder and Director of Planet Drum Foundation since 1973, was one of the first ecologists to recognize the importance, on an increasingly urbanized planet, of developing sustainable cities and was the originator of the concepts in current usage of the terms "bioregion" and "reinhabitation;" and,

Whereas, In 1986 Peter Berg, via Planet Drum Foundation, brought together knowledgeable individuals to discuss sustainable urban public policy goals which led to the publication of *Green City Program for the San Francisco Bay Area* which in turn led to the creation of the San Francisco Department of the Environment and its Sustainability Plan; and,

Whereas, Peter Berg developed the Green City Project to educate, coordinate and network the involvement of the general public in environmental activities including the Green City Calendar, a central clearinghouse for environmental, sustainable activities and a vital source of information for all San Francisco Bay Area residents; and,

Whereas, From 1993–2011, Peter Berg through Planet Drum Foundation and the Green City Project carried out Education + Action Programs and Bioregional Education Workshops for teachers, students and residents that have included a broad array of activities: watershed restoration, planting school gardens, initiating recycling systems at schools, and materials reuse in art projects; and,

Whereas, Peter Berg's work has awakened personal ecological consciousness, fostered increasing environmental awareness, and aided residents in developing ecologically sustainable lifestyles; and

Whereas, Peter Berg unexpectedly transitioned to his next plane of existence on July 28, 2011 leaving behind a lasting legacy that will be sustained by both the

Planet Drum Foundation and the Eliot and Peter Berg Endowment Fund; it has now, therefore, been

Resolved, That, in recognition of his vision, dedication, and leadership, the people of the City and County of San Francisco by and through their Board of Supervisors honors Peter Berg, for his powerful contribution to the residents, government, and civic life of San Francisco, and hereby proclaims:

October 1, 2011 as Peter Berg Day in San Francisco
Enacted by the Board of Supervisors on September 20, 2011
Witness my hand and official Seal:
Supervisor Ross Mirkarimi

FIGURE 3 "Diggers Freed" was the front-page headline that accompanied this San Francisco City Hall photograph, *San Francisco Chronicle*, November 30, 1966. The newspaper identifies the men as (from left): Robert Morticello, Emmett Grogan, Pierre Minnault, Peter Berg, and Brooks Bucher.

Source: © Bob Campbell/San Francisco Chronicle/Corbis

FIGURE 4 Peter Berg, working on *Free City News*, San Francisco, 1967 or 1968

Source: © Charles Gould Photography

FIGURE 5 Peter Berg clamming,
California, 1969

Source: © Charles Gould Photography

FIGURE 6 Conundrum Creek, Colorado, 1972. Back row (from left): Chuck
Gould, Jane Lapiner, Sierra Simpson, David Simpson, Judy (Goldhaft) Berg,
Peter Berg, Destiny Kinal; Middle Row: Kerry Simonson, Aaron Rosenberg,
Gabriel Cohen, Todd Simonson; Front Row: Joshua Tree, Honey, Omar
Simpson peeking over the dog, Ocean Berg, Solange Gould, Gillian Handleman

Source: © Charles Gould Photography

FIGURE 7 Reinhabitory Theater, 1977—Peter Berg as Lizard, Kent Minault as Coyote

Source: © Erik Weber

FIGURE 8 Planet Drum Foundation office, 1990. From left: Peter Berg, Crofton Diack, Marie Dolcini, Judy Goldhaft

Source: © Charles Kennard

FIGURE 9 "Peter Berg: A Man with an Urban Bio-vision" (*Noe Valley Voice*), Billy Goat Hill, San Francisco, 1990

Source: © Charles Kennard

FIGURE 10 Peter Berg (right) interviewing Giuseppe Moretti, Italian bioregionalist, on the banks of the Po River in Italy, 1994

Source: © Judy Goldhaft

FIGURE 11 Peter Berg, Three Gorges Dam, China, 2001
Source: © Judy Goldhaft

FIGURE 12 Peter Berg listening to Oscar Enrique at Fanny De Baird school in Ecuador, 2010. Oscar was one of nearly sixty students who participated in Planet Drum's *Bioregionalismo* afterschool education program that year.

Source: © Clayton Plager-Unger

FIGURE 13 Peter Berg and Judy Goldhaft in their home, San Francisco, 2010

Source: © Eve Quesnel

PART 3

Bioregional travels around the Pacific Rim

WALKING INTO THE RING OF FIRE

Peter Berg carefully makes his way across hot lava at Volcanoes National Park in the Hawai'ian Islands. Molten magma from the planet's core collides with ocean water, producing plumes of steam and forming new land, which will anchor life in the ongoing processes of creation. Berg's reverential tone turns suddenly ominous when he catalogues the unprecedented damage that humans have caused to the biosphere in the past two hundred years. This piece, published in 1993 in a special issue of Chicago Review *on North Pacific Rim cultures, compares the impact of volcanic eruptions and human-caused changes such as deforestation and desertification.*

The Hawai'ian Islands were formed by volcanoes in the center of the Pacific Basin's "Ring of Fire," a great circle of more than two hundred and fifty active and many more dormant erupted mountains that stretches from the tip of South America up to the Aleutian Islands and down the ocean's other side through Japan to New Zealand. It roughly traces the edge of the Pacific Tectonic Plate whose geological contention with adjoining plates in the process of continental drift is the basis for the Ring's volcanic action.

The Islands' unique location at the middle of the Ring might account for the massively strong force that continues to be exerted in their construction. The highest Hawai'ian volcano, Mauna Loa, began to climb from 18,000 feet deep on the ocean floor about three million years ago. Two-thirds of its history was consumed just to break through the Pacific's surface into daylight. Since then it has spewed lava regularly to eventually gain an altitude of 13,796 feet above sea level. Mauna Loa's present combined height of just over six miles qualifies it as not only the largest volcano but the tallest mountain from base to top of any kind on the planet.

When eruptions occur, they create fresh landscapes of the type that can be seen today around Mauna Loa's more active neighboring peak, Kilauea. During a lava flow the land surface that previously existed is seared clean of life, and an infant-like series of biological stages follows. Obvious signs of recent incubation are visible everywhere: unvegetated sides of craters, black stripes running down green hillsides, acres of cinders, and black sand beaches created from wave-pounded cooled lava.

Plants venture onto this lifeless terrain in a series of clearly defined steps. Ferns are among the first in most places. Elegant silver-swords appear singly in high zones. They are totem species of biotic reoccupation that advance soon after lava cools to take advantage of water-collecting low spots. The first wave of trees includes the rangy and adaptable wiliwili whose light but strong wood was used by Native Hawai'ians to make surfboards. Extremely slow soil accumulation and favorable positions away from the wind and facing the sun will gradually allow more species to join until the result may be a tall, dense, dripping rainforest with multiple canopies, each featuring different plants with gigantic specimens that are unduplicated anywhere else.

Hawai'i's wet and warm climate could harbor almost any terrestrial life form, and it has hosted a continuous series of new arrivals since initially appearing above the waves. The first were transported by sea and wind or grew from seeds in bird droppings and probably originated nearby in older Pacific islands. Once established they gradually evolved into an astonishing range of about two thousand indigenous plant and animal species. Around one thousand years ago the first human inhabitants sailed in from central Polynesia bringing food plants such as taro and breadfruit, and domestic animals including dogs and pigs. Some of these, like the *kukui* (candlenut) tree, prospered so well that they can be found throughout the islands.

Immigrant species kept arriving at a slow pace in the same way that coconuts continue to float onto beaches, and a gradual accommodation of them by the original plants and animals and those brought later by Polynesian pioneers resulted in numerous relatively stable and richly diverse ecosystems. But when Europeans and Americans began arriving, just a little over two hundred years ago, the rate of addition of new species accelerated much faster and brought chaotic effects whose eventual outcomes can only be guessed. Native plants and animals were overrun in many places as extinctions regularly followed the introduction of exotics. Even relatively new invaders have subsequently been put to bay by more recent arrivals. Glycene vines which were planted as cattle fodder in the 1970s are already thickly blanketing Maui at the rate of hundreds of acres every year, shading out practically everything underneath them including lantana vines which preceded glycenes in the same role only a few decades earlier.

The overall evolutionary impression Hawai'i presently gives is of a constant barrage of new life elements forced into an already heavily loaded mix of ancient and more recent entities that were only partially harmonized with each other. Compared to relatively static areas with harsher weather, such as New England or northern Europe where many of the new human invaders originated, Hawai'i is now a biological free-fire zone in which anything can happen when a foreign species is introduced, and little of it can be anticipated. Today's commonplace sights such as whole plains of cactus or a mongoose glimpsed suddenly slipping into a macadamia grove simply didn't exist before this century. Native Hawai'i is being overwhelmed by conditions that will remain completely unresolved for a long time to come.

The rush of contemporary ecological change that makes any "natural" area suspect of being only a temporary condition becomes evident within a few days of travelling through the islands. Even so, nothing compares with the mind-wiping shock of earth-induced transformation that occurs when molten lava explodes in the ocean.

I had opened an evening eco-storytelling show at the Kilauea Theater high up in the cool clouds covering the volcano with a spontaneous invocation: "I pledge devotion to Madam Pele / and Kilauea Volcano wherein she dwells / one ever-lasting fire / creating lava and new land for all." It was pointedly intended as a more fitting tribute to the place than the United States Pledge of Allegiance, even if I was an inexperienced albeit respectful outsider. Acknowledging Pele—the potent goddess who Native Hawai'ians believe makes her home within their volcanoes—might have seemed presumptuous by a visitor but it became thoroughly appropriate the next morning when fresh flows from Kilauea were reported to be streaming into the Pacific. I felt summoned by the place itself to be a witness to this quintessential island-forming event and headed for the coast near Kalapana as quickly as I could.

The nearest road to the flow led through Volcano National Park and ended abruptly where it had been buried under eight feet of swollen-looking black rock. Climbing up on that shiny bulging mass, I could see a white plume of steam where lava was meeting the ocean and rising to several hundred feet above the coastline a mile or so away. The surface of the recently cooled lava at my feet was still so unweathered that delicate silica fibers ("Pele's hair") which rain and wind would soon sweep away were sticking out prominently. Heat shimmers still rose above holes in the surface that were venting molten pools several feet below. Luminous green, purple and silver patches of reflected sunlight seemed like northern lights on the night-black stone. Raw sulfur that had separated out as the magma material cooled made occasional yellow streaks in the uneven surface which was by turns flat and smooth, grainy and pitted, folded like dough, or exquisitely rippled as though a bolt of silk had been gracefully draped across the ground. Halfway through the walk I felt warmth building in the rubber soles of my shoes and calculated that if they began to melt, I would have to head back rather than chance running further forward to look for a cooler place.

Near the steam plume there was a junk sculpture of twisted rusty steel girders remaining from a former park visitor's center that had been obliterated by heavy flows only a few months before. It created a bombarded World War II beach effect heightened by some shattered and half-toppled palm trees that were still smoking.

Only a few yards from the pathetically inadequate park structure stood a native temple site constructed of uncemented, tightly fitted volcanic stones that was several hundred years old and survived because lava had flowed around rather than over it. Why it had been spared seemed both obvious and portentous.

Just beyond the temple on what would have been the route of the buried road (surrealistically intact for only a few feet directly in front of the ancient site) was the new live flow. It wasn't running from the top of Kilauea but had pushed through from under a weak spot toward the bottom of the volcano's slope the way underground water sometimes emerges as a spring. The orange-red lava formed into thick rope-like lengths that moved so slowly they appeared to be still and laid onto the solid rock like jelly. They were broiling hot, throwing off gray puffs of smoking gas or flaming up briefly before disappearing under the edge of some cooled surface to reappear further below. The radiant flush on all of my skin that faced the lava river felt like a steam bath or sweat lodge.

Paradoxically, a park ranger stood in this distinctly nonhuman setting farther down where lava slowly pooled before running under a heaped earlier flow and then oozing into the ocean. Thick pluming steam billowed behind him, emitting muffled booms that resembled distant artillery fire. I looked to see what he wore on his feet and gladly noted they were conventional leather hiking boots with pressed rubber soles, which meant my shoes would last after all. Closer proximity to the steam cloud clarified why there had been small stinging sensations on my face and arms during the walk out. Wisps of sulfurous-smelling steam were occasionally blown back inshore and the burly, lobster-skinned white-haired ranger would wave a hand in front of his nose.

"Sulfuric acid. I won't work lower without a mask."

"Are you here to keep people back from the cloud?" I asked.

"I'm showing anyone who shows up how to cross the lava. Just move quickly across the gray top of the shield that's formed over the molten stuff. Don't stop. Don't fall down. It's 2500 degrees if you disappear into a hole in the shield, so don't worry. It'll be over fast and life was never a sure thing anyway."

An odd-humored homily was even less expected than his actual presence.

In front of me lay a glowing stream about fifty feet wide that was variously colored bright red, orange, yellow-white, or ashy gray depending on how thin the lava sheet was, whether it had stood in one place for a minute longer than the rest, or if a breeze had just passed over that particular spot. A broken trail of dark gray shield was barely maintaining itself against the hotter colors of nibbling lava. Sweat from the intense heat began running freely down my back and legs. I smelled smoke from the soles of my shoes and became angry at my obsessiveness in questioning their ability to endure.

The prospect of continuing further without seeing someone do it first or carefully mapping the hot spots should have melted my resolve if not the shoes, but the opposite happened. A wonderstruck state I felt when first walking toward the plume and imagining its powerful source returned. Instead of wariness I felt drawn forward with a transcendent sense of being elevated in the air. The first few steps were taken slowly to gauge how soft the shield was, but then I began to move faster and confidently searched ahead for steam vents or wrinkled places that could trip me up. Acceptance of the fantastic reality—"I'm actually stepping on lava"—completely shut out disbelief. Walking an inch or less above the hottest substance I had ever seen seemed more like floating over it.

"Remember, don't stop," yelled the ranger. "And don't try crossing that *aa*." He referred to a type of newly cooled lava with a pointy, gritty surface allegedly named for the pained sound one makes walking on it barefoot. "It'll slow you down and give the heat more time to work on your shoes."

I took a side route that required jumping onto a small gray mass surrounded by a trickle of orange lava like a rock sticking up from a creek. A quick leaping step from there led to solid ground that was actually the far bank of the lava flow. It was too hot to sit down and review the course I had followed across, so I kept walking and looked uphill at where the braided hot magma began. I was even more impressed by the eruption's sheer power than before and marveled that it had ever relented enough to be crossed anywhere in the path of descent.

The ocean shore near the source of the steam was a sharp-edged but relatively shallow cliff. A piece of it had recently sheared away and rocked in the waves like a broken ship. Pebbles had been ground off and surged forward around it with each pulse of water in the same pounding and rumbling process that created the surrounding beach of glinting black sand.

The area where molten lava was actually reaching the ocean was only a few feet wide, but it held the most densely compacted scene of natural alchemy imaginable. As the glowing mass entered sea water it created a high rolling boil that hissed into sprays of steam with slight variations of color from white to yellow and gray. The actual point of contact was obscured by these billows, but sometimes lava could be seen underwater still glowing red like hot iron. Bubbling discolored ripples spread out from the spot in a fifty-foot wide arc of dark tan before gradually returning to normal deep blue. The exploding sounds were much louder close-up, emitted by sea-cooled pieces of lava that snapped apart as they contracted. Black cinders flew out from within the steam and dropped into the water in splashing bursts.

I was experiencing the most primal collision of fire and water on earth, magnified by the intense temperature of magma from the planet's core and an unlimited expanse of Pacific Ocean. My mind humbly discarded thoughts as they arose to leave itself open to the deep essence that was expressing itself. Rising into an otherwise cloudless sky, the slim line of white steam that had been the guidepost to this amazing occurrence was a sign of earth-making from before the time of organic life. It was an image evoking not only union of two universal elements, but also the creation of the other two, scalding air and new earth. I knew why I felt so reverential, barely able to keep from being burned by the impulse to get closer to this ancient source of newly created land. This is how our living world began and the process has never stopped. Rock that was unavailable as a foundation for inhabitation is freshly layered onto the coast, increasing the size of the island and creating an underwater anchor for plants that will in turn attract brilliantly colored fish and provide material for beaches that will grow dune plants and eventually those from further inshore.

Right then was the beginning of part of the earth, and it begins again and again and again.

Our planet can absorb the incredible blasts of volcanic eruptions and the disruption they create because it has done so countless times in the past. Broiling heat, acidic gas, sky-obliterating smoke clouds, and buried jungles are part of both continuous and evolutionary life processes. The biosphere has not only become well adapted to them, it depends upon them.

The changes humans are creating are different. As with rapid ecosystem alterations in the Hawai'ian Islands over a time span of only two hundred years, the consequences of many of our other recent unprecedented interventions into the biosphere are unknown. Deforestation, desertification, soil erosion, water and air poisoning, global warming, and ozone layer depletion are effects on a scale approaching those of the last major Ice Age. We as a single species are blindly altering the conditions of all life without any real sense of the magnitude of danger brought by our acts. We are destroying life faster than the earth can create it.

GUARD FOX WATCH TAKES ON THE OLYMPICS

Peter Berg and Kimiharu To

"Nobody wins the games if nature loses!" is the slogan of Guard Fox Watch, an organization that Peter Berg cofounded with Kimiharu To of Japan to monitor and report on the ecological damage caused by the 1998 Winter Olympics in Nagano. Berg and To draw a set of guidelines to avoid negative impacts on future Olympics and suggest beneficial ways to create the means for future sustainability. The pair of press releases reprinted here calls the Nagano Games' theme of "Respect for the Beauty and Bounty of Nature" an "empty promise," itemizes the negative ecological impacts of the event, and recommends specific steps for post-Games remediation of natural systems of the Nagano Bioregion and local human ecology. Guard Fox Watch articles on Nagano and subsequent Winter Olympics are available on Planet Drum's Eco-Eye on the Olympics webpage. Given their enormous popularity and the media fest surrounding the Olympics, Guard Fox Watch's position will strike many readers as cantankerous and misguided—that is, until they allow themselves to consider the justice of the cause.

Guard Fox Watch Statement I

Statement of concern regarding the ecological impact of the Nagano Winter Olympics (Globalist Games)

The ecological impact of the upcoming Winter Olympics in Nagano has become an urgent concern of local residents, environmentally-conscious citizens of Japan, and a growing number of people throughout the world. The present measures for "coexistence with nature" do not remotely satisfy reasonable standards for protection against many threats to life systems posed by the Games. In addition, there are important priorities for long-term sustainability in the region that have not been addressed.

Land, highway and other development for staging the Games has already inflicted high ecological costs. Massive further damage will soon occur through sheer numbers of attendees at events which will adversely affect air, water, soil, and ecosystems in significant ways. Although they are only two weeks long in duration, the legacy of these last Winter Games before the 21st Century will be the greatest ecological disaster in Nagano's bioregional history.

The theme of "Respect for the Beauty and Bounty of Nature" is an empty promise that totally fails to adequately address the seriousness of this situation. GUARD FOX WATCH will observe the negative impacts of the Games and assess their ecological damage. We will issue periodic warnings about particularly dangerous activities in order to prevent their reoccurrence, and provide ongoing reports over the two week period. We will also propose guidelines to avoid the negative impacts of future Olympics and other large sports events and suggest beneficial ways to create the means for future sustainability when they are held.

Nobody Wins the Games If Nature Loses!

Guard Fox Watch Committee

(Feb. 4, 1998)

Guard Fox Watch Statement II, 14 February 1998

After one week of the Nagano Winter Games, it is obvious that some outrageous ecological impacts must be stopped immediately:

1) Use of salt and other chemicals to clear ice and snow at event sites and to keep major roadways open 24 hours a day must cease at the present huge scale. There are many other means to effectively treat ice and snow that don't involve such highly destructive consequences for ground water, rice field soil, and towns downstream.
2) Trash burning at lodges, restaurants, and town garbage facilities must be forbidden for the remainder of the Games due to excessive air pollution such as presently occurs in Hakuba Valley and other places.
3) Personal automobiles must be banned on the roads near event sites where they cause traffic jams with engines running up to half an hour that contribute significantly to acute current air pollution.
4) "Recycling" bins at event sites actually recycle nothing in themselves but provide an inexpensive means to sort trash using audience assistance. One bin choice proudly announces "burnables" which eventually contribute to air pollution. Other choices (especially "plastic") may not be sent to the most ecological recycling destinations. Recycling processes must be immediately disclosed, reviewed and modified.

GUARD FOX WATCH has established two main areas for determining ecological impacts that need to be assessed for future remediation, restoration and reparations for damages: a) natural systems of the Nagano Bioregion, and b) local human ecology.

Natural systems that are most obviously affected are:

1) Water. Snow is handled with shovels and bulldozers but it isn't dirt, it's water. Snow melts into local soil, water drains and channels, eventually ending up in agricultural irrigation water and rivers. It carries along everything dropped on it including highway salt, snow-bonded auto exhaust chemicals and incidental wastes such as tire rubber, grease, antifreeze, and battery acid, as well as all forms of noxious litter thrown away by hundreds of thousands of people participating in the Games or attending them.
2) Soil. Erosion from building 115 kilometers of new roads for the Winter Olympics will be extensive in the steep and geologically sensitive Nagano mountains.
3) Ecosystems. Native plant and animal communities have been cut open with new roads and disrupted or destroyed by clearcutting forests and bulldozing land for construction. Animals are presently frightened away by night lighting and crowd noise during their most difficult survival season.

Human ecology impacts include:

1) Economic displacement. Any employment of local people and increase in Nagano business attributable to the Games is temporary. Sufficient jobs in regionally sustainable industries are still lacking. Burdensome taxes incurred by roadbuilding and construction for the Games is inequitably assigned to Nagano residents alone.
2) Garbage. Hakuba alone is slated to handle 87 metric tons of additional waste because of the Olympics (a figure that will undoubtedly be exceeded). Garbage burning is an inappropriate method of disposal even under ordinary conditions.
3) Water supplies. Usual uses were vastly multiplied. Supplies are diverted for human use from native ecosystems.
4) Energy. Increases in unsustainable fossil fuel energy use. Air pollution by autos.

GUARD FOX WATCH recommendations for dealing with the devastating ecological aftermath of the Olympics for natural systems are to neutralize the roadside and watershed effects of chemical pollution, undertake thorough erosion monitoring and control, and restore and maintain native plant and animal communities. In order to repair damage to human ecology and create a sustainable future for Nagano, we urge shifting the costs of construction to organizers and sponsors of the Games, instituting genuine and thorough recycling programs, developing energy sources that are renewable rather than polluting fossil fuels or dangerous nuclear power, converting all water systems to recycle gray water, and awarding subsidies for new businesses and jobs to create these sustainable alternatives.

Nobody Wins The Games If Nature Loses!

BIOREGIONALISM COMES TO JAPAN

An interview of Peter Berg by Richard Evanoff

Richard Evanoff, a professor of environmental ethics at Aoyama Gakuin University in Tokyo, conducts an intellectually stimulating interview with Berg, covering topics that include deep ecology, personal lifestyle, international trade, self-sufficiency, political decision making, and globalization. In this interview, published in Japan Environment Monitor *(June 1998), Evanoff prompts Berg to answer some common criticisms of eco-localism, including charges of insularity, exclusiveness, and parochialism. Berg's pointed answers may have the effect of "[setting] off a large-scale explosion in the brain," precisely his intention.*

The term "bioregionalism" was first popularized in the 1970s by the ecologist Raymond Dasmann and activist Peter Berg. Berg was in Japan this past winter investigating, together with Japanese activist Kimiharu To, the ecological damage caused by the Nagano Olympics. *The Japan Times* ("Ecology of Nagano seen coming in last," February 12, 1998) quoted Berg's reference to the event as the "greatest ecological disaster in Nagano's bioregional history." To criticized the games for being run in the interests of multinational corporations, television broadcasters, and developers with no citizen input, despite the fact that it is citizens "who must pay for a four-lane highway and airport they don't need." Farmers will also suffer from pollution of their rice paddies and the native species of Nagano will be damaged.

The Planet Drum Foundation, founded by Berg and others in 1973 to advance bioregional ideas, publishes the biannual journal *Raise the Stakes*, sponsors educational and cultural activities on bioregional themes, and provides networking services for bioregional activists, including a directory listing 250 bioregional groups around the world. The organization has helped to develop the Bioregional Association of the Northern Americas and sponsors a biannual continental gathering of bioregionalists. Its publications include *A Green City Program for the San Francisco Bay Area and Beyond*, *Reinhabiting a Separate Country*, and *Discovering Your Life-Place: A First Bioregional Workbook* [. . . .]

The following interview was conducted in Tokyo and introduces readers to some of the key ideas of bioregionalism.

EVANOFF: What exactly is bioregionalism?

BERG: A bioregion is a geographic area defined by natural characteristics, including watersheds, landforms, soils, geological qualities, native plants and animals, climate, and weather. These characteristics are continuous; in other words, when there are changes in these characteristics you've gone from one bioregion to another. Obviously these borders are soft and wide, as opposed to linear and sharp in the present geopolitical sense of "boundary." Bioregionalism includes human beings as a species in the interplay of these natural characteristics. It promotes an inhabitory attitude by which humans adapt themselves to the natural characteristics of a bioregion in an appropriate way. At this point in history such an attitude exists only among so-called primitive people or as a matter of historical record. For most people on the planet today it would be necessary to become a reinhabitant in order to fit into the natural characteristics of the bioregions they occupy. A bioregion is a geographic terrain and a terrain of consciousness. It is a cultural idea based on characteristics usually associated with the natural sciences. Put simply, a bioregion is a "life-place," the natural place around you that's alive and contains your life as well as the lives of other species.

EVANOFF: There seems to be a perception, at least among some, that the environmental movement is about preserving pristine wilderness areas with little or no human interference. You seem to be working, however, towards a harmonization of nature and culture.

BERG: Bioregionalism is proactive. It is carrying the concept of a life-place into the activities and goals of human society, as opposed to protest. Environmentalism has been a protest-oriented activity based on attempting to deal with a destructive industrial society. On the one hand, it tries to preserve pristine wilderness areas for their own sake and, on the other, to keep water and air clean for the sake of humans. Bioregionalism goes beyond both of these. In a bioregion there are different zones of human interface with natural systems: urban, suburban, rural, and wilderness. And each of these has a different appropriate reinhabitory approach.

EVANOFF: What kind of changes in lifestyle will be necessary if people want to live in harmony with bioregions?

BERG: The bioregional idea at first seems to be a nature or outdoors-oriented view. In fact, it is a fairly profound philosophical perspective because it addresses basic civilization questions: who am I, what am I, and what am I going to do? In the context of the biosphere, a person as a member of the human species interacting with other species is a fundamental premise of bioregionalism. So what you do is to reconceptualize your relationship with the elements of the planetary biosphere, other people, society, and the exigencies of contemporary life. Carrying out a bioregional lifestyle is to apply reinhabitory directions to the basic necessities of life. Where does my food come from? What's my relationship to the water that I use? What's my relationship to the soil? What's my relationship to native ecosystems? Am I using materials that are from the bioregion where I live for house construction and the fabrication of products? Am I learning about the life-systems of the place where I live and about how my own life ultimately depends on them? Am I learning how to live in a place in a long-term, sustainable way with bioregional self-reliance as a guide? There are a lot of ways to apply the bioregional idea.

EVANOFF: A lot of the things we consume these days are not locally produced but imported via the global market, and it's sometimes difficult to trace out the connections. What kind of critique does bioregionalism offer of global trade?

BERG: The connections are actually fairly easy to trace out. It's the combination of them that's hard to keep up with. I know that the coffee I drink could come from several different places on the planet, that it's harvested in a certain way, and I know that ships carry it. What makes it difficult are the eco-energetics of the cups, of the heating source used to make the coffee, of the water that goes into it. All of those eco-energetics become extremely complicated. Right now, these eco-energy inputs cost more than we know because the ecological damage hasn't been assessed. The bioregional worth of things as opposed to the negative ecological footprint simply hasn't been investigated. It hasn't been one of those things that a big R&D project has been designed to find out—and it should be! What people can do about it in a practical way is to try to find out what the local products are, what the costs are, and to make decisions about what they consume and what they get involved with based on that. It's possible to do this with joy rather than puritanical morality. In fact, when I walk down the street in the Shasta Bioregion in San Francisco and see a native plant or tree, it's quite exciting. It's thrilling!

EVANOFF: How far do you want to go with self-sufficiency? Should communities become entirely self-sufficient? Would that preclude any possibility of international trade?

BERG: We're talking about a direction here, not a dictum—as much self-reliance as possible and as much of a real cost analysis of exports and imports as possible. For example, when you export agriculture, you export soil and water, as well as some species of domestic plant. You transport it using some energy source and you package it. All of these things have real costs that aren't reflected in the price.

EVANOFF: One aspect of bioregionalism seems to be the transformation of consciousness on a very personal level.

BERG: We often assume that we're capable of divining models that somehow will be or should be employed by the general public to initiate some sort of enormous change based on a critical evaluation of the present situation. And we often feel that these models can have efficacy in some grand historical and socially progressive way. But I'm not sure this is true. I believe that most people are in a trance, a deep trance having to do with the nature and requirements of industrial society. You get up in the morning in an essentially disinhabitory environment. You deal with the requirements of getting your body and mind together in ways that are completely dissociated from their origins in nature—you only see water coming out of a tap. You get out on the street with people you've learned to be wary of and adopt an anonymous identity. You get on some means of public transportation about which you know nothing. The subway is rattling through the geology of the city, but it's not geology you see, it's advertisements. Then you get off, and you're dealing with these other people on the basis of relationships that are dictated by power and command. You fulfill your role in the operation, using a lot of mechanical signals. You get through all that, go back home, watch television, and go to bed. Now, if you haven't been in a deep trance, where exactly have you been? We're talking about at least 50% of the population. They take respite by going to foreign places where they absolutely destroy the landscapes without even knowing it. To escape from this trance, they go mess up Hawaii. That's what we're dealing with. This is the famous, average, normal, reasonable human being that we assume is out there. So why do we pretend to have models that might be useful to these people and believe that it's possible to create some sort of social movement based on something like the Paris Commune? Where do we get this crap? What hope do we have? How should we go about it? As an activist-thinker in a situation such as talking to a university class or a group of businessmen or public policy people, I simply try to create a mental condition that will have the effect of an explosion in their brain. I could talk paradigm-talk all day, and it would bore me. I try to set off a large-scale explosion in the mind of the person or audience I'm dealing with. If I'm lucky and the explosion does occur, I don't know where the pieces are going to settle. The reason I'm doing this is because I feel as though I'm an agent provocateur who is pursuing his own survival in a trance-driven society that wants to deprive me of any of the little measly human-natural interactive possibilities that I can experience. That really is where I'm at.

EVANOFF: How exactly do you go about shocking people?

BERG: One way to shock people is to say that they aren't going to do anything to save the earth if they aren't doing something around them right now. The earth isn't just the rainforest or the Amazon jungle or the whales or the hole in the ozone layer alone. The earth is also where you are. To so-called primitive people the world is local-cosmological, not planetary. The direction of our present civilization is to turn the earth into a garbage dump and then abandon it, to turn it into an uninhabitable smoggy sewer and then leave it. To a large extent what we're doing is committing suicide as a species. Another shocking thing is for people to realize how impoverished they are in spite of the illusion of material success, that their relationships with others are often bad and that they can't depend on very many people. In the U.S., the majority of the population is just two paychecks away from homelessness. That should send a shiver of fear through anyone! Everyone is extremely close to that edge, which includes insanity, neurosis, unhappiness, and bad health. I think most people are aware that they're committing a sort of soft-shoe planet-murder simply through their lives.

EVANOFF: Some people criticize the environmental movement for emphasizing changes in lifestyles rather than changes in political structure.

BERG: That's a false opposition. You can't change the political structures without changing the description of the person and what their anticipations and intentions are. During the French Revolution, most people had no idea what freedom was. What they were saying was that freedom was the direction they wanted to go in. They simply wanted the situation to be something other than what it was then, but they had no idea what it was going to be. In the same way a life of identifying with the human species, of an eco-centered basis of decision-making and public policy, of identifying with wild nature in a planetary context is something we have no idea of. A person now in late industrial society can say there is a possible world to go to, not utopia, but relieving the oppression and suffering of the present. It's a process, and it involves different relationships and activities, as well as disavowing certain political and economic structures and putting faith in others, or at least saying that I'll put my faith in trying to make this alternative work rather than put my faith in hoping that this present dominant structure continues.

EVANOFF: Is there in fact a utopian element in bioregionalism?

BERG: I think there's a utopian element in human consciousness. I think there was a utopian element in the Stone Age. People have always dreamt together of a resolution of problems and difficulties. Medicine is utopian—that a cure is possible for disease. Magic is utopian—that a miraculous outcome can occur. Art is utopian, that you can produce something that others will be inspired by aesthetically.

EVANOFF: How do you assess the current state of the environmental movement?

BERG: The environmental movement is over. I actually believe it ended on Earth Day in 1972, and in fact historians will probably say that. Environmentalism had always been the handmaiden of late industrial society. It was a way to preserve the material benefits of industrial products and processes while mitigating the effect of developing those products and carrying out those processes. Clean water and clean air were the epitome of the environmental movement. We had rivers that caught fire and air that was causing cancer. Even ordinary environments were visibly affected by industrial processes. It's not surprising to me that a lot of old-line environmentalists have felt assailed by the deep-ecology, bioregional, whole-systems perspective because single-issue environmentalism was a way to get through the day. It was a way to deal with that soft-shoe planet-murder. You could take a bath in your environmentalism and feel good. Environmentalism simply won't be a twenty-first century consideration.

EVANOFF: So where's it going?

BERG: There are two major activities that will replace environmentalism. One is restoration ecology—not in the academic sense, but as practiced by residents: urban people, suburban people, and rural people. Ecological restoration projects are much more comprehensive human activities than first imagined. When people first hear of ecological restoration, they think, oh, some nature project that I do on weekends. But in fact, restoring an urban creek is a major undertaking and is an essential activity for a reinhabitory perspective in a city, and has multiple implications. The other direction is urban sustainability. We have become an urban species. More than half of us live in cities. So we have to become renaturalized as urban residents. In other words, we have to regain our species perspective and expand it, even while living in dense multistoried areas. Urban sustainability is not just a watchword. At present most municipal governments put urban sustainability below the top ten issues that they're involved with. But within a very short time it will rise to the top three or so, and I believe eventually become the central issue for decision-making and policy directions regarding employment, health, education, welfare, transportation, energy, and so on. The central component of all these concerns is sustainability.

EVANOFF: What is the Green City Project?

BERG: We're trying to raise consciousness and help people get involved. We connect volunteers with 450 groups in the Bay Area. We publish a calendar of events that has activities for every day of the year. The idea is that school children, the elderly, working people, people of all classes and ethnicities, can become involved in some aspect of urban sustainability, such as tree planting, neighborhood empowerment, appropriate transportation, celebrations, and culture. Culture is particularly important: art and murals depicting native species, libraries, public sculptures, and events connected with watching natural phenomena, such as the rising of the sun at the equinox or solstice. I tell people that the future mayor of San Francisco will one day walk onto the Golden Gate Bridge, with all the traffic stopped, to lead the Salmon Welcoming Celebration on the day in fall when salmon return to spawn from the North Pacific into San Francisco Bay and up the Sacramento River, with thousands of people dancing and making music, wearing salmon costumes, eating smoked salmon, and saying "Welcome back brothers and sisters!"

EVANOFF: Those kinds of cultural activities seem so rich compared to most of the pastimes that dominate modern life.

BERG: The appreciation of culture inherent in the bioregional perspective involves the very values that are most prized by art and antique collectors. They are unique, diverse, participatory, personal. They are the most highly valued things, yet people are unaware of the potential of ordinary everyday experience, and think of it as somehow going back to wearing a loincloth.

EVANOFF: How do you see public participation in terms of the political decision-making process? On the one hand, bioregionalism advocates local participation, but on the other, so many decisions about what's going on in the world are made by multinational corporations and international organizations such as the World Trade Organization. The local and the global are often in conflict with each other. Decisions might be made by a multinational to close down a factory in a particular community, for example, and the community can be devastated by that. Do you see the two coexisting side by side?

BERG: There are many possibilities for effecting change. The variety that I'm most fond of and I think is the most authentic is when people undertake through their mutual decision-making to create a situation which they feel is desirable or beneficial and fits in with their idea of bioregional reinhabitation. When they do this, all kinds of interaction will occur with the dominant society. To give an example, when residents of the Shasta Bioregion tried to carry out a salmon restoration project on their own, using their own backyards as the site for water tanks for eggs to hatch so that salmon could be put back into the creeks where they had become extinct, they were prevented from getting eggs from female salmon by the California Department of Fish and Game, who had no way to see that activity except as poaching! Isn't that a wonderful contradiction? It really exposes the conflict.

EVANOFF: What about globalization?

BERG: Protest is necessary because as globalization increases there are inroads into things like personal privacy and community cohesion that are extremely destructive. So protesting, regulating, and defending against globalization is extremely important.

EVANOFF: Do you see bioregionalism as something that's going to disrupt the dominant society?

BERG: The dominant globalist society believes that it has ultimate dominion over anything that it chooses to have dominion over. That's the situation at present. If you put together the heads of major multinational corporations and gave them a list of possibilities for getting involved with communities, or individual and social behavior, they would be able to go through the list and think of ways in which they could dominate any of those situations. Public relations and advertising people already do that. They ask themselves, is there a way that we can get into the bedroom of every married couple so that they all use a particular product, do a particular thing, stop doing something else. That's their present perspective. And the reason that they've had such extraordinary success is because they've just blasted communities, blasted human taste, befuddled people, cast illusions so dense that people just don't know what's going on— their mouths are open. Bioregional activities run against this, and they're not the only ones that run against this. Native economies and cooperative endeavors do as well. I've been to globalization forums where there have been literally hundreds of representatives with a tremendous range of reaction to globalist imposition. As bioregionalist solutions are counterposed to industrial solutions, they by necessity run against globalist imposition.

EVANOFF: Can the bioregional sentiment prevail against it?

BERG: Here we're dealing with values. If we can establish activities that have values associated with them that people don't want to lose, or that they feel they've contributed in establishing, then we can establish some ground. I believe there is an essential, dichotomous conflict between eco-localism in general, of which bioregionalism is a form, and the globalist multinational corporate push. In the twenty-first century we'll see that conflict. I hate to use the word "war" but we're already seeing it. The Zapatista rebellion in the Chiapas region of Mexico is completely formulated around resistance to globalist imposition on the part of eco-local social groups. But I've also seen it in what could be called suburban situations in Mexico, for example in the town of Tepoztlán in an event that's called the "Golf War," where citizens resisted the building of a resort and golf course that would use communal water. The plan had been approved illegally by the state and national governments and rights were given to multinational corporations which the governments did not have the authority to give. I was there a year ago and there were still roadblocks to prevent the army trucks from coming into town. Local people resisted the project to the point that they ousted their bribed city councilmen. They now call themselves the Free, Autonomous and Democratic Municipality of Tepoztlán. You can also see the trend towards localization in the falling apart of Yugoslavia and the Soviet Union, and the realignment of social groups in Africa and Asia.

EVANOFF: It seems that the people who advocate globalization get a lot of political mileage out of the rhetoric that we're "bringing the world together" and creating a global society based on peace and harmony. At the same time criticisms are sometimes made against eco-localism on the grounds that it's going to promote insularity, ethnic exclusiveness, religious fundamentalism, and the creation of cultural enclaves in which people are going to be isolated from each other. In the media and so forth all of this makes globalism seem appealing while making something like bioregionalism look insular.

BERG: The dominant oppressive group can always do extraordinary things to divide, conquer, and corrupt authentic, viable local structures. There probably isn't anything that globalism offers that shouldn't be questioned or negotiated from a bioregional point of view. Some areas of global cooperation may be more acceptable than others. The hole in the ozone layer, for example, is the kind of problem that has to be solved by people occupying various places on the planet. There are potential benefits from global cooperation in areas such as these. It's extremely hypocritical, though, for multinational corporations to pretend to be bringing the world together.

EVANOFF: How about the charge that bioregionalism encourages people to go off into their own little communities and not become cosmopolitan?

BERG: The richness and authenticity that is the reward of bioregionalism requires exactly that kind of going into the place where you live. I can walk down a country lane and be thinking about the world tennis matches or I can be looking at the particular native trees that are right in front of me. It doesn't matter where the world tennis matches are being held but the trees being there does matter. They can't be anywhere else. They have to be there. This is where they evolved. So there's information selection that is in fact insular or that isolates you from other information. Now, does that necessarily breed parochialism? I've heard people say that parochialism and xenophobia may not be that bad, but I personally think that they are. I believe that they are restrictive. So I look for a meta-level of bioregional identification: the bioregion is my window on the planetary biosphere and the means for participating in it. So, yes, this stream that comes through the area that I'm standing in is unique to this place, but that water is joining up with the water of the whole biosphere by mingling with other watersheds, by going to the ocean, through evaporating as clouds and coming back as rain. Just the idea that every molecule of water on the planet has been used and reused again and again is a marvelous cosmos-establishing experience. So, the "joys" of chauvinism are easily replaced by the magic of larger biospheric and cosmological participation.

EVANOFF: So we're connected both geographically with people and life in other bioregions and historically with the past and future.

BERG: Exactly.

EVANOFF: Despite what seems to me to be a lot of unnecessary ideological conflict between the various schools of environmental philosophy—deep ecology, social ecology, ecofeminism, and the like—people in each of these groups seem to be attracted to at least some aspects of bioregionalism. Deep ecology, for example, is big on promoting a change in cultural attitudes and personal consciousness, while social ecology emphasizes decentralized municipal decision-making. Do you see bioregionalism as being a mediating force that might be able to unify or bring together some of these disparate theoretical perspectives?

BERG: One reason why these new ecological, philosophical formulations have been attracted to and have subsequently incorporated a bioregional perspective is because bioregionalism offers an authenticating foundation for the whole ecological premise. People these days are putting the word "eco" in front of everything precisely because they don't want to be identified with the old power and resource-manipulating ethos. Reinhabitation as a practical activity does have a fluidity that is unifying. A person can have an ecological perspective but for that person to be able to do something with others and have a social relationship based on an ecological perspective, there must be a social understanding (not an academic or technical understanding) about what our mutual territory is, where we are, and what we relate to each other about. The bioregion comes in as a common vista—this is what we can talk about! Let's talk about the restoration of the natural systems that we live in as a long-term goal, with all of these various perspectives—the social perspective, the gender perspective, the diet perspective, the cosmological perspective—having something to contribute. Words such as "bioregion" and "reinhabitation" shouldn't be seen as the property of some narrow theoretical perspective but as public language.

EVANOFF: What's your interest in Japan?

BERG: The Sacramento River goes into San Francisco Bay and into the California Current and the North Pacific. Salmon which swim in our rivers also swim past Hokkaido Island. We're on the same latitudinal lines as Japan. So it's no longer possible for me to have a "United Statesian" identity. I have to have both a Shasta Bioregion identity and a North Pacific Rim identity in planetary terms. On the one hand, I can say that I'm a citizen of the city of San Francisco, in the county of San Francisco, in the state of California, in the United States of America, in the so-called "free world." Or I can say that I live in the Islais Creek Watershed, of the San Francisco Bay Estuary, of the Shasta Bioregion, of the North Pacific Rim, of the Pacific Basin, in the planetary biosphere of the universe. In this latter way of thinking, which I much prefer, Japan and America are transpacific relatives.

EVANOFF: How would bioregionalism apply to Japan?

BERG: Well, historically Japan has this great nature philosophy that I can be inspired by. But since the war Japan has had a productivist, modern, competitive system that functions only at the cost of personal freedom, ecological damage, and a really nasty attitude outside the boundaries of the country towards other people's resources and bioregions. There are many segments of Japanese society, however, that are aware of this on numerous levels—of the need for greater personal freedom, greater ecological responsibility, and a harmonious interaction with other people on the planet. Attitudes about peace, nonviolence, and spirituality among the Japanese people are extremely strong. I gave a bioregional tour of Hakuba Valley to local residents and we stood up on a cliff about a thousand feet high looking down on the whole watershed. We had just seen the springs and were observing native plants vs. exotic, water coming into the rice fields, the damage of the Olympics construction, and the power of the watershed. It's a very steep valley, you know. You could tell what the forces are by looking at the flood plain of the river. It's ten times the width of the river on both sides and it's pure rock and gravel. That means that when the snow melts, the water is just roaring through there because of the gravitational pull. That's one of the reasons why Hakuba Valley is so delicate—all the water ends up in the river. There's no place for it to go, no seepage. So here is the natural template of this watershed that was given by natural forces and that people adapted to, and now we're looking at a phenomenon—the Nagano Olympics—that will rewrite the ecological history of this area. This is the historic episode, the modern history-making event of that area. After the Olympics leaves, people will count the future in terms of this event. We can either live harmoniously with this natural area or we can allow it to be degraded and destroyed. It really is a spiritual question. After the tour a woman came up to me and said that she was a teacher but had lost her purpose in teaching. Now, however, she had something to believe in and something to teach the children. "In everything I do I'm going to make this a part of their life," she said. Japanese people have this spiritual dimension which I find absolutely astonishing.

EVANOFF: What exactly do you hope to achieve with respect to the Olympics?

BERG: We're going to try to assess the damage using socio-cultural rather than natural-scientific tools. What I'm hoping personally is that some basis for reparations can be established. The upshot is that this kind of large-scale sporting spectacle promotes a "society of the spectacle" that lasts for a very short time but has a devastating effect on the long-term prospects of natural landscapes. This can't go on. This is an important instance of globalism vs. bioregional sustainability and it has to be opposed.

CHINA'S EPIC CONFLICT OF CAPACITIES

In this dark travel essay posted on the Planet Drum website, Berg shares eyewitness observations and launches a no-holds-barred critique of China's massive industrialization and especially of the Three Gorges Dam Project, under construction in 2001 when Berg visited the Yangtze River. This dystopian dispatch quotes a local resident who comments, "China is like the Titanic. The current regime believes it is invulnerable, [but it is] about to hit an iceberg." The only possibility for a positive outcome that Berg can muster amid the "eye-burning, throat-scratching, nose-stuffing smog" is to wonder if the Chinese people will begin to feel that the Mandate of Heaven has been withdrawn from the Red Dynasty.

A regrettably familiar scenario is playing out on an ominous scale in China. It is a struggle between frenzied industrial capacity building, and the ecological carrying capacity that is necessary to support a future society. To dismiss the significance of this nation's present conflict by saying that the same thing is happening everywhere would be likening a candle flame to a forest fire.

China has achieved an extremely large amount of industrialization in just fifty years. It isn't necessary to quote statistics. Look in your clothes closet, investigate the hidden components in electronic appliances, or just empty your pockets and most likely some Chinese manufactured products will appear. They are everywhere.

The cost of this momentous surge has been enormous environmental damage at home. Boats leaving Shanghai's city center dock to begin a trip up the Yangtze River are shrouded in eye-burning, throat-scratching, nose-stuffing smog. The only water actually visible is directly beneath the ship's rail. The striking new multistory needle-shaped communications building that pierces a large shining sphere midway to the top dubbed "The Pearl of the Orient" lying just across the river in Pudong can barely be seen through the haze blanket.

Surely the air must clear up further down the river. But it doesn't. All afternoon, steadily through the night, and through the next day and night, a gray curtain shrouds unbroken shorelines of smudged smokestacks, noisy power plants, rusty container freight booms, drain pipes spewing discolored liquid, squat factories, coal piles, and grimy rail yards. For more than a hundred miles the principal variation in air pollution from one of China's largest industrial cities is its odor. There are distinct bands of stench that reflect burnt cardboard, coal smoke, braised metal, wood smoke, diesel fuel, or baked minerals.

Although it is poisonous to life forms in general and especially injurious for human beings, air pollution as bad as this can eventually be reduced or practically eliminated if there is a will to do so. Unfortunately, further travel several hundred more miles up the Yangtze provides overwhelming evidence that China is following a completely opposite path. The grotesque Three Gorges Dam Project (3GDP) when it is initially completed in 2003 will throttle the river for over a thousand miles upstream and drown an inimitable part of Chinese cultural history along with a long-recognized part of the world's natural heritage. The renowned and inspiring canyons of Three Gorges will be submerged by a wall-to-wall lake. Imagine turning the Grand Canyon into a landfill and topping it off with garbage. It is an equivalent loss, and the ecological impact will be even greater.

The 3GDP is a guiding symbol for what some feel will be the upcoming Chinese Century. "The fight of man with the [sic] nature for water resources" proclaims the inscription on a new monument above the dam construction site. It could just as well read "for everything." The 21st century will be a head-whipping era of accelerated urbanization in previously countryside-based China. Erection of new buildings is so feverish that no daytime cityscape is without the sight of several construction cranes. A dozen could be spotted in one quick glance even through the polluted air of Shanghai. Nighttime city views are never without dozens of small brilliant white beads from welding torches pricking the darkness.

There are dreary large black and white signs everywhere along the Yangtze banks proclaiming "135 meters" (for the reservoir's depth in 2003) or "175 meters" (for the ultimate drowning in 2009). If the same brutal honesty prevailed in cities, there would be billboards proclaiming "135 million tons of garbage," and "175 thousand pounds of air and water pollution." Much of the rural population is slated to be moved off of the land (where more than half now live) to cram new buildings by the hundreds of millions. If this grim fantasy is realized, there should also be billboards listing dried up rivers, mowed down forests, ruined farm land, and sewage tainted seas. (80% of China's human waste is dumped into rivers and ocean bays.)

This isn't solely an outsider's view. Resident critics bravely express similar and even more fatalistic outcomes. A particularly direct comment was, "China is like the Titanic. The current regime believes it is invulnerable and is about to hit an iceberg." What will be the first cracking point? Ecologically informed urban observers point to strains on water supplies. Beijing's rivers are already exhausted from a five to ten times jump in population (depending on how it's counted) and a huge increase in industry over the last half-century. Drinkable water is sharply limited nation-wide and can only become more scarce. Lack of water is a planet-wide problem that may be felt most deeply here.

The 3GDP's mission is to control flooding on the Yangtze, provide irrigation, and supply one-tenth of the total electrical power for China's one and a quarter billion people. The largest dam ever built also has the greatest potential for problems: unprecedented water pressure from the world's most vast reservoir, severe silt build-up from the perpetually brown Yangtze, and vulnerability to geological events. There is a sharp division of engineering opinions about the dam and ensuing hydrological phenomena. Catastrophic failure shouldn't be ruled out. Even without it, the damage that will eventually be done by uprooting over a million people and flooding their cities and farms, submerging nine-tenths of the known ancient artifacts of the Yangtze Valley, and many other negative repercussions of 3GDP can stir fateful doubts about the government.

Is there any possibility for a positive outcome? The present regime deems itself "communism with Chinese characteristics." One Chinese characteristic is to believe that rulers prevail through the Mandate of Heaven, which is unsuspectingly taken away from or bestowed on different groups. The turnover is usually preceded by a natural disaster such as famines or floods. The massive amount of overbuilding and technological/industrial capacity building currently underway symbolized by Three Gorges Dam may inadvertently cause such a calamity. Suppose people begin to feel that the Mandate of Heaven has been withdrawn from the Red Dynasty, and it no longer balances the needs of The Middle Kingdom. The debts to ecological capacity must ultimately be met, and may come due faster than we could hope.

COLORS ARE THE DEEDS OF LIGHT

In this 2005 dispatch from Kyoto, Berg summarizes a talk that he gave at Seika University. Berg attributes his title, "Colors Are the Deeds of Light," to a phrase by Johann Wolfgang von Goethe. By comparing the show of hands on questions such as how many students own television sets or cellular phones or have seen a trout in a creek or a fox in the wild, Berg awakens the students to the fact that, unlike their grandparents, they were born into the Industrial Era. Statistics on waste (the average Japanese young person will discard thirty-five computers and mobile phones and twelve washing machines in his or her lifetime) cast a pall over the room that even Berg's positive alternatives for the future could not lift. The evening is redeemed at dinner over bowls of soba noodles and glasses of beer when two of the quietest students in the class confront Berg with challenging questions, showing that they have learned to think for themselves. Their questions press Berg to further articulate the bioregional perspective.

The persistent edge of metal cornered buildings cutting into the eyes and days of businesslike Japan seems everywhere dominant and unforgiving, but the overlaid human environment also crowds in resilient minds that can wondrously rebound from those daily slashing encounters. This happened in Kyoto last night.

Eco-philosopher Yuichi Inouye's combined classes of 150 or so Environmental Sciences students had filled a hall at Seika University yesterday afternoon to hear my talk on bioregional sustainability. Seika is a good place to try out new ideas so I began some comments about our present historical moment by asking how many owned television sets. Every hand was raised.

Then an opposite experience: how many had seen a trout in a creek? A little over half as many. How many owned a personal computer? All again. Seen a deer in a forest? An even half. Owned a cellular phone? All. Seen a fox in the wild? Now less than half. Their grandparents had been born before there were televisions, PCs or cell phones and most had probably seen all three wild animals. They were born into the Industrial Era whose end was being signaled by the information devices that the grandchildren now universally owned. It had been a blighting time for biospheric life on the scale of the last Ice Age. The new epoch could hopefully take a turn for the better.

But was there actually improvement so far? Not according to a European Union report on Waste from Electrical and Electronic Equipment (WEE). Yuichi translated the list of 553 pieces of equipment that each young Japanese person in the audience would discard during their average 78 years of life: 95 small household appliances such as vacuum cleaners and toasters, 55 consumer items (TVs, video camcorders, DVDs, etc.), 35 computers and mobile phones, 12 washing machines (TWELVE! Yuichi was astonished), 10 refrigerators, and 6 microwaves. Enough to cover five acres of land. If everyone on the planet consumed at this level it would take three earths to support them. So much for the promise of the post-industrial age.

I next steered toward positive alternatives for the future although the inertia of those dismal facts seemed to prevent changing course completely. It took the surprise presence of old friends like Kim To, his wife Izumi with their new baby girl, Noriko who volunteered at Planet Drum's San Francisco office, and Ken Rodgers from *Kyoto Journal* to finally exorcise the pall.

Inouye is a consummately involved educator and in typical style arranged a two hour seminar answering questions from students, faculty and interested guests to immediately follow the talk. Their intriguing range of interests included difficulty finding jobs in sustainable fields, dying towns on the "back door" side of the country's main Honshu Island facing the Sea of Japan, how local communities should take over projects started by outside NGOs, and even the unfortunate advent into the United States of elaborate Japanese toilet systems with bottom-showering devices. One of the subjects that stood out was the importance of getting out of buildings and going into natural settings to show features of watersheds, native species and other bioregional characteristics. It is possible to see the core of watershed dynamics simply by following a path that leads downhill. Any plant encountered is either native or exotic, and usually shows obvious indications of the way it relates to local features such as availability of sunlight. Kicking up dust can reveal some soil characteristics. And something unplanned but noteworthy will always happen to the participants. A bird or other animal will show itself. A tree will have signs of a fire or lightning strike. There will be new blooms or a spray of mushrooms or webs with crazily decorated spiders. It is an infallible certainty that interesting things can be seen on any occasion.

Two women sophomores sat throughout this marathon Q & A without saying anything except to converse with each other. On the way out I mentioned this to them playfully not even sure they understood English. Inouye overheard and in his perpetual Teacher of The Year role stayed behind to solicit their reactions to the preceding events. "They really have a lot of serious concerns," he reported excitedly. "I invited them to dinner with us to question us in a less public situation." (I believe he even paid for their dinner. Students often visit with his family at home and stay the night if it gets too late.) We talked about unrelated but specifically Japanese subjects walking to a *soba* (buckwheat noodle) restaurant. The fact that they both had pink kimonos at home, whether they would marry within the next ten years (Japanese women are rapidly abandoning traditional obligatory roles), and superstitions about *onis* (devils) that are common throughout the countryside.

Once in the restaurant over *tempura*, bowls of noodles and copious glasses of beer the level of discussion shifted completely. Chiaki confronted me about a remark concerning the globalized phenomenon of eating bananas everywhere in the world although they only originate from a few tropical locations. She ate a banana every morning. What makes something globalized and why is that negative? If all globalized phenomena were negative we would oppose the Internet, I responded. But we don't because globalization of information has manifold benefits. Besides that the Internet is free. Economic globalization is completely different. It exploits and drains resources in one part of the world (usually poorer) for the benefit of other parts (usually richer). If the Internet was economically globalized it would only come with a fee.

Now Madoka, the other student, unburdened herself of what had become a contention with fellow environmentally oriented students. Recycling was overrated, she espoused. It is mostly meaningful in developed countries where there are large enough volumes of specific discarded materials such as glass or aluminum to warrant pickups and processing. But shouldn't that be the last resort because it required so much labor and consumed vast quantities of energy? Wouldn't it be better to reduce use or reuse materials beforehand, and build products that last longer rather than continually grind them up? Those are important aspects of consumer waste that should get more emphasis than recycling.

You're right and less developed countries have a natural culture of reuse for many objects such as glass bottles that are emptied of soda one day and seen the next as a container for gathered honey sold on the street, I responded. The isolation of recycling is also a problem. It has resulted in vast amounts of old newspapers in the US, for example, that don't yet have a use where they're collected and end up sold to places as far away as China carried by diesel-burning ships. Recycling should always include provision for local remanufacture of salvaged materials at least into objects for community use such as newspapers transformed into government office paper products, demolished building rubble reconstructed into park benches, or hundreds of other possibilities. Governments should be required to incubate businesses for these functions if they don't already exist.

Something extraordinary had happened at our table. Both students brought up specifics but they were actually avidly questioning the general process of logic in the areas of their concerns. A sub-theme about the purpose of education had hung over the day's classroom sessions and dogged us into the night. Here was the answer. Their questions were colored panels in the stream of an original point of light that was simply the practice of thinking for oneself. I whispered, "Yuichi, you've taught them to think. You must be proud." He shook his head, "Proud for them, not for me."

With time slowed down by the relaxed pleasure of seeing vivid evidence of his patient shepherding, I witnessed the next episode from an almost alpine vantage point. Chiaki began by contending my characterization in the seminar of corporate culture's obsession with the game of golf as environmentally destructive and imitatively uncreative. It was actually psychologically beneficial as a way of relaxing from stressful work conditions, and people enjoyed themselves enthusiastically playing golf. Leave them alone at it, she urged. Madoka agreed.

On our way to the restaurant I had asked about their parents' careers. Chiaki's father was a Mitsubishi corporate executive and Madoka's worked six days a week in a self-owned construction business. I was suspicious that we were in fact discussing their fathers' game and they felt a duty to defend family members, but I said nothing while Yuichi began to move the subject into the same logic-searching framework as before. Golf actually enforced corporate culture rather than providing an escape from it, he insisted. There was a high degree of company worker socializing involved, and a kind of unrealistic bubble surrounding their play that isolated them from the rest of the world. Strolling in pursuit of a ball on a heavily landscaped course is monotonous compared to a nature hike or hill climb, I suggested. The students previously stated an urgent need to remove obstacles that prevented businesses from becoming more sustainable, but didn't that mean urging more sustainable expressions of corporate culture as well? I came out with it. Their fathers played golf, didn't they? Not surprisingly they nodded yes.

Dinner was over by then but there was something else. Their parents disapproved of their interest in ecological sustainability and the overall open-mindedness they had begun to express. Even their hometown friends thought they were becoming abnormal. How could they feel better about this unforeseen situation? Something struck me just then about their predicament. Their parents probably would think Yuichi and I were odd as well. They would see us as hippy-like and narrow in interests. But actually we were quite different in our styles and approaches, not rubber-stamped imitations of each other, and our lives were culturally rich in philosophy, art, poetry, and community involvements that their parents probably knew nothing about. The young women would have to begin building up their own interests and goals for accomplishment as well. An independent life followed independent thinking. Outside we thanked each other for the evening with a level of sincerity more typical of musicians after playing a piece together.

FINDING THE FUTURE IN THE MUD

From Nagoya, Japan, where he was invited to give a series of presentations in 2005, Berg files a report that enunciates far-reaching ecological prophecies. By 2025, Berg forecasts, cities will be the norm for at least three-quarters of human habitation, but they will be completely transformed. Most food will be produced locally using former factories, warehouses, and office buildings; water will be reused several times; energy will be increasingly small scale and come from local renewable sources of natural flows; technology will be advanced and adaptive; and wild nature will flourish in the city. Berg concludes this far-reaching vision with a story about children playing in the mud at the Fujimae Wetland. Saved from becoming a garbage landfill, the mud flat becomes a place of discovery and natural wonder for children.

A small evening event in Eco Life Plaza located far away from Aichi Expo released a vision that guided the next week of presentations here. This is a brave earthly outpost in Sasashima Satellite of downtown Nagoya's sprawling De La Fantasia amusement park. The venue was a nearby club bearing a name that seems a stunningly perfect example of the strangeness English can have in Japan, Ding Dong Dang. Billed as a panel discussion on what we may unfold by 2025 and pitched toward the Star Festival occurring that week and its custom of writing wishes on pieces of paper that are pinned onto tree branches (audience members were asked to do this), there was a potential from the beginning to enunciate far-reaching ecological prophecies.

Twenty years into the future is a full generation and therefore capable of evolving vast social and cultural shifts, if modern history to this point is a guide. I chose to list some basic prognostications at the beginning, in spite of their potentially radical sound, and explain afterward why they seemed destined.

Cities will be the norm for at least three-quarters of human habitation but they will be completely transformed, I predicted. Approaches to satisfying basic human needs will change dramatically to fit a dominantly urban location. Most food will be produced in or immediately close to cities using former factories, warehouses, office buildings, and other industrial structures, as well as streets that have been half torn up to only run one way. Half of the water will be reused from stores that have themselves been reused several times before. Energy will be increasingly small scale and come from local renewable sources of natural flows that are only barely utilized at present: ocean waves, tides and currents; air thermals; perhaps even sound waves. Materials for construction and manufacturing will mainly come from reused and recycled materials (in a similar way as water). Finally, wild nature will flourish in the city where restoration of plant and animal species, ecosystems and habitats will be accepted as part of normal urbanite identity.

Why is it safe to anticipate these changes? Cities are becoming so large and numerous, and consequently covering so much land area, that they will represent the main factor for considering the entire planetary environment. Fossil fuel, the ignition source for industrial development, will become scarce to the point of luxury, with a liter of gasoline comparably priced to a liter of olive oil. A major result will be that human life will be more localized. Globalization has simultaneously unleashed its opposite of devolutionary decentralism as well. There will be more autonomous local governments and smaller if not fewer of the present nation states. The new governments will have natural boundaries encompassing watershed areas and bioregions in which cities will be managed as part of the particular natural geography. There will be more forms of culture, economy and even monetary currency, unique to each local area.

Some edges of these thoughts had arisen before but after that evening I felt sure of the whole vision. It isn't the false boosterist promise of Infinite Progress promoted by consumer and corporate interests, but it isn't the grim catastrophic forecast of Industrial Collapse either. There is no reason to believe that food, water, energy, and materials can't have a cultural and ethical basis that surpasses what we know from today's questionable mainstream lifestyle. (A visit to less developed places inevitably arouses admiration for the warmer relationships between people, artfulness of daily life, superlative food, and pleasures in general.) There isn't reason to believe that society will be any less advanced technologically either. The majority of today's most promising advancements use smaller levels of materials and more sophisticated methods. In short, a future based on the finite nature of the biosphere doesn't have to be finite in its creative possibilities.

A sense of this ecologically-based future came with a visit to the rescued Fujimae Wetland that stands as a symbol of Tokai Bioregion (the greater natural area surrounding Nagoya).

Slated in the 1980s to become a garbage landfill, it became the focus of citizen resistance to losing the last remnant of once-rich local marshes of Shonai River's estuary. Atsuo Tsugi, Director of Fujimae Ramsar Society, led Earthday Everyday's Naoto Anzai and Jennifer Kwong, and me out onto the low tide mud. We pulled off our shoes, rolled up our pant legs and followed a group of forty or so fourth-graders with their teachers and some volunteers who were already busy finding samples of tidal life.

They dug with both hands past the elbows to find clams, crabs and ghost shrimp. Shrieks of discovery mixed with shouts to come see what was found. I kept track of one possessed girl who at various times could be seen digging up fifty clams, then switched to gathering crabs, stood up to her knees waving arms in a game to wildly keep balance, spontaneously threw mud into the air, and protested about leaving when it was time to go. A boy couldn't stop digging holes with a shovel and was working his way far from the group when called to leave. They were all totally absorbed with gray mud squishing between toes, dirty hands, animals wiggling between fingers, walking stiffly and carefully.

Teachers showed pans full of animals that included oysters and barnacles from hooped frames placed to observe growth rates and patterns. The children were definitely more attentive than is usual in a classroom, adding their own comments and experiences to the demonstration that was more a history of their outing than an ordinary lesson. "I also feel like a child when I'm on the mudflat," Atsuo confessed.

What a startling contrast to the amusement park where Eco Life holds out its small lifesome corner. Black asphalt obliterates even the smallest amount of soil. Parents drag sulking children from ride to booth, chewing on paper-wrapped fast food and examining entrance prices. Pokémon World is the main draw. Colored lights flash on yellow and red plastic machines, uninteresting automatic music plays, electronic pings and bongs sound in the vacant air. Metal rails mark boundaries and orange cones guide traffic.

This isn't really a place for discovering but another controlled site for consumption and relating to commercial culture. Here parents who don't know what to do with their children can be satisfied that at least their expectations from advertising can be fulfilled, some money spent as proof of earnestness.

The mudflat is a true guide to the children's future. Saved from garbage, it saves their individuality while saving their place in a natural community. It saves their lives.

INSTRUCTIONS FROM MOUNTAINS AND AN ISLAND

After spending three weeks struggling with the daunting ecological realities of Tokyo and Nagoya, Berg in this 2005 dispatch visits Toyooka, a mountain village in the Nagano Prefecture, and Oshima Island, which has an active volcano that erupted in 1986. The people of these small, out-of-the-way places take on the big question of what kind of life can and should be lived considering technological and environmental changes occurring to our species and the planet in general. Berg finds the creativity of the people inspiring and an ecological future for these places entirely feasible.

The mountains of Nagano Prefecture are a significant part of Honshu Island's spine and the headwaters of major rivers running to both the Japan Sea and Pacific Ocean sides. They have been both a source and refuge for Japanese culture throughout its history, holding an aura of oldness and authenticity that give the rocky streams and steep forests a kind of authority as well as serenity. This is where mist rises from the shadows of valleys at dawn and interrupts the certainty of brightening peaks with foggy illusion.

Boundlessly creative Hitoshi Yoshida resonates with the source quality of this place. He has switchbacked through several communities in Nagano since leaving Tokyo's paved-over ground around a decade ago. His nose has now led to Toyooka Village in the southern mountain region and an opportunity provided by the local government to transform the small closed university into a new learning center for an ecologically centered way of life. I'm there with a group of people he chose for their ability to light up different parts of this underground cave of possibilities. Ranging from activists to small business operators, we address the problems and solutions of ecological and economic sustainability for mountain communities like Toyooka Village that have been losing population to the big cities and whose economies are shrinking with the advent of globalization. But there is much more at stake here. It is what kind of life can and should be lived considering the technological and environmental changes occurring to our species and the planet in general. Yoshida is taking on the big question from a place small enough to yield practical results. His group of only four students enrolled so far is joined by a wonderful array of local supporters including the village's supremely competent mayor, a high school teacher and his class of only six third year students, local businessmen, visitors from other parts of the mountains, and some mothers with children. Our several days long seminar was nothing if not real.

Talks and discussions were about relating to nature, making the energy and cultural infrastructure of communities more ecological, home soy sauce making, canning delicious native *k-ichigo* (tree berry), and using cooking *saki* as a food. We broke off to visit an abandoned small village that once held seventy families, gather and eat wild mountain *walabi* (ferns), view surly native boars raised in pens, observe snake catching techniques for the essential ingredient in medicinal *mamushi saki* taken for numerous complaints, and stop unexpectedly at Abu (poison bee) River with a blue pool beside a naturally square granite boulder to hear its story of a farmer who regularly saw two naked mountain girls bathe there but regrettably told local villagers who created a crowd that scared them away.

At one point I reflect dreamily how the seemingly passive forest actually pulses relentlessly with land shaking in tectonic grunts, dirt and rocks falling down, trees billowing gases, water running and sucked up plant stems, worms dissolving earth and passing it through their tube bodies as soil, insects devouring wastes and each other, pollen blowing, flowers opening and closing, ferns uncoiling, fish sucking slime off stream rocks, birds nibbling omnivorously and defecating everywhere, boars plowing up the ground, deer mowing leaves of everything they can reach.

The gathering was a nowever event. Something changeless can lead us through changes.

Oshima Island by way of Tokyo Bay is the final stop on this visit. Atsuo Shiga is a cultural adventurer who sees vast possibilities for healing large city populations on the still half-sustainable island where an intermittently active volcano last spewed lava in 1986. He leads what he calls "a shrine tour" completely around the 50 or so kilometer diameter shoreline that includes a magically preserved 15th century worship site as well as camellia forests, sharp-edged lava cliffs and black sand beaches, visually striking *ajisai* (hydrangea) flowers with multiple blue pistil centers offset by long stemmed four-petal white flowers (they uncannily resemble a pop hairstyle here that has balls shaking on wires away from the head), two mating *tobi* (ospreys) glide above and two more fly up and over us from the roadtop. "It is a sign that we're doing the right thing," Atsuo says.

An insight about comparative ecologies occurs to me because of the quick shift between Nagano and Oshima (and possibly the presence of Atsuo's frenetically inventive mind). The island has four times as many natural features. The volcano at the center, the ocean beyond, and between them the coastline, along with the forested slopes that are similar to Nagano's single feature. I imagine the coastline redone in a painting as a single line with an accompanying stripe for the ocean and mountainsides and the volcano at the center radiating out above them all. A new image for Oshima as a sustainable place, dedicatedly restoring forests, and formerly abundant coast and ocean life. Sea water pollution could be reduced immensely through a zero waste policy, farms could provide all of the vegetables consumed, and alternative energy sources especially wind could supply all the needs currently fed by fossil fuels. Fish are a staple and sea vegetable harvesting already employs dozens of local inhabitants. Visitors who are presently a hundred times as numerous as residents over a year would be invited to participate in those eco-activities along with hiking, volcano watching, swimming, beaching, and diving.

I spent three weeks struggling with the daunting ecological facts of massive Tokyo and Nagoya. Toyooka Village and Oshima Island are doable and inspiring.

PART 4

Ecological restoration in Ecuador

CONSERVATION, PRESERVATION AND RESTORATION IN ECUADOR

This essay, originally published in Earth Island Journal *in 2001, takes readers to Bahía de Caráquez, a city of forty thousand that suffered devastating natural disasters in 1998, from El Niño mudslides to an earthquake. Berg recounts how he became involved in efforts to repair damage, while setting up an office/apartment for Planet Drum Foundation in Bahía in 2000. One night shortly after his arrival, unnumbered hordes of whirring crickets flew into the unscreened apartment and weighed down the netting that covered Berg's bed, the persistent insects crawling just above his eyes and mouth and pressing down upon his body, an unforgettable initiation into the tropics. Work by Berg and Bahía residents gets under way quickly, continuing restoration of mangroves, replanting the mud banks with indigenous plants, and forming Ecology Clubs for the area's youth, soon to become the next generation of* bioregionalistas.

ECUADOR—Bahía de Caráquez is a small city but its regional importance magnifies its size. It is the municipal center of an entire *canton* (large county) that holds several urban *parochias* (suburban towns). It is the terminus of a four-lane highway, a port for the ferry and water taxis across Rio Chone Bay, a center for manufacturing and shops, a haven for professionals, and a destination for thousands of both Ecuadorian and gringo vacationers.

During the fierce winter storms of 1998, several hills towering over Bahía nearly completely slid away. Surging mud quickly flattened a low wall of fieldstones, over-ran the narrow storm drains and swept away houses on its way to fill in the shore of the bay. More than a dozen people were killed in the mudslide that devastated the barrio of Maria Auxiliadora.

Approaching on a road that was deep in flowing mud during El Niño rains of 1998, there is no break in the slender strip of houses beside the bay that constitutes most of this city of about 40,000 people. The hillside becomes more perpendicular until it rises 75 feet-high at an average angle of 45 degrees. The face of the slope is gullied to various depths, with the severest cuts carved five-feet deep. The soil is light orange clay and more prominently visible than the sparse shrubs and small trees on top of it. What is remarkable is that much plant life exists here at all.

Last September, city engineer Ivan Aguirre drove me through Astillero barrio and Leonidas Plaza to make an initial survey of land slippage from El Niño rains and the earthquake. At Sixto Duran Bellan Boulevard, we took a right and followed a dirt road to the top of a hill. Ivan got out and gestured for me to join him.

The ground at our feet was step-like from land subsidence. Suddenly the ground ended at the lip of a cliff that fell away more than 125 meters below us. It was a genuinely astonishing moment. We were humbled by the magnitude of fallen earth that started its slide two years ago from the point where we were standing. "Did you hear it?" I asked Ivan.

"Oh, at first it was so loud!" He put his hands over his ears and made a hoarse creaking sound. "Then it went 'shwoo-schwoo-schwoo' for a long time." His hands made repeated pressing-down movements in front of him. I could feel what he was describing in my stomach as though I was on a roller coaster.

Night of the living bugs

I had originally come to Ecuador in February 1999 to attend an International Eco-Gathering and help local *ecologistas* repair damage from extreme El Niño storms and an earthquake. On January 29, 2000, I returned to Astillero to set up Planet Drum's new office/apartment in Leonidas Plaza and participate in a reforestation project that partnered the US-based Planet Drum Foundation with the local Eco-Bahía Learning Center for the Environment.

When I left the considerable comfort of the Casa Grande guest-house and moved into the field office, I discovered that, despite a succession of promises, six window spaces still weren't covered by screens. I had no idea of the adventure that lay in store.

When the rainy season begins in Ecuador, a powerful biological message resounds throughout the insect world. It may be a burst of sexual energy, it may relate to their homes being flooded in ground burrows, but crickets (called "grillos") become visible in numbers that are beyond calculation.

It was the night after the rains began. As I went to bed at 10 o'clock, a patter of light thudding spread from outside the windows to the walls and floors of my room. I had brought tent-shaped insect netting on the previous trip. Feeling like a gringo hypocrite and hypochondriac, I brought it to the new place thinking that mosquitoes might be a special problem because of the open windows. I have seldom been as grateful for such a relatively small item.

The insects seemed to be giant flying cockroaches and the first few gave me the familiar high-tension apprehension that those insects can cause. I grabbed the netting and draped it over the bed. Now hundreds began hitting the windows with flat-sounding bangs that I thought would break the existing glass. Whirring crickets flew into the room and hit the walls and netting. They crawled just above my eyes and mouth. My knees went up automatically, to create a kind of ceiling of netting above my body while I waited for the invasion to subside. But it didn't.

So many crickets accumulated that they began to weigh down the net above me. I shrugged and punched to dislodge them, which succeeded to a degree but may also have been the reason that a few got underneath and began jumping with rapidly oscillating wings across my face. It was difficult to make the decision to lift the netting and slap away those intruders. I took the chance in a quick, confused, whirling dance, ignoring as much as I could the crunch of squashed crickets underfoot. I brushed away those that crawled up my legs with frantic downward karate-style chops.

Back in bed, I tucked the netting around my body and hoped that the level of cricket numbers wouldn't increase and that no other insects would appear. I was wrong on both accounts. Cricket bodies hitting the walls and floor began to sound like radio static and mosquitoes began biting through the netting stretched against my knees that acted as short tent poles. If I slept at all that night, it was flat on my back with gnawed knees in the air.

I got up at dawn to the barking of dogs and crowing of roosters. The crickets weren't flying anymore. I brushed some off of my clothes and dressed inside the netting. A dozen fell out of my boots.

Chino (a boatman who saved several people swept into the bay during the mudslides by pulling them out hair-first) helped me hang the netting properly by string and nails above my bed. There's still no desk, chairs, or dresser, but it's the tropics, and pluses quickly outweigh the minuses.

A view from the hill

There's a barrel of rainwater on the roof-patio (a typical Ecuadorian amenity even in low-income houses). The view on one side looks toward the Bird Islands in the bay. On the other, a perfectly conical mountain—intact, without any sign of slides and covered with seemingly untouched native vegetation.

I boarded a shared taxi to Bahía and found Patricio Tamariz, who was escorting a Guayaquil TV crew. The reporter asked to film an interview at La Cruz, at the foot of the now-slanted cross that stands atop Bahía's highest hill. Slides of rain-soaked soil left a precipitous drop at the base of the cross and the earthquake had fissured the hilltop. The next earthquake or El Niño will surely carry away half of what remains.

The reporter asked what sparked the eco-city idea. I related the need to reconstruct the storm-damaged city and how making it more ecologically sustainable became the theme. "It's the first bioregional eco-city," I added, pointing down at sites that featured continuing restoration of mangroves in the river and replanting indigenous plants on land buried by the mudslide.

"How long will it take for the eco-city to be realized," he asked. "It isn't like flipping on a light switch," I replied. The Ecology Clubs of 100 eight- to twelve-year-olds came to mind. "In five years, they will be teenagers with the background and potential for completing the transition. That's when you'll see the true eco-city bloom."

Tomorrow we start the revegetation project in the Maria Auxiliadora barrio. Eduardo, Nicola, Marcelo, and I had an enthusiastic meeting about how many of which species to grow. Today I went to the main market to buy large used feed-bags at about four cents each for hauling sawdust mulch.

This is what I mean about pluses. The landlord maintains a sawmill on one side of the building where the cricket episode took place and there's a second mill on the other side. The whine of sawblades is banshee-like for five seconds every few minutes all day long, but we'll have all of the free acidic mulch we'll need to hold in water and neutralize the alkaline clay for young seedlings.

Restoration begins

The "re-wilding" of Maria Auxiliadora began with a haphazard slowness that strummed my nerves. Marcelo wasn't where he said he would be at 2 PM to help me load 150 *algarrobo* plants that Flor-Maria Duenas donated from her accumulation of about 1,000 seedlings. Patricio was supposed to be there with a truck, and wasn't. We were losing daylight for planting and the situation concerning volunteers from the barrio was uncertain. I had bought sodas and cookies for 50 workers and brought them by triciclo to load into the non-existent truck.

Suddenly the impasse began to blow open like a dam that can't hold back an overfilled reservoir. Marcelo arrived and we loaded up. We drove to Maria Auxiliadora not knowing what reception was waiting.

We arrived to find a few of Marcelo's friends and Luis Duenas, a partner of Eduardo Rodriguez in Eco-Bahía Centro's reforestation committee. Marcelo had spent the morning chopping close to 500 *hobo* and *muyullo* lengths to stick into the ground as plantings. We unloaded quickly.

A steeply pitched break from a ridgetop would be the starting point. A triciclo arrived to haul seedlings and cuttings to that point and then men from the barrio appeared to help. Flor-Maria had spread word that wages would be paid and we eventually had 20 or so helpers. She also joined us, leading about ten small children.

The work now became a serious project with Marcelo and Luis working in different areas, planting trees at a distance of three to four meters. Marcelo directed a mixed pattern of planting for *hobo*, *muyullo* and *algarrobo*, while Luis ingeniously guided their placement along *contoursos* (contours) to create the effect of terracing when the trees were larger. All the work was done without mechanically disturbing the soil, which we all agree, goes against our best bioregional interests.

Workers jimmied posthole diggers into the ground of hillsides that were angled at 45 degrees. In the three hours we had remaining before sunset, they set 200 *hobo* sticks in the soil, some in front of twisted and broken house walls. One hundred and fifty *muyullos* were planted in alternating spots, and 150 *algarrobos* were placed between them.

Muyullo and *algarrobo* are native trees. Their roots grow deep to help hold the clay. When the clay soil absorbs rainwater, it becomes super-saturated and can break away under the pressure of the increased weight.

Residents, mostly children, joined in chopping *muyullo* branches and pounding them into the ground, digging holes for foot-high *algarrobo* seedlings, adding some grass and other plants found nearby, and spreading wet sawdust at the bases for mulch.

While we were hard at planting, Flor-Maria had begun organizing a new Ecology Club that grew to about 30 children. We served them sodas and cookies. She continued teaching, perched on a sack of sawdust. Her earlier tiredness had been completely reversed. She decided to stay for their benefit and it totally revived her.

The project began more successfully than I could have imagined. The day's job covered five to six acres. The replantings were about three-feet high and bright green six months later. Enough thrived to give the impression that after one or two normal rainy seasons, this small section of hillside will have a fairly dense cover of plants and a better chance to withstand the next El Niño. And it can provide a foundational habitat for restoring whole indigenous ecosystems.

I asked the group of local workers whether the barrio would respect our labors and leave the revegetation area intact, and they stated that they would. We are actually creating a complete covering of indigenous plants that can hold the soil and provide a wild corridor through the city.

"Revegetation" not "reforestation"

Here are some of the factors that make this work on only a few hectares of earth so significant. To start with, it consists of either denuded small cliffs or piled-up mounds of mainly sub-surface clay soil remaining from nearly the worst kind of mudslides. Whatever works here can probably work anywhere. The land that can be restored with our revegetation method may encompass as much as one-third of Ecuador's entire coastal region.

All of the plants used in the project are natives of the indigenous dry neotropical forest. *Paja macho* grass is one of the primary plants, *algarrobo* and *muyullo* bushes are from the second stage and *guayacan*, *hobo* and *Ferdnan Sanchez* trees are found in the climax forest.

Plants from each stage play a different role in erosion reduction. The forest that results from the mixture as soon as five years from now (along with native volunteers such as the vigorous *frutillo* trees that already dot the project site) will be a rich habitat for native birds and other animals.

Why do we insist on calling it "revegetation" instead of "reforestation"? The reasoning behind this seemingly regressive choice of terms is that Ecuador's natural indigenous dry-neotropical forest is a wondrously diverse phenomenon.

These complex ecosystems can shift with near abruptness from tall trees on the wet side of a hill to thorny brush only a few feet across a knife-edged ridge on the dry side. The forest floor can range from bare dust to spongy humus within a couple of steps. Tree species may be stunted in one spot and overly large in another.

Fern-like plants, requiring relatively high levels of moisture, grow close enough to be seen in the same glance as pole-shaped cacti (creating an unnerving visual effect of mixed-up biomes).

There are slender vines with thorns growing on the sides that resemble spear points and are wider than the diameter of the plant. Elegant white tree snails the size of cockles climb along stems and branches everywhere. Lines of leaf-cutter ants, each bearing similar sized green pieces that are larger than themselves, march along like members of a flag-carrying precision musical band.

Any attempt to duplicate what can be found in a few hectares of native forest would have to be enormously painstaking and most likely prohibitively expensive—if it could truly be accomplished at all. If one can't actually recreate this remarkable forest, why puff up the endeavor with the high-sounding term "reforestation"?

Planet Drum's project is more sensitive to native features than most planting efforts. If these methods were followed in all of the applicable eroded places, they could eventually help regenerate a significant part of the indigenous coastal forest.

HOW TO BIOSPHERE

Why would a San Francisco bioregionalist set up a field office in Ecuador and become involved in an ecological restoration effort so far from home? In this 2001 dispatch from Bahía de Caráquez Berg explains that because Bahía formally committed itself to become an eco-city, it can show the way toward creating model ecological urban areas. Rather than seek heavy industrialization, Bahía could help to establish "a valuable path toward planethood," pioneering sustainability through green cities, enlightened agriculture, and restoration along with preservation of natural areas. Berg envisions that future economic benefits for Bahía will come not so much from exploiting resources but by generating information about them through education facilities and visitor sites. This piece reveals what is at stake for Peter Berg in extending Planet Drum's purview to the equator.

Coastal Ecuador seems to breed imaginative future scenarios. It could be the sheer biological richness of the country, mixed with hard-pressed economic necessity, but something definitely inspires a sense of starting over in new and different ways. People aren't generally inhibited about having large visions.

One Bahía friend enunciates new ideas as a constant aspect of our conversations. Here's one that flashed out while I was describing how the houses ruined by mudslides were incorporated into the design of paths for the revegetation park in María Auxiliadora barrio. "Why don't we have a museum there with displays about El Niño and the earthquake in 1998," he said. "There are plenty of photos for an entire panorama. And not just the damage. All of the weather conditions that produced the rains, and the geology underlying the earthquake. With descriptions of dry tropical forest plants and animals that people could see right outside. A big map with bioregional features of all kinds: Rio Chone, Niño and Humboldt ocean currents meeting offshore, rainy and dry seasons, soil types. You know those circular depressions that are the remains of water catch basins from the ancient times? Well, they're being viewed from space by archeologists and other scientists who are trying to find patterns for water availability. We could follow all kinds of satellite information like that." "Why not?" I said.

I was talking to someone else who owns a *reserva* (natural preserve) about the differences in accessibility for visitors to public land versus private land. "My land will be public," he declared with earnest certainty. When I replied with a confused look, he described a future corridor made up of wild and reforested parcels that would be joined together as a chain of dry forest along most of the coast. It would be an enormous preserve given something like park status and assigned interpretive centers and guides every so often. As far as I know, this is a personal dream that only people he has spoken with share. Now I share it as well.

Both of those visions have a common root in a distinctly Ecuadorian sensibility. I don't think they are mere fantasies but achievable in the 21st century the way dreams of mass-produced automobiles were in the 20th. This place doesn't have to follow the same course of development as elsewhere.

It's time to start thinking like parts of a whole. The unified biosphere of our planet is a fact, and we should be acting accordingly. Each of us may live in just one place, or a few places at most, but it is obvious that we absolutely depend on the whole for basics of life like air and rainfall. Less noticeable but hugely important are the world-wide physical systems that support us such as ocean currents with their role in nurturing sea life, or the earth-girdling zones of life from the polar caps to the equator that temper major aspects of how we eat, build, dress, and countless other adaptations.

Of all the shared interactions with planet-wide phenomena, the most compelling and mysterious are relations with other living things. We are involved with plants and animals at every moment, from bacteria in our stomachs to the food that fills them. It may often seem that living entities relate most strongly to conditions found in their immediate area, but exchanges with distant species and forces are also essential. Bird migrations from Africa to Europe and the Arctic to the Amazon point out those faraway links. Food chains joining krill to shrimp to fish to bears and humans extend across oceans and far up river estuaries to mountain streams. All biological activity is open-ended in this way to some degree. We don't know all of the ways and certainly can't see them, but everything alive is interdependent with everything else.

So, how to biosphere? It's not just something between all of the people on earth, difficult as that is. How do we consciously involve ourselves with the interrelatedness of all life? These aren't useless questions. In a relatively short time our species has increased in numbers and impact to the point that we can cause serious alterations of the biosphere such as global climate change. We need to know how to share the earth so that we don't destroy the foundation of our species in other life forms and natural systems.

Coastal Ecuador could help establish a valuable path toward planethood. Rather than seek heavy industrialization, it could pioneer sustainability through green cities, enlightened agriculture, and restoration along with preservation of natural areas.

This area is particularly suited for a foundational biospheric role. Features that are intentionally built into a greenhouse in other places are found naturally. A daily mid-heaven arc of the sun that doesn't vary for more than a few degrees all year. Abundant water during the rainy season. High humidity. No frost; sixty degrees Fahrenheit would be considered extremely cold. Storms are generally mild.

Wild fruits such as *hobo* and *pechiche* abound and are consumed by nearly everyone to some degree. Papayas, plantain, limes, and many other staples require no more attention than occasional water. There is an astounding range of other crops that need a little more care, ranging from potatoes to rice and cabbages to passion fruit.

It is a primarily agricultural society now, and this is a desirable and practical direction for the future. The greatest ecological benefits would be realized through a large-scale shift toward organic food production that is sustainable in terms of soil and water. As world food standards move away from pesticides and artificial fertilizer, this would also be the most profitable route.

Another major direction is in restoring and maintaining unique biodiversity. The coast is mainly in a part-wild condition although there are still intact wilderness places. For these singular species to survive, they require reforestation, re-introduction of both plants and animals, and greatly increased protection of habitats including the shore and ocean. Future economic benefits will come not so much in exploitation of resources but in generating information about them. Natural sciences research centers in every bioregion, of course, but also a multitude of unique education facilities, and visitor sites expanded to include working restoration projects.

Cities still have manageable populations in terms of sustainability. Bahía de Caráquez (like Cotacachi in the mountains) can show the way toward making model ecological urban areas.

With the whole biosphere critically requiring a respite from devastation, coastal Eco-Ecuador will benefit everyone.

LAGALOU: TO GET THINGS DONE WITH FEELING

Having done ecology work in Ecuador for six years, Berg steps back in this 2006 essay to reflect on significant differences between countries of the northern temperate zone and less industrially developed places nearer the equator. In Ecuador Berg notes two active economic systems, one based on money, the other on the nonmonetary lending and borrowing of goods and services among kinship and friendship networks. Berg invents the term "lagalou" to describe this nonmonetary society that is able to manage without the industrial-style infrastructures of the North, structures that, while efficient, are impersonal and create isolation. In contrast, societies with lagalou are highly social, and the exchanges that sustain life—picture a bustling marketplace, a crowded public bus, a boisterous family gathering— are pervaded with feeling, "the music that moves bodies in a dance that gets things done." Berg wonders how the North might relearn lagalou, speculating that the post-peak oil future may accelerate beneficial changes of this sort much faster than we can presently imagine.

Inhabitants of the Northern Temperate Zone who return from visits to places nearer the Equator are often more relaxed and open to people and events around them. Passengers on airplanes and boats tend to laugh and use their hands more. They aren't as likely to react as though they've been personally invaded if someone bumps into them. Even more tolerant of crying babies. It's not just a vacation syndrome since this expansive attitude illuminates business as well as tourist trippers whether from North America, Europe, Russia, China or Japan.

The cliché is that more southerly based people are "warmer" but that's a superficial explanation. It's not just the warmer climate either. A deeper emotional level must be involved because many visitors actually suffer some degree of reverse culture shock when they return. They can be chilled and constricted by the society they find at home. It requires a certain amount of adaptation to re-enter. Some even feel a powerful antipathy amounting to actual revulsion and dis-identification. They no longer wish to be associated with the mainstream culture that originally nurtured them.

Travelers to Mediterranean countries can come back with some degree of at least temporary transformation, but those who go to less industrially developed places in South America, Africa, Southeast Asia, or elsewhere are liable to be especially affected. What is the basis for this condition that can threaten previously held values to the point of wanting to discard them? Does it have significance for societies in general?

Keeping to just the sentimental level of how "welcoming" or "generous" more southerly people seem to be won't provide the answers. A more challenging starting place would be to look at situations that seem to be uncomfortably different.

For six years I have done ecology work in Ecuador that involves a lot of moving around from place to place. It's made me acutely aware of the strong physical contrast in roads. Riding in a vehicle there inevitably involves sensing the road surface along the way. Potholes or missing sections, bad repairs with dissimilar materials, cracks, bumps, mud, gravel, dust, rocks . . . are continually communicated up from the wheels. Holding on to something or several different parts of a vehicle simultaneously to avoid smashing into the roof or dashboard is more often than not an essential part of the ride. Bouncing around on the seat causes the scenery of bright green tropical forest or fields of evenly planted banana trees and tall groves of leaning bamboo to jump as though filmed through a handheld camera while running. Worn springs cause body jolting that is greater than a traveler from outside may have ever experienced. A bone-rattling trip in a near terminal condition vintage Land Rover from Quito to a fantastic remote cloud forest reserva-with leafy room-like spaces holding pink and purple orchids and multitudes of air plants was also unforgettable as a series of crescendoing mountain road impacts.

Smooth asphalt that is taken for granted in most of the U.S. presents an opposite experience, really a non-experience. Drivers steer with one hand holding a cup of hot coffee or a cell phone, even writing in a note pad, with little regard for the tame surface beneath them. A sensation of the actual road is an unusual and intrusive event. Roadness simply isn't felt. The street outside my house in San Francisco was torn up and repaved repeatedly in a frenzy of maintenance over the last year by invading armies of yellow clanging metal-treaded machines and blank-range firing jackhammers. Each separate addition of water mains or gas lines or new curbs required tearing up and then carefully restoring pristinely smooth pavement.

This very non-feel of what's under the wheels that begins for me upon riding to my house from the San Francisco airport has become through absence of sensation an immediate reminder of huge differences in other expectations. It represents a gaping disparity in services that also exists with electricity, water, telephones, street lights, Internet, supplies on store shelves, deliveries . . . a list that can easily become much longer. In most places in Ecuador they are liable to be frequently interrupted for fairly long periods.

"Infrastructure" is the common term for the collection of amenities that makes things function easily. It's a strictly functional word that over-simplifies what is actually involved. Those enabling functions such as electricity, piped water and roads represent a significant part of the labor and expense of living in societies that maintain them. A great percentage of the human work performed and money paid goes for them, much greater than their users realize. Vast amounts of salaries, taxes, tolls, fees, and other charges need to continually pour out like new asphalt. At least a quarter and often more of an average person's salary—a minimum of one week of a month's work—pays the bills involved.

To command such enormous outlays of labor and cash there has to be a strong social agreement about the intention to continue using infrastructures and a need for them to be constantly operational. People must believe that there are many things that simply cannot be done without them. This is the underlying factor in panic about "peak oil" that views the future without petroleum as catastrophic. Infrastructures are not just functional entities to make a car trip smoother or start a stove burner or access a website (all heavily dependent on fossil fuel products). They actually represent powerful foundational social beliefs, intentions and priorities.

In Ecuador the playing out of social beliefs, intentions and priorities has a different emphasis. Some of the principal considerations are also startlingly different. Things get done but the society is able to manage without industrial style infrastructures. For lack of an existing term to describe this I offer "lagalou." Think of music that helps to move muscles in a complex dance. Ecuadorian society moves along on lagalou.

Families of relatives are extremely important to Ecuadorians. They may be more important than anything else. One's family is large and can number at least hundreds of members. Seeing the same eyes or nose or mouth shape shared by dozens of people can be disconcerting. It is true that there are generally more children per household making more sisters and brothers, but that isn't the main reason for the vastly larger size. It is who is included. All grandparents and great-grandparents have high positions of course, but their siblings and more distant relations are also counted. First uncles and aunts are usually as close as mothers and fathers, and all of the members of the families of their mates are added in. Cousins of any degree may be as close as brothers and sisters. All of the relatives from both the mother and father's sides are part of the total. It isn't unusual for someone to catch a name in a conversation and interject, "Did you say Velez? Is that the family of Carlos Velez? We're related. His uncle is married to my grandmother's cousin."

Families have ultimate lagalou in Ecuador. An extensive family not only provides a large share of one's comfort and stability, companions and entertainment, assistance and opportunities, it also gives many otherwise for-pay services. It can feed you and lend money. It gives you a place to stay and for that reason may also determine where you travel. If something is needed either to borrow or purchase it commonly first involves searching among members of the family. It finds mates, jobs, connections, government positions, and practically anything else. The family has continuing and over-arching presence. Workers often miss days on a job to help out when family members become sick. When I told someone that I, as many people in the U.S., only had a few close relatives it was taken as though a plague must have destroyed the rest. I received a genuinely pitying look and was told, "I feel sorry for you." A memorable symbol of how deep the blood of family relations runs came after a woman graduated from a university and at a party in her honor was presented with a framed "diploma" stating her family as the awarding institution. The family wasn't going to be left out of her matriculation. She keeps it on the wall alongside the official document.

In comparison, life in industrially developed countries is much more self-contained. People think of themselves as primarily private individuals and anxiously guard their personal spaces and lives. Consequently they are completely dependent on supporting services, and often pay exorbitantly for necessities that are commonly given free of charge in a society with lagalou.

This isn't a description of a romantic tropical paradise, and Ecuadorians aren't uncritical of the conditions in their country. It only has thirteen million people but migration to Spain alone has been close to half a million in the last ten or so years and continues at a high rate. The standard of living ranks in about the middle for all nations on the planet and the reality of that statistic means that money is in painfully short supply. (An example of the literal truth of this is when small stores and restaurants often send someone to another commercial establishment to make change for a customer's paper note used to pay the bill.) People don't enjoy losing electric power, water cut-offs, road closures, missing deliveries, short store supplies, bad roads, or other breakdowns.

When interruptions occur, however, there is less complaining and things continue with surprising ease. Few commercial establishments are so dependent on infrastructures that they have to close down. Lagalou takes over. Pre-modern cultural practices survive just beneath the surface and they re-emerge quickly with little anxiety. Candles shine from windows in all of the nearby houses when electricity is cut off. If water stops coming out of the pipes an elaborate alternative system takes over. Most homes and businesses have large portable water containers on hand that can be filled at wells. There are cisterns built into the basements of many houses that can be recharged by water trucks. Buckets appear beside sinks and in bathrooms to transport water for washing dishes and flushing toilets. Conservation measures such as soaping up with the faucet off and watering plants with leftover rinse water automatically come into play.

Another main source of lagalou is the fact that there are two active economic systems. Money is the basis for only one of them. The other is non-monetary, a kind of lending and borrowing of goods and services. Family membership may be involved but usually many circles of friends are included as well. Typically it works like this. Most city people know or are related to someone in the countryside. When there is a shortage of money those country connections are visited to augment supplies of food. City people commonly take buses to travel to the country and perhaps help out on a farm, returning with various amounts of produce that can include live chickens, meat, eggs, cheese, vegetables, fruit, and so forth.

When country people come to the city to sell their produce or buy equipment they can stay with friends or relatives. Some member or other of the households involved may make trips as often as every week. The whole complex exchange can be accomplished without using any money except for remarkably low bus fares. People in the countryside have local arrangements among themselves for trading equipment, labor and supplies by helping with harvests, borrowing pack animals and machinery, joining construction projects, and many others. In a similar way city people may trade health care for house repairs, and so forth.

In industrially developed countries where people lead more isolated lives, the exchange of money is required for almost all economic functions. When things are desired that are beyond a person's means they are acquired through credit, and when money is low it is owed or borrowed.

Lagalou is more than just getting things done. Everything that lagalou does is done with feeling. Let's return to the less than comfortable example of experiencing the road surface. There's more to be felt than just jolts and shakes by the rows of passengers holding babies, sacks of fruit, live chickens, bottles of honey, and mysterious cartons tied with rope. Buses and trucks are much more prevalent than in more developed places where private automobiles outnumber other forms of transportation. Buses are extremely cheap, and convivial. On-board Latin dance music is usually playing. Fellow passengers are helpful with directions. Private vehicles (both cars and trucks) usually transport more than one person unlike the pattern in more developed countries. Because the passengers are relatives, friends, or grateful strangers there is amiable conversation during the ride. Self-expression is inevitable. Hands wave as voices rise and laughter erupts. Revelations take place. Valuable information is exchanged, and business takes place. A ride is seldom just accomplishing travel to a destination. Because the trip has lagalou you feel the other passengers along with the road.

Lagalou also operates in the most common forms of trade. Marketplaces are hugely interactive and feature unusual products and services (haircuts and shoes along with vegetables). More foods are raw rather than processed and their quality is evident to the eye and nose. Fresh produce and fish comes from open stalls rather than coolers with week-old goods. There are different prices for the same item from one stall to the other, haggling thrives, and deals are made. Even individual shops away from the main markets usually have some of these same characteristics, and vendors pedal carts full of vegetables, strings of crabs, baked goods, toiletries, and other necessities through neighborhood streets.

The difference between lagalou and purely functional infrastructures is inestimable. Infrastructures are efficient but alienating and inner-directed, like the sound of a recorded voice instead of a real person. Lagalou is assimilating and outer-directed, always involving other people and their lives.

It seems obvious that it is desirable to have the kind of advantages that families and alternative economies possess, and not abandon them for the imagined benefits of more efficient but impersonal enabling and facilitating services. But is this realistic? Northern Temperate Zoners usually imagine that Equator dwellers would readily imitate their model if they could and that only economic disadvantages keep them in lagalou.

That's an opinion that may be based more on what has been lost in industrialized societies than what is still cherished in those that function with lagalou. Families have shrunk to a minor role. Money and credit are essential. Trade is strictly cash and carry. A re-creation of extended familial relationships in another form would be needed to restore lagalou, and exchanges of goods and services would need a different foundation. There is a hint of this in "tribes" of friends that support each other. Mutual childcare groups, living cooperatives and eco-villages also come to mind. Joining barter clubs, using local currencies, and patronizing worker-owned collectives or consumer supported farms can substitute for some cash-only transactions. A greater devotion to restoring natural ecosystems and other features in places close by to where people live is an undoubtedly helpful practice for overall sustainability. Increasingly expensive energy supplies in fossil fuel dependent societies may accelerate these and other beneficial changes much faster than can be presently imagined. The most important element is feeling and for that there are only rare examples at this point in what must be seen as the over-industrialized Northern Temperate Zone. For exposure to true lagalou one has to go closer to the Equator where it is still the music that moves bodies in a dance that gets things done.

THE CORE OF ECO-TOURISM

Berg opens this 2006 dispatch from Ecuador with a paradox: "How can there be 'world' identity and preservation of diverse cultures at the same time?" He muses on the profitable business of eco-tourism in a world being rapidly transformed by globalization. The eco-tourist's visit inevitably becomes part of the force for the disappearance of authentic, place-located cultures and intact ecosystems, the very thing that the eco-seeker came to see. Berg argues that there is only one alternative that would benefit natural places and that is for visitors to volunteer and join in the recovery of places that have been damaged or threatened, be they forests or tide pools, deserts or coral reefs.

There is an intriguing cultural paradox mixed in with the conflicted assortment of values and human experience that have evolved from contemporary globalism. How can there be "world" identity and preservation of diverse cultures at the same time? Eating fusion-nationality food, working as an importer of flowers from Ecuador, discussing Saudi Arabian Islamism, wearing running shoes made in China and a shirt from Indonesia, using a Taiwanese cell phone, and driving a Japanese car assembled in Tennessee.

There is still an actual Viet Nam, Ecuador, Saudi Arabia, China, Indonesia, Taiwan, Japan, and Tennessee. They have distinct ongoing languages and cultures. The megapolitan Los Angeleno, New Yorker, Londoner, Berliner, and Tokyo resident speaks at least one language but it is increasingly polyglot and transitory. The culture of globalism is synthetic and indefinite, based more on the process of change than on solid content.

World culture mixers aren't just in major cities. From work-seeking immigrants to "world music" enthusiasts, electronics shoppers to television news viewers, the feel of global participation is spreading everywhere. Émigré communities are found in small towns now, and new artistic undergrounds occur overnight in abandoned villages and remote islands. It isn't a trend but a thoroughly transforming wave.

The world is subordinating the place. Technology is replacing geography. Authentic place-located cultures are disappearing or changing. This means that any destination where a visitor goes is in rapid transition. What is the central issue of eco-tourism given this accelerated transformation?

The ecologically minded visitor, guest or whatever euphemism suits the tourist industry has a higher quotient of globalist influences than the local people. Usually the visited areas are lower in income and consumption levels as well. They are also more natural or wild than where the eco-seeker lives. These may in fact be the conditions that underlie the need for eco-tourism in the first place.

But the culture of place that the visitor sees is eroding. It is blowing away along with hillside soils stripped of forests and over-grazed by cattle for export. Native social forms of human reciprocity with natural systems and indigenous wildlife are often collapsing in a quest for commodities and lifestyles such as those portrayed on television.

The eco-tourist comes to see natural features and undertake experiences in wilderness areas that are vanishing through misuse and neglect. The eco-visit inevitably becomes part of the force for their disappearance. Regardless of reassurances from tour operators about the greenness or sustainability features of their stay, the guests are helping to destroy the host places that they came to see.

There is only one alternative that can benefit natural places. It is for visitors to join in the restoration, maintenance and protection of ecosystems and other natural features, whether they be forests or tide pools, deserts or coral reefs, elephants or bower birds. Eco-visitors must act as eco-volunteers and participate in the recovery of places that have been damaged or threatened. They can do this by performing needed work while they are touring: tree-planting, water testing, litter removal . . . anything that needs more hands and spare energy. When they return home they can undertake other supportive activities based on actual experiences and knowledge about what is being lost.

This is an opportunity for some level of authentic identification with a place that may be otherwise absent in globalist culture.

The City Planning Department of Bahía de Caráquez is including our Bosque en Medio de las Ruinas "wild park" in Maria Auxiliadora barrio as part of a planned natural and scenic trail for residents and eco-visitors (along with the hilltop point of La Cruz barrio and the new mirador in Bella Vista barrio). If successful this plan will upgrade the Bosque with an entranceway visitor's center, improved paths and bamboo stairways, and plant identification markers. It is a good means for preserving the erosion-controlling trees planted over the last five years and sheltering habitat they create for wildlife (there are now more birds and butterflies in the Bosque than any other place in the city). At a meeting with our staff and a representative of Maria Auxiliadora last week they agreed to maintain and expand the native species planted in the park and to hire local barrio residents as builders, guides and maintenance workers. We are conceiving of ways for visitors to contribute to the overall ecosystem restoration effort there.

"RIGHTS OF NATURE" IN NEW ECUADOR CONSTITUTION, 2008

Ecuador's 2008 constitution is the first constitution in the world to grant "Rights of Nature." In this dispatch of the same year, Berg wonders why this milestone in human history occurred in Ecuador, a country previously unknown for advanced ecological policies, and he speculates that two factors may be relevant: the monumental presence of Nature itself in Ecuador and Ecuadorians' cultural flair for change. Whatever the reason for its place of origin, Berg heralds Ecuador's new constitution as a trail-blazing governing document for the planet.

Ecuador has just ratified a new constitution overflowing with innovations that make it a trail-blazing 21st Century governing document. Environmental awareness and protection are recognized on a particularly high level in response to present day revelations about local destruction of habitat and species as well as planetary climate change. These are covered as extensively as might be hoped for in sections of the new document titled "Good Life" and "Biodiversity and Natural Resources." But there is more than even environmentalists have previously sought. It is the first constitution in the world to grant "Rights of Nature."

Nature in Ecuador is now recognized to fully possess the "right to exist, persist, maintain and regenerate its natural cycles, structure, functions and its processes in evolution." To ensure these rights the government is responsible for "precaution and restriction measures in all the activities that can lead to the extinction of species, the destruction of ecosystems or the permanent alteration of natural cycles."

The concept isn't brand new. Wilderness advocates and leading ecologists such as Raymond Dasmann pleaded to grant legal rights to Nature nearly half a century ago, and it has been the subject of numerous "deep ecology" and some law articles and books. What is new to the point of near incomprehension is that this idea is now part of Ecuador's national purpose. Consider the broadest possibilities for interpretation. Don't the processes of resources extraction, manufacturing, energy production, large-scale agriculture, mass transportation, housing development, and nearly all other operations of contemporary society interfere with wild Nature? No one yet knows what laws will follow to carry out the intent of the new constitution, or how they will be applied. Imagine when the U.S. constitution first granted life, liberty and the pursuit of happiness. We will have to wait to discover what "Rights of Nature" actually means. This much is clear, the prospects for human consciousness have just widened considerably.

How did this happen in a country previously unknown for advanced ecological policies? There are at least as many themes in the national character of Ecuador as in any other country, but two stand out with undeniable clarity. One is that it has a continuous basis in Nature that is close and powerful. The other is that Ecuadorians are able to adapt rapidly to changes—ideas, technology, and fashion. It may have taken time for them to see the effects of large-scale environmental destruction but they have decided to stop it now in the firmest terms.

The grand scale of Ecuador's natural attributes and their significance to the rest of the world is a fixture in the national mind. A transit across the country starts with the Galapagos Islands offshore where Darwin formulated his evolution theories, continues to the coast on the Pacific Ocean which is often unpeopled and wild, moves inland to cloud forests with world-leading numbers of unique birds, plants and insects, ascends to extremely high peaks and major active volcanoes in the Andes Mountains, and finally encounters vast and dense Amazon Basin rain forests feeding oxygen to the planet's atmosphere. It is no accident that the country is the only one named for an earthly phenomenon, the equator that was first discovered there.

The speed of change can be neck-breakingly excessive. The worst result has been a long history of fast boom-bust agricultural innovations in this food-producing nirvana, most recently ruinous shrimp-farming that denuded habitat-harboring mangroves and pollutes main estuaries. Rapid transition can also bring undoubted benefits like Guayaquil's startling reversal from the worst-rated urban area in the world only ten years ago to today's notably attractive and amenable largest city in the nation. To keep Ecuador's equilibrium, almost half of the population still remains culturally indigenous with loyalties to traditional communities, and most people retain allegiances to large families that have a prevailing influence in social and economic relations. These socially conservative factors act like ballast as Ecuador roars past.

The monumental presence of Nature itself and a cultural flair for change account in a large part for how "Rights of Nature" came to be, and will likely continue to shape the way they are interpreted in the legal laboratory of constitutional law.

OUT OF THE BLUE, EVEN MORE GREEN: UNEXPECTED BENEFITS OF RESTORING BIODIVERSITY

In this upbeat report, published in Kyoto Journal *in 2010, Berg offers a decade's-end review of Planet Drum's revegetation efforts in Bahía, recapitulating some of the unanticipated benefits that followed. Local school kids, barrio residents, and international visitors participated and learned about ecosystem restoration. Berg concludes optimistically: "When we work to restore or protect biodiversity we discover many additional and valuable ways—often unexpected—to achieve a sustainable future."*

Any action taken to restore a place's natural biodiversity can also spark further beneficial changes that will come as a complete surprise. Here's what else has taken place since Planet Drum Foundation decided to replant native trees in the Pacific Coast city of Bahía de Caráquez, Ecuador after severe El Niño rains triggered disastrous mudslides.

The first site chosen for restoration was in a neighborhood that happened to be near a school. Its students came to help out, learned about local dry tropical forest plants, and later formed an eco-club. The location was eventually declared a municipal "wild park" and staircases were built from recycled wood that lead to paths designed for nature-loving visitors. The replanted area has attracted native birds, butterflies and even anteaters, so that whole ecosystems have started to recover.

A greenhouse was built to grow a variety of plants for restoring more sites where trees had been uprooted by mudslides. Local residents were employed to produce sapling trees and to oversee plantings. Seeds for this purpose were gathered from trees that were still standing amidst the devastation. In addition, household food wastes were collected to produce compost for making the soil more fertile. Empty plastic soft drink bottles were cut and repurposed as containers for growing plants. Volunteers from other countries came to assist and in turn learned about plant nursery work and local natural ecology. Landowners got involved because they wanted to replant trees on ruined parts of their properties. Newspapers and radio stations reported about the project, thus educating the general public. Neighborhood residents then started their own groups to plant trees. And Bahía de Caráquez became known as an eco-city. International visitors arrived to observe the restoration work so that they could carry out similar restorations back home.

It is now eleven years later and thousands of trees are growing tall and spreading their roots deeply into the soil, helping to control erosion, rebuild local ecosystems, and reduce siltation caused by eroded soil that threatens aquatic life in the river estuary that borders the city. These new trees continually produce oxygen and store carbon, helping reduce greenhouse gases that contribute to worldwide climate change. Hundreds of students and volunteers have learned about ecosystems and how to restore biodiversity. The whole Ecuadorian city now knows that natural restoration work is underway and residents attend presentations and celebrations to support it. Nearby cities have begun their own replanting programs.

Biodiversity includes many species and ecosystems, and there are usually a greater number of types of native plants and animals than might be expected to exist within any geographic area. Complex interrelationships exist between them that are barely understood. Resident species of plants and animals frequently encounter newcomers who wander in as well as regular migrants, such as birds that usually live elsewhere. Biodiversity means an extremely large number of life forms behaving in a nearly inexhaustible variety of ways.

We are one of those life forms and depend on the others to support us. When we work to restore or protect biodiversity we discover many additional and valuable ways—often unexpected—to achieve a sustainable future.

FIGURE 14 Plaque honoring Peter Berg. (See English translation on facing page.) This plaque hangs in City Hall, Bahía de Caráquez, Ecuador.

Source: City Hall, Bahía de Caráquez, Ecuador © Clayton Plager-Unger

THE AUTONOMOUS DECENTRALIZED MUNICIPAL GOVERNMENT OF CANTÓN SUCRE ON BEHALF OF CANTÓN SUCRE, MAKES RECORD OF ITS UNENDING GRATITUDE TO MR.

Peter Berg

Father of Bioregionalism
Founder of Planet Drum Foundation
Icon in the Global Environmental Community
Proponent of the Sustainable Urban Model (Green Cities)
Friend of the Present and Future Citizens of Bahía de Cáraquez

(October 1, 1937–July 28, 2011)

In 1999, he helped pioneer the Eco-City citizens' movement after the El Niño and earthquake disasters, in order to reconstruct Bahía de Caráquez in harmony with the natural systems it harbors. He emphasized the following principles:

- That the human species should identify itself within its community and not as independent from other existing forms of life
- That citizens should be conscious of their natural resources
- That they have a duty to replenish them
- That Intergenerational Solidarity should be the legacy of our existence

Thank you Peter …
Your efforts have been an inspiration to Cantón Sucre, to Ecuador, and to visitors of the World.
Long Live the Eco-City!

Dr. Carlos Mendoza Rodríguez
Mayor of Cantón Sucre
Bahía de Caráquez, May 4, 2012
(translated into English by Lauren Yero)

PART 5

Tributes

PETER BERG—AN APPRECIATION

Saul Yale Barodofsky

My first memory of Peter is of walking together on the beach in Santa Barbara in 1967. I had just finished a run of L.A. Provo (our provocation street theater group) and was resting up, after too much acid, in the Montecito hills. Peter and some buddies were visiting Santa Barbara on Digger business.

We had heard of the Diggers, and I was already a fan. Digging up the "roots of society" and replanting a more equitable social model was all the rage then. We were also just a little bit in awe. They had so many helping hands to put on their "presentations," and in L.A., there were only three of us to do ours (plus some erratic help from our ladies).

I remember later hanging out in San Francisco en route to my living on Mt. Shasta and meeting many of the family, especially Judy Berg, Peter Coyote, Vinny Renaldi, and Emmett Grogan—Emmett later on came up to Shasta to come down from a rather long run with heroin—he succeeded.

Later, when I had been on Mt. Shasta for almost a year (studying with Mother Mary, an American psychic), Peter visited me just to assure himself that I was not under the influence of a cult. I wasn't.

During one of her teachings, Mary saw him across the room and asked me who he was. When I told her, she directed me to protect him: "He is one of the Progenitors of the New Age. Guard his back, and protect him with your life." Of course I told Peter and Judy what my instructions were, and with their bemused permission I put an amulet facing their entrance and a picture of Mother Kali on their refrigerator door. They still have the amulet.

The next day Peter called me. "What in the Hell did you get me into?" he cried. "I got all these crazy dreams with Indian women and swords and lions." I was so pleased it was working.

I visited Peter and Judy on a more or less regular basis. I always felt their welcome, even when they had no fixed home of their own and were living in a basement in San Francisco—my dog and I were made welcome.

I remember coming down from Mt. Shasta and walking in on a planning meeting for the Ring Around the Pentagon demonstration. Judy welcomed me, and I became a fly on the wall. Peter, Ram Dass, Allen Ginsberg, Allen Cohen were people I remember being there. I have a clear memory of Ram Dass asking Ginsberg a serious question: "I get all these letters," he said. "They say they're about to kill themselves unless I can help them. Any suggestions?" Ginsberg replied, "When this happens to me, I just put the letter on my forehead, and say OMMMMM!"

Later during that same meeting there was a loud knock on the door. Everyone tightened up. "Who's there?" "Abby Hoffman" came through the door. "Who in the hell is Abby Hoffman?" was our reply. "I'm the guy who stopped the clock on the New York Stock Exchange," he responded. (To those suffering senior moments, Abby and some friends threw a few hundred one-dollar bills onto the floor of the exchange, and the resulting furor caused the exchange to close all trading until they gathered up all the dollar bills.) Naturally, he was admitted to the meeting.

My training on Mt. Shasta was in alternative medicine, and I practiced acupressure, herbology, chiropractics, sending and transmutation of energy, and anything else that I could learn.

The Digger family, now called Free City, accepted me as the Free Doctor and put me to work.

I did general stuff: headaches, stomach problems, menstrual pain, and back pain. I also introduced granola (raw) and chia seeds (for extra energy) to the community via the Communication Company. Peter had been given a rare (at that time) video camera, and he did a video of me doing my sort of chiropractic healing thing.

Years later, after I had moved into the rugs and textiles of the women of the Silk Road (1978), Peter started calling me "Heal and Deal." He still does.

Once Peter asked me to join him in visiting an old friend and artist, Billy Batman. He was concerned that Billy was too deep into heroin and might fall off the world. I agreed, and we went a-calling. I imagine that Peter's most persuasive job was with Billy, rather than with me.

I did a general scanning and started on his feet, trying to get an idea of just how impacted he was and if any thing was radically out of balance.

As I started to apply pressure, I looked at him and asked, "Any pain here, or here, or here?" "Pain," he responded, "Saul, I haven't felt my feet in years." I stopped my diagnosis and started to offer advice on maintaining his health—extra drinking water, regular soaking baths, and stretching out the body. Billy was very polite, as he listened. Peter felt he probably wouldn't do them but thanked me anyway.

I remember Peter (almost incoherently stoned) directing us in midnight plastering "1% Free" posters all over downtown San Francisco. It was an amazing night, and at the end I was amazed that we had survived—again.

A few years later, I was studying with "Sufi Sam," and I got a call from Judy. "Peter has really screwed up his back. He's in a lot of pain. Can you help?" I went to Sam and asked him to "bless" my hands. After I told him why and what Mary had said, he agreed and put his hands over mine. I felt so much power flowing into my hands I was afraid to touch anything lest it drain off. One of my friends agreed to drive me to their house and even opened doors for me.

When we got there, Judy let us in, and as I went to see Peter, I could see he was in serious pain. Judy took off the sheet covering his back, and I placed my hands just over his spine (not touching him). He almost leaped out of bed. "What the f— did you do to me?" he said. "This felt just like it did when I stepped on a man-of-war in Florida." I took that as a hopeful sign that Sam's energy was flowing through me. Peter did get better, but only after a spinal fusion.

Peter has never disparaged my path, be it spiritual or alternative healing. As he said to me on Monday, when I was leaving San Francisco, "You know I don't believe in any of this stuff. But I do believe in you."

Thanks Peter, I believe in you too.

December 17, 2010
Charlottesville, Virginia

PETER BERG AND JUDY GOLDHAFT AND THE REINHABITORY THEATER

Peter Coyote

Some time around 1973 or '74, Judy Goldhaft (Peter's wife) convened a group of ex-Mime-Troupers and some actors from the Fireside Theater in Minneapolis, an entire theater company that moved west after seeing us perform and entered our gravitational field here. Biologists and ecologists had known for some time that political demarcations of counties and states had virtually nothing to do with the way in which the Earth organized itself. Peter and biologist Raymond Dasmann had done and continued to do a great deal of groundbreaking work thinking through and articulating the implications of that fact for human culture and politics. For instance, in common plant-animal-climate communities, people tended to live somewhat similarly because of the common biological-climate base underlying their culture, so northern California has much more in common with southwestern Oregon than it does with southern California. Peter and Ray created a map of the United States based on dominant plant communities and popularized the subject with a term they coined for political work—bioregions. Before very long, bioregionalism rapidly became an accepted way of looking at the world, and, due to Peter and Judy's work promulgating it through a magazine called *Planet Drum*, bioregional groups began to form, meet, and plan together, all over the country.

Peter also coined the term "reinhabitation" to describe the process of learning how to live in a place according to the dictates of the place itself. If culture was going to thrive and not desecrate the Earth (still an open question), European immigrants would have to relearn much of the ancient wisdom and place-specific lore of the Natives they'd driven off and how to reintegrate these bioregions and a new culture, enabling us to live there in a sustainable, harmonious manner.

Both Peter and Judy and their gaggle of friends, among whom I include myself, were, whatever else we may have been, creative artists at the top of our game. The theater where we had all met in the early 1960s and that we had brought to prominence had achieved national fame due to several cross-country tours and a prestigious OBIE award from New York City's *Village Voice* newspaper.

Most of this new core group had left the Mime Troupe in the late '60s to form the Diggers and raise the stakes of the political pressure we exerted on global capitalism by undermining the culture that it had created. Exploring the possibilities and potentialities of a counterculture that was not based on premises of profit and private property seemed not only the right thing to do but imperative, and after our city-based Digger band decided what we needed to do, most of us broke away from urban life and moved into rural areas to explore new styles of life and economy. Peter and Judy chose to remain in San Francisco and make that the focus of their work.

Prior to Judy's convening of the meeting under discussion, we had for many years been spread far and wide, somewhat isolated from one another. Now we were back together in San Francisco, eager to play, and Judy had an idea for some sort of cultural expression of reinhabitory and bioregional ideas, something akin to what we had done together in the Mime Troupe around left-wing politics—zany, fun, but evolved around a core of political content that made it meaningful.

We began meeting in a large room at a complex called The Farm. Nestled between two busy streets and partially shaded by a freeway overpass, it was literally an urban farm. People grew vegetables and raised animals there and dedicated the facilities and their labors to teaching local schoolchildren about Nature. They offered us a large, empty meeting room where we first convened to do . . . what? No one knew.

Artists generally proceed initially by hunches—they make a gesture, write a phrase, draw a line, or move their bodies and then step back and evaluate the implication of what they have just done. Then they repeat the process. This "creative process" is common to virtually all the arts. If we were going to create a cultural event that had a relationship to our bioregion, we would have to know the local history—not a Eurocentric version but the creation myths and legends of the original inhabitants. We began poring through Native stories, looking them up, reading them to one another, and experimentally "putting them on their feet" to find dramatic or comedic possibilities.

Nothing about this dry description of our process prepared our number for watching two of our members, crouched, with forearms raised chest-high to simulate forepaws, sniffing one another's butts, raising their legs to pee like coyotes, then seamlessly connecting animal challenge to a human status competition by comparing wristwatches. As we had done so successfully in the Mime Troupe, following the laughter of our peers was the surest gauge of whether or not we were on the right track.

We spent days at the zoo watching animals and learning to imitate them and translate their behavior with our human bodies. To ancient legends, we added send-ups of our own counterculture foolishness on the part of back-to-the-land hippies—things we had all seen and experienced in the various rural communities in which we had lived. From these tales evolved the story of Branch and Crystal, two do-gooder, hapless back-to-the-landers, and their crazed methedrine-fueled chickens (which, if memory serves, I played with startlingly intimate knowledge of the effects of methedrine on avian nervous systems). In this fashion, trying and failing, coached by Judy's quiet encouragement and insistence and Peter's mad-cap and insightful illuminations, bursting like flares in the group mind, we assembled "a show." It was something of a miracle. We had discovered a way to discuss two new concepts—bioregionalism and reinhabitation—in the same wacky manner we had once conscripted to discuss political issues in the San Francisco Mime Troupe.

Form and content are indivisible. This is a fancy way of saying that the way you describe something or the manner in which you accomplish a task becomes part of the meaning of the task. We did not want to create a "product" with our Reinhabitory Theater but wanted to lend support and entertain others who were thinking like us. That meant moving to where they were living and performing in venues available there. We began to perform in local movie theaters, fields, parks, virtually any venue we could get, taking the show "to the people" as we had done in the Mime Troupe. And, the people "got it" on the first pass and loved us for expressing their lives and thoughts in such funky, comedic, and insightful ways. Reinhabitory Theater reflected the new culture that was trying to establish new roots "in place": in the hinterlands and cities of California. Our stories were part mythic, part goofy, as current as marijuana farming and as ancient as the Native tale of the Bear and the Lizard. Ancient but contemporary, if you can imagine indigenous myths enacted by Laurel and Hardy.

For me personally it was a lovely time. I am, by nature, a storyteller and performer, but during the Digger years, our group ethos about anonymity (refusing to pursue fame) and living without money made me eschew performance and the conflicted, contradictory problems of publicity and adulation they brought with them. I was determined to remain loyal to my Digger clan and our values, but, for an actor, it also meant being disloyal to my nature.

Reinhabitory Theater was my stepping stone back into public life and the opportunity to exploit my talents and have opportunities I had missed. There is no doubt in my mind that I would never have pursued my career as an actor had it not been for this intermediate warm, affectionate immersion in the warm bath of friendship and camaraderie, exploring the implications of life on Earth . . . which always occurs in some site-specific *place*.

"Everything Changes" is the immutable law of creation. Life, family, economies, eventually intervened, and after a good run of several years, some folks had to get jobs, some moved away, and the Reinhabitory Theater Company eventually evaporated. The ideas it articulated and the emergent culture it identified did not, however. They were direct by-products of the fertile imaginations and unrelenting intellectual efforts of Peter and Judy. Thanks to our efforts and support, they were now cast into the air to float as freely as dandelion seeds, to land and sprout where they would. To Peter and Judy, I would quote our late mutual friend, poet and Digger-friend Kirby Doyle in his poem, "Ode to John Garfield"—"Look, your lessons blossom."

Mill Valley, California, August 2011

ELEGY FOR PETER BERG

Jim Dodge

Here is an "Elegy for Peter Berg . . ." in the form of a ku, a poetic form that began as a teaching device and evolved into a literary form through use. (A teacher in the Caucus Mountain Mystery Schools [where the non-Christian traditions retreated during the persecutions of the seventeenth century] grew tired of long, abstract answers from her students and began limiting replies to seven syllables.) The two major rules for the ku are (1) no more or less than seven syllables, and (2) the title must be longer than the poem.

Some practitioners also confine subject matter to any possible associative extension of ku—that is, "coo" as doves do, or "bill and coo," thus love and seduction/courtship as a subject, or "coup" as in overthrowing a government, thus poems of revolution, and so on. The Iowa Actualists promulgated this rather silly subject restriction, but Actualist purists insist on it.

You'll note an additional ku added to the first, making this the first of a new form, the Two-Part Ku, or Chain of Ku, or, with Aretha on the soundtrack, a Chain of Fool Ku.

> A Two-Part Elegy for Peter Berg Disguised as
> Good-Natured Tweaks of My Bioregional Cohorts—
> Especially the Males—Regarding Their Choices of
> Totem Names, Nicknames, and CB Handles
>
> I
>
> Fewer eagles,
> More algae.
>
> II
>
> Lot less bears,
> Way more berries.

REMEMBERING PETER

Susan Griffin

As I was moved to learn recently, whales habitually congregate in one area of the ocean to compose a single piece of music together.

Did Peter know this? It would not have surprised him. The phenomenon validates what he had been saying for decades. He understood so early and so cogently how we all collaborate, in the songs we sing and the thoughts we think not only with each other but, by virtue of our very existence, with where we are. With place.

Whale songs would of their nature contain so much: the briny taste of sea water, for instance, or topographical features of the ocean floor over which they float as they sing, even the particular weather of the area. The sound that emanates from these majestic creatures (the larynx alone the size of a vending machine) reflects all that sustains them.

That not just forests and rivers but also songs are part of what defines a region was one of the great contributions Peter Berg made to the way we imagine ourselves and the Earth today. Before Peter got hold of it, the word "bioregion" was a mostly technical term used to denote a particular conservation area. Peter enlarged our thinking by including in the definition not only every form of life, animal and vegetable, along with terrain and weather within a watershed, but also human culture. In this way, he was contributing to a revolution in twentieth-century consciousness: we were beginning to see that human creativity does not stand apart from the Earth but rather resonates with the land where we live, including the paths water takes as snow melts and flows down from the mountains.

From this angle of perception, it becomes clear that we are not *on top* of (or apart from) nature but *of* nature, embedded, our loftiest ideas arising from the Earth. Made of clay, we have been generated and shaped not only by our parents but also by the ten thousand beings of Hindu scripture, by all the life that surrounds us.

"Europeans came as invaders clearing terrain for an occupation civilization," Peter wrote in an early *Planet Drum* publication. Once "man" falls from the top of the *Scala Natura*—the medieval "great chain of being" that placed humanity on top of a descending scale of animals, plants, and minerals—many other hierarchies are also undermined, among those the idea that European civilizations were superior to the original cultures and civilizations of America.

I came across my first copy of *Planet Drum* almost by accident. Reading those fiery philosophical and political declarations on the soft pages of newsprint, I felt an astonishing resonance, as if something long dormant and as yet unnamed were coming to life inside my soul. I don't know the year precisely—it was sometime between 1970 and '72—but, appropriately, the memory is in my body. (*Your body is home*, Peter wrote in 1970.)

I know it was daytime: an afternoon light streamed from the south-facing windows. I had recently been reading Emma Goldman and had put down my copy of *Planet Drum* and turned to the bookshelf on my left to retrieve a copy of the first volume of her autobiography, *My Life*. In what is something like an intellectual ritual, as I leafed through the pages, I could feel a strong electrical force between Goldman's ideas and what I had just read in *Planet Drum*. There was something here I knew, something in this connection, something I could not yet delineate, though from the strength of the feeling, I sensed it was significant. It was at this moment, a lifelong search began.

Planet Drum arose from the Diggers, a movement in San Francisco that called for the end of business as usual, including capitalist exploitation. The Diggers used to bake bread in tin cans and give it away free on the streets. Like Goldman, they were anarchists, and, like her, too, (though unlike the violent black suits that disrupt peaceful protests today) they believed in peaceful tactics.

They existed as part of a larger motion sweeping up so many of us in the '60s and '70s, a collective trajectory that if truth be told really began a decade earlier, in the '50s, with the Beat generation, whose ground zero was San Francisco. The poetry of *Howl*, with its outcry against complacency, Michael McClure's call to our mammalian nature, Diane di Prima's celebration of wolves, and Bob Kaufman "dreaming of wild beats," all still ringing in our ears.

Just as Emma Goldman once demanded, this was a revolution that danced. Peter's broadside for *Planet Drum* read like poetry. In fact, the Diggers, which included the actor Peter Coyote, began at a theater, the Mime Troupe, located then in the Mission district of San Francisco (a place coincidentally where I had studied when I was few years younger). And as a radical act of social change, they performed free theater in the street.

Poetry, theatre, anarchism, ecology, civil rights. The air was rife with new visions. For me, these were the formative days of my own feminism. Listening to and telling stories in my "consciousness-raising" group, reading books that had been previously ignored or neglected because they were written by women, reviving the many suppressed histories of women, I found my own awareness growing almost too fast for me to contain. And in this awareness there was a series of hunches, inclinations, what the French novelist Nathalie Sarraute once called *tropisms*, pointing me in directions that I could not entirely map or even name yet.

In the same way that I was drawn by Peter Berg's writing in *Planet Drum*, I was electrified by a film I saw in 1974. Set in the place where I grew up, Los Angeles and the San Fernando Valley, *Chinatown* depicted the struggle over water rights that had occurred in 1937, six years before I was born. A series of machinations instigated by William Mulholland resulted in the diversion of water from the Owens Valley to the San Fernando Valley, reducing a once-verdant land to desert and transforming a desert to habitable and thus valuable land. The shadowy men behind these transactions made millions. But this was just the subplot of the film, the background subtly shaping the main plot, a story of a woman who had been sexually abused by her father and was trying in vain to protect her daughter from the same fate.

The nexus from which my own work was to spring was all there. The idea of a watershed that I had first encountered in Peter's writing, connected to oppression, power, and rape. In 1972, I had written an essay positing that rape is motivated not by simple sexual drive but rather by the psychological (and socially constructed) desire to dominate. Now, two years later, I was to begin a new book, *Woman and Nature*, where I would connect the attempt to dominate and control nature with the domination and control of women.

Peter was a not feminist in the early years. But he got there more quickly than many men. The process of thought is social and collaborative, but we don't all come to the same insights at the same time. We are like relay racers, shifting the baton from one hand to the other. I know Peter learned a great deal eventually from feminism, as did feminists from his work in ways both large and small. I am thinking now of that outrageously ironic group called the Guerrilla Girls, artists, activists and critics who dressed in gorilla suits, while appearing unannounced at various events to protest wanton and widespread discrimination against women in the arts. The term "guerrilla theater," to which they added a new chapter, was first coined by Peter Berg.

Eventually, in a later book, *A Chorus of Stones*, I began to write about war and gender. I don't know if I had already read the words in "Homeskin," Peter's broadside dated 1970, that were listed under the heading "Man-Made." Nevertheless I am startled at their prescience, as I read them now: "Perpetual global war as a primary industry."

I never knew Peter Berg well. But his presence was very important to me, has become in fact, like the bioregion of northern California where I have lived most of life, a part of me. *Re-Membered.* Like Beat poetry, his words are still ringing in my ears while I continue adding my part to the great song we are all, like those whales, composing together, the waters of consciousness held by the watersheds we inhabit, our dreams woven on wild looms.

(An expanded version of this tribute appeared under the title "You Are Where You Live" in the Winter 2013 issue of *YES! Magazine*.)

DIAMOND THUNDERBOLT, BIOREGIONS OF ECOLOGICAL TRUTH: HOMAGE TO PETER BERG

David Haenke

At the end of July 2011 I was on the road in Michigan (in my home bioregion of the Great Lakes), and in midcourse of the process of writing this essay, when I got word of Peter Berg's death from Stephanie Mills, a primary writer in ecology and bioregionalism and longtime friend of both Peter and myself. Even though I was well aware he was in treatment for lung cancer (he and I had corresponded about this a couple of months earlier), I had no clue that he was so close to passing. The news was a sorrowful shock to me and changed the tenor of many things, such as my life, the bioregional movement, and, as I did not set out to write an epitaph, this writing.

More than once I got to do Peter's jumping exercise with him. As part of one of his inimitable presentations, he would lead a group of people, usually standing with him in a circle, to physically jump up out of whatever geopolitical unit they were in at the time (e.g., "California," "Illinois," "USA") and then come back down into their bioregion (Shasta, Great Lakes, Ozarks). It was a powerful exercise, phase shift, from one terrain of consciousness into another. Afterward he always left it at that, no jumping back. We jumped with Peter up out of a broken nation and came down home forever into a whole other one. When we go far enough into bioregional mind, no good reason to ever come back out.

Whether or not it's exemplified here by any particular merit, I have thought and worked exceptionally much on this homage to Peter. (Usually, no matter what the occasion, I dash writings off in a single draft without much editing.) It is a daunting task to, in any number of words, attempt to cover the vast and deep life region that was—and remains in his memory and body of work—Peter Berg. A book or two could and may well be written just on the subject of his seminal role in the development of the '60s counterculture and his talents as an activist performer and social innovator, as with the Diggers, where he and his wild crew of coyotes, more than one a Peter, characteristically went for the radix elemental of freedoms: personal, political, economic: free everything dispensed as performance piece of great and funny seriousness, real stuff dispensed for the benefit of living beings.

Vajra: adamantine diamond thunderbolt. I tender an ecocentric definition: an encompassing whole truth powerful as frozen lightning, singularity, realized divination of the reality of nature/the nature of reality, so powerful as to be radiantly densely palpable to all the senses, held in the hand, turned this way and that, infinite number of facets more than reflecting but actually containing all that is known, can be known, and unknown.

The universe, here in this corner of it, has as "its most intimate expression of itself, . . . this tiny planet. . ." (Thomas Berry, *The Dream of the Earth*, 163). Here *in* Earth (not "on" it, as David Abram observes) nested jewel boxes, one within the other, are elemental vajras spinning out of nature truly expressed as ecology: functional reality, truth, intelligence, sanity: all ecological in nature. Ver . . . verde . . . verdant . . . green truth . . . green vajras. . . . The roots of ecocentrism.

The relatively recent arrival—a favorable mutation—of ecocentric mind (in the late 1960s as far as I can tell) is epochal and necessary.

Peter Berg is on the short list of the pioneers of our species in this awakening from the exterminist nightmare of anthropocentrism, the hall of mirrors that has possessed the human mind and driven us to use our evolutionary gifts to exploit other forms of life with an ecocidal ferocity that clearly leads to our own destruction.

Some pioneers, such as Gary Snyder, have their most known work primarily in the realms of the mind, poetry, philosophy, even as he has always rigorously lived and practiced his ecological values on the ground at home and long advocated for sustainable approaches in a wide range of areas, including forestry and technology; Snyder has explored, articulated the bioregions of the mind early, and, like no other, is seamlessly interwoven into the warp and weft of bioregionalism. Arne Naess and the founders of Deep Ecology, as an extension of their philosophy, engaged in varying forms of resistance—deep environmentalism—to the machinery of destruction. Thomas Berry followed his childhood vision of the meadow into the elemental nature of religion.

Radical necessity for the Earth in extremis is in implementation of the vision, where the vajra gets ever more palpable: *functional ecocentrism*, discernment and extrapolation from ecological laws and principles of design scenarios for every aspect of human life: economics, politics, technology, agriculture, forestry, architecture, education, and so on; systemic reconfiguration of human life at all levels. (No more theory necessary!)

In discernment and development of critical elements of above, the pioneers' list gets even shorter; for example, Allan Savory (holistic resource management, starting with grasslands), John Todd (ecological engineering), Mollison and Holmgren (Permaculture), and the founders of ecological agriculture and forestry (Allan Savory: "I have no theories.").

Following further into the prime mandate for functional truth, Peter Berg's discernment of bioregions/bioregionalism holds a singular place. The collected elements of the work of ecologically based systemic reconfiguration, in order to function with optimal ecological integrity, require a context consonant with eco-spatial differentiations of the Earth itself: bioregions, and bioregionalism as the integrator of all ecological design modalities. In the special unified field of Peter's mind and practice, art, planet drumming, activism, performance, and tearing up the San Francisco street to plant the native species of Shasta Nation, all things elementally discerned and necessary fuse into bioregionalism.

And there's much more here. I believe Peter saw this same thing that quite possesses my life. . . . Inherent in the bioregions is an ancient, anti-entropic, flaw-less, and indeed magical ecological economy, billions of years in refinement, that runs 100 percent on sunlight, creates endless florescence of life of endless abundance, wastes nothing/recycles 100 percent, and is, in the words of Thomas Berry, "self-propagating, self-nourishing, self-educating, self-governing, self-healing and self-fulfilling" (*The Dream of the Earth*, 166). It is for humans to discern how this works (we have indeed done this for some crucial systems) and, in alli-ance with the operant modes of the bioregions, to fold ourselves in, and this is probably the only way that we can continue to be here in the Earth. As Thomas suggests, the prime template for *governance* is here (and, I suggest, politics too). It's all in the Codex Bioregionalis, where magic, divination, art, photosynthesis, science, logic, reason, intelligence: all come out of and converge in nature, the template and home for devolution into ecological decentralization . . . and bio-regional nations. Peter's beloved Shasta Nation. Ozark Nation. Cascadia Nation. Anahuac Nation. Gulf of Maine Nation. Edwards Plateau Nation. Great Lakes Nation. Katuah Nation. KAW Nation. Amble Toward Continent Congress (Peter Berg, "Amble Towards Continent Congress," *The Great Blafigria*, 1976, vols. II & III). Turtle Island Confederation of Bioregional Nations. With Peter's invitation as a roadmap, we did so amble to Continent Congress, first in 1984, North American Bioregional Congress I, Tallgrass Prairie, just northwest of the Ozarks. Continen-tal Bioregional Congress has remained in session ever since through ten meetings. We contemplate the eleventh.

When and where the ecological thunderbolt first struck Peter I don't know. But I'm sure it was realization, for in my experience bioregionalism has not come from invention but is more an epiphanic remembrance of ancient "figures of rela-tion," a term Peter often used. But from whatever place of beginning, his relent-less primal drive (he was a primal guy!) powered by his mind nonpareil to the live foundations of palpable truths sent him into a realm mostly untrammeled by humans of neo-European origins or those associated with appurtenances of "modern" "civilization"—this realm of the pioneers of functional ecocentrism. Here he discerned and divined the numinous vajra of how and indeed why the Earth physically delineates its body ecosphere, the bioregions, and how, from right out of the nature of bioregions, comes a new and ancient way of life for our species, of a whole cloth, all-encompassing, depthless, specific, palpable truth pervasive, something way beyond theory but, and necessarily so, applicable and capable of being implemented in all the appurtenances of ecological design: rein-habitation and its greenprints. Reinhabitation, not only of bioregions but of Earth itself.

The bioregional revelation can possess, and has possessed from my own experience, fully and ecstatically, mind body soul, and I believe it did for Peter from the first transmission of who-knows-when to his last breath. I believe the template of bioregionalism's ecstatic nature awaiting in his mind may have played fully into his original passion and performance of the arts of freedom on the '60s streets of San Francisco and given it vibrant ground and source.

He translated not just the idea but the ecological decentralist roadmap to implementation of a way for the humans to stay here on the planet and taught it brilliantly through all manner of performance—on stage, at a lectern, by the written word—and by pulling up the concrete on the street in front of the Planet Drum house to plant native trees and the seeds of green cities.

Peter Berg did not invent bioregionalism. Again, it's immanent in Earth reality and can only be recognized, remembered, translated, interpreted. Somewhere in the historical swirl of bioregionalism coming into current conceptual form, between Peter, Allen Van Newkirk, and Raymond Dasmann, the term was probably coined (before that Carl Sauer's work did a lot to prepare the ground). That bioregionalism is the most powerful and necessary realization in all of human existence and that Peter Berg did more than anyone else by far to translate it vibrantly into the human realm makes his life work epochal.

Ascription of "force of nature" to a person is much overused. If Peter Berg's life became the benchmark for such an ascription, it would be far less used. Peter was indeed a force of nature. With all that implies. Just like his bioregional vision. One of Turtle Island's Holy Coyotes. For myself it was of the greatest of honors to have worked with him in the bioregional movement, though it was not at times easy, and why should it have been? I think of Peter, his wild nature, and how he might have seen an eventual bioregional nation, like his beloved Shasta. Back in the early '90s I wrote a piece called *Wild Civilization* and how such a concept relates to bioregionalism and a bioregional nation; an excerpt: "Wild civilization is far from perfect, hardly utopian. It is not 'New Age.' It is rough, intense, variously rugged, uncertain. Just like life. Only you can breathe the air, drink the water, and have as peers some interesting, but not necessarily human neighbors."

I think of younger Peter in the '70s in the early fires of creation with his cohort of no-less-amazing incandescently brilliant bioregionalist front-wave rider changeling friend & ally co-biorevolutionaries, his life partner Judy Goldhaft, Freeman House and David Simpson of the Mattole, Jerry Martien, Jim Dodge, Jerry Gorsline . . .

"At this moment, Peter Berg and David Simpson . . . are chaining up to get over the pass and into the Missoula basin from the west. They will participate in an alternative energy and agricultural conference and spur our regional-identity bundle efforts ever onward." (Bob Curry, "Letter to Blafigrians," January 1976, *The Great Blafigra Is*, Vols. II & III, p. 32)

Goodbye, Peter, and thank you beyond all measure
for what you did
and what you left with us.

David Haenke
Sheppard Ridge,
Bryant Creek Watershed,
Ozarks Bioregion,
Turtle Island,
Earth September 2011

BIOREGIONALISM AND RIVER OF WORDS

Robert Hass

[TAPED CONVERSATION WITH ROBERT HASS, OCTOBER 11, 2013, BERKELEY, CA]

You know, I can't tell you how and when Peter and I first met. I've been trying to think about it. I know that I heard him speak several times on several occasions before I was ever introduced to him to say hello. And I don't think I ever much more than said hello. Some time, I would guess in the early 1980s, I first heard him speak. I was, in those days, reading Gary Snyder, of course. And I was reading the writing of Wendell Berry on getting back to the land in Kentucky. As one of the things I was interested in, I was reading environmental writing. I don't remember when Gary first published "Coming into the Watershed," that essay, and when I heard Peter. But I think I heard Peter before I read the essay.

But at some point in those years what Peter was saying began to crystallize for me. I was not interested in going into the mountains and living off the grid, and I wasn't going to be a farmer. I had friends, two couples, who read Wendell Berry and went to Kentucky and tried to farm, raise sheep, raise tobacco, which seemed really admirable—that back-to-the-land moment in the 1970's.

I was thinking, I guess, about how to make a life as a writer, a poet. I found myself thinking about the fact that most people live in cities. I grew up in the Bay Area. I love the natural surroundings, but I also love the city and the rhythm of that life. And I was married, I had children, I was going to make a living as a teacher. And so, as a writer, my relation to the natural world was a bit troubling to me, because it seemed that the kind of nature in nature writing belonged, for most people, myself included, to weekends. Which is I think the case in industrial and postindustrial society, to a very large extent. For most people, the relationship to what we used to call the wild is recreational. In both senses. That is, go out, play and have fun, but also in the other meaning of a place to recreate, to re-create yourself spiritually, imaginatively, and in other ways. And I thought, well, poetry belonged to that. But I hated the idea of poetry belonging to weekends, you know?

So hearing Peter talk about bioregionalism made it clear to me that there was long-term political work to do around the relationships among wild places, urban life, suburbs, the energy flows through interlocking or overlapping environmental systems, and it gave me at least a way for thinking about how to think about those issues.

And then I read fugitive things. This was for me kind of at the edges of a life. I was trying to make my way as a poet and earn a living and raise a family. I spent a lot of time on weekends teaching myself my place, hiking with my wife and kids, and a lot of summer time in the mountains. Doing that life that I had envisaged— being a Confucian during the week and a Taoist on weekends, as someone said of an old Chinese poet. And it really was not until the mid-'90s that I felt like I was able to do anything in the way of environmental activism. And so, when I got the strange job of being poet laureate of the United States, I was the first person from west of the Mississippi who'd ever held the position, and it seemed like an opportunity.

The obligations of the laureateship are just to give a poetry reading and to curate a reading series on Capitol Hill. But they give you money to have one kind of conference or something. Rita Dove, who had preceded me, got together a bunch of scholars to talk about the black migration out of the South into northern cities in the era of Ku Klux Klan, which was a really cool thing for her to do.

And I thought, well, I'm from the West, I should do something about the tradition of nature writing. And then I talked to Gary Snyder about how we might put it together. And he said, well, let's think in terms of watersheds. And I thought, okay, now I understand what I could do. I could do a conference on bioregionalism, which I had been reading about but was on the backburner for me. And so we tried to invite everyone we could in the country who was thinking about this subject.

So in some ways it was a celebration of Peter and his ideas, which were at the core of the event, which turned out to be really interesting. I had just met a guy named Bob Boone who had started the Friends of the Anacostia River project. The Anacostia is the other river, besides the Potomac, that creates DC. And it's the one that flows through the black neighborhoods of DC. And Bob Boone showed me the sewer maps and the flood control maps of DC, pointing out to me that whenever there is a heavy rain in Washington, the old 19th-century conjoint storm sewer system overflowed, and the sewage from the Federal Triangle, that is from Congress, Treasury, the Supreme Court, flows right into the Anacostia and drifts slowly through the poor black neighborhoods, while conservative congressmen are on TV, waving, pointing their fingers, and saying they're going to get the governments off people's backs.

So it turned out to be a stupendous metaphor for thinking ecologically about the place you live in, its energy systems, and the way it flowed through. And the repair and the remodeling of that system, after many years' work by Bob Boone, has been approved by Congress. Some of the funds are held up, but the process is actually starting. And, of course, all the cities in the country have nineteenth-century storm sewer systems. None of them may be such a perfect Dickensian metaphor as the one in Washington.

But anyway, so Peter was there. Gary Snyder was there. Terry Tempest Williams was there. Ann Zwinger was there. Stephanie Mills was there. Barry Lopez, Peter Matthiessen, Bill McKibben, Jim Galvin for Wyoming. A lot of very good people. We asked tons of people and they came, and it was great. But, I realized at that point, by the time I was finding my way around, that Washington is a city of lobbyists. That's its main industry, and the reporters on the newspapers are profoundly cynical about it, and I understood that this event was going to happen and be over, and that was it. Which turned out to be the case. The first night of the conference Peter Matthiessen spoke to about seven hundred people in a church on Capitol Hill about the destruction of the habitat of half the world's cranes and tigers and many migratory birds and the *Washington Post* the next morning had on the culture pages a story about a bunch of young male Republican staffers who meet every year on the anniversary of the sinking of the Titanic to drink cognac and smoke cigars.

And so trying to think about what to do about it, Pam Michael, who was working for—had been the KPFA radio person—was working as the public relations person for International Rivers and she got me together with people there. I had been thinking that there were three things we really needed to do. We need to get to schoolchildren. We need to do it in an interdisciplinary way that was fun for them. I was thinking about the fact that, because the teaching of literature involved either the teaching of poetry or the teaching of drama or the teaching of fiction, that with very few exceptions, Thoreau's *Walden* being one of them, nature writing, the tradition of natural history writing, has no place in the curriculum, when it would be at the core of the kind of education that Peter Berg was imagining.

People would not just know the way energy flowed through their systems, they'd know the way that it had been imagined in the past. A bioregional education would include the ecology of a place and its literature. It could include the history of botanical drawing in that place, the history of mapping in that place; it would be interested in understanding the relation between cultures and economies. There are a lot of people who had been thinking about this. Planet Drum had been doing that kind of work for years, but it had not gotten into the schools of education. And it had not gotten into the classrooms. So Pam and Owen Lammers, the director of International Rivers, said let's put together some money and start a program, a contest, to get kids to make art and poetry about their watershed, and we'll put together booklets of how to teach natural history, how to do art education, how to teach kids to write poems about the world around them. This was 1996, and not much was going on in the schools except corporate green-washing. That's changed in the last fifteen years, and during those years Pamela Michael and her organization have been holding this contest in hundreds and after a while thousands of schools. They pick winners in every age category—from kindergarten through twelfth grade—artists and poets. They publish books every year of the children's poetry and art and put thousands of the books in classrooms all over the country. So that, in many parts of the country, I forget how many—it would be interesting to talk to Pam, but in thousands of classrooms in the country—it's just part of what they do now in the spring. Make art about their watershed, which involves, of course, coming to understand what a watershed is, to be introduced to that way of feeling where they are on earth. To imagine bioregionally. So this is one of the ways in which Peter's ideas have crept into the world.

PETER BERG

An excellent lizard man

Joanne Kyger

Fingers. Paws. Fingers. Paws. Fingers!

Lizard Man wins, so we have five fingers

to write this down

and turn the page

I saw the Reinhabitory Theater perform this piece of history, on a Sunday, over on the other side of the lagoon at Audubon Canyon Ranch in May 1977. With Silver Fox and Coyote making the world. Singing it into existence. Jumping onto it. A big clod of dirt.

How did they learn such animal graces? Judy Berg, as the cougar, says they practiced a lot.

It became an identity.

Then we came back to my house and had a chicken barbecue. That was part of a joke, too.

The following year, 1978, *Reinhabiting a Separate Country–A Bioregional Anthology of Northern California* was published. It is one of the most important books I have. Teaching an awareness of life in a "bioregion"—a word originated and used by Peter and Raymond Dasmann. One becomes a detective of place, of history and geography, "natural" boundaries usurping sharp political lines. A way to recognize the authenticity of the "local." Certainly in West Marin, where I live, it led to the production of organic farms, organic dairies, and an astonishing "green" awareness.

Peter has visited, many times, the small town where I reside, which has always lived within its watershed. New water meters stopped being issued in 1971 when growth was starting to overtake water supply. One tiny but year-round running stream, which begins way up in a canyon, provides the only fresh-water source in the area. The water from there is now stored and collected in two giant water tanks and behind two small earth dams. Needless to say, everyone is aware of and practices conservation of water.

Then the town was sued by the powerful Pacific Legal Foundation, which demanded water rights for owners of undeveloped property. After a prolonged court case, the town won. A town needs only to provide water, to the best of its ability, to those residing within its watershed. No "borrowed" water.

A "bioregional" solution. A word that has given political and cultural credence to what we now call "sustainability." One participates in a "live in place" identity—with a practice of an interrelated consciousness of animals, land and water.

For me, Lizard Man is still turning the pages of history, always with a local and hands on approach.

July 30, 2011

REMEMBERING PETER BERG

Martin A. Lee

It's not often that you meet someone who actually changes how you see things, someone who changes the way you think about the world. Peter Berg was such a person.

When I first met Peter, in 1979, I didn't know that he was instrumental in introducing ecology to the American Left. I didn't know of his pioneering work as a bioregional philosopher-activist with the Planet Drum Foundation. I didn't know that he had written and directed plays for the San Francisco Mime Troupe and that he had coined the phrase "guerrilla theater." I only knew that he had been associated with a group called the Diggers in San Francisco in the mid-1960s.

I was writing a social history of LSD (*Acid Dreams*), and I wanted to know more about the Diggers, an anarchist cadre that provided free food for "hippies" in Golden Gate Park during the heyday of the psychedelic era. So I arranged to visit Peter and his partner, Judy Goldhaft, at their home in San Francisco's Noe Valley. My intention was to interview them and record their Digger stories. Peter, however, didn't want to talk about the 1960s. He wasn't nostalgic about those years, and he wasn't one to rest on past laurels.

I didn't learn much about the Diggers that day (that would come later). I never even turned on my cassette recorder. But the meeting was hardly a bust. We spoke for several hours, and when I left my head was spinning. Peter dazzled with words and ideas. He articulated a brilliant, overarching, integrative vision, a kind of unified field theory of ecology, culture, and living-in-place, a notion to conjure with.

Peter Berg was way ahead of the curve. Ten years before the end of the Cold War, he emphasized the dangers of "global monoculture," a homogenizing juggernaut initially obscured by the binary logjam of East versus West. When "globalization" became the target of worldwide protests after the demise of Soviet bloc Communism, Berg provided a roadmap for moving beyond the postmodern, nation-state morass. "Bioregions," he counseled, "are appropriate locations for decentralization."

Berg insisted that a bioregion should be understood as a cultural as well as an ecological concept. A radical decentralist and an innovative green thinker, he deserves a place of honor in the pantheon of American anarchism along with Thoreau and the Wobblies. But Peter eschewed "isms"—they were so nineteenth century—and he was eminently pragmatic and forward-looking.

And feisty. And intense. And more than occasionally outrageous, as when he and Judy ripped up a portion of their urban sidewalk and turned it into a native plant garden.

Peter and I became close friends after our first conversation. It was a great privilege to share his confidence over the years. On every solstice and equinox, he would mark the change of seasons by blowing on a conch shell. It was the sound of resistance calling, a cry for sanity and renewal, and an homage to the wilderness that will colonize the scars we leave behind.

FAMILY

Malcolm Margolin

I'd see Peter Berg only now and then, but I always enjoyed his solid, gruff, four-square, down-to-earth manner. His ideas, like his manner, seemed to have grown out of the soil; they were sound, relevant, and practical, and in an important way they helped me understand what I was doing and explain it to others.

Since the early 1970s I've been writing and publishing regional material—the literature and histories of particular places. A special interest and personal passion has been my work in the California Indian world. For the past thirty-five years I've been hanging out in the shade of oak trees listening to stories, and I've been tramping through mountains, deserts, riverbanks, seashores, valleys, and woodlands of California with people whose ancestral link to this land goes back thousands of years. I have visited places where the first people emerged from the ground to inhabit the world; I've been shown rocks that in the time before this were living beings and that still retain power and memory. Look! Here's the footprint of the great bird who strode the earth when its surface was still soft. I have been introduced to the fragments of old calendars that governed the rhythm of daily life: when the elderberry blossoms we can no longer collect shellfish, the chirping of a certain wren announces the coming of the salmon. Knowledge so deep as to be inseparable from its place.

After years of what the anthropologist Clifford Geertz characterized as "deep hanging out," I've learned a few things. Perhaps the most important thing I've learned is how adaptable people can be. Every so often I catch a glimpse of the image behind the mass media ads and political campaigns, the assumption that we are a species with fixed needs to be filled and that we require a certain level of material goods and social complexity to be happy. But that's not what I've seen in my California travels. In old California people in favorable places lived in large villages with complex social structures. In the deserts and other less abundant environments they lived in small clans that traveled great distances. People who lived along the rivers had salmon, and they felt fortunate in their wealth. Those who lived along the ocean shores had shellfish, and they felt fortunate in their wealth. Those who lived in the mountains had pine nuts, and they felt fortunate in their wealth. Those who lived in the desert had chia, and they felt fortunate in their wealth. California is a land of many environments and, within those environments, micro-environments, and each of them fostered a different way of being. What blessed diversity! How many different pathways to fulfillment!

In truth I would have carried on my "work" (how odd it feels to call this love affair with the world "work") without Peter, but he did something for me for which I'll be forever grateful. In pre-Peter times these pockets of local knowledge and custom would have been dismissed as provincial. People who stuck close to their land were hillbillies and hicks. And those of us who wrote about their life were regarded as romantic and irrelevant. But once Peter put forth his concept of bioregionalism, I was no longer a nostalgic hippie lost in the boonies. I was now a member of a movement. I was now part of a larger family, a family of poets, naturalists, artists, and thinkers. It was a family that Peter created, and even though I don't show up very often at family functions it's a family I'm proud to be part of.

MANY HAPPY RETURNS, RIGHT?

Duncan McNaughton

Along the lagoon road toward Stinson Beach
about half way I guess someone had run
down a raccoon. Four or five vultures were
standing around, another dining. I
don't recall seeing them standing around
like that before. Dignified as deacons
looking on, shiny black robes, scarlet hoods.
Having flown in from beyond human
vision. I don't believe they do it by smell.
Generally silent, etc.,
but I pulled over anyway to chat.
Five hours or so ahead of the big June
moon fattening over San Francisco.
One thing led to other things. Inquiries.
She's in a band, I said by way of explanation of the relationship and
the tattoos. Guys will do anything to
do anything. Offhand, nonchalant, both
warily. An actress too, minor stuff,
usually a bad girl, is pretty
much how the day turned out, Peter.

Good luck, pal. I think they do it by awareness.
                                                    Bolinas
                                                    2012

IN MEMORY OF PETER BERG

Stephanie Mills

When Eqbal Ahmad died, in 1999, Edward Said ended his fine memorial to his friend and colleague "His friends grieve inconsolably," a heartrending phrase that began reverberating in my mind when I learned of Peter Berg's death. Then came these lines from one of Jim Dodge's *Piss-Fir Willie Poems*:

> The hardest work you'll find in this world
> Is digging the grave for someone you loved.

The struggle to accept the reality of Peter's demise and even to hint at what his life and work meant to me has been that kind of hard.

In 1970, as a young activist, I was already witnessing the radical import of ecology being leached out of environmentalism. The environmental movement was becoming instrumental, managerial, and centralist, distancing itself from the counterculture and comporting itself as though late industrial civilization could and should continue its trajectory, but in a lite clean cosmopolitan fashion. Power relations between *Homo sapiens* and other living creatures, between researchers and the laity, bioregions and nation-states, consumers and subsistence peoples, and other structural issues weren't up for discussion downtown.

Vexed, I began work on a manuscript titled *Whatever Happened to Ecology?* Shortly thereafter, I discovered that what had happened to ecology was bioregionalism. It was a more fitting response to the planet's ecosocial crises than lobbying the Feds to ensure that things got worse less quickly.

Planet Drum was the vehicle for my introduction to bioregionalism, and Peter Berg was the driver who welcomed me aboard. Early on, Peter's genius and ultra hipness overawed me. He didn't let my trepidation skew a respectful collaboration that grew into genuine friendship. Over the years I spoke at some of Planet Drum's conferences, contributed occasionally to *Raise the Stakes*, and, thanks to Peter's initiative, co-guest edited a bioregions issue of *CoEvolution Quarterly* (No. 32, Winter 1981). It was an education. Bioregionalism—the congresses, the worldview, the practices and rhetoric—changed my life and shaped my own writing, speaking, and teaching.

Bioregionalism makes such good sense that it now, if under many other names, has the quality of obviousness. But it had to be thought up, and Peter Berg, never content merely to theorize, was a leading theorist. "Visionary" is an overworked term, but Peter was that, and intellectually rigorous, too. He articulated his ideas with a poet's care and an organizer's discipline. Which is why, along with its paramount biocentrism, Peter's opus is durable goods.

"Who am I? Where am I? and What am I going to do about it?" was the bioregional activist's catechism. The fundamental requirements of sustainability were: "Restore natural systems, satisfy basic human needs, and develop support for individuals." Carve those in living rock.

Utterly devoted to his purpose, persistent in his work, Peter Berg was nevertheless a rare ecological activist being devoid of piety or Puritanism. More pagan, he was viscerally attuned to biogeography and natural history—the peregrines, the yerba buena, the serpentine, the fogs, and the seismicity of Shasta bioregion. With like intensity, he savored journeys and art, food and drink, writing and teaching, and his family's life.

Peter was geopolitically aware and astute but expended little intellectual energy on breaking news. He was sharply aware of the severity of the ecological crisis but didn't found his rhetoric on disaster. His work focused on our being one species-kind, inhabiting diverse bioregions, capable, through our cultures, of life-enhancing participation in the planet's ecology.

Once when I was batting about some apocalyptic ideas for an upcoming talk, he said, "Don't start by opening a can of worms." Ever the bioregional organizer, he knew not to begin by appalling your listeners and diminishing hope.

Wonderful to say, after I moved from San Francisco to Leelanau County, Michigan, my friendship with Peter and Judy persisted and deepened through correspondence, phone calls, and, when I visited the Bay Area, stays at their home. The folder holding decades of postcards, letters, and dispatches from Peter is a trove of quick perceptions and deep reflections.

"Talked to Roshi at this temple for 2 hrs. about direct revelations from nature," wrote Peter in March 2001, on the back of a postcard from the Tofuki-ji temple in Japan. "Good insights!"

In addition to the travel vignettes, wide-ranging wit, and enthusiastic bulletins about Planet Drum's programs, Peter's letters also brought kindly concern and real understanding. He could be gallant!

When I last visited, in late March 2011, Peter and Judy came to the airport motel to pick me up. Peter, physically diminished but dashing in his fine black beret, emerged from their Prius with a Douglas iris to bestow, a flower from his cherished and highly significant sidewalk native plants garden.

The timbre of Peter's voice was always fine. During that last visit, Peter talked and talked, more compellingly than ever. Now the voice was hoarse. He needed an oxygen lanyard most of the time. Nevertheless on that last visit, in the course of a classic Berg and Goldhaft outing to meet some wildness in San Francisco, we whirled up to the saddle of the Twin Peaks. The sight of the Pacific sundown wind currying the lush newly reinstated native grasses on a hillside called forth plenty of voice for Peter's wonder and joy.

For the loss to the bioregionalist community and the world of this brilliant guide and for the loss of such a dear friend, I grieve—but I doubt that Peter would long countenance the inconsolability.

HOWLING WITH PETER BERG, A TRIBUTE

Giuseppe Moretti

It was a September day in 1991, late in the afternoon, when I reached the front door of Planet Drum. The door was open, and inside there was a man seated at a desk phoning. I recognized who he was, but I'd never heard his voice before; a thundering voice, I would say, speaking without pause, every word precise as if chiseled in marble.

I had just landed in San Francisco from Milan, Italy, and my instructions were to reach the offices of Planet Drum; the plan, drawn with Crofton Diack, a Planet Drum staff member, was to spend the night there and leave the next day for the Napa Valley, where the First Shasta Bioregional Gathering was going to happen. The man at the desk finally put down the phone and, turning to me, asked, "Are you Giuseppi?" "Yes," I said, and a great smile illuminated his round face. That was the beginning of my long friendship with Peter Berg, which lasted all the rest of his days on this planet.

After that event I came back home resolved to propose the idea of bioregionalism in Italy. I was not a writer nor a journalist (I was and still am a peasant farmer here in the Po river watershed bioregion); in fact, I'd never written anything, anywhere; nevertheless, I started a newsletter called *Lato Selvatico*, the medium I used to spread the bioregional vision here in the Italian peninsula, despite critics who argued the idea was inappropriate for Europe. "America," they said, "is America, and Europe is different." I was pretty aware of the cultural and ecological differences, but our rivers, our mountains and valleys were asking for the same concern that every river, mountain, and valley in the world, including those in America, were asking for: a new kind of attention, a new kind of relationship with the life-places where we live. "The bioregional idea is not an American idea. It is a biospheric idea and the biosphere is something we all share," Peter Berg said, in his 1994 interview with *Lato Selvatico*.

In the fall of 1994 Peter and Judy came to Europe for a series of conferences and performances, and they kindly accepted my invitation to come to Italy. Thanks to a small circle of friends who had come together around *Lato Selvatico*, we were able to set up talks all over Italy: Mantova, Bologna, Ravenna, Roma, Napoli, and Firenze set off our bioregional expedition. The unconventional wolf howl with which Peter usually started every talk was a sign for the audience that something different was going to happen—no more simple "save the environment" or "plant a tree." In fact, Peter took the people on a journey, asked that they re-imagine themselves and their life in term of bioregions, a new way to live on the Earth. The idea was "to save the parts if we want to save the whole." For us, now students of bioregionalism, his words nourished our minds and spirits, but for the mainstream environmentalists things stayed as they were. In an article that appeared in *La Nuova Ecologia* (January 1995) he was called a "provoker," and the bioregional idea was dismissed as "defective, without historic perspective and possibility of alliances." We all can imagine where this sort of myopia comes from.

Two years later, in 1996, we set up the Rete Bioregionale Italiana, as a "common ground" (a network) for people and groups to share ideas, experiences, projects and emotions, to develop appropriate cultural, spiritual, and material practices of life in harmony with our own places, our own bioregions, the other bioregions, and ultimately the planet Earth. Our first work together was a book, *La Terra Racconta*, on the bioregional concept, with instructions on how to design the map of our individual bioregions. We included Peter's masterpiece, "Finding Your Own Bioregion" (extract from *Discovering Your Life-place*).

Peter came two more times to Italy, the first for a conference at the University of Pisa, with meetings and radio interviews in Milan. The second time with Judy in February 2003, as Guard Fox Watch, the sister group of Planet Drum, created in defence of the watersheds in which the Winter Olympic Games were going to happen. I already knew Peter's fame as a fighter: back in Digger times they called him "the Hun." The Olympic Games Committee of Turin 2006, which invited Guard Fox Watch to monitor the preparations for the Games, didn't know Peter and found all their data, skiing outlines, and Olympic structures contested by this man who not only had the local ecosystems, the local communities, and their economies in mind but also the greater Po River watershed—"what happens upriver has influence downriver." The parts were never so distant. Peter continued to report all the negative evidence—registered at Nagano (Japan) and Salt Lake City (Utah), the sites of the previous two Olympic Games monitored by GFW—produced by the current Olympic procedures. A complete report on the bioregional impact and the ecological implications of the Games, including a whole set of recommendations, has since been produced and sent to the Olympic Committee, which they of course haven't taken into consideration, though I'm sure they won't easily forget Peter Berg.

At this point a question comes up: how is it that the bioregional proposal, suggesting we "save the parts to save the whole," that we try "to seek harmonious ways to relate to natural systems in the places/bioregions where we live," that we rethink the cities "from gray to green," that we "find sustainable ways to satisfy basic human needs" and so on, doesn't get, if not support, at least some acknowledgement from mainstream cultural/political institutions? Even, as we've seen, environmental organizations look at bioregional proposals with suspicion and mistrust. To me the bioregional proposal looks like good sense, more or less the same concept as taking care of our own homes, our own families, the general wellbeing of the community where we live. We all can agree on this. (The differences come of course in how large we consider our home, our family, our community.)

Okay, we all know the anthropocentric tendencies of the world we live in, all know how much the economies, the models of production and consumption, the cultural and political dogmas, permeate people's lives. We all know the contradictions of modern living. Notwithstanding, and possibly at the heart of it all, there is something missing from the modern human being that dramatically limits his view.

What did Peter Berg have that his environmental colleagues or people in general don't have? For me it's just a matter of practice, or better, of a certain kind of practice. We all can say we love the world, but if we have never known the world in our hearts, it will be very hard to see the deer, the mountain, the river, or our neighbour, the local community, our lover, the bakery, the furniture maker . . . as part of ourselves, and so, as we all are, part and unreplaceable elements of a very specific set of relations. What Peter used to call the bioregion.

We did remain in contact all these years. I sometimes went to see him and Judy in San Francisco. I published his articles, and he published my bioregional reports from Italy. He was particularly supportive in our recent turmoil and change from the Rete Bioregionale to the new Sentiero Bioregionale.

Peter Berg was a man of strong character, aware of the political, economic, and social complexities of the actual world. He knew how to be pragmatic, never stopped believing in the potential of the bioregional idea to offer society a concrete possibility to renew herself. Peter had the imaginative power which let him translate his ideas into actions. Never banal or repetitive, but creative, poetic, and a great fighter for the Earth.

To finish I would like to remember also the human side of Peter Berg. At the time of his first visit here in 1994—during a break in the bioregional tour—he, Judy, my then-wife, Graziella, and I went to Venice. After visiting San Marco plaza we went along the Grand Canal, gondolas everywhere, taking passengers for rides. Looking at the scene, Peter came to me and, whispering, said (I don't remember his exact words), "I know it may look bourgeois, but gondolas for us are mythic—I don't care how much it costs, I would like to take Judy for a ride and you two also."

So, off we all went in a gondola, howling!

Bioregione Bacino Fluviale del Po
July 6, 2012
Translation revised by James Koller

FORGING A NEW PATH: EVOLUTION OF ECOLOGICAL RESTORATION IN BAHÍA DE CARÁQUEZ

Clayton Plager-Unger

The ability to exchange ideas does not necessarily depend on the language one is speaking. Peter Berg made a huge impression on the local population in Bahía de Caráquez, a small city on the coast of Ecuador, with only a beginner's level of Spanish comprehension. Peter introduced new ideas about ecology and human activity to a population that had just been hit by devastating mudslides, which were followed by a 7.1 Richter earthquake. The raw force of nature had shaken residents to the core. In the aftermath, residents were exceptionally willing to reevaluate their relationship with the environment. Peter entered Ecuador with his bioregional clairvoyance like a confident actor taking the stage.

While navigating civil unrest, faulty infrastructure, and tropical diseases, Peter promoted Planet Drum's vision of reinhabitation and ecosystem restoration. The nascent eco-city movement was just taking form, as was Planet Drum's permanent field presence. Workshops, studies, and collaborations with national and international volunteers were the preliminary steps toward developing the native plant Revegetation Project and Bioregional Education Program. These initiatives continue to grow, gain support, and raise awareness to this day.

Not content with accepting the world around him as it was, Peter invented and used new words and expressions throughout his life. He realized that creating a new ecological consciousness out of a global, industrialized society would require a new vocabulary, regardless of one's native tongue. In order to understand the idea of "bioregionalism" one must first question his or her place in Planet Earth's biosphere. How do people get food, water, shelter, and energy? Where do resources come from, and where do they go? The phonetic awkwardness of the word "bioregionalism" is exacerbated only by one's isolation from the natural cycles of his or her surrounding environment.

In the province of Manabí, where Bahía is located, residents are accustomed to frequent power outages, lack of running water, and unreliable transportation, among any number of other inconveniences that are typically associated with "underdeveloped" regions. As a result, community and individual self-reliance are especially high. Whether they are aware of it or not, bioregionalism is a large part of their daily life.

It's difficult to walk down the street in Bahía without bumping into or stumbling over tangible examples. Hundreds of ecological taxis—tricycles designed for carrying two to three passengers or the equivalent load—transport people and goods around Bahía not because of an environmental mandate or to reduce carbon emissions but because drivers can make a daily wage doing it. Bamboo and thatch are widely used in construction. Craftsmen work in shops that spill onto the sidewalk. They repair appliances, machinery, and tools with whatever pieces of scrap materials are on hand.

Despite the fact that accomplishing the simplest task can easily turn into a monumental undertaking due to unexpected obstacles that abound, it is immediately apparent that in Bahía there is a large potential for promoting bioregional activities. The excitement of sharing his bioregional vision in contrast to the myriad daily hardships, challenges, and setbacks is palpable in the dispatches Peter wrote during numerous visits from 1999 through 2011.

During one of Peter's initial visits to Bahía de Caráquez, in 2000, he was attacked one night by a swarm of flying crickets, whose population violently erupts each year around the beginning of the rainy season. The episode became the focus of one of Peter's first dispatches. Even though a well-placed mosquito net and some window screens would have greatly reduced the dramatic effect of the story, the point remains significant; the wildness of nature in the tropics of Ecuador is in your face, literally. A fainter-hearted person would have caught the first flight back to his or her home country, never to return again.

In 2008, Peter and Planet Drum received a renewed sense of inspiration when Ecuador adopted the rights of nature in its new, first-ever popularly approved constitution. The country named after one of the most fundamentally defining characteristics of the planet became the first to give constitutional rights to nature, or *pachamama*—Quichua for "the space where life exists." Quichua expressions, such as *sumak kawsay* "good living," abound in the new constitution. In a section called "Soil" in the chapter on "Biodiversity and Natural Resources," the government states that it will "develop and promote . . . revegetation projects that avoid single-crop farming and preferably use native species adapted to the area."

Interestingly enough, Ecuador now considers itself a pluri-national state, and the new constitution formally recognizes the various indigenous groups that inhabit its territory. In fact, the struggle for these rights is related to the civil unrest that Peter witnessed in 2000, when indigenous groups marched on Quito and participated in the forceful removal, with help from the military, of President Jamil Mahuad.

Throughout this time, Planet Drum continued to move forward with its ecological restoration initiatives. The native plant nursery grew in size and production. Selection of species for revegetation was honed to focus on the most effective species for erosion control, habitat creation, and community engagement. Over the years, dozens of local landowners collaborated in the planting of tens of thousands of native trees. Hundreds of schoolchildren participated in the Bioregional Education Program, learning about bioregionalism and how to apply those ideas to Bahía. Peter was an integral part in organizing and participating in numerous conferences, workshops, gatherings, parades, and celebrations.

In November 2010, the last time Peter came to Ecuador, he had lung cancer, traveled with an oxygen machine, and, instead of traveling directly to Bahía, ended up in the hospital in Guayaquil with anemia complications resulting from ongoing chemotherapy sessions. The purpose of his visit was to plan the Bioregional Sustainability Institute, which is a synthesis of Planet Drum's projects set in a formal academic context where students receive school credit for learning about and hands-on practice of bioregionalism.

In his final dispatch from Ecuador, he laid out the design for "A School to Retrieve the Future." With its unique and intact natural systems, Bahía becomes the setting for high-level bioregional education. Planet Drum's experiences shared with local residents and the knowledge gained about ecosystem restoration are the basis for educating students so that they can become bioregional educators and practitioners themselves in order to spread bioregional wisdom wherever their lives may lead them.

The city of Bahía continues to strive to become the ecological city that Peter helped plan for in 1999 and is now considered the nation's premier ecological city. Peter's contribution to the city was immortalized in November 2012 when the city held a ceremony in his honor and unveiled a plaque at the entrance of City Hall that recognizes the dedication he gave to Bahía and calls him the "father of bioregionalism."

Peter had a gift of perception that allowed him to make observations at a glance that most might spend a large portion of their life pondering. He recognized that Bahía has an irresistibly high potential for ecological restoration (reinhabitation). To this day, I am approached by a wide variety of locals who met Peter years ago and distinctly recall their interactions with an older white man who wore a pony tail and shared ecological wisdom with whoever would listen to his imperfect Spanish.

November 2012

PETER BERG

Kirkpatrick Sale

I knew Peter, of course, through the bioregional movement, of which he was such an important pioneer, and together we worked hard to, as it were, put it on the map. We met at the First Bioregional Congress in Missouri in 1984 and I was taken—as who was not?—by his dramatic stage presence even when there was no stage and by his unlimited dedication to our environmental cause. We met at many bioregional affairs in subsequent years at least through the 1990s, and though I turned my attention to other kinds of politics, Peter never flagged or drifted and led Planet Drum as the primary organization of the movement until his death.

What I wrote down when I first learned of Peter's passing was this: "Peter was a decenter man than many realized, and almost as important as he thought he was."

Decency counts for something, and he wouldn't have inspired as many as he did without it, even at those times in the congresses when we got into some fairly heavy debates or grew absent-minded from perhaps an ingestion of herbs or tired of the new people who always needed so much bringing-along. He was always honest in all my dealings with him, straightforward, and as often as not able to find humor in what was otherwise a moment of tension or difficulty.

As to his role in the movement, I take nothing away from his dedication, persistence, and energy when I say that I never was much taken with his writing, for of course that was not his primary talent, no matter how well he made *Raise the Stakes*, for quite some time, into an important outlet for bioregional thinking.

I must confess to a profound disappointment that the bioregional movement did not have even more an impact than it did, but we all know that sowing ecological wisdom in an age of self-indulgent capitalism is a difficult project. And, by God, we did what we could, and we did educate and inspire many thousands of people, in this country and elsewhere, and we put a concept onto the political-environmental agenda and into the ecological literature that will live on, no matter what, to be found and learned anew when the moment comes, after the collapse of the system, when people will want to know the best way to live in harmony with the Earth.

THE MECHANICS OF REINHABITATION: REMEMBERING PETER BERG ALONG THE BIOREGIONAL TRAIL

David Simpson

It is not unusual for there to be a gap of considerable emotional distance between the exaltation that accompanies important human scientific or intellectual discovery and the humdrum, day-to-day level of behavior that surrounds the lives of the discoverers. The theme of the quotidian nipping at the heels of the momentous has many variants, and often it is in the completely ordinary that great things find their choicest breeding ground.

There was nothing ordinary or drab, though, about the lives we lived together in random collectivity in the 1960s and into the early 1970s. Nor could anyone suggest that Peter Berg's day-to-day communications, then or at any other point, were lacking in drama, content, or color.

If from time to time friends and nemeses of Peter found annoyance in his outpouring of rhetoric, it was usually in terms of form more than of meaning. The barrages he regularly unleashed on audiences, witting or otherwise, were sometimes thunderous and intimidating. In actuality, they were driven by his need to keep communicative pace with the rate and intensity of his internal discoveries on the perversions of imperial America. Peter was before all else a man of visionary ideas. A close second was his uncanny capacity for challenging intellectual dishonesty and dismembering rationales for the status quo, no matter how subtle.

A factor contributing to the intensity of all of our actions and perceptions in the brief, fiery Digger incarnation (1966–68) was an unspoken competition with one another—always the men. The object of such competition was to strike the first or most damaging blow (to "count coup") against whatever shibboleth of repressive, war-driven, pre-'60s society fell within our sights. We attacked by instinct what we thought were pathologies of an immoral status quo. Once the counterculture grew and provided a protective cover both in numbers and in commitment to basic, shared ideologies, we upped the ante and attacked with yet less reserve.

Even in such a tribe and in a time where wild iconoclasm was normal behavior, Peter stood out. It earned him the sobriquet of "The Hun" in some circles for his unrelenting, take-no-prisoners assaults on the murderous hypocrisy and dishonesty that were on their way to become the norm in mainstream American culture. (The image of The Hun had been reinforced when Peter had his head forcibly shaved in early 1967 by the Las Vegas police after they arrested him for, as he described it, driving a car with Indians in it.)

As virulent, clever, and necessary as Peter's attacks on existing cultural norms were, his real creativity in the end was reserved for the far more constructive envisioning of what the terms for a livable future might be and what steps might help us get there. Sometimes eccentric, often bawdy or wrapped in a scathing humor, Peter's leaps into the future were reliably prophetic and, in the end, absolutely serious. The task of explicating a comprehensive and somewhat practical set of ideas that could allow for the development of a sustainable culture was to become central in Peter's focus after 1972.

Simplicity, poverty, and old trucks

A factor in our evolving ideology early on was our self-elected commitment to a state of personal impoverishment or "simplicity." It was part and parcel of our bedrock concept of who we were and what we were doing in the world—a natural outcome of our virulently anticommercial lifestyles, to say nothing of our commitment to the value of "Free."

In our shared intellectual framework, wealth, even a mild version of it, or security might have drawn us away from the acting out of our shared ideals. It might have challenged the solidarity we felt with the masses of people worldwide who were excluded from the comforts and conveniences of the burgeoning American middle class. Its gain was almost always an illegitimate distraction from the real work. At worst, it was a false idol that had the capacity to lure us back into the painfully repressive arena of pre-'60s consciousness.

Doing without the comfort of money and the prosaic grounding that the pursuit of wealth required didn't exactly lubricate the wheels on which our world turned. It certainly didn't endear us to average middle-class Americans who, upon encountering the obvious pleasure we took in our nonremunerative "work" (contrasted with the tedium of their commercially oriented lives), often found themselves affronted. The fact that this work during the Digger era basically involved the redistribution of resources might have contributed to this pique.

Since this is in the end a story of searching, travel, and migration, nowhere did this subtle trade-off of freedom for material comfort play out with more impact than in the constant demand our ancient vehicles—chariots of cultural warfare and spiritual exploration—made on us to keep them running. The price? Busted knuckles, grease-stained clothing, hours spent in the oily mud under leaky old trucks, and a more or less complete surrender of the luxury of wide social approbation. (No one was thanking us for being poor and greasy.) The reward? A truck running by one's own hand that did not require keeping a job just to pay for, a healthy acquaintance with California winter mud, and a questionable but nonetheless strong sense of righteousness that was to carry us well out onto the road home.

It seems unlikely from this remove that the mobility required for a significant segment of an entire generation to find a place on the planet could have been accomplished in this fleet of beat-up old pickup trucks, derelict school buses, and rust-bucket panel vans. It was in these that we bombed around San Francisco in the heady days of the counterculture, hustling for or "liberating" the materials necessary to forge even a semblance of a social safety net for the disaffected youth swarming the city. And it was in these same rusty behemoths or ones just like them that we, a little later, were to travel far out over the landscape in our intuitive quest for places where we might take root. Ultimately, in an ironic turn, the necessity to keep our vehicles running and our eyes on a new, more primitive kind of future helped ground us in a functional, even meditative relationship to the everyday world around us. It could be said that niggling mechanical demands—our feet of clay—actually helped lift us to heights of spirit achievable few other ways.

Stockholm

In June 1972, Peter Berg traveled to Stockholm, Sweden, to witness the United Nations Conference on the Human Environment. It was the UN's and, for that matter, the nations of the world's first major effort to deal with environmental issues on a planet-wide basis. (Peter had recently come to prefer the term "planet" as opposed to "globe" or "world" or even "Earth." He spent a fair amount of time just then explicating what alternative nuances accrued from whatever word you chose to describe that comely "blue marble" photographed from the Apollo satellite later in 1972.)

According to many observers, Stockholm marked a major turning point in the development of the world's environmental politics. Of course, prior to the first Earth Day, in 1970, there had been no broad or in any way state-sanctioned recognition that environmental politics on a "planetary level" were even necessary. The Stockholm event was the first formal international forum where governments, multinational corporations, and large, often newly created environmental organizations traded pronouncements about the environment. They even joined together to make the first of what was going to prove to be a long series of high-sounding, even astute, but, in the long run, weightless statements to the world.

For the first time, though, such words as "sustainability" and "stewardship" found currency on the largest stage. It should be kept in mind that despite the various tokenisms that were to come out of Stockholm, this period of environmental foment from 1967 through Earth Day to Stockholm and beyond did yield considerable fruit within the United States. A spate of landmark environmental legislation—quite radical from the perspective of today—was passed during the Nixon years (e.g., the Clean Air Act, Clean Water Act, Endangered Species Act, the foundation of the EPA). One might attribute the level of openness to change at that point in history to a lack of full recognition as to what sustainability was actually going to require of us.

Peter, meanwhile, was to return from his trip imbued with a renewed sense of mission provoked as much by what he found missing at the conference as by what had been represented. The first Planet Drum "Bundle" was published less than a year later. It represented an effort to forge a new perspective from disparate elements and social critiques. This perspective studiously avoided tendencies among then-current conservation directives, tendencies that rendered environmentalism ineffective at slowing the depredations of free-market industrial capitalism on the planet. At every turn the environmental agenda was threatened with cooption by the very people and institutions that had caused the problem to begin with.

Behind us, casting a long shadow, sat a history and a dominant frame of reference haunted by the archaic politically drawn boundaries upon which nation-states have been founded. There was a strong need for this established geographical and psychological perspective to give way so that the underlying shapes of the biosphere and the realities of the natural world might be felt. This task was almost feverishly political. We sought a perspective that transcended anything resembling the artificial geopolitical boundaries within which we had grown up. We saw ourselves working in the service of an emerging consciousness based in planetary reality and the terrain of our own psyches.

This budding perspective pointed at how humans might reclaim an appropriate role in the natural world, something other than that of industrial leech sucking on the tender flesh of the mother planet or brute creatures that, left unregulated, could not help but desecrate the last remnants of our "wilderness" heritage—while all the time reproducing without measure.

The environmental movement right from the start was far more effective at identifying and decrying wrongs done to the planet one by one than it was at envisioning a different relationship of humans to nature. Without that new vision, though, we were stranded, unable to even approach sustainability. The environmental movement, such as it was in 1972, seemed to be seeking a simple on-off switch.

There was, though, no switch available to us by which we could simply turn off industrial capitalism. We were all, to some degree, caught in its brutal web. All environmentalism could do short of an impossibly radical challenge was to tinker around the edges, protecting a few of the remaining "wilderness reserves," applying desultory regulatory schemes, or simply lamenting our losses.

The effort at developing a workable alternative perspective—at re-envisioning and reinvigorating the place of humans in the natural world—was to fall to a growing cadre of place-based thinkers and activists, many of whom were to be mobilized by Planet Drum, the central legacy of Peter and Judy Berg.

The quiet migration

If 1972 signaled the official awakening of consciousness about the environment, it also lay right in the midst of a period of great but largely unheralded transiency, a veritable migration of tribes, collectives, families away from the perceived dead ends of Middle America. It was a migration mostly but not exclusively of young people outward from the great cities of America, and especially from the Queen City of the '60s, San Francisco—a New Age diaspora.

It is an irony that the greatest economic growth period perhaps in civilization's history—which had hugely expanded the American middle class—produced in only its second or third generation a whole cohort that largely rejected the values that made for such an enormous economic and distributional success. The currents that we swam in were dangerously contrary, filled with unseen reefs and back eddies, intensifying the febrile spirit in which we had first launched our journeys.

Conundrum Creek and the importance of spirits

It was brandy, a small amount of very strong brandy rationed out with great care, that played the enabling role in our tale. Brandy, though, was the last thing on our minds the fresh chilled morning of that last Saturday in November 1972 when we—the Bergs in their van and we in our house-truck—finally kicked the blocks lose and began to trundle down the road, pulling away from our camp on Conundrum Creek. We followed the flow of Castle Creek, which drained the north face of Castle Peak rising behind us to the south to an altitude of more than fourteen thousand feet. The Maroon Bells rose majestic in the southwest, glowing in the morning sunlight.

A few miles below our abandoned camp, Castle Creek fed into a larger tributary of the Colorado River valley, the mildly overnamed Roaring Fork River. (The dominant roar it has come to emit in its forty-nine-mile course from the joining of its tributaries to its confluence with the mainstream Colorado at Glenwood Springs is that of commerce.)

There at the confluence of several grand slopes ideal for that most dashing of human athletic pursuits sat Aspen, Colorado. It was not yet a colossally overbuilt haven for the extremely rich but rapidly on its way to becoming the standard. Our fates, as principled paupers and prospective people of the land, lay north and west down the Roaring Fork to Steamboat on the Colorado itself and then west along the great Colorado's inner gorge shared with Interstate Highway 70 that ran from Denver toward Salt Lake City and the far West.

Almost a month earlier, Jane and I, our three children, Gaby, Omar, and Sierra, along with two other boys, Todd and Kerry, who were friends of the family, had traveled from Humboldt County, California, to Chuck and Destiny Gould's home above Conundrum Creek near Aspen, Colorado. We drove a 1955 two-ton Chevy truck with a funky but handsome recycled redwood cabin built onto the bed and out over the truck's cab. It was a bulky, slow-moving artifact of our backwoods Humboldt landscape, but in the shapes of its roof and body and the various paraphernalia hanging from the sides there were clear intimations of the earlier pioneers' Conestoga wagon or the timeless gypsy caravan. Most noticeably, the long half-crescent windows on either side above the cab bore a calculated resemblance to the eye of the Raven as it was depicted in Kwakiutl and other Northwest tribal imagery.

We crawled in stately fashion from our backwoods mooring in the cutover redwood and fir forest out onto the contemporary American highway with its generous pre-1973 speed limit of 70 mph, a speed we reached only on long, straight downhill reaches and even that with trepidation about our ability to bring the beast to a timely stop if one suddenly became required.

Chuck Gould and Destiny Kinal, with whom we had been close during the latter part of the Digger period in San Francisco's infamous Haight Ashbury, had established a semi-temporary home for themselves in the Rockies. They happily allowed the place to be used as a sort of way station for whichever family friends might be passing through on their way to the nascent communes of the southwest or on the long run to the East Coast. (The counterculture as it existed outside the cities then was still a thin web of outposts.)

The house the Goulds had rented nestled in the aspen and blue spruce forest along Conundrum Creek, one of the mighty Colorado River's thousands of feeder creeks. This one at its mouth just below our camp was maybe 1,500 feet in elevation above Aspen. Aspen's elevation was 7,900 feet.

Chuck and Destiny were unusually enterprising people as well as generous friends and had arranged work for us down the hill from Conundrum. Jane was to teach a dance class at the mildly exclusive Aspen Health Club, and I was offered construction work with Chuck, helping to build Aspen's first community school.

Jane's and my hope was to make enough money in a few weeks of work to get us through the better part of winter back in Humboldt. It was a reasonable ambition given that our needs were few. Even back then before it was hardly Aspen, a lot more money existed there than in the little Pacific coastal timber towns around which we lived. The whole rural landscape of northwestern California had been largely abandoned after the big trees were gone.

We had parked our rig in a small clearing in the aspen forest at the base of the hill upon which Chuck and Destiny's house sat. Meals were shared up at the much warmer, more spacious house on the hill with Chuck and Destiny and their daughters, Gillian and Solange.

There was great pleasure, as I recall, in those meals and the long conversations afterward around the fireplace into which Chuck fed a steady supply of aspen logs. The kids were thoroughly wrapped in each other's company, and it was sweet and comforting for us old friends and communards to be together again after a long absence. The intense philosophical intimacies and shared political passions bred in the glory years of the past decade were easily rekindled. We were deeply social creatures too long disallowed from freely swimming together in what had become our healthiest medium, each other's companionship.

The Bergs arrived a few days later and from the opposite direction. The crossing of our schedules was completely coincidental—meeting near Aspen had been in neither of our original travel plans. Peter and Judy had been calling in to the Goulds from the road but hadn't been able to pin point a time of arrival. Our old trucks reliably got us places but rarely according to a predictable schedule. Peter and Judy were traveling back west with their two children, Aaron and Ocean, after a year-long eastern sojourn (which included Peter's foray to Stockholm). Their vehicle was a large, squat International Harvester Carry-All painted a dank eggplant purple, a creaky old UPS van clearly gone rogue.

Two days before their arrival in Aspen, it seems, while still on the flat eastern Colorado plain, the Bergs had started hearing a whirring noise emanating from the rear of their engine compartment, which sat beneath a cowling inside the cab of the vehicle. They felt it was entirely unwise but nonetheless necessary to ignore the noise and plow ahead in hopes that the problem would not grow to a crippling dimension until they were safely with friends or at least close to them.

The mainstream zeitgeist as it pertained to the road in that era was both more antagonistic toward obvious social mutants like ourselves—and our outmoded and often illegal vehicles—and more permissive. It might have been that a dim memory of Dust Bowl migrations on America's highways produced a tolerance of a style of travel as subversive as ours. It did not, though, provoke easy familiarity. It made family travel in the vivid and demanding way we did it possible, but we were also more vulnerable to ending up stranded in inhospitable surroundings. It was good—even necessary—to have friends along the routes we plied. More than friends, really—People, as in "Our People," as in the new tribalism. Friendship made hospitality a nice option. Being of the same people made it mandatory.

On their way up the very last hill to Chuck and Destiny's the whirring sound coming from the Bergs's vehicle became an outright clanging. The purple van pulled into the clearing below the Goulds on Conundrum Creek in a clatter of distress. Before we had thoroughly hugged and concluded the happy warbling of renewed affections, we were collectively thrust deep into the prosaic world of truck mechanics. Our combined mechanical wisdom soon produced an analysis that the problem with the van was the throw-out bearing that helps activate the clutch. It had loosened with wear and begun to come apart. The fact that the Bergs made it up the long grade from the Roaring Fork with such a sorely worn mechanism was just short of miraculous. Perhaps it could provide the basis for a new holiday sacred to orthodox proto-bioregionalists. (How do you say "Eternal Throw-Out Bearing" in Hebrew?)

It had brought them unto safety and with only one small but significant consequence—the worn bearing at the very last stage of its disintegration, perhaps just yards from the parking spot itself, had allowed the drive shaft to wobble and gyrate. The clanging and the intense vibration had cracked the bell housing, an essential metal casing that protects the flywheel. Significant repairs were required, and they were going to happen, by necessity, right there in that frigid high alpine clearing where the van now sat side by side with our house-truck and Chuck's smaller GMC flatbed truck of similar vintage.

Through the application of our combined mechanical knowledge (often limited to advocating strategic applications of duct tape and bailing wire), the three men decided that we should fall back on the wise policy that had come to be our tradition in face of breakdown—Retreat and Celebrate. It could have been an added hexagram in the I Ching: *When the axle of the ox cart is broken and one cannot cross the waters, great or otherwise, the Superior Man does not try to force events but instead Retreats to eat and drink with friends and Celebrate around the fire.*

The addition of the Bergs to the company in the nights that followed stoked the preexisting bonhomie into a full-on joy, a renewal of the Digger-Free Family spirit in front of that roaring aspen fire. Minor abrasions from past low-grade competitions and accidental slights endemic to on-again-off-again collective living were long healed or forgotten. We reveled in each other's company.

An extended and intense conversation developed over the course of our time together. It was directed toward what might be next in the context of a shared history for us all—assuming we would get past the busted bell housing and throw-out bearing. Thoughts elicited from Peter's trip to Stockholm in June of that year and his brief entry into international environmental politics were still drumming steadily in his head awaiting a flowering.

So was another long conversation initiated during a visit in Nova Scotia that Peter had paid to poet and radical social activist Allen Van Newkirk just before the trip to Stockholm. It was in those conversations that the term "bioregionalism" was first bandied about. At the time, it was more a description of appropriate ecological partitioning rather than any sort of guide for how humans might better relate to the natural world. It would develop that capacity only later after the completion of a wider ongoing discussion, one that included famed California ecologist Ray Dasmann and legendary poet Gary Snyder.

The rediscovery of nature

There were many genies released by the '60s, but none, thank God, so difficult to put back in its bottle as a heightened awareness of the nature of the given world. Nature itself for all intents and purposes had been discovered anew and in a richness and complexity far outside the reach of musty textbooks and academic laboratories. Diverse, enormous, infinitesimally detailed, exquisitely patterned, outright pulsing with sensuality—this newly rediscovered creation, this vast panoply of color and sound, smell and touch, of what was around, beneath, outside, within us—rocked our awareness profoundly. A vastly more ornate biology, including powerful sexuality, was an essential part of the reconnection. Many of us might at this distance wish to deny it, but it was LSD and other psychedelics that had forced open our eyes and revealed the previously incomprehensible nature of nature. It had shaken us to the core and at the same time established the necessity for finding reliable footing—new and unassailable relationships and identities—in this ever more complex natural world.

This new awareness was to color every system, discipline or language previously devised by civilization to help us understand and explain nature and society. Philosophy, for instance, became eco-philosophy. Perceptions about our relationship to the natural world were sought now in Plato's cave. History came to be as much about the story of humans' impact on nature as on one another. Every natural science became almost overnight far more sophisticated and complex in light of the new awareness. Young scientists found meaningful challenge in digging ever deeper into their disciplines. New perceptions kindled new vocabularies capable of communicating what was being learned so rapidly through newly sensitized systematic observations. It made the myriad losses to the natural world we had witnessed even in our brief lives—the smothering under concrete so many sweet places we had ran and played in as children—ever less tolerable.

Economy was for the first time paired in some advanced thinking with ecology, and economic models in which growth was the dominant force were thrust up against a newly vitalized concept: sustainability. We in our inner-city enclaves and warrens at that time had felt strongly from the outset that the enormous machine of the industrial capitalist economy could not, for much longer, be sustained. Its insatiable appetite for profit and growth doomed it to more or less perpetual internal and external warfare and pushed it hard up against the real limits of the natural world and against the indigenous people and land-based cultures that still protected parts of it.

This budding awareness, by 1972, was also the source, when heeded, of a kind of modesty that had been largely absent in the past among our industry and empire-building forbearers. It was a recognition of how little we knew and how much we needed to know before we could arrive at an understanding and an interpretation of events that would enable us to find our rightful place spiritually and economically in this vast newly revealed inheritance. And finding that place was likely to be crucial in salvaging humankind and its fellow species from the fires of our own extermination.

One thing was clear; there was no going back. Unmoored from the disintegrating scene in SF and incapable of holding a strong center or a cohesive ideological focus for any length of time, we, the Digger/Free Family, might already have been reabsorbed by mainstream culture one person or one family at a time. That culture, of course, would had to have gained antibodies to make us more digestible than we had originally been, or we would have had to be inoculated with a larger tolerance for what had grown to be morally and spiritually ever less tolerable in the heart of the repressive, war-driven culture. But it had not and we had not. The trails back into "respectable" America, its fixation with Vietnam and its vast disinterest in sustainability, were closed to us as surely as any high mountain pass in winter.

Peter Berg and the Digger ethos

Modesty was not the first word you would use to describe Peter Berg or, for that matter, any of the young men and, in some ways, women who identified with the concepts and actions that defined the Diggers. The whole Digger ethos seemed at times to be founded to some degree in an unshakable certainty of purpose and a machismo elan. Given how we acted in those early days of intense new cultural manifestations—the subtle swagger that seemed to be a crucial element of our adaptations and their impacts on the world around us—it is remarkable that as many of us survived as did. In truth, the line between the cultural warrior and the out-and-out rogue was fine.

Peter had always been something of a contrarian, a gadfly, whose ability to irritate was eclipsed only by the penetrating clarity of his thinking and the incisive power of his metaphors. He had a prodigiously original mind capable of a sometimes prophetic quality and the kind of color that was largely lacking in the mainstream intellectual discourse. Such discourse indeed paled into black-and-white before the rush of the era's visceral excitements. Peter thought and communicated with a verve and a passion that were antidotal to the weak soup we'd previously been fed.

Peter's rap was an ongoing, often rapid-fire, imagery-rich critique of American materialism and the tedium and drabness of bourgeois life. To conform to it required mute acceptance of seemingly endless, brutal warfare, at that particular moment in Vietnam. Dealing with warfare, in this analysis, became a factor more of culture than of politics or economics. America's was literally a culture of war. Liberating oneself from conformity to the dominant culture was an effective way to free oneself of its habitual political tyranny and passion for war. Long hair or tie-dye dresses were hardly badges of courageous dissent, but they did set one at a greater distance from the M-16 and PTSD.

In the late Mime Troupe, early Digger days, Peter's was a powerful clarion call to liberation of self through cultural rebirth and actions consonant with it. If the Haight and the powerful cultural revolution that took root there had a political commissar, it was Peter. Mix his ability with contemporary liberationist language, old-line Marxist-Leninist critiques of bourgeois values, and a dose of the outrageous, bawdy humor that few others could muster, and the result was a potent and original sociopolitical amalgam. When it didn't rise to achieve visionary cohesion, his rap at least left you with a smile. It was, finally, a powerful call to action. We didn't know much, but we intuited that action challenging the cultural status quo was demanded of us.

What we talked about at Conundrum

When we sat around those brilliant aspen fires five or so years later and shared notes on past visions and visions yet to come, Peter was earnest on a new level. Here in this mountain retreat post-Stockholm, he was still challenging, funny, and acerbic, but he was on the verge of what was to become the most compelling and entirely serious set of perceptions his life would contain. The importance of paying proper deference to these perceptions and his sense of how great were the stakes seemed to have produced an unusual moderation in Peter. We were all growing up.

One of the things that is so interesting about Stockholm, the first fully international effort to deal with environmental disrepair, was that right off the bat it set the terms and the limits for dialogue between interests (government, large commercial interests, civil society, indigenous peoples). It delegated, by some consistent instinct, varying power and position within this emerging framework to those interests.

These still-uncodified structures and limitations to access to power within the larger dialogue were to remain a relative constant in future UN environmental efforts whether convened under the concept of Sustainable Development (Rio and Rio+) or as the Framework Convention on Climate Change (UNFCCC COP's). The rich nations—back then mostly America, European countries, and Japan—referred to as the "first world" and later as the "developed nations," quietly held the reins of real power, to the frustration of the "third world" and the "developing nations." They have made of the UN, in its environmental manifestations, a servant to the goal of controlling and sustaining wealth through cooption of environmental language and concepts and further subjugation of local cultures and economies.

Several long-range problems concerning environmentalism emerged in Stockholm. One was the corporateness of the large "world" environmental organizations. A prime example was the International Union for the Conservation of Nature (IUCN), based in Geneva. At the time, the chairman of the board of the IUCN was one of the cagier oil barons of his day, Robert O. Anderson, CEO of Atlantic Richfield. This cozy board-sharing relationship, it seemed to Peter, was emulated by the environmental movement's larger international players. It was a previously unheralded revolving door that potentially called into question primary motivations and capacity for straight dealing.

Another problem that was not yet quite out of the closet then but coming related to large environmental organizations themselves and to the directions of environmentalism in general. A principal orientation of the environmental movement was the protection and preservation of still-unspoiled wild systems or of some species that were close to extinction. On another tangent were environmentalists' narrow focus on controlling the human population and its impacts on the planet.

Humans, in relationship to any of these perspectives, were seen as creators of the problem. Solutions often had to do with terminating or severely limiting this influence on select landscapes, sometimes by terminating the very presence of humans. This solution too often rationalized the curtailing of influence of indigenous peoples and peasant agriculturists whose ecological and cultural relationships to their environment were many generations deep and in fact were often the primary reason the ecosystems were still intact. They were viewed then, and often still are, as a force for ecological damage—as if there was a perfect natural state that preexisted all human impacts, an original, more or less permanent ecological balance and well-being. This failure to distinguish the uses indigenous and land-based peoples made of their environment from those of large, externally based economic interests has helped perpetuate great injustices and resulted in ecological disasters on an enormous scale.

What Peter encountered in Stockholm turned out to be motifs and structures that were to order the flow of the international environmental dialogue for decades to come and provide the basic undergirding of efforts by the UN and other lesser international forums to control and contain that dialogue within bounds that were acceptable to the great economic powers. Part of this right from the start had to do with access—who would be granted access to decision making at these events and who would be excluded. The forum was undeniably important because it was attended by representatives of most of the world's governments. Conflicts arose, though, because of a basic dynamic; the major impetus for opening a dialogue over specific problems, or for noting that problems existed at all, usually came not from government, especially those of the developed nations, or from industry and commerce, but from what is commonly referred to as Civil Society.

At these gatherings, Civil Society is largely composed of individuals and non-governmental organizations working at various levels and scales, deeply committed to dealing with environmental and social problems, some specific and some not. Governments in these forums, especially those of the developed nations, seemed too likely to represent national commercial interests working to evade the costs of effective environmental responses. Real problem solvers seemed to be underrepresented or forced to the margins of deliberations.

At its more roughhewn fringes where people actually lived, Civil Society included indigenous peoples, peasant farmers, traditional agriculturists, campesinos, and other inhabitants of place-based and land-based communities. Large industrial and commercial interests whose extractive processes were the cause of many of the problems (with which the Conference was convened to deal) were much more likely to be represented in the formal UN-sponsored forums than were critics drawn from these communities whose landscapes were being negatively impacted.

The UN processes became, piecemeal and indirectly, a forum for limiting demand for effective environmental action. (The United States was to become the leading obstructive force in UN processes established to deal with climate change.) These processes also proved themselves resistant to concepts and initiatives that would have allowed land-based communities at least a portion of power to determine their own destinies or even to guarantee their own survival. This was especially so when rights of land-based people or impoverished urban communities imposed limits on the ability of large commercial interests to exploit a resource, gain access to cheap labor, or dump pollutants into neighboring water, soil, and atmosphere.

The rights of indigenous and land-based peoples were crucial in the short and the long run to more than their cultural survival. Observance of those rights was central to the protection of ecosystems. Mainstream environmentalism had somehow missed this age-old connection between healthy indigenous cultures and healthy landscapes. Many models for action, even for the least corrupted environmental initiatives, were based on the desire to protect wilderness and endangered species. They missed this crucial connection of human culture and the land.

Peter was keenly aware of the shortcomings and inequities of the UN process that were already on display in Stockholm. These severe limitations on environmental and social effectiveness forced a question: if the United Nations, the ostensible repository of the power and wisdom of the combined governments of the world, was not going to effect changes that survival of species, ecosystems, and cultures required, who was? How could local, land-based people and cultures gain the power necessary for their survival? The health of their lands, it had started to become clear, depended upon access to that power.

In the end, it was the basic nature of the forum itself—representative of nation-states coming together to solve the planet's problems—that was the problem. States existing within their politically drawn boundaries, along with their corporate allies, exercised almost complete extractive sovereignty over natural systems within those boundaries. They tended to form a crude overlay shorting out the subtle, complex circuitry of ecosystems by which the planet sustains its resiliency.

Modern industrially developed economies instinctively seek homogeneity, simplification, and the replication of identical cultural shapes and forms regardless of the vast complexity of the landscapes they cover. Nation-states as manifestations and defenders of large economic interests do not respond to ecological signals first and foremost, if at all. In this light, how to realign society and cultures with the pulse and flow of underlying nature was to become the central question and one that the UN by the very way it is constituted was unable to answer or even understand. This understanding awaited the development of a truly "bioregional" vision.

Back to reality

But before these great planetary issues could be forced into the world dialogue, there was the matter of obdurate physical reality at the microcosmic level. What stood between Peter and Judy and the launch of their new publication, with its crucial explication of the limits of world environmentalism circa 1972, was a clutch, a throw-out bearing, and a bell housing. It was in dealing with these mechanical factors, for however many days it required in our cold Conundrum Creek redoubt, that our collective clock was going to be set.

It didn't take us long to dismantle the clutch plate, but the International Harvester bell housing has some peculiarities that made it a challenge to free it from the drive train. We finally had to loosen the rear motor mounts and jack up the engine block a little before the busted bell housing, which it turned out was fabricated in two parts rather than the more typical one, was free. Then arose the question of where to find a replacement.

The trucks much favored by our crew in the mid-'60s—Chevy, GMC, and occasionally Dodge pickups and small flatbeds manufactured between, let's say,

1947 and 1955—required an almost constant replenishment of parts. Even if new parts were still manufactured, their cost would have been prohibitive. Our only hope lay in auto and truck dismantlers or wreckers—junk yards.

Junk yards once existed in abundance in sprawling, blighted, postindustrial landscapes on the seedier edges of small towns and cities alike. They are a sub-culture within themselves that provides a crucial service to those who lead eco-nomically marginal but honest existences at society's fringes. At one point this amounted to a substantial percentage of our fellow Americans and may do so once again as the middle class continues to shrink. Junk yards were extremely vulner-able to the approach of wealth and its ability to regularly replace entire fleets of cars at the first signs of aging. Gentrification was a quick death to the world of the auto dismantler and the colorful, knowing characters who peopled it.

Around Aspen, junk yards even back then tended toward the boutique. Auto dismantlers had been tacitly shoved elsewhere by the irresistible force of surg-ing real estate values. We found it necessary to extend our search deep into the Colorado countryside. It wasn't until we hit Rifle, a town 60 miles up the Colo-rado from Glenwood Springs and perhaps 120 from our Conundrum camp that we finally hit pay dirt—an old International Carry All—a gorgeous gem sitting forlorn and alone in the half-frozen mud at the back of a wrecking yard just out of town. Removing the bell housing was a slow, cold, muddy task, but we were motivated by an anticipation that we might actually accomplish our mission.

It took us only another day back at Conundrum to get the new bell housing in place, but it turned out to be a costly day because the rebuilt clutch plate had to go on first. In this process, one of us, who need not be singled out, forged ahead without proper communication. It was with the intention of furthering our work that he had climbed under the truck and began tightening up the nuts on what he thought were the bolts that secure the clutch plate to the whole mechanism. The problem was that instead of getting a socket onto one of the clutch plate mount-ing bolts, he got it on to one of the adjustment nuts on the pressure plate itself. We were not to understand the full implications of this until the next morning, after we had secured the bell housing and all the mounting bolts. When we finally fired up the truck and tested the clutch, fully expecting, in our innocence, forward motion, nothing happened. The truck stood stationary despite numerous attempts to activate the clutch and shift into gear.

Why it did this was just then eons beyond our limited capacity to diagnose. We were fortunate, though, to find by telephone a mechanic of considerably more experience than our own. Turns out that the adjustment nuts on the pressure plate were supposed to be set with an arbor press, a heavy-duty press weighing several tons that establishes exactly equal pressure throughout the clutch. Without such evenly set pressure, established by the settings of the nuts on the mounting plate, the clutch would not engage and the truck would continue to go nowhere.

The nearest shop with an arbor press was in east Denver, a couple hundred miles off and, we discovered, closed on the weekend, which was just about to start. By way of throwing us poor dogs a bone, the mechanic who provided this information suggested that if we were desperate we could try to find the right combination of pressure on the clutch adjustment bolts on our own, using only hand wrenches. He forewarned us, though, that the combinations of pressure on the three nuts were nearly infinite, and only the exact one would work. What choice had we but to try?

Thus began one of the most odd and tedious episodes in our collective mechanical experience. The next several days were composed of the same ritual, parts of which were ripe with tedium: have breakfast, after which Peter, Chuck, and I descended to the trucks and started a small campfire a little distance from the van's radiator. Then we swept the night's accumulation of snow from around the bottom of the cab of the truck so that we could crawl underneath. Then we got out The Jar.

This was an old-fashioned, heavy glass jar from another era, probably fished out of an old homestead dump, that contained a pint of a slightly cloudy, viscous white liquid. I had had the prescience to stop on the way out from Humboldt at a place way back in the coastal mountains known as Whisky Hill, where friends had established in recent years a dependable still and proceeded to delight their neighbors and destroy their own livers.

The booze with which I left Whisky Hill after some proper horse-trading was amazingly potent, a double distilled apple and pear brandy that its makers claimed to be 180 proof, that is, 90 percent pure alcohol. At the start of each day we were to spend on the frigid ground under the van, we turned to The Jar. We limited ourselves to little more than a wetting of our tongues at each turn. Additional microscopic inhalations were rationed throughout the cold day. That the booze lasted until the end of the endeavor was a matter of both the sheer concentrated power of the stuff itself and the totally uncharacteristic discipline the three of us applied to our intake. Its sustaining capacity added to the quasi-miraculous aspect of events and further justified our vaunted new celebration, the Festival of the Eternal Throw-Out Bearing.

Fortified by fire within and without we traded off tasks, one of us at a time climbing under the van to take very small, measured turns on the pressure plate bolts. Then another of us, sitting at the wheel, would start the truck and try to engage the clutch. The third person would mind the fire. After a few rotations, we would all warm up in front of the fire for a moment and take a tiny sip of brandy. No one got stuck under the truck for long. It was truly cold by then at that altitude, and the trees were laden each morning with new-fallen snow. It was much colder yet again lying on the ice underneath the truck. Frostbite and exposure threatened, albeit casually, but we had courage, fortitude, warm meals up at the house—and The Jar.

This went on literally for five days. It started to get outright spooky, especially when the falling snow seemed to lay a mantle of almost supernatural silence over the scene. I remember Peter making up nonsense songs trying to sustain a little cheer, but it often felt like the three of us were lost in an endless loop from a Japanese art film or that we were captives of some jealous mountain God who had cast a spell on this silent, motionless little clearing. We sometimes felt we were doomed to this pointless routine; turn the ratchet—start the truck—let out the clutch—no movement—turn off the truck—turn the ratchet—and on— forever or until spring, whichever came first. Our thoughts thusly addled festered into despair. Would we never return home to Humboldt or San Francisco or anywhere? Had we again drawn the attention of the Furies? Would there be no reckoning with Stockholm, no Planet Drum, no bioregional perspective, no watershed restoration?

It wasn't until the fifth day, with the remaining brandy little more than a film on the inside of the bottle, that we finally broke the ice, as it were. After the 401st or 576th or whatever twist of the wrench, the clutch suddenly engaged with the engine running. The truck moved. It actually moved! Back and forth—several times. Oh joy! It was as if the light and life had suddenly reached into our chilly glade. The spell was broken and the very last drop of brandy was applied to the beginning of the first celebration of the Festival of the Eternal Throw-Out Bearing. That took place after the patient wrenchmen returned victorious to the warmth of family and fire at the house up the hill. Thanks to our slender but somehow effective mechanical capacities, there would be a future for us.

The next morning we gathered our combined nine children, two dogs, and six adults for a photo. Chuck, one of the great photographic recorders of the late Digger era, set his camera on automatic trigger and got into the picture in time. High on mountain air and truly joyful companionship, we all felt an exhilaration that is clearly written on the faces in the photo. The flow of good spirits had been loosed once again by companionship, a reinvigorated sense of historical purpose, and, of course, the freedom to get back on the road.

So after saying our goodbyes and our warmest thanks for the Goulds' grand hospitality and their arrangement of employment and the long mechanical residency, we pulled back the blocks and trundled out of the little canyon, following the Castle Creek Road down toward the Roaring Fork Valley and on to the Colorado itself.

Caravanning

Peter and Judy and Jane and I had decided earlier at Conundrum that when the Bergs' van was road-worthy, we would travel west together. Traveling in tandem in old trucks had by that time become common practice among our people— we called it "caravanning"—a way of communalizing travel. One guiding logic for the evolution of the new-age caravan was that a state patrolman or local law enforcement, though excited by a potential trove of violations, would be less eager to make a traffic stop harassing several questionably legal old trucks than one of them. (It would be like stopping a small village from an undetermined but potentially dangerous foreign country. You just didn't know.) It was an especially useful method of travel when many of us were searching together for land to go back to. It was also insurance that if you broke down there would be somebody to drive you to the nearest junk yard.

For this trip, running as it did in the shadow of the Eternal Throw-Out Bearing, the Bergs and we planned wisely to caravan at least as far as Nevada City, where California Highway 20 angles off Interstate 80 toward Lake County and Humboldt. Peter was eager to get back to San Francisco, find a place to live, and start working on the new publication. We had commitments in Humboldt that would ultimately lead us to the Mattole Valley and the development of watershed restoration as a key component of reinhabitation. We made a tentative plan to come down later in the winter to help get out the first publication, whatever it was to be.

So here we were, filled with a sense of mission, our two ungainly vehicles rumbling heavily down the canyon of the upper Colorado, retracing the steps we'd taken ten days ago in search of a bell housing. At Rifle, we turned north up Colorado Highway 13 toward Meeker then west on 64, which led up onto the great intermountain plateau and the junction with Interstate 40. Long after nightfall on that late-autumn trip, the roads were busy. The oil and gas boom that before long was going to envelop this plateau country was already swinging into action. There were many large trucks on the road, hauling massive drilling gear and millions of feet of pipe destined to penetrate deep into the earth beneath the plateau. We were still thirty years or so out from familiarity with the term "fracking," but its grim predecessor, oil shale extraction, was just then starting to wreak havoc.

The late-autumn ride through Utah and especially on Highway 50 through Nevada was mind numbing, long and quiet. Even the kids, who swapped back and forth in various combinations between the Bergs' rig and ours every time we stopped for gas, were wistful and largely silent in face of the steady grayness of sky and the sheets of thin snow that were driven back and forth across the otherwise dry countryside by the chill winter winds.

Coming into the valleys of northern California from Nevada in winter is literally going from black and white to Technicolor. The same season that had rendered the Great Basin of the Intermountain West a sere, grey, snow-blown landscape had turned California's enormous Central Valley and the foothills of its tributaries verdant and rich. Early-fall rains that year had hurried along the annual regreening of the landscape. Except in the high Sierras themselves, winter temperatures averaged twenty to thirty degrees warmer west of the long north-south range of mountains than on the east slope and in the Great Basin.

The Bergs' path and ours separated finally. Peter and Judy went on following Interstate 80 through the Sacramento Valley and into the Bay Area and the city. We drove due west on California State Highway 20 through the Central Valley and up into the Lake country, over to 101 and then north to Humboldt.

Many important things were to follow. Peter and Judy, of course, with the help of a number of people, went on to create a series of publications we referred to as "Bundles." They were composed of separately designed and printed pieces—essays, poems, maps, and such—bundled together in a common envelope under the rubric of Planet Drum.

The Drum of the title was one that came down to us through a very old drawing of a Sami (Lapp) shaman. The instrument depicted had a number of symbols painted on the taut skin of its wide head. A flat circle made of the collarbone of a reindeer sat loose on the drum. When the shaman beat the drum, probably from below, the circle of bone bounced and moved over one after another symbol. The shaman, in a sort of trance influenced by an intoxicant made from fermented reindeer milk, read and interpreted the progression of the symbols and the messages they were delivering from the spirit world. The shaman's drum was a powerful image that helped define an enterprise that promised prophetic insight and might provide a key to assist in planetary survival.

Some would argue, though, that reality would have been as well or even better represented had the shaman's drumstick and the circle of reindeer bone looked more like a socket wrench and vise grips. Maybe the prophetic shaman's true American place was out near Rifle, Colorado, where the beat-up old International Carryall no doubt still sat in the snow, in Buddha-like quietude at the back of the wrecking yard where we found the replacement for Peter's busted bell housing. Or maybe we were already being guided in the alpine cold along Conundrum when, over and over and over, bereft of all hope, we turned the nut on the clutch pressure plate ever so slightly. It's good to be true to one's roots.

Postscript—Back to the un: What bioregionalism is and isn't

Peter and Judy visited here in Petrolia a few weeks before Peter passed away. It was midsummer, a glorious time. He was inordinately upbeat and clearheaded, and we began letting ourselves think that maybe he could keep going, albeit in a physically reduced state, and continue to be part of our lives for a while. Peter had cheerful conversations with several of the many people in our valley that he had befriended over the years of visiting here, sharing in the intellectual developments of our restoration work and teaching at our high school. Peter had always understood our watershed-wide efforts at restoration in the Mattole as a central aspect of the work of a reinhabitory community.

Peter, Judy, Jane, and I had a last, long, intermittent conversation that spanned the week. Jane and I had recently traveled to several Conferences of the Parties—COPs, UN-organized summits dealing with climate change—and to another conference on the same subject organized by the government of Bolivia. (Evo Morales had called for a "People's Conference on Climate Change" in April 2010, a few months after the painful failure to make progress at the Copenhagen COP in late 2009. The Cochabamba event produced a set of principles that most of the activists, numbering in the tens of thousands, signed onto and that laid out steps necessary to deal successfully with climate change. The Cochabamba principles were presented to the UNFCCC. They were ignored.)

The UN events were sad, troubling affairs. They seemed set up to create the illusion that the governments and business leaders of the world were dealing responsibly with this inestimably grave threat. They were like elaborate circuses in which the clowns were not funny—expensive shows in which all had their assigned roles, even the most radical critics of the process and the scientists whose ongoing bleak assessments ostensibly provided the fuel. Neoliberal, business-friendly, free-market models still dominated the discourse. Carbon trading had been added to the portfolios of energy managers, a bit of sleight of hand that did not bode well for land-based communities in the South but promised a brief run of new profits for investors in the North—that is, until the deception was thoroughly exposed.

People representing local and regional communities were still largely denied any kind of real power and in fact were most often treated as obstacles to sustained access to resources by large investors, distant corporate entities, and compliant elites at home. Continued dominance by these powers was still very much guaranteed while at the same time atmospheric, terrestrial, and marine ecosystems continue to unravel in response to the unimpeded upward trajectory of CO_2 levels. The model for UN action put in place first in Stockholm in 1972 had endured intact up to and beyond COP 17 in Durban and Rio II. It can only be interpreted as colossal hubristic misjudgment based on the indefensible presumption of . . . what? That science was routinely wrong? That a few people will be so rich they won't need a functioning planet?

Peter and I were in complete agreement that whatever legitimacy the UN might have had as the agency for real dialogue and real action to protect the planet was by now simply gone up in smoke. Where did that leave us?

There had been over the last decades of the twentieth century a number of gatherings under the flag, so to speak, of Bioregional Congresses, and they were among the most inspiring and meaningful events or parties in which many of us had taken part in since the '60s. But no mass political movement evolved or could evolve from such a foundation. Launching a truly bioregional initiative at this point through current political structures would be like trying to get close to the earth by pitching a canvas tent on top of a thick pad of reinforced concrete. Reinhabitory directives would be too easily subsumed if funneled through a system that was created to corroborate and sustain the unsustainable.

Bioregionalism, in other words, was a deeper notion than could be easily manifested through standard political mechanisms. It was and is buoyed by a groundswell of new understandings of ancient relationships relative to the natural world that are as profound and ineffable as the Dao—nameless truths revealing themselves in intuitive flashes or in the grim spasms of the heart encountering loss of the world part by part.

Instead of a political movement, bioregionalism has become the base of a philosophical landscape in which localism and a belief in building the culture of place provide guiding directives. It is at the core of a new unforced social instinct for sharing that grew in our communities in face of the ethical deterioration and loss of legitimacy of larger political and economic structures and processes. It offers both a practical reciprocity and a spiritual reenchantment without which the halls of our being are poorly lit. It promises a fulfillment that is based on constant rediscovery and sharing of knowledge of local ecological processes and holds out the key for adapting ourselves and our institutions to them. Bioregionalism is a force rather than an entity, one that will grow in effectiveness as generations succeed one another and our understanding of our places on the planet grows. It alone can bring us, even in our old trucks and soiled clothing, closer to home. In his inimitable, sometimes joyful, occasionally overbearing, and frequently profane way, Peter recited for us under the apt cover of bioregionalism the siren call of the sacred, of the land, the planet—a call welcoming us home.

(David Simpson's tribute is part of a longer essay that will be published by Planet Drum Books.)

PETER BERG, COUNTERCULTURE, AND THE BIOREGIONAL IMPULSE

Gary Snyder

I first got my start at matching my visionary and scholarly impulse to rethink North America with the actual landscape when I started snow peak mountaineering in the Pacific Northwest. One can't help but see large spaces of mountains, a few rivers, and think—there are no political boundaries on this, it is a matter of its own shapes and lineaments.

Later, as a student at Reed, I came across A. L. Kroeber's "Cultural and Natural Areas of Native North America" with its marvelous pouch of maps in the back (Tribal boundaries, four maps of differing Vegetation Areas, Native Cultural Areas, and Physiographic Areas of Native North America) and saw it as a guide to better understanding what North America was and could be. It also proved to be an introduction to a perspective on the entire planet. I ordered and bought a copy, and still have it and use it, in spite of the magic of G.I.S. (U. of Ca. Press, 1947)

Then I spent some years in East Asia, mostly Japan. In letters and a few essays my friends and I pursued this line of thought further, if lightly, and when I returned to the West Coast for good, in 1968, I was soon in touch with Peter Coyote, Jim Dodge, Jerry Martien, and Freeman House and soon met Peter Berg.

There was a large gathering, at Muir Beach early in 1969—when Sandy Stewart still ran a restaurant there—and I met Peter Berg then. I right away liked his sparky, funny, fiercely questioning streak and noted that he looked liked Lenin.

Soon after (even while I was busy staging up to go to the Sierra Nevada and planning the building for the Kitkitdizze house), Peter spoke of his Planet Drum project, and though I was drawn into mountain carpentry and local community-building labors for many years, I tried to stay in touch.

Peter's circle developed around him, his lovely wife, Judy Goldhaft, perfected her sinuous water dance, and they all began to do workshops from place to place—dances—games—and participating in sexy salmon drama. *Raise the Stakes* got started. And David Haenke and many others were holding bioregional gatherings in the Ozarks, in Kansas, and in various places—we had one in northern California—it was a lively time. Peter and I were once invited speakers up in Missoula, talking our watershed and community ideas to a host of scholars and counterculture people at the University.

Somebody else will have to do that history, but what I remember was that Peter himself was always at the core of so much. Other groups elsewhere flourished, but San Francisco remained the center of much bioregional thinking for many years. By the same token, my area got deeper into its own local work—the Yuba River watershed, forestry, wildlife, and water issues, and the return of a few larger mammals like cougar and bear as well as the now ever-present wild turkey. I was less in touch with Peter and Judy in the last two decades but well-employed locally, as well as periodically visiting the burgeoning local bioregional groups in Japan. Peter Berg maintained his unique style, language, wit, and occasional critical probing, through it all and to everyone's advantage. A hardy, scrappy, supersmart and sardonic alpha, Peter provided leadership and made a contribution that has been immeasurable;

and what a guy.

3. III. (Girls Day in Japan) 2012

PETER AMONG THE DIGGERS

Starhawk

I like to think I met Peter Berg in the spring of the Summer of Love, during Easter Week of 1967, when I was sixteen years old. My friend Hilda and I had persuaded our parents to let us fly up to San Francisco on our spring break and stay with her cousin Dottie who lived in the heart of the Haight Ashbury. We told our parents we were going to tour college campuses. Actually, we knew what was happening in the Haight—luckily, they didn't. Or at least, they wouldn't have, had *Life* magazine not chosen that particular week to run a feature on the hippies of the Haight. It came out while we were away, and we faced the consequences when we got back. But that's another story.

Haight Street—what an amazing, intoxicating street it was for a girl from L.A.! Crowded with actual people, not just cars—people watching one another, strutting and strumming and breaking into spontaneous dances, strolling and trolling for spare change, the men with their hair drooping down over collars and mustaches waving, the women in draperies of torn lace and tattered velvets, the shops full of incense and cheap treasures from the East. And there were cafes, where people sat and had conversations, and you might meet a poet! And the park, just down the way, with drums pounding all day and a perpetual dance in progress.

I fell in love with San Francisco on that trip. It took me another seven years to move up here, but once I made it, I stayed. It's my city, the place where I sank roots. And so it's fitting that on that very first trip, I interrupted our intoxicated wanderings through the magic of the streets to fulfill my first semiprofessional writing assignment—to interview the Diggers for the University High School *Worrier*, our underground newspaper—named in contrast to the official high school paper, *The Warrior*.

One of the storefronts on Haight Street was a free store—a dark warren of bins of clothing and used goods where you could wander in and take what you needed. Above it, the Diggers had their headquarters. They gave out free food and promoted the radical idea that people were actually entitled to live, to eat, to take shelter, and to adorn themselves just by virtue of being alive.

Hilda and I tromped up the stairs. We entered a dark loft filled with stacks of papers and old couches and talked to older men—in their twenties or thirties!—with their hair tied back into ponytails and their mustaches curling with the electricity of new ideas. I can't swear that we interviewed Peter himself, but I like to think we did. At this distance of time, I remember we spent much of the afternoon talking to a parade of people who came in and out.

And we came away with a set of ideas that were to shift my path in life. We learned about the historic Diggers, who in 1649 took over land on St. George's Hill in England and began to farm, without permission or legal ownership. They believed that land and resources were a common treasury, that it was a crime to exploit the Earth or hoard its riches. And the Diggers of 1967 emulated their ideas. They were the forerunners of the squatters, of Food Not Bombs, of the Really, Really Free Market, of so many attempts to put the lie to capitalism by practicing radical generosity.

When I think of Peter, I think of those qualities of generosity and freedom. Giving generously of himself, he was free to think beyond the usual categories, not just to step beyond the box but to challenge the box itself. Why do we draw lines and boundaries, he asked, that are disconnected from the natural world? Why don't we think about bioregions, instead, linked to watersheds and climate and the real features of the land?

When I next encountered Peter, I was grown up and still writing. I would meet him at events in San Francisco and at bioregional gatherings. What I love about the bioregional movement is that it, too, transcends the usual boundaries. The gatherings were rich with ceremony and song and culture, not just speeches. At each one, I made new, lifelong friends.

Peter was a huge influence in my life, my work, and my writing. In particular, my futuristic novel, *The Fifth Sacred Thing*, attempted to imagine a bioregional, ecologically balanced, diverse, and just culture arising in San Francisco. The city becomes almost a character in the book, and that bioregional sense of connection to place and community is at its heart.

I spent many years working and organizing against the corporate globalization that allows companies to roam the globe in search of ever-higher profits and ever-lower standards of safety and quality of life for workers. For me, the bioregional movement was always the alternative, the quest to take root in a place and commit to it, to learn its natural and cultural history, its plants and animals, its birds and soils, its waterways and its winds. Activism can be draining and demoralizing when you are constantly protesting *against*. Bioregionalism gives us a glimpse of what we are taking action for.

Today, climate change has spawned a new awareness of the vital importance of the local. We are lucky to have Peter's legacy and the rich harvest of his many years of work, writing, and thinking to help guide us through these crucial times.

IN TRANSPACIFIC FRATERNITY: PETER BERG'S PLANET DRUMMING IN JAPAN

Kimiharu To

Among the various environmental activists and thinkers who have visited Japan, Peter Berg has enjoyed exceptional popularity. As Peter reports in his first dispatch from Japan, "Bioregional ideas have been accepted at surprisingly high levels in this country." For my countrymen, Peter's ideals did not transmit a fresh ecological approach. Rather, they were an intimate gift for activists, educators, community organizers, students, and others who consciously and unconsciously sought re-inhabitation in Japan.

His elaborations and stories helped re-animate our place-attachments, philosophies and traditional praxes that were being rapidly eroded by Japan's post–World War II urbanization and modernization. Furthermore, Peter's frankness, humor, and keenness toward cultural issues made his messages all the more plausible and attractive. Peter's methods were uncommon in the Japanese context, especially his mapping workshops and field tours. They called for expressing and exchanging views and talking about feelings and concerns about one's life-place, and they helped restore our imagination and commitment toward our own bioregional praxis. My occasional task of translating Peter's talks had me contemplating my own culture revealed through his perception and thoughts.

Similarly, for Peter, I suppose, his engagements with Japan and with the 1998 Winter Olympic Games were an extension of his own adventurous biospheric and cosmological bioregional identifications. Thinking back on my conversations with Peter and tracing his writings, it appears to be an inevitable unfolding in the course of his life story. The following is a reminiscence of his footprints upon a path we shared for a time.

Ceremony

In the summer of 1995, when I first met Peter during the Deep Ecology Summer Workshop held in northern California, I asked Peter to give my fellow

Japanese a series of talks on bioregionalism. I was then living in Hakuba, a village of the Nagano prefecture, located about 350 kilometers northwest of Tokyo. I was translating an anthology of Deep Ecology while working as an in-residence care-taker and apprentice farmer at a *minshuku* (ski lodge) and as a mountain ranger. The steep, beautiful alpine valley of Hakuba, the home of about nine thousand residents, was rapidly changing as it prepared for the upheaval of the 1998 Winter Olympics. A handful of residents who shared a concern about the impact of this event on the village's future decided to put together Peter's events for October 1995.

During his one-week visit, Peter stayed with me at the lodge and gave talks, workshops, and a field tour. His visit was well received, I recall, although the owner of the ski lodge, Tadashi Yamagishi, had shown little interest in both my and Peter's work. Besides being the lodge owner, Mr. Yamagishi was rather an important person in the village since he worked full time at the local post office and on weekends took care of his rice paddies and vegetable fields. But one day toward the end of Peter's visit, Mr. Yamagishi decided to bring us along to a small fire ceremony being held to prepare for a local sporting event that Mr. Yamagishi was sponsoring. Mr. Yamagishi said this fire ceremony might be interesting.

It was held at night in a tiny Shinto shrine in a small, very old and remote settlement called Aoni, hidden in a deep forest and rugged valley, where there are only about ten households, all built in the traditional thatched-roof style with wooden frames. There was no recognizable change relative to the pending Olym-pic Games.

Just as we arrived at the *kagura-den* of the shrine, where sacred music and dance are usually conducted, a few local youths were making a fire by using sticks and small cedar boards. About a dozen of Aoni's residents were sitting cross-legged around the fire. After the fire caught and settled, the coals were spread and a whole salmon was thrown onto the embers. While waiting for the salmon to cook, the group talked about the rice harvest, the weather, wild mushrooms, and the fire. Locally brewed sake was poured directly from large two-liter bottles into ordinary teacups. Peter was very attentive, and when he received a teacup of sake, the group pretended not to watch, but they were sneaking glances at how a foreigner might drink sake. Peter was the only foreigner and, perhaps for some of them, the first foreigner they'd encountered. At that point, we were with them in their circle, but only provisionally, because we'd been invited by the lodge owner.

After the salmon was cooked, its burnt skin was removed. Then, it was placed on a large cypress board, salt was sprinkled on it, and the board was passed around. Each person ate the salmon meat with fingers while the person sitting beside him or her held the board. They passed the salmon around and around and continued drinking sake, and Peter did just as they did. They kept talking as if we were not there. This sequence of drinking, eating, holding, and occasional sake-pouring maneuvers involved a sophisticated set of group dynamics and com-munications. Peter whispered to me a few questions about the procedure and the group's hierarchy.

At the end of the ceremony, Peter spoke to me about the American Indian ceremonies he had attended, and then he told me to say, "This is exactly how the Indians do." A few quiet moments of contemplation and comfort passed. The foreign guest had suddenly been recognized as an intimate and a knowledgeable person having authority. As he and I made our way back from the shrine, walking in complete darkness, participants came with us to ask Peter questions, and Mr. Yamagishi, upon our return to the lodge, invited Peter to talk further over a drink. Peter's sensitivity and clarity about what had occurred that evening in Aoni had gained him entrée into Hakuba's mainstream society.

Since then, the word "Aoni" became our buzzword for the entire Hakuba experience. After Peter's return to San Francisco, he elaborated on this encounter in his letter, suggesting that "This can be a major symbolic moment in transforming consciousness about the human roles in the biosphere for Japan and other parts of the world."

Nobody wins if nature loses

The name Guard Fox Watch (GFW) came out during the discussion that Peter and I had upon his return visit to Hakuba in 1998, ten days before the Games were to begin. Upon our arrival, we discovered and were somewhat amazed by various genres of anti-Olympic activism that had developed, including actions by anarchists and other groups that seemed opposed to anything connected to the government. We went the rounds, listening to different groups and what they were trying to do. Their messages seemed scattered, and in the end, Peter and I agreed not to simply converge with but rather to be distinctive from these groups. In the hurried moments before the games began, we began brainstorming ideas for our name. We knew we must make sure that our standpoint was with bioregionalism. In our conversation, Peter and I first talked about deities and their missions and touched upon the name *Daikoku,* a Japanese folklore deity whose name is also the name of my residential district in Nagano. That led us to *Kokopeli*, the coyote deity associated with Native American culture and that was used as the title of Nanao Sakaki's then-new book, which eventually guided us to our decision to settle upon *fox*. Peter and I decided to use *fox* because of its cultural connotations, such as the deity *Inari* under the Japanese Shinto, associated with the guardian and messenger aspects.

The GFW engagement is, of course, a form of applied bioregional praxis. Since the Nagano Games, Peter and other GFWers have visited other Winter Olympic venues one to two years prior to the Games. We press local organizers, the International Olympic Committee officials, and other concerned residents to obtain a series of baseline measurements in relation to various environmental factors, such as energy and water consumption, air and water quality, traffic density, solid waste disposal, wildlife populations, and so on. Without such baseline data, we argue, it would be impossible to prove whether the stated goal of a net positive environmental impact for the Winter Games has been achieved. Also, we stress that the event should be a showcase of the most ecologically advanced event planning, building, and restorative works. GFW is supported by a loose network of people who question the ecological and social consequences of the global winter sporting quadrennials as they each are held in different mountainous, ecologically vulnerable regions.

Tracing when Peter started thinking about the other side of the ocean. I found a poem, *San Francisco Bioregional Chant*, written in 1974, in which Peter had used the Japanese word for ocean current, *kuro shio*, so I surmised that he perhaps had long held an interest in Eastern cultures. After his initial visit in 1995, Peter came to Japan five or six times; he kept visiting, and we kept inviting him. For many of its adherents, bioregionalism had meant staying in one place, but Peter showed through his Japanese engagements that a universal thread could be found in bioregionalism. Considering the people whom Peter met during his visits and how those connections led to his bioregional restoration and education program in another place in the Pacific Basin, Bahía de Caráquez, Ecuador, his engagement with Japan was an accidental but inevitable magic not only for his Japanese audience, for me, and for Peter, but also for the idea of bioregionalism and the planet Earth.

PETER BERG, REGIONAL PLANNER

Robert Young

Peter Berg was many people. As the poet Walt Whitman said of himself, he "contained multitudes." A partner, father, writer, activist, performer, friend, poet, and visionary—many different biographies could (and should) be written about Peter. And when they are written, again, to paraphrase Whitman, the real Peter Berg will never get in the books, at least not completely.

In my life, Peter played the role of employer and mentor. Beginning as an intern at Planet Drum, I was introduced to Peter's ideas on bioregionalism. Through a somewhat circuitous career path that eventually brought me to becoming a planning scholar and practitioner, I gained deeper insight into the value and importance of Peter's thought and activism. As a result, I will try to comment on just two aspects of Peter Berg—his contribution to the field of regional planning and to that of anarchist theory.

Through his work with Raymond Dasmann and Judy Goldhaft, Peter's articulation of bioregionalism enhanced and expanded the breadth of community and regional planning. Although it is unclear to me the extent to which he read or was familiar with the ideas of the Anglo-American planning tradition, with amazing acuity Peter grasped and drove to greater conclusion the ideas of foundational planning theorists and practitioners such as Patrick Geddes, Lewis Mumford, Ebenezer Howard, and the Regional Planning Association of America (RPAA).

There is much that Peter Berg and Patrick Geddes, widely considered to be the founder of modern regional planning, had in common. Both were an anathema to most institutions, both set an independent course of inquiry, writing, and civic engagement, and both saw theater and the arts as a vital means of expressing new social ideas. Perhaps most significant, however, was their focus on the watershed as a key organizing principle of society. As Geddes noted in his 1904 address, "Civics: as Applied Sociology": "Such a river system is, as geographer after geographer has pointed out, the essential unit for the student of cities and civilisations."

Peter was indeed a "student of cities and civilizations," and, through bioregionalism, he seized and expanded upon this essential fact.

Geddes named the synthesis of the physical and life sciences and cities with their regions "geotechnics" and saw it as a path toward the eventual achievement of "biotechnics": "the time," as David Shillan wrote, "when life values should predominate over money or any other purely material valuation." While this definition resonates well with Peter's critique of technology, money, and materialism, Berg brought a richer conclusion to Geddes's and Geddes's apostles' objectives. Where they saw a fully realized modernist humanity as the eventual prime beneficiary of such a society, Peter radically broadened this perspective.

Peter's vital contribution through bioregionalism was to restore the centrality of life—all life—to regional planning. Whereas most regional planners have offered a human-centered focus aimed at greater rationalization and efficiency in the use of resources—albeit toward an elevated quality of life for the common person—Peter charted a less myopic course. As its name reflects, Peter's concept of bioregionalism instead centers on life (including but not limited to solely human life) and the cycles upon which it depends. As such they become both the source and the recipient of Peter Berg's idea of regional planning.

The implication of Peter's shift in focus is significant. For Geddes, to a degree, and especially for his acolytes such as Lewis Mumford and for the RPAA (and many contemporary environmental organizations), nature conservation is a defining aspect of advanced, environmental civilization. Peter, instead, advocated reinhabitation. This strategy aims at resolving the contradiction between society and nature, transcending their antagonisms in favor of achieving a mutually supportive evolution. In pursuing this higher synthesis reinhabitation provides paths in which life, rather than the accumulation of capital or power, is the fundamental organizing principle of society. By doing so it brings a more nuanced aspect to the work of conservation and restoration and heightens the legitimacy of native, endemic cultures, and ecological relationships in regional planning.

Peter's bioregionalism also understood the importance of cities. Like Ebenezer Howard, best known for his book *Garden Cities of To-Morrow* (1902) and considered a principal founder of modern town and city planning, Peter grasped the necessity of integrating cities and their hinterlands. For Peter the purpose of this relationship was not simply proximity or connection but transformation. Rural productive systems such as forestry, agriculture, and fisheries could, through reinhabitation, move from depletion or managerial domination to systems of "natural provision." Peter argued that this shift, coupled with efforts to create "green cities" through localizing urban nutrient, material, and energy cycles, would enable human settlements to reunite with the rest of the natural world as a positive force in the healthy evolution of ecosystems.

By restoring its ecological relationships, this transition politically liberated the city-region in two fundamental ways. First, it freed rural inhabitants from the need to act as the city's colonial overseers, coercively managing previously diverse and interdependent ecosystems as plantations paying tribute with their lifeblood to the ever-growing imperial metropolis. Second, it liberated urban centers from their status as imperial overlords, thus opening new cultural and technical opportunities for the city's regional self-provision. Freed from this Janus-like combination of coercive relationships, rural and urban culture could, through reinhabitation, enter into a new set of regional ecological and social relations marked by mutually supportive growth and development.

In addition to his contributions to the evolution of regional planning, Peter Berg also made significant contributions in the realm of anarchist thought. Although anarchism has many threads and Peter could be described as having added to several of these, in regard to planning he contributed directly to the development of anarcho-communist theory.

Early agrarian rebels such as Gerrard Winstanley (an organizer of the original seventeenth-century Diggers movement in England) planted the initial concepts of anarcho-communism. The Diggers' pamphlet, *The True Levelers Standard Advanced* (1649), and extralegal actions at St. George's Hill in Surrey and elsewhere presented an ideal of small, egalitarian, agrarian communities operating in harmony with the Earth. Later, developed into a component of modern socialist thought by the Italian section of the First International, anarcho-communism was further advanced by the nineteenth- and early twentieth-century Russian anarchist writer and activist Peter Kropotkin. To the ideal of anarcho-communism Kropotkin contributed a governance structure of egalitarian human relations suited for a society that had achieved advanced industrial and agricultural capabilities. He described these relations in the realms of production and political association through works such as *The Conquest of Bread* (1906) and *Fields, Factories, and Workshops of Tomorrow* (1912).

Kropotkin's colleague, the French geographer Élisée Reclus, provided a spatial context for human community development by identifying watersheds as a key to understanding and organizing society. Throughout his writings Reclus described the influence of geography and landscape in shaping distinct human societies and ecological relationships.[1] Patrick Geddes, contemporary colleague to Kropotkin and Reclus, graphically represented these relationships in his groundbreaking illustration of "The Valley Section" and in his call for regional and civic surveys as the basis of proper planning.

Peter Berg added a further dimension to the contributions of Reclus, Kropotkin, and others concerning the governance and spatial context (politics and place) of anarcho-communism. The ideas and work of nineteenth-century (and earlier) anarcho-communist writers and activists focused primarily on liberating the oppressed agricultural and industrial masses. They envisioned regional federations of agro-industrial communes embodying a new commonwealth of labor whose scientific approach to developing the tools of production would consummate the true emancipation of human potential.

While Peter shared anarchism's dispositions toward hierarchy, the state, and wage labor, he clearly expanded its constituency to include, more directly, the broader community of life. Through his writings in this book, as well as

Envisioning Sustainability (2009), the Planet Drum periodical *Raise the Stakes*, and his performance work with Reinhabitory Theater, Peter articulated an egalitarian social order in which animal and plant communities and, indeed, ecosystems themselves share sovereignty with human society.

While nineteenth-century (and contemporary) socialists largely view nature through a benign or paternalistic perspective where scientific methods are harnessed to efficiently plan, manage, and conserve "natural resources" for the betterment of a more widely enfranchised human community, Peter was out for bigger game. Establishing life itself and the ecological cycles that support it as the fundamental object of social liberation, he advocated the development of bioregional/watershed-based planning integrating the voices of all members of the community, human and beyond. In so advocating, he made the regional community, long articulated by the anarcho-communists as the most natural association of human society, embrace all of its inhabitants—human and nonhuman—as its true citizens.

These are two aspects of Peter Berg's diverse and elusive legacy. Its various strands, crossing and reshaping disciplines and borders, will continue to grow and influence the evolution of society along myriad paths. While Peter made significant contributions to the field of regional planning, anarchist thought, and activism, these are only fragments of his fuller influence and person. Throughout he explored and advocated a deep connection to the planet, to life and its cycles. As perhaps his own comment on his legacy and the most direct way to find it, Peter might himself have quoted Whitman: "I bequeath myself to the dirt to grow from the grass I love / If you want me again, look for me under your boot-soles."

Note

1. Reclus's works such as *History of a River* (1869) was an early exposition of watersheds as a coherent perspective for comprehending and organizing society. He further articulated these ideas in books such as *The History of a Mountain* (1881) and the *New Universal Geography—The Earth and Its Inhabitants* (1894).

SEEING DEEP: A REMEMBRANCE OF PETER BERG

Seth Zuckerman

The middle-aged man with the weather-beaten face leaned his weight onto the handle of the shopping cart, trying to make out what I was saying. "A bayo-ree-shah-what?" he said, his voice slurring.

"A bioregionalist," I repeated, "you see, you're really a bioregionalist." He shifted more of his weight onto the cart, and it started rolling at me. I side-stepped. "Look, you recycle," I said, pointing at the cans in the shopping cart. "You make use of locally available resources. You even drive an alcohol-powered vehicle!"

The scene was a talent show—a cabaret of sorts—at the Fourth North American Bioregional Congress in Squamish, British Columbia, in 1988. Peter had been kind enough to portray a wino in the skit I'd sketched out and to teach me a few commedia dell'arte moves for our act.

It wasn't the first time I'd learned something important from him. Four years earlier, Peter had set me up on a blind date with the place that I would eventually come to call home. Come visit me there while I'm staying with Freeman House, he'd said, I think you'd like it. He described the pioneering salmon restoration work under way in that northern California valley and the proximity of the wild to people's everyday lives. His invitation launched my love affair with the Mattole watershed and its human community, a bond that continues to this day.

At first, I had to nurture that connection as a long-distance romance from my shared flat in San Francisco, a few blocks from the Planet Drum world headquarters in Peter and Judy's basement. While I puzzled about whether and how to reassemble my life in the Mattole, they were kind enough to rope me into some Planet Drum projects. The first time I marked the winter solstice holiday was at the foundation's "Celebrate the Longest Night" benefit at the California Academy of Sciences in Golden Gate Park. That event was the public launch of the Green City Project, which led to the *Green City Handbook* that Peter coauthored with Beryl Magilavy and me.

But my most vivid memories of Peter from that era are the times he and I pruned fruit trees together in the city. Peter had learned his technique from an arborist in the Mattole, advertised his services in the neighborhood, and wanted help on some of the larger jobs. Tackling an overgrown apple tree, he'd marvel at the caliber of wood we were leaving on the ground. "This is logging," he'd say. It appealed to the perception he harbored of the rural and the wild hidden beneath the concrete of the city, a perception I was happy to join him in.

For all of Peter's rustic visions of the urban landscape, he did not conceive it as a Jeffersonian idyll. To him, the city blocks could be read more accurately as feudal fiefdoms, and Peter never forgot that he came from serf stock. He bid the jobs for a fixed price, so his hourly wage depended on our working efficiently. If I was being a little too careful—taking too long to decide where to cut or snipping twice where once would have sufficed—he'd chastise me and remind me that we had to move faster so that he could preserve whatever advantage he had negotiated from the landed gentry in whose backyards we were working.

It's an outlook he brought to his intellectual work, too, and tried to impart to me as well. One time, Peter received a request from a European publisher who wanted permission to reproduce an older essay of his. The publisher had listed the copyright forms it needed signed and notarized but hadn't offered a reprint fee. Peter strategized to come up with his next move. "We don't usually go to such lengths unless there is some money involved" was his considered response. That brought out a cash offer, Peter told me with satisfaction, generously sharing survival skills that would help me in my work as a freelancer.

Years passed for me in San Francisco—writing for a variety of magazines, enrolling in graduate school, but still pining for the Mattole. Eventually, I turned to another Mattolian to whom Peter had introduced me, David Simpson, and asked whether the Mattole organizations needed any research done, since I was looking for a topic for my master's project. The MRC was just finishing a study of old-growth forests, David said, but was curious about second-growth stands, which made up 90 percent of the forest in the Mattole. Might I be interested in coming up to research their possible role in the social and ecological future of the watershed? He had just secured a modest amount of funding, and I jumped at the chance to try cohabiting with the watershed of my dreams.

Once I moved there, however, I started to wonder whether Peter had painted an overly rosy picture of EcoSuperHeroes saving salmon. The "community" that had seemed so united from a distance was revealed up close as heterogeneous and pluralistic, sometimes bitterly divided, and, most painful to me as a twenty-something idealist, not all absorbed single-mindedly in restoration. Egos and perceived prerogatives occasionally disrupted the work even within the core of the restoration movement. The Mattole might have been the paragon of bioregional "reinhabitation" that Peter touted, but that didn't make the tree planting less muddy or the squabbles any less messy. I had my share of "what have I done?" moments, like the time my prearranged cabin lease fell apart the day after I had deposited my first load of belongings there.

Over time—as with any long-term relationship, I suppose—I came to understand the place, my colleagues, and our common effort with more complexity and nuance. As the years went by, I realized that it wasn't superficial ignorance that had led Peter to talk up the Mattole. He saw beyond the surface layer of the projects under way with fish, trees, and schoolchildren and past the hardpan of human weaknesses, all the way to the deeper commitment that drove my new neighbors to care so profoundly for their watershed. What he saw there resonated with the fierce love he felt for the places that this green planet is made up of, each unique, like his own treasured Shasta bioregion, each deserving of its own cadre of bioregionalist caretakers and creators.

STRATEGIES FOR REINHABITING THE NORTHERN CALIFORNIA BIOREGION

Ernest Callenbach's best-selling novel Ecotopia *(1975) imagines an eco-logically sustainable future society in northern California, a region that seceded from the United States to become a separate country known as Ecotopia. In 1976, with Callenbach's assent,* Seriatim: Journal of Ecotopia *began publication, edited by Bruce Brody.* Seriatim, *a word meaning natural succession, is a journal "about the Ecotopian bio-region located in the Northwest corner of the American continent where an environmentally-attuned, stable-state society is emerging.* Seriatim *aims to document and foster the growth of that society" (*Seriatim*). In 1977 Peter Berg's "Strat-egies for Reinhabiting the Northern California Bioregion," based on a lecture that Berg had delivered to employees of the State of California's Office of Appropriate Technology, appeared in* Seriatim *(volume 1, issue 3). Ecologist Raymond Dasmann submitted Berg's essay for republication in the British periodical* The Ecologist, *but the editor found it baffling. Das-mann then offered to revise Berg's essay and resubmit it to* The Ecologist *as a coauthored piece, and it was accepted and published as "Reinhabiting California," reprinted as the lead essay of this collection. For those who may be interested in comparing the two versions, Berg's original* Seriatim *essay appears here.*

It's an attractive and reasonable prospect, in many ways ideal, but hardly radi-cal considering that ideas and activities for living-in-place have probably been a major influence on the practical forms and inspirational visions of human societies for most of our species' several million year history.

Unfortunately for the native people, wild species, and diverse regions of Ecotopia, living-in-place went into eclipse here when Europeans "discovered" this continent. A directly opposite theme quickly became dominant; short-term exhaustive exploitation of the land.

Natural life-support systems in nearly every region of Ecotopia have been severely weakened within a few hundred years. The regions' wealth of diversity—plants and animals whose variety and quantity amazed the first explorers—has been largely spent and altered toward a narrow range of mostly nonnative crops and stock. Chronic misuse has ruined huge areas of rich farm and range land. Wastes from absurdly dense industrial concentrations have left some places almost unlivable.

Human life ultimately depends on the continuation of other life, regardless of the "endless frontier" delusion and Invader mentality that came to dominate Ecotopia. The mentality that removed one native people and species after another to "make a living." Living-in-place is not only a more attractive and reasonable prospect, it has become necessary if people intend to stay on in any of Ecotopia's regions without further modifying them in even more dangerous directions.

Reinhabitation refers to the spirit of living-in-place within a region that has been disrupted and injured through generations of exploitation. It means becoming native to places by developing awareness of their special life continuities, and undertaking activities and evolving social forms that tend to maintain and restore them.

Reinhabitation is neither a specialized field nor an "ecology lifestyle." It is simply becoming fully alive in and with a place.

Useful information for reinhabitory living-in-place comes from a wide range of immediately regional and generalized planetary sources. Studies of local native inhabitants, the history of cities, conservation, comparative farming methods, water project plans, ethnopoetics, energy utilization reports, native species studies, biogeography, and early settlers' stories reveal essential aspects of living within a given place. Reinhabitants can apply this background to determining personal livelihoods and community economics, establishing criteria for assigning social priorities and making political decisions, and developing relationships with other species.

Bioregion defines a specific place with reference to the conditions that influence all living things within it. A particularly good starting point for a reinhabitory perspective because it describes both a place and a terrain of consciousness; the place and ideas about living in it combined.

Scientific measures of the limits of various natural zones are extremely helpful in locating a bioregion. Fairly definite patterns of accord between areas indicated in geological surveys, soil composition analyses, inventories of flora and fauna, watershed maps, and meteorological observations can establish the extent and variations of a continuous regional life-place.

The final boundaries of a bioregion might best be ultimately decided by the people living in it. Natural sciences tend to exclude the activities of human life, but a bioregion could be defined as a human species realm of living-in-place. For example, the migratory routes of Pacific salmon extend across the ocean between Asia and North America, but the people of northern California consider the salmon that spawn in their rivers to be native there. The fish are part of the northern California bioregion, but the whole North Pacific is not.

There is a distinct resonance among living things and the factors influencing them that occurs specifically within each place on the planet. Defining a bioregion is a way to describe that unique resonance.

In biospheric terms, belonging to a bioregion may be the most desirable inter-dependent way for people to relate to the whole planetary environment. We would be responsive to the whole by maintaining the parts.

The northern California bioregion

A map of North America's land forms provides a striking image on the continent's western margin of the enormous Central Valley bowl; the heart of the southern Ecotopia bioregion.[1] It is clearly outlined by a nearly unbroken circle of moun-tains: the high Sierra Nevada to the east, Tehachapi Mountains south, Pacific Coast Range along the ocean, Klamath-Siskiyous north. The whole bioregion actually extends further westward to include the coast, the Farallon Islands offshore, and part of the Pacific Ocean itself at least as far as the California Current.

Enormous plant zone changes echo the mountainous boundaries. These moun-tains act as rainmakers by catching clouds streaming off the Pacific. Consequently, heavy winter showers and spring snow-melt runoffs bring much more water to northern California plant life than to that in neighboring bioregions east and south. More plant species exist here than further north because there is a more temperate climate and a wider diversity of habitats.[2]

Point Conception is a natural break-point for the bioregion's southern border; a significant number of northern California's plant species markedly diminish south of Point Conception and eastward along the line of the Tehachapis to the Sierra Nevada. Plants of the Great Basin deserts contrast sharply with the forests on the western slopes—the crestline of the Sierra can serve as northern California's east-ern limit. The northern border starts from the last reaches of the Sierra and arcs west past the volcanic peaks of Lassen and Shasta that hold off the high desert beyond. From there it continues through heavy forests in the Klamath Mountains nearly straight west to the Pacific and the northern limit of coast redwoods around the Chetco River Valley in Oregon.

Distinct watershed characteristics also reflect southern Ecotopia's mountain containing wall and the heavy rainfall it provides.[3]

Place is alive

Knowing where it is tells something of what the bioregion is, but a map of the place is like an anatomical drawing of a human being; the body without its real substance. Reinhabitants also recognize an active identity, the life the place is leading.

The land forms, vegetation, and watersheds that point to a distinguishable northern California bioregion form supports for its ongoing life cycles. Snow-melt in the Sierra washes down soils to create the rich top layer of the Central Valley. Micro-organisms spawned in that soil drift out of the watershed, providing food for shellfish and abundant schools of ocean fish close to shore. The low flat Central Valley heats us faster than the higher surrounding hills pulling in cool Pacific air and fog as essential precipitation for luxuriant plant growth just one ridge back from the windy coastline. The swiftness of the coastal rivers clears away mud, enabling steelhead and salmon to find clean gravel spawning beds.

Overcast wet winter and desert-dry summer are administered each year like opposing cures over the living strands that bind the bioregion together. Spring floods fill ponds and invite a profusion of life: late summer drives them out to dust again. The bioregion's body metabolism shifts, speeds up, slows down, and shifts again.

There is a regional complex of naturally adapted groups of plants existing like cells reproducing themselves in a living body. Each has a spectrum of herbs, shrubs, and trees which long ago became dominant in specific places by successfully re-seeding themselves in the particular set of water, soil, weather, and multi-species conditions existing in those spots. There is a narrow band of redwood and ferns along the coast; fir-spruce-cedar throughout the Coast Range, Klamath-Siskiyous, and Sierra; oaks and bunch grass in the valley, tule and Cottonwood in the Delta—to name only the most prominent in a few formations. They are the climax species of natural successions occurring in those areas, the plants most likely to maintain themselves there.

Northern California has an unusually great number of very restricted sites with comparatively rare or oddly-mixed plants. Unless the site has been overrun with invader plants introduced from another bioregion or bulldozed and paved by an invader mentality, the original plants keep establishing themselves. Rare or common, they are natives, and if only the barest remnant of native plant life remains it will be moving toward reinhabiting its special area.

Strategies for fitting in

People have been part of the bioregion's life for a long time. The greatest part of that time has been a positive rather than negative experience for other life sharing the place. In describing how as many as 500 separate tribal "republics" lived side by side in California for at least 15,000 years without serious hostility toward each other or disruption of life-systems around them, Jack Forbes points out a critical difference between invaders and inhabitants. "Native Californians . . . felt themselves to be something other than independent, autonomous individuals. They perceived themselves as being deeply bound together with other people (and with the surrounding non-human forms of life) in a complex interconnected web of life, that is to say, a true community. . . ."[4] From this idea came the basic principle of non-exploitation, of respect and reverence for all creatures, a principle extremely hostile to the kind of economic development typical of modern society and destructive of human morals.

Reinhabitants are as different from invaders as these were from the original inhabitants. They want to fit into the place—which requires preserving the place to fit in to. Their most basic goals are to restore and maintain watersheds, topsoil, and native species; elements of obvious necessity for in-place existence because they determine the essential conditions of water, food, and stable diversity. Their further "future primitive" aims might include developing contemporary bioregional cultures that celebrate the continuity of life where they live, and new region-to-region forms of participation with other cultures based on our mutuality as a species in the planetary biosphere.

Moves to accomplish reinhabitation of northern California would have to take into account the nature and limits of the place, the ways people have dwelt here and the way they live here now, and priorities for restoring the bioregion's natural systems. Shifting to a reinhabitory society requires basic changes in present-day social directions, economics, and politics.

Social directions

Our real "period of discovery" has just begun. The bioregion is only barely recognized in terms of how life systems relate to each other in it. It is still an anxious mystery whether we will be able to continue living here. How many people can the bioregion carry without destroying it further? What kinds of activities should be encouraged? Which ones are too ruinous to continue? How can people find out about bioregional criteria in a participative way so that they feel it is for their mutual benefit rather than an imposed set of regulations? Bioregional research and education would confront these problems and accept participative terms for their solutions.

Natural watersheds would receive prominent recognition as the frameworks within which communities are organized. The network of springs, creeks, and rivers flowing together in a specific area exerts a dominant influence on all non-human life there; it is the basic designer of local life. Frequent floods in northern California remind us that watersheds affect human lives as well, but their full importance is actually much more subtle and pervasive. Native communities were developed expressly around natural water supplies and tribal boundaries were usually set by the limits of watersheds. Pioneer settlements followed the same pattern, often displacing native groups with the intention of securing their water. Cattle ranching, agriculture, and even the growth of cities are directly related to the availability of water.

Defining the local watershed and restricting growth and development to fit the limits of immediate water supplies would become primary directions of reinhabitory communities. They would view themselves as centered there and responsible for the watershed.

The San Francisco Bay Region has always been a population center because of the confluence of rivers coming into it and its proximity to the ocean. The comparatively recent burgeoning of cities there is directly tied to the advantages of being at the mouth of southern Ecotopia's largest watershed, but Bay Area communities have been mindlessly irresponsible about preserving the conditions that permit them to be there.

As long as these communities view themselves as being somehow outside the bioregion they will proceed to turn the Bay into a deadly sump. But if they transfer their identity from "the world" back to the region, if San Franciscans can see themselves in San Francisco Bay–Sacramento River Estuary/Pacific Coast Range/North Pacific Rim/Pacific Basin, we will be well on the way toward building a reinhabitory society.

Economics

Southern Ecotopia is naturally rich biologically. It may be the richest bioregion in North America. Present-day economics here are generally based on exploiting this richness for maximum short-term profits. The natural systems that create conditions of abundance in the region are both short-term and long-term. There's plenty of water and it usually comes every year. There's plenty of good soil but it took hundreds of thousands of years to form. There are still some great forests left but they grew over centuries; very few have recovered that were logged a hundred years ago.

Reinhabitory economics seek sufficiency rather than profit. They might be more aptly termed "ecologics" since their object is to successfully maintain natural life-system continuities while enjoying them and using them to live.

Most current forms of economic activity that rely on the bioregion's natural conditions would continue in a reinhabitory society, but they would be altered to account for the short and long-term variations in their cycles.

Southern Ecotopia's Central Valley has become one of the planet's food centers. It's a naturally productive place; northern California has a temperate climate, there's a steady supply of water, and the topsoil is some of the richest in North America. But the current scale of agriculture is untenable in the long-term. Fossil fuel and chemical fertilizer can only become more expensive, and the soil is simultaneously being ruined and blown away.

There needs to be massive redistribution of land to create smaller farms. They would concentrate on growing a wider range of food species (including native food plants), increasing the nutritional value of crops, maintaining the soil, employing alternatives to fossil fuels, and developing small-scale marketing systems. More people would be involved, thereby creating jobs and lightening the population load on the cities.

Forests have to be allowed to rebuild themselves. Clear-cutting ruins their capability to provide a long term renewable resource. Watershed-based reforestation and stream restoration projects are necessary everywhere that logging has been done. Cut trees are wastefully processed; tops, stumps, and branches are left behind, and whole logs are shipped away to be processed elsewhere and sold back in the region. Crafts that use every part of the tree should be employed to make maximum use of the materials while employing a greater number of regional people.

Fisheries have to be carefully protected. They provide a long-term life-support of rich protein, if used correctly, or a quickly emptied biological niche, if mishandled. The separation between fishermen and departments with authority over them perpetrates an anachronistic state of conflict. Catching fish and maintaining the fisheries have to be seen as parts of the same concern. Reasonable catches and protection of ocean-river migrating fish spawning grounds should become a bioregion-wide responsibility.

Reinhabitory consciousness multiplies the opportunities for employment within the bioregion. New reinhabitory livelihoods based on exchanging information, cooperative planning, administering exchanges of labor and tools, intra- and inter-regional networking, and watershed media emphasizing bioregional rather than city-consumer information could replace a few centralized positions with many decentralized ones. The goals of restoring and maintaining watersheds, topsoil, and native species invite the creation of many jobs to simply un-do the bioregional damage that invader society has already done.

Politics

Beginning with the Spanish Occupation, northern California as a bioregion has been obscured by a succession of alien super-identities. Political boundaries have always been superimposed so the area's identity was reduced to "Part of New Spain" or an arbitrarily designed chunk of land obtained from Mexico.

The bioregion that exists largely in what is now called northern California is finally visible as a separate whole, and, for purposes of reinhabiting the place, it should have a political identity of its own.

The bioregion cannot be treated with regard for its own life-continuities while it is part of and administered by a larger state government. It should be a separate state.

As long as this bioregion belongs to a larger state it will be subject to southern California's demands on its watershed. (The Feather River already runs into a pipe and from there to Los Angeles.) Its control over use of the Central Valley will be pre-empted by policies tailored for Imperial Valley monoculturism. From a reinhabitory point of view, both are bioregional death threats.

The bioregion has political interests like protecting fishing rights off its coast, restoring spawning grounds in its rivers, and properly handling its unique forests.

In addition, elections over the last decade have shown a distinct difference in voting sentiments between northern and southern California counties. It is likely that this difference will continue and increase on vital bioregional issues while the population weight in southern California will prevail.

As a separate state, the bioregion could redistrict its counties to create watershed governments appropriate to maintaining local life-places. City-country divisions could be resolved on bioregional grounds.

Recognizing this autonomous bioregion will provide a space for us to address each other as member of a species sharing the planet together and with other species.

Endnotes

1. *Landforms of the United States* (map). Erwin Raisz, Boston. Also, *Landforms of California and Nevada*, by Raisz.
2. *Potential Natural Vegetation of the Coterminous United States.* A.W. Kuchler, Serial Publication J6 American Geographical Society, New York, 1964.
3. *"Biographical Influences on the Northern California Bioregion."* Arthur Okamuro with Dennis Breedlove in P. Berg (ed.) *Reinhabiting a Separate Country:* Planet/Drum. San Francisco, 1976. Prepared for California Arts Council.
4. "The Native American Experience in California History." Jack D. Forbes, *California Historical Quarterly,* September 1971, pp. 234–242.

PERMISSIONS

Berg, Peter. "Bioregional and Wild!" *The New Catalyst* (1989/1990). Reprinted by permission of Ocean Berg.
———. "Bioregions." *Resurgence* 98 (May/June 1983): 19. Reprinted by permission.
———. "Celestial Soulstice 2010." *Planet Drum Foundation.* 2010. Web. Reprinted by permission of Ocean Berg.
———. "China's Epic Conflict of Capacities." *Planet Drum Foundation.* August 2001. Web. Reprinted by permission by Ocean Berg.
———. " 'Colors Are the Deeds of Light'—Johann Wolfgang von Goethe." (Report #1, July 5, 2005) Kyoto, Japan. *Planet Drum Foundation.* Web. Reprinted by permission of Ocean Berg.
———. "Conservation, Preservation and Restoration in Ecuador." *Earth Island Journal* (Spring 2001): 25–27. Reprinted by permission.
———. "The Core of Eco-Tourism." (Dispatch #3, September 20, 2006) Bahía de Caráquez, Ecuador. *Planet Drum Foundation.* Web. Reprinted by permission of Ocean Berg.
———. "Figures of Regulation: Guides for Re-Balancing Society with the Biosphere." *Eco-Decentralist Design.* San Francisco: Planet Drum Foundation, 1982. Reprinted by permission of Ocean Berg.
———. "Finding the Future in the Mud." (Report #2, July 10, 2005) Nagoya, Japan. *Planet Drum Foundation.* Web. Reprinted by permission of Ocean Berg.
———. "Green City." *North American Bioregional Congress Proceedings, Bioregional Congress II, August 25–29, 1986.* Forestville, CA.: Hart Publishing, 1987. 72–75. Reprinted by permission of Ocean Berg.
———. "How to Biosphere." (Report #3, September 7, 2001) Bahía de Caráquez, Ecuador. *Planet Drum Foundation.* Web. Reprinted by permission of Ocean Berg.
———. "Instructions From Mountains and an Island." (Report #3, July 22, 2005) Nagano Prefecture, Japan. *Planet Drum Foundation.* Web. Reprinted by permission of Ocean Berg.
———. "Introduction to Interview with Maria Soledad Vela About 'Rights of Nature; in New Ecuador Constitution." (Autumn Dispatch #1, October 16, 2008). *Planet Drum Foundation.* Web. Reprinted by permission of Ocean Berg.
———. "Lagalou: To Get Things Done with Feeling." *NewOrleansCanThriveBlog.* 2006. Web. Reprinted by permission of Ocean Berg.

————. "Learning to Partner with a Life-Place." (Ecuador Dispatch #1, June 12, 2004). *Planet Drum Foundation.* Web. Reprinted by permission of Ocean Berg.

————. "A Metamorphosis for Cities: From Gray to Green." *City Lights Review #4.* San Francisco: City Lights Publishers, 1990. Reprinted by permission of Ocean Berg.

————. "Out of the Blue, Even More Green: Unexpected Benefits of Restoring Biodiversity." *Kyoto Journal* 75 (2010). Reprinted by permission of Ocean Berg.

————. "The Post-Environmentalist Directions of Bioregionalism." *Poetics of Wilderness Proceedings.* Wilderness Issues Lecture Series 2001. Ed. Roger Dunsmore. Missoula: University of Montana, 2001. 166–173. Reprinted by permission of Ocean Berg.

————. "A River Runs Through It." *Environmental Action* 14.9 (May 1983): 20–21. Reprinted by permission. Environmental Action http://www.environmental-action.org/

————. "San Francisco Bioregional Chant." San Francisco: Planet Drum Broadside, 1974. Reprinted by permission of Ocean Berg.

————. "A San Francisco Native Plant Sidewalk Garden." *Growing Native Newsletter* July/Aug. 1991. Reprinted by permission of Louise Lacey.

————. "Strategies for Reinhabiting the Northern California Bioregion." *Seriatim* 1.3 (1977): 2–8. Reprinted by permission of Ocean Berg.

————. "Walking into the Ring of Fire." *Chicago Review* 39.3/4 (1993): 161–67. Reprinted by permission.

————. "A White Paper on San Francisco's Future and the Natural Interdependence of Pacific People." *City of San Francisco*, 11 Nov. 1975. 20–21.

Berg, Peter, and Kimiharu To. "Guard Fox Watch Statement I: Statement of Concern Regarding the Ecological Impact of the Nagano Winter Olympics (Globalist Games)." 4 Feb. 1998. *Planet Drum Foundation.* Web. Reprinted by permission of Kimiharu To.

————. "Guard Fox Watch II." 14 Feb. 1998. *Planet Drum Foundation.* Web. Reprinted by permission of Kimiharu To.

Berg, Peter, and Raymond Dasmann. "Reinhabiting California." *The Ecologist* 7.10 (1977): 399–401. Reprinted by permission.

Evanoff, Richard. "Bioregionalism Comes to Japan: An Interview with Peter Berg." *Japan Environmental Monitor* 97.4 (June 1998). Web. Reprinted by permission of Richard Evanoff.

Helm, Michael. "An Interview with Peter Berg." *City Miner* (Summer 1978): 5–7, 28–33. Reprinted by permission.

Jensen, Derrick. "Peter Berg." *Listening to the Land: Conversations about Nature, Culture, and Eros.* San Francisco: Sierra Club Books, 1995. 198–207. Reprinted by permission of Derrick Jensen.

PETER BERG BIBLIOGRAPHY

Peter Berg wrote in a variety of genres: essays, poems, plays, broadsides, manifestoes, letters, editorials, forewords, book reviews, film reviews, tributes, video narration, blog posts, posters, policy, screeds, lectures, and more. His works have been published in periodicals, newspapers, books, and websites. Planet Drum Foundation, which Berg founded in 1973, carries on an active publishing program, and Peter Berg served as its visionary director and editor until his death, in 2011. Berg was interviewed many times throughout his career, and some of the interviews were transcribed and published. Much of Berg's published writing is difficult to locate because many of the venues in which he published are not indexed in searchable databases.

We offer this bibliography as an aid to scholars and others interested in following the Peter Berg paper trail. Cheryll Glotfelty's research assistants, Andrew B. Ross and Tyler Nickl, performed the initial research for this bibliography, accessing materials in the Planet Drum Foundation collection in the University Archives at the University of Nevada, Reno, perusing the Planet Drum Foundation website, and consulting databases. Glotfelty expanded the original draft, adding materials that Judy Goldhaft located in Peter Berg's personal files and in Planet Drum Foundation's archives.

This bibliography lists Peter Berg's published writings in English as well as published interviews with Berg that appeared in print. It does not list unpublished manuscripts or unpublished lectures or radio, TV, and video interviews that were not published as transcriptions. It does not list translations of Berg's work into other languages or secondary works about Peter Berg. Serious scholars looking for material beyond this bibliography should contact Planet Drum Foundation. Despite our best efforts there are undoubtedly publications by Peter Berg that escaped our notice, and we would appreciate being notified of them.

This bibliography is organized into the following categories. Items within each category are ordered chronologically.

Categories

Books
Journal, Magazine, and Newspaper Publications
Publications in Books
Published Interviews
Miscellanea
Plays
Planet Drum Website Publications
Essays
Dispatches (Ecuador; Asia; Other Locations)
Poems
Tributes

Books

Reinhabiting a Separate Country: A Bioregional Anthology of Northern California. Peter Berg, ed. San Francisco: Planet Drum Books, 1978. Print.
Renewable Energy and Bioregions: A New Context for Public Policy (with George Tukel). San Francisco: Planet Drum Foundation, 1980. Print.
A Green City Program for San Francisco Bay Area Cities and Towns (with Beryl Magilavy and Seth Zuckerman). San Francisco: Planet Drum Foundation, 1989. Print.
A Green City Program for the San Francisco Bay Area and Beyond (with Beryl Magilavy and Seth Zuckerman). San Francisco: Planet Drum Foundation, Wingbow Press, 1990. Print.
Discovering Your Life-Place: A First Bioregional Workbook. San Francisco: Planet Drum Foundation, 1995. Print.
Envisioning Sustainability. San Francisco: Subculture Books, 2009. Print.

Journal, magazine, and newspaper publications

"Daytime Paranoia Becomes a Joke at Night." *Free City* Set 2. San Francisco, 1967. Rpt. on *The Digger Archives*. Web.
Davis, R. G., and Peter Berg. "Sartre through Brecht." *Tulane Drama Review* 12.1 (Autumn 1967): 132–36. Print.
[Berg, Peter.] "Free City Bloodlight." *The Digger Papers. The Realist* 81 (Aug. 1968): 22. Web.
"Trip Without a Ticket." *The Digger Papers. The Realist* 81 (Aug. 1968): 3–4. Web.
"Grounds & Surrounds." Planet Drum Bundle 2. San Francisco: Planet Drum, 1974. n.p. Print.
"A White Paper on San Francisco's Future and the Natural Interdependence of Pacific People." *City of San Francisco* 11 Nov. 1975: 20–21. Print.
"Amble Towards Continent Congress." Planet Drum Bundle 4 (1976). Print.

"Strategies for Reinhabiting the Northern California Bioregion." *Seriatim* 1.3 (1977): 2–8. Print.

"Reinhabiting California." (with Raymond Dasmann). *The Ecologist* 7.10 (1977): 399–401. Print.

"Soft Borders." *Raise the Stakes! The Planet Drum Review* 1.1 (Fall 1979): unnumbered cover page, 1. Print.

"Northwest Nation: An Interview with Doug Aberley." *Raise the Stakes! The Planet Drum Review* 1.1 (Fall 1979): 2. Print.

Rev. of *An Baner Kernewek* (The Cornish Banner) [magazine]. *Raise the Stakes! The Planet Drum Review* 1.1 (Fall 1979): 3. Print.

"Raise the Stakes!" *Raise the Stakes! The Planet Drum Review* 1.1 (Fall 1979): 6. Print.

———— and Linn House. "Are the Rockies Too Big to Worry About?" Introduction to Bundle 6 (1979). Print.

"Renewable Energy & Bioregions: A New Context for Public Policy" (with George Tukel). Planet Drum Bundle 7 (1980). Print.

"Report From Quebec": Christian Lamontagne interviewed by Peter Berg. *Raise the Stakes! The Planet Drum Review* 1.2 (Winter 1981): 1–2. Print.

Rev. of *Sámid Aednan* by Norwegian Sami Association. *Raise the Stakes! The Planet Drum Review* 1.2 (Winter 1981): 15. Print.

Rev. of *Rootdrinker*, by Alan Casline (ed.). *Raise the Stakes! The Planet Drum Review* 1.2 (Winter 1981): 15. Print.

Rev. of *Upriver Downriver* (newsletter). *Raise the Stakes! The Planet Drum Review* 1.2 (Winter 1981): 15. Print.

Rev. of *All Area* (journal). *Raise the Stakes! The Planet Drum Review* 1.2 (Winter 1981): 15. Print.

"Editor's Statement: The Next Step." *Raise the Stakes! The Planet Drum Review* 1.2 (Winter 1981): 16. Print.

———— and Stephanie Mills, guest eds. Special issue on "Bioregions." *Coevolution Quarterly* 32 (Winter 1981). Print.

"Devolving Beyond Monoculture." *Coevolution Quarterly* 32 (Winter 1981): 24–30. Print.

"Interview with Jimoh Omo-Fadaka and Fatima Omo-Fadaka." *Coevolution Quarterly* 32 (Winter 1981): 39–40. Print.

"How a Language Could Be Political." Peter Berg talking with Gwynfor Evans. *Coevolution Quarterly* 32 (Winter 1981): 44–47. Print.

"South Australia: An Interview with John Stokes." *Raise the Stakes! The Planet Drum Review* 1.3 (Summer 1981): 4–6. Print.

"Renewable Energy to Renew Society: A Talk by Peter Berg." *Raise the Stakes! The Planet Drum Review* 1.3 (Summer 1981): 10–11. Print.

"Freedom to Be Respectful." Interview with Russell Means by Peter Berg. *Raise the Stakes! The Planet Drum Review* 5 (Spring 1982): 12. Print.

Rev. of *In Search of the Primitive* by Stanley Diamond. *Raise the Stakes! The Planet Drum Review* 5 (Spring 1982): 14. Print.

"Introduction." Eco-Decentralist Design Planet Drum Bundle. San Francisco: Planet Drum Foundation, 1982. Print.

"Figures of Regulation: Guides for Re-Balancing Society with the Biosphere." Planet Drum Bundle 8 (1982). Print.

"Starting Over: NABC 1." *Raise the Stakes! The Planet Drum Review* 6 (Winter 1983): 4. Print.

"4th World: 2nd Assembly." *Raise the Stakes! The Planet Drum Review* 6 (Winter 1983): 6. Print.

"Bioregion and Human Location." *All Area* 2 (Spring 1983). Print.

Rev. of *Koyaanisqatsi*, by Godfrey Reggio (dir.). *Raise the Stakes! The Planet Drum Review* 7 (Spring 1983): 13. Print.

"Searching for the Future: Policies and Actions for Today." Proceedings of the 3rd Triennial E. F. Schumacher Conference, Newsletter (May 1983): 9–11. Print.

"A River Runs Through It." *Environmental Action* 14.9 (May 1983): 20–21. Print.

"Bioregions." *Resurgence* 98 (May/June 1983): 19. Rpt. *East West Journal* (Jan. 1984). Rpt. with the title "Living in Place." *Elmwood Quarterly* (Winter 1993–1994). Print.

"More Than Just Saving What's Left." *Raise the Stakes! The Planet Drum Review* 8 (Fall 1983): 1–2. Print.

"Homing In: Community Self-Determination." Interview with Bo Yerxa. *Raise the Stakes! The Planet Drum Review* 8 (Fall 1983): 3, 6. Print.

"A Change We Can Afford: Toward a Bioregional Economics." Interview with Shann Turnbull. *Raise the Stakes! The Planet Drum Review* 8 (Fall 1983): 4–5. Print.

Rev. of *An Baner Kernewek* (The Cornish Banner) [magazine]. *Raise the Stakes! The Planet Drum Review* 8 (Fall 1983): 13. Print.

"Volcanoes Make Good Neighbors (but shouldn't Portland move?)" Robert Curry interviewed by Peter Berg. *Raise the Stakes! The Planet Drum Review* 9 (Spring 1984): 2–3. Print.

"Amble Towards Continent Congress." (excerpted version). *Raise the Stakes! The Planet Drum Review* 10 (Summer 1984): 8–9, 12. Print.

"Prints & Sign." *Raise the Stakes! The Planet Drum Review* 10 (Summer 1984): 12. Print.

"A Bioregional Fantasy of Future Cities." *Environmental Action* 16.7 (May/June 1985): 12. Print.

"Growing a Bioregional Politics, Excerpts from a talk by Peter Berg." *RAIN* 11.5 (July/Aug. 1985): 14–16. Print.

"Celebrate the Longest Night." *Raise the Stakes! The Planet Drum Review* 11 (Summer 1986): 1–2. Print.

"Growing a Life-Place Politics." *Raise the Stakes! The Planet Drum Review* 11 (Summer 1986): unnumbered 4-page insert (following p. 8). Rpt. as "A Call to Bioregionalism: Growing a Life-Place Politics." *Ecology Center Newsletter* 21.9 (Sept. 1991): 1–4. Print.

"Coming of Age in Bio-topia." Guest editorial. *Not Man Apart* Sept./Oct. 1986: 3. Print.

"Watershed-Scaled Governments and Green Cities." *Land Use Policy* 4.1 (Jan. 1987): 5–10. Print.

"Emerging States: A Bioregional Directory." *Raise the Stakes! The Planet Drum Review* 12 (Spring 1987): 1. Print.

"Lording it Over the Biosphere." Rev. of *To Govern Evolution: Further Adventures of the Political Animal*, by Walter Truett Anderson. *Futures* 20.1 (Feb. 1988): 89–91. Print.

"Native Plants." *San Francisco Chronicle* 2 March 1988. Print.

"A Green City Vision for the Bay Area." *The San Francisco Bay Guardian* 22.26 (13 April 1988): 15. Print.

"Crucial Conflict." Letters. *New Options* 48 (May 1988): 5. Print.

"Peter Berg." Guest editorial. *Whole Earth Review* (Winter 1988). Print.

"Walking the Border Between Native and Non-native Cultures: Malcolm Margolin interviewed by Peter Berg." *Raise the Stakes! The Planet Drum Review* 14 (Winter 1988–1989): 2–4. Print.

Rev. (with Judy Goldhaft) of *Urban Wilderness: Nature in New York City*, by Jean Gardner and Joel Greenberg. *Raise the Stakes! The Planet Drum Review* 14 (Winter 1988–1989): 14. Print.

"Borders." *Raise the Stakes! The Planet Drum Review* 14 (Winter 1988–1989): 16. Print.
"Starting Over Without Columbus." *Raise the Stakes! The Planet Drum Review* 15 (Fall 1989): 1. Print.
———— and Kirkpatrick Sale. "Thoughts for a World at the Edge." *The Journal of Wild Culture* 2.2 & 3 (Fall 1989): 14–23. Print.
"A Pragmatist's New City." *L.A. Weekly* 1–7 Dec. 1989: 41. Print.
"A Critique of Earthquake Reporting." Peter Berg interviewing Jerry Mander. Printed as an insert to a Planet Drum *PULSE*, 1989. Print.
"A Metamorphosis for Cities: From Gray to Green." *City Lights Review* 4 (1990). Rpt. *Trumpeter* 8.1 (Winter 1991): 9–12. Rpt. *Putting Power in Its Place*, ed. Judith Plant and Christopher Plant. Philadelphia: New Society Publishers, 1992. Print.
"Transit Tip #2, Travelling Off the Grid." *San Francisco Bay Guardian* 10 Oct. 1990: 25. Print.
"Transit Tip #5, Think About Where You Are." *San Francisco Bay Guardian* 10 Oct. 1990: 28. Print.
"Transit Tip #9, A New Kind of House Call." *San Francisco Bay Guardian* 10 Oct. 1990: 40. Print.
"What is Bioregionalism?" *Talking Leaves* (April 1991): 5–6. Print.
"What is Bioregionalism?" *The Trumpeter* 8.1 (Winter 1991): 6–12. Print.
"Transpersonal Ecology and the Varieties of Identification." *The Trumpeter* 8.1 (Winter 1991): 6–12. Print.
"Recreating Urbanity." *Raise the Stakes. The Planet Drum Review* 17 (Winter 1991): 4. Print.
Rev. of *The Practice of the Wild*, by Gary Snyder. *Raise the Stakes. The Planet Drum Review* 17 (Winter 1991): 12. Print.
————, Beryl Magilavy, and Seth Zuckerman. "Greening Our Cities." *Co-Op America Quarterly* (Spring 1991). Print.
"Falcons and the Mutual Benefit Life Building—An Inner City Fable." p. 8 of article "The Beat Goes on, Planet Drum Foundation in Action." *Permaculture International Journal* 40 (June–Aug. 1991): 6–10. Print.
"Expanding Ecology." Rev. of *Renewing the Earth: The Promise of Social Ecology. A Celebration of the Work of Murray Bookchin*, by John Clark (ed.) and *Discordant Harmonies: A New Ecology for the Twenty-First Century*, by Daniel B. Botkin. *Futures* 23.6 (July/Aug.1991): 673–675. Print.
"A San Francisco Native Plant Sidewalk Garden." *Growing Native Newsletter* July/Aug. 1991: 13–15. Print.
Rev. of *Renewing the Earth: The Promise of Social Ecology*, ed. John Clark. *Futures* 23.6 (July–Aug. 1991): 673. Print.
Rev. of *Discordant Harmonies: A New Ecology for the 21st Century*, by Daniel B. Botkin. *Futures* 23.6 (July–Aug. 1991): 673–75. Print.
"San Francisco Bioregion." *Our Generation* 22–23 (1991). Print.
"Post-Environmentalist Origins." (From an address presented at the "Symposium on Biodiversity of Northwestern California." 28–30 Oct. 1991, Santa Rosa, CA). *Raise the Stakes. The Planet Drum Review* 18/19 (Winter 1991/Spring 1992): 1, 21. Print.
Rev. of *In the Absence of the Sacred: The Failure of Technology & The Survival of the Indian Nations*, by Jerry Mander. *Raise the Stakes. The Planet Drum Review* 18/19 (Winter 1991/Spring 1992): 18. Print.
Rev. of *Mindwalk,* by Bert Amadeus Capra. *Raise the Stakes. The Planet Drum Review* 18/19 (Winter 1991/Spring 1992): 20. Print.
"Shasta Bioregional Gathering Opening." *Raise the Stakes. The Planet Drum Review* 20 (Fall 1992): 1. Print.

"Government Agencies' 'Bioregional' Plan: Action Response" (roundtable participant). *Raise the Stakes. The Planet Drum Review* 20 (Fall 1992): 9–10. Print.

"The Bioregional Vision." *The Eco Echo*. Newsletter of the Mount Shasta Bioregional Ecology Center (Fall–Winter 1992–93). Rpt. in archives of the *Mount Shasta Bioregional Ecology Center* website. Web.

"Walking into the Ring of Fire." *Chicago Review* 39.3–4 (1993): 161–68. Print.

Rev. of *Video Mind, Earth Mind: Art, Communications & Ecology* by Paul Ryan. *Raise the Stakes. The Planet Drum Review* 21 (Spring/Summer 1993): 13. Print.

Letter to the Editor, *The San Francisco Chronicle*, re: "Environmentalists Should Look Ahead" by Walter Truett Anderson. 26 Nov. 1993. Print.

Rev. of *Boundaries of Home*, ed. Doug Aberley. *Raise the Stakes. The Planet Drum Review* 22 (Winter 1993/1994): 12. Print.

"Living in Place." *Elmwood Quarterly* (Winter 1993–94): 17–18. Print.

"Putting 'BIO' in Front of Regional." *Landscape Architecture* 84.4 (April 1994): 59–61. Print.

"Earth Block/Ciudad Verde Greens Carnaval." *SF Weekly* 1994. Print.

"Put 'BIO' in Front of Regional." *Raise the Stakes. The Planet Drum Review* 23 (Summer 1994): 2, 5. Print.

"Where Poems Come From: An Interview with Jerry Martien." *Raise the Stakes. The Planet Drum Review* 23 (Summer 1994): 6. Print.

"Planet Drum Foundation." 1995. *Shaping San Francisco's Digital Archive @ Foundsf*. Shaping San Francisco, 2012. Web.

"Thinking About the Biosphere and Getting Bioregional: David Suzuki Interviewed by Peter Berg." *Raise the Stakes. The Planet Drum Review* 25 (Winter 1995/1996): 1–3. Print.

"U.N. at 50: Time for a New Perspective: A Talk by Peter Berg." *Raise the Stakes. The Planet Drum Review* 25 (Winter 1995/1996): 4–5. Print.

"Three Green City Glances at Japan." *Raise the Stakes. The Planet Drum Review* 25 (Winter 1995/1996): 7. Print.

"European Visit Fuels Bioregional Fervor." *Raise the Stakes. The Planet Drum Review* 25 (Winter 1995/1996): 8. Print.

"Franco Beltrametti: A Sketch." (memorial) *Raise the Stakes. The Planet Drum Review* 25 (Winter 1995/1996): 10. Print.

"Schooling in a Wild Preserve: D. Tompkins Interviewed by Peter Berg." *Raise the Stakes. The Planet Drum Review* 26 (Fall 1996): 7, 9. Print.

"The Green City: Hands-On Activist Award." *Raise the Stakes. The Planet Drum Review* 26 (Fall 1996): 15. Print.

"The Genuine Sprit of Localism." *Resurgence* 183 (July/Aug. 1997): 52–53. Print.

"Bioregionalism Meets Local Autonomy in Mexico." *Raise the Stakes. The Planet Drum Review* 27 (Summer 1997): 6–7. Print.

Rev. of *Biopiracy: The Plunder of Nature and Knowledge*, by Vandana Shiva. *Raise the Stakes. The Planet Drum Review* 27 (Summer 1997): 12. Print.

"Bioregionalism Versus Fascism: A Conversation About Place, Ethnicity, Globalization, and the Waning of the Nation-State." Conversation with Martin A. Lee. *Raise the Stakes. The Planet Drum Review* 28 (Spring 1998): 1–2. Print.

"Postcards from the Olympics' Underside." *Raise the Stakes. The Planet Drum Review* 28 (Spring 1998): 4. Print.

Rev. of *The Saltmen of Tibet*, by Ulrike Koch (dir.). *Raise the Stakes. The Planet Drum Review* 28 (Spring 1998): 8. Print.

"More Than Just Saving What's Left." *Raise the Stakes. The Planet Drum Review* 29 (Winter 1998/1999): 2. Print.

Rev. of *Ecology: A Pocket Guide*, by Ernest Callenbach. *Raise the Stakes. The Planet Drum Review* 29 (Winter 1998/1999): 12. Print.

"*Raise the Stakes* Did Just That." (editorial). *Raise the Stakes. The Planet Drum Review* 30 (1999–2000): 1. Print.

"Recreating Urbanity." *Raise the Stakes. The Planet Drum Review* 30 (1999–2000): 2. Print.

"Ecuador Green City Revisited, August '99." *Raise the Stakes. The Planet Drum Review* 30 (1999–2000): 12. Print.

Rev. of *Totem Salmon: Life Lessons From Another Species,* by Freeman House. *Raise the Stakes. The Planet Drum Review* 30 (1999–2000): 14. Print.

"Conservation, Preservation and Restoration in Ecuador." *Earth Island Journal* 16.1 (Spring 2001): 25–27. Print.

"What is Bioregionalism?" 2002. *Cascadian Independence Project.* Open Cascadian Collaborative License, 2014. Web.

"The Bioregional Approach for Making Sustainable Cities." *Urban Green Tech* (Tokyo). 2004.

"Restoration in Coastal Ecuador." *The Permaculture Activist* 51 (Feb. 2004): 58–60. Print.

"Lagalou." *NewOrleansCanThriveBlog.* 2006. Web.

Rev. of *On Gandhi's Path: Bob Swann's Work For Peace and Community Economics*, by Stephanie Mills. *Planet Drum PULSE: A Voice For Bioregional Sustainability, Education and Culture* (Summer 2010): 13. Print.

"Out of the Blue, Even More Green: Unexpected Benefits of Restoring Biodiversity." *Kyoto Journal* 75 (2010). Web.

"Peter Berg: In His Own Words." *Planet Drum PULSE: A Voice For Bioregional Sustainability, Education and Culture* (Fall 2011): 5–12. Print.

Publications in books

"Planetedge." *BAMN By Any Means Necessary: Outlaw Manifestos and Ephemera 1965–70.* Ed. Peter Stansill and David Zane Mairowitz. Hammondsworth, UK: Penguin, 1971. 60–67. Print.

"Borne-Native in the San Francisco Bay Region." *Living Here,* Frisco Bay Mussel Group, 1977. Print.

"Reinhabitating California" (with Raymond Dasmann). 1977. Rpt. *Reinhabiting A Separate Country: A Bioregional Anthology of Northern California.* Ed. Peter Berg. San Francisco: Planet Drum Books, 1978. 217–20. Print.

"Reinhabitory Theater." *Reinhabiting A Separate Country: A Bioregional Anthology of Northern California.* Ed. Peter Berg. San Francisco: Planet Drum Books, 1978. 186–91. Print.

"Lizard and Coyote." *Reinhabiting A Separate Country: A Bioregional Anthology of Northern California.* Ed. Peter Berg. San Francisco: Planet Drum Books, 1978. 192–94. Print.

"Introduction." *Devolutionary Notes*, by Michael Zwerin. San Francisco: Planet Drum Books, 1980. Print.

"On Being Our Own Anthropologists." *City Country Miners: Some Northern California Veins.* Ed. Michael Helm. Berkeley: City Miner Books, 1982. 245–48. Print.

"Raise the Stakes!" [poem]. *City Country Miners: Some Northern California Veins.* Ed. Michael Helm. Berkeley: City Miner Books, 1982. 249. Print.

"NABC/Green Politics." *Green Politics: The Global Promise.* Ed. Charlene Spretnak and Fritjof Capra. New York: E. P. Dutton, 1984. Print.

"More than Just Saving What's Left" (from *Raise the Stakes!* 8 [Fall 1983]). Rpt. *The Alternative Press Annual, 1983*. Philadelphia: Temple University Press, 1984. 323–26. Print.

"Green City." *North American Bioregional Congress Proceedings, Bioregional Congress II, August 25–29, 1986*. Forestville, CA.: Hart Publishing, 1987. 72–75. Print.

"Preface." *Strawberries in November: A Guide to Gardening in the East Bay*, by Judith Goldsmith. Berkeley: Heyday Books, 1987. Print.

"The Roots of Bioregionalism: An Interview" (Peter Berg and Judy Goldhaft in conversation with Seth Zuckerman). *Third North American Bioregional Congress Proceedings, Held August 21 to 26, 1988 by the banks of the Cheakamus River, Paradise Valley, Squamish, Ish Bioregion, Pacific Cascadia (British Columbia, Canada)*. San Francisco: Planet Drum Foundation, 1989. 50–53. Print.

"A Green City Program with a Bioregional Perspective: Developing the San Francisco Green City Plan." *Green Cities: Ecologically Sound Approaches to Urban Space*. Ed. David Gordon. Montreal: Black Rose Books, 1990. 281–88. Print.

"Creating Green Cities." *Call to Action: Handbook for Ecology, Peace, and Justice*. Ed. Brad Erickson. San Francisco, Sierra Club Books, 1990. 159–61. Print.

"More than Just Saving What's Left." *Home! A Bioregional Reader*. Ed. Van Andruss, Christopher Plant, Judith Plant, and Eleanor Wright. Philadelphia: New Society, 1990. Rpt. *Habitat, Australia* 19.2 (April 1991): 32–33. Rpt. New Catalyst Books, 2008. 13–16. Print.

"Reinhabiting California" (with Raymond Dasmann). 1977. Rpt. *Home! A Bioregional Reader*. Ed. Van Andruss, Christopher Plant, Judith Plant, and Eleanor Wright. Philadelphia: New Society, 1990. New Catalyst Books, 2008. 35–38. Print.

"A Green City Program for San Francisco Bay Area Cities and Towns." *Home! A Bioregional Reader*. Ed. Van Andruss, Christopher Plant, Judith Plant, and Eleanor Wright. Philadelphia: New Society, 1990. New Catalyst Books, 2008. 104–09. Print.

"Growing a Life-Place Politics." *Home! A Bioregional Reader*. Ed. Van Andruss, Christopher Plant, Judith Plant, and Eleanor Wright. Philadelphia: New Society, 1990. New Catalyst Books, 2008. 137–44. Print.

"Beating the Drum with Gary." *Gary Snyder: Dimensions of a Life*. Ed. Jon Halper. San Francisco: Sierra Club Books, 1991. 376–91. Print.

"Bioregional Cultural Awareness." *Proceedings of the Symposium on Biodiversity of Northwestern California: October 28–30, 1991*. Berkeley: Wildland Resource Center, Division of Agriculture and Natural Resources, University of California, 1992. 215–16. Print.

"Foreword Regarding the Ecological Crisis." *Video Mind, Earth Mind: Art, Communications, and Ecology*, by Paul Ryan. New York: Peter Lang, 1993. xvii–xviii. Print.

"Foreword." *In Cold Margins: Sustainable Development in Northern Bioregions*, by J. M. Jamil Brownson. Missoula, MT: Northern Rim Press, 1995. i–iii. Print.

"The Post-Environmentalist Directions of Bioregionalism." *Poetics of Wilderness Proceedings*. Wilderness Issues Lecture Series 2001. Ed. Roger Dunsmore. Missoula: University of Montana, 2001. 166–73. Print.

——— and Judy Goldhaft. "Peter Berg and Judy Goldhaft." *Environmental Activists*. Ed. John F. Mongillo and Bibi Booth. Westport, CT: Greenwood Press, 2001. 16–20. Print.

"Bioregionalism." *Encyclopedia of World Environmental History*. Vol. 1. Ed. Shepard Krech III, J. R. McNeill, and Carolyn Merchant. New York: Routledge, 2004. 145–47. Print.

Published interviews

Wolf, Leonard, and Deborah Wolf. "Peter Berg." *Voices from the Love Generation.* Boston: Little, Brown and Company, 1968. 246–63. Print.

Helm, Michael. "An Interview with Peter Berg." *City Miner* (Summer 1978): 5–7, 28–33. Print.

Penn, Shana. "Green City: An Interview with Peter Berg," *The Elmwood Newsletter* 3.1 (1987). Print.

"The Roots of Bioregionalism: An Interview." Peter Berg, Judy Goldhaft, Seth Zucker-man, and Freeman House participating. *Third North* American *Bioregional Congress Proceedings.* The North American Bioregional Congress, 1989. Print.

"Bioregional and Wild! An Interview with Peter Berg." *The New Catalyst* (Winter 1989/1990): 12–13. Print.

Plant, Christopher, and Judith Plant, eds. "Bioregional and Wild! A New Cultural Image . . ." *Turtle Talk: Voices for a Sustainable Future.* Philadelphia: New Society Publishers, 1990. 21–30. Print.

"Weeds in the Cracks: Why the Bioregional and Green City Movements Give Me Reasons for Hope." *New Dimensions* 17.2 (March–April 1990): 4–6. Print.

Weinberg, Bill. "Interview with Peter Berg." *High Times* (April 1993): 50–55. Print.

Jensen, Derrick. "Peter Berg." *Listening to the* Land*: Conversations about Nature, Culture, and Eros.* San Francisco: Sierra Club Books, 1995. 198–207. Print.

Chepesiuk, Ron. "Peter Berg: From Digger to Environmental Activist." *Sixties Radicals, Then and Now: Candid Conversations with Those Who Shaped the Era.* By Ron Chepe-siuk. Jefferson, NC: McFarland, 1995. 118–32. Print.

Berrios, Steven. "Bioregionalism—An Interview with Peter Berg." *Tidal Tales,* 10.3 (May–June 1997). Newsletter of the Hayward Shoreline Interpretive Center, Hayward, CA, 1997. Print.

"Ecology of Nagano Seen Coming in Last." *Japan Times* 12 Feb. 1998. Print.

Evanoff, Richard. "Bioregionalism Comes to Japan: An Interview with Peter Berg." *Japan Environmental Monitor* 97.4 (June 1998). Web.

Sloman, Larry. Quotes from an interview with Peter Berg. Chapters 3 and 4. *Steal This Dream: Abbie Hoffman and the Countercultural Revolution in America.* Doubleday, 1998. Print.

Hesse, Stephen. "Beating the Bioregion Drum: Putting People Back into Ecology (inter-view with Planet Drum Director, Peter Berg)." *Japan Times* 21 Sept. 2005. Print.

Kisseloff, Jeff. "Peter Berg: The Digger." Interview. *Generation on Fire: Voices of Protest from the 1960s, An Oral History.* Lexington: UP of Kentucky, 2007. 137–51. Print.

Hamlin, Jesse. "Summer of Love: 40 Years Later / Peter Berg and Judy Goldhaft." *SF Gate* 20 May 2007. Hearst Communications, 2014. Web.

Miscellanea

"Homeskin." Planet Drum Broadside, 1970.

"Automated Rites of the Obsolete Future." Planet Drum Broadside, 1972.

"Reinhabitation Message from the Pacific Coast, North America." Planet Drum Broadside, 1974.

"A San Francisco Bioregional Chant." Planet Drum Broadside, 1974. Rpt. *Poetry Flash* Archive. Web.

"Amble Toward Continent Congress." Planet Drum *Continent Congress* Bundle #4, 1976.
"Interdependent Message to Participants, Observers, and Conferees Gathered at the U.N. Habitat Conference, June 1, 1976." Planet Drum Broadside, Aug. 1976.
"Worksheet for Bioregional Planning." Planet Drum Broadside, 6 March 1978.
Listening to the Earth. Symposium Poster. Art Michael Myers. Berkeley, CA: Designed by Sharpshooter Studios. 1979. Web. Oakland Museum of California. Oakland Museum of California, 2013.
———— and George Tukel. "Renewable Energy and Bioregions, A New Context for Public Policy." California Office of Appropriate Technology. Sept. 1980.
"Amble Towards Continent Congress." (poster/map). 1992.
"Talk by Peter Berg at 'Watershed: Writers, Nature, and Community.'" Washington, D.C. 19 April 1996. Rpt. Peter Berg, *Envisioning Sustainability*. San Francisco: Subculture Books, 2009. 227–31. Rpt. *Poetry Flash* Archive. Web.
"Invisible Except for a Nervous System." 1996. *Poetry Flash* Archive. Web.
"Shasta Bioregion Winter Solstice." 1997. *Poetry Flash* Archive. Web.
"Solstice Solo." 2003. *Poetry Flash* Archive. Web.

Plays

Information about Peter Berg's scriptwriting has been provided by Judy Goldhaft, Planet Drum Foundation.
Il Candelaio is an adaption of Giordano Bruno's play of the same name, written by Peter Berg for the San Francisco Mime Troupe, performed in the park, followed by arrest for not having a permit to perform in the park, 7 Aug. 1965.
Centerman is a dramatization of Wolfgang Borchert's short story *The Dandelion*, which Peter Berg wrote, directed, and produced for the San Francisco Mime Troupe, 6 March 1966.
Search and Seizure is a play Peter Berg wrote and directed for the San Francisco Mime Troupe, 19 June 1966.
Out Put You is a play Peter Berg wrote, directed, and produced for the San Francisco Mime Troupe, Sept. 1966.
Olive Pits by Lope de Rueda is a play Peter Berg and Peter Cohon (Coyote) adapted and performed in for the San Francisco Mime Troupe 1966. In 1968 it won an Obie Award.
What's That, A Head? was a puppet play Peter Berg wrote with Barbara LaMorticella for the San Francisco Mime Troupe.

Planet Drum website publications

Publications listed below are accessible on *Planet Drum Foundation* website. www.planetdrum.org.

Essays

"Amble Toward Continent Congress." Planet Drum Continent Congress Bundle, 1976. Web.
"Guard Fox Watch Statement I: Statement of Concern Regarding the Ecological Impact of the Nagano Winter Olympics (Globalist Games)." 4 Feb. 1998. Web.
"Guard Fox Watch II." 14 Feb. 1998. Web.
"Call to Action: Help Stop the Greenwashing of the Winter Olympics: Make the 2002 Games in Salt Lake City Ecologically Sustainable." 2002. Web.
"Bioregionalism (Defined and Updated 2002)." 2002. Web.
"Quick Bioregional Quiz." 2002. Web.

"Why Take on the Winter Olympics, and What Came of the Effort?" 11 Feb. 2002. Web.
"The Bioregional Approach to Making Sustainable Cities." (Also published in *Urban Green Tech* [Tokyo] 2004). Web.
"Learning to Partner with a Life-Place" (Ecuador Dispatch #1, 12 June 2004). Web.
"New Weather and You." *The Messenger* 2006. (*The Messenger* is published by Independent Arts & Media as part of the Seventh Annual Expo for the Artist & Musician.) Rpt. on the Planet Drum Foundation website.
"Review of Francois Truffaut's *Shoot the Piano Player.*" 7 March 2007. Web.
"The New Green Deal of 2009." 2008. Web.

Dispatches

Ecuador

1999

"Latitude 0 Degrees, 36 Minutes South" (Report from Ecuador #1, 11 Feb., 1999).
"'Will It Rain Forever?' (Flor-Maria Tamariz)" (Report #2, 12 Feb., 1999) Bahía de Caráquez, Ecuador.
"Two And a Half Doses of Realidad" (Bahía de Caráquez, Ecuador Eco-Gathering Report #3, 16 Feb., 1999).
"Eco-Bahia Support Group Forming" (Letter #1, 17 Feb., 1999) Bahía de Caráquez, Ecuador.
"3rd World or 3rd Planet?" (Bahía de Caráquez, Ecuador Eco-gathering Report #4, 18 Feb., 1999).
"Letters of Support Requested" (Letter #2, 20 Feb., 1999) Bahía de Caráquez, Ecuador.
"'Put some air into our lungs!' (Bahia audience member)" (Bahía de Caráquez, Ecuador Eco-gathering Report #5, 21 Feb., 1999).
"Viva Eco-Bahia!" (Bahía de Caráquez, Ecuador Eco-gathering Report #6, 25 Feb., 1999).
"At the Threshold of a Sustainable Future" (Ecuador Eco-Gathering Report #7 San Francisco, California, 24 March, 1999).
"Ecuador Green City Revisited, August 1999."

2000

"The Peaceful Roar" (21 Jan., 2000).
"Growing Into the Dry Tropical Forest" (27 Jan., 2000) Bahía de Caráquez, Ecuador.
"Why Did I Come To Ecuador To Live With A Lumber Mill On Each Side Of My House?" (Leonidas Plaza, 29 Jan., 2000).
"Ojala!" (Leonidas Plaza—Bahía de Caráquez, Ecuador, 30 Jan., 2000).
"A Natural Hothouse" (5 Feb., 2000) Bahía de Caráquez, Ecuador.
"Rebellion Comes to Bahía a Month Late, But Nonetheless Verdad" (14 Feb., 2000) Bahía de Caráquez, Ecuador.
"The Restoration of Bahía is Underway" (9 Sept., 2000).
"Ecological City Plan for Bahía De Caráquez, Ecuador" (11 Sept., 2000).
"From a Park to a Plan" (14 Sept., 2000).
"Unsorted Impressions" (16 Sept., 2000).
"Two Steps Forward Without Any Backward" (22 Sept., 2000).
"Why 'Revegetation' Rather Than 'Reforestation' . . . and Where?" (27 Sept., 2000).

2001

"Report on Bahía de Caráquez Hillside Erosion Suitable for Revegetation Using Plantings Without Physical Alterations of the Landscape" (Rio Chone Border From Astillero to Kilometro Ocho—Excepting El Toro Watershed) (23 Jan., 2001).

"Moving Several Levels Higher" (Report #1 from Bahía de Caráquez, Ecuador, 23 Jan., 2001).

"Still More Levels" (Report #2 from Bahía de Caráquez, Ecuador, 28 Jan., 2001).

"Destiny Under a Florid Sky" (Report #3 from Bahía de Caráquez, Ecuador, 1 Feb., 2001).

"A Remarkable Week for Pacha Mama" (Report #4 from Hotel Pais Libre, Canoa, Ecuador, 4 Feb., 2001).

"Maniaca and Loco," including an essay "The Culture of Complaint" (Report #5 from Bahía de Caráquez, Ecuador, 13 Feb., 2001).

"History With Some Inevitable Loose Ends" (Report #6 from Bahía de Caráquez, Ecuador, 18 Feb., 2001).

"Counsel From an Unusual Source" (Report #1, 23 Aug., 2001) Bahía de Caráquez, Ecuador.

"Now and Future Water" (Report #2, 30 Aug., 2001) Bahía de Caráquez, Ecuador.

"How to Biosphere" (Report #3, 7 Sept., 2001) Bahía de Caráquez, Ecuador.

"Transforming Trash to Fruit Trees" (Report #4, 10 Sept., 2001) Bahía de Caráquez, Ecuador.

2002

"Rain Included at Extra Cost" (Winter 2001–02 Report #1, 7 Feb., 2002) Bahía de Caráquez, Ecuador.

"Carnival Heat" (Winter 2001–02 Report #2, 12 Feb., 2002) Bahía de Caráquez, Ecuador.

"Dancing Public Revegetation onto Private Land" (Winter 2001–02 Report #3, 17 Feb., 2002) Bahía de Caráquez, Ecuador.

"The 'Bear' in the Bosque and Other Outcomes" (Winter 2001–02 Report #4, 22 Feb., 2002) Bahía de Caráquez, Ecuador.

"Closing Circles and Emerging Angles" (Fall 2002 Dispatch #1, 21 Sept., 2002) Bahía de Caráquez, Ecuador.

"Governments International, National and Across the Street" (Fall 2002 Dispatch #2, 25 Sept., 2002) Bahía de Caráquez, Ecuador.

2003

"Ecuador and Planet Drum Undergo Major Transitions" (Winter 2002–03 Dispatch #1, 17 Jan., 2003) Bahía de Caráquez, Ecuador.

"Revelations in a Cattle Slough" (Winter 2002–03 Dispatch #2, 19 Jan., 2003) Bahía de Caráquez, Ecuador.

"Natives are Harder" (Autumn 2003 Dispatch #1, 12 Nov., 2003) Bahía de Caráquez, Ecuador.

"Re-emerging Indigenas" (Autumn 2003 Dispatch #2, 13 Nov., 2003) Bahía de Caráquez, Ecuador.

"Reiterating the Ecological City" (Autumn 2003 Dispatch #3, 15 Nov., 2003) Bahía de Caráquez, Ecuador.

"For Indoor Use Only—A Meditation" (Autumn 2003 Dispatch #4, 20 Nov., 2003) Bahía de Caráquez, Ecuador.

"Pique y Pasa (Choose What You Like)" (Autumn 2003 Dispatch #5, 22 Nov., 2003) Bahía de Caráquez, Ecuador.

"Wild & 'Wild' Encounters" (Autumn 2003 Dispatch #6, 26 Nov., 2003) Bahía de Caráquez, Ecuador.

2004

"Learning to Partner with a Life-Place" (Summer 2004 Dispatch #1, 12 June, 2004) Bahía de Caráquez, Ecuador.

"The Next Five Years Begin on a Dry Note" (Summer 2004 Dispatch #2, 19 June, 2004) Bahía de Caráquez, Ecuador.
"Close Call, Solemn Solstice" (Summer 2004 Dispatch #3, 23 June, 2004) Bahía de Caráquez, Ecuador.
"Seeing the Future in the Past, Again" (Summer 2004 Dispatch #4, 26 June, 2004) Bahía de Caráquez, Ecuador.
"How a Day Passes Here" (Summer 2004 Dispatch #5, 28 June, 2004) Bahía de Caráquez, Ecuador.
"A Re-birth of Ecologics" (Summer 2004 Dispatch #6, 30 June, 2004) Bahía de Caráquez, Ecuador.

2005

"Eco-Bahia Becomes an Adult at the Age of Six" (Dispatch #1, 23 Feb., 2005) Bahía de Caráquez, Ecuador.
"Land Found But Not Quite Located" (Dispatch #2, 3 Sept., 2005) Bahía de Caráquez, Ecuador.
"At Last, The Hard Part" (Dispatch #3, 5 Sept., 2005) Bahía de Caráquez, Ecuador.
"Careers of Improvisation—Part I" (Dispatch #4, 7 Sept., 2005) Bahía de Caráquez, Ecuador.

2006

"Winter's Wet Green Heat" (Dispatch #1, 10 March, 2006) Bahía de Caráquez, Ecuador.
"Reality Checks" (Dispatch #2, 12 Sept., 2006) Bahía de Caráquez, Ecuador.
"The Core of Eco-Tourism" (Dispatch #3, 20 Sept., 2006) Bahía de Caráquez, Ecuador.

2007

"On the Way to a Road" (Dispatch #1, 12 March, 2007) Bahía de Caráquez, Ecuador.
"New Accomplishments, Partial and Complete" (Dispatch #2, 22 March, 2007) Bahía de Caráquez, Ecuador.
"Dispatch #3" September SF PDF Staff Visit—2007 [Excerpts from Letters] (Sept. 2007).

2008

"Tropical Winter Sketches" (Dispatch #1, 17 March, 2008) Bahía de Caráquez, Ecuador.
"National Transformation Can Inspire Local Progress" (with Eco-Mandato [mandate] 2008) (Dispatch #2, 24 March, 2008) Bahía de Caráquez, Ecuador.
"A Celebration and A Reflection" (Dispatch #3, 5 April, 2008) Bahía de Caráquez, Ecuador.
"Introduction to Interview with Maria Soledad Vela About 'Rights of Nature' in New Ecuador Constitution" (Autumn Dispatch #1, 16 Oct., 2008) [interview in Winter 2008 *Planet Drum PULSE*].
"An Experience of Social Worth" (Autumn Dispatch #2, 17 Oct., 2008) Bahía de Caráquez, Ecuador.
"A Slice Through Layers of Days" (Autumn Dispatch #3, 25 Oct., 2008) Bahía de Caráquez, Ecuador.

2009

"In the Season of Rising Expectations" (Dispatch #1, 16 Feb., 2009) Bahía de Caráquez, Ecuador.
"Discovering the Status of Some Things to Come" (Dispatch #2, 22 Feb., 2009) Bahía de Caráquez, Ecuador.
"How *Eco-Bahia* Was Rescued" (Dispatch #3, 25 Feb., 2009) Bahía de Caráquez, Ecuador.

2010
"A School to Retrieve the Future" (Dispatch #1, 18 Nov., 2010) Bahía de Caráquez, Ecuador.

Asia

2001
"Bioregionalism Finds Eager Audiences in Japan." Aug. 2001.
"China's Epic Conflict of Capacities." Aug. 2001.
"Big Horizon Mongolia." Aug. 2001.

2004
"A Prescription for Japan's Cities" (Dispatch #1, 26 Sept., 2004) Northwest Pacific Main Islands.
"Finding the Path Off the Road" (Dispatch #2, 7 Oct., 2004) Northwest Pacific Main Islands.
"Tokyo Typhoon: Vestiges of a People and a River" (Dispatch #3, 15 Oct., 2004) Northwest Pacific Main Islands.
"Restoring Ecology From the Inside Out" (Dispatch #4, 18 Oct., 2004) Northwest Pacific Main Islands.

2005
"'Colors Are the Deeds of Light'—Johann Wolfgang von Goethe" (Report #1, 5 July, 2005) Kyoto, Japan.
"Finding the Future in the Mud" (Report #2, 10 July, 2005) Nagoya, Japan.
"Instructions From Mountains and an Island" (Report #3, 22 July, 2005) Nagano Prefecture, Japan.

Other locations

"Finding a Bioregion in the Sea" (8 Oct., 2006) Peace Boat off Baja, California.

Poems

"Hudson Loan" (2005)
"Celestial Soulstice 2010"

Tributes

"Standing on a Street Corner Doing Nothing is Power." Tribute to Gregory Corso. Read at a memorial, 24 Jan., 2001.
"Ray Dasmann's Way to See." Bahía de Caráquez, Ecuador, 6 Jan., 2003.
"Painter Hiroshi Yoshida's Bioregional Perception of Place." March 2005.
"Some Encounters with Murray Bookchin." Aug. 2006.
"Meeting Thomas Berry, Biospherean." 2008.
"Overview of John Berger." 16 Oct., 2008.
"Nanao Sakaki." 2008. (Includes a dispatch from Japan, 2004).

INDEX

Note: Locators for illustrations are in italics. Locators for entries found in endnotes and followed by "n," (e.g. , 132n).

FIGURE 15 Peter Berg at the Third North American Bioregional Congress, Ish Bioregion, Pacific Cascadia, 1988

Source: © Judy Goldhaft